"The Muses Females Are"

LOCUST HILL LITERARY STUDIES
NO. 20

Locust Hill Literary Studies

1. *Blake and His Bibles*. Edited by David V. Erdman. ISBN 0-933951-29-9. LC 89-14052.

2. *Faulkner, Sut, and Other Southerners*. M. Thomas Inge. ISBN 0-933951-31-0. LC 91-40016.

3. *Essays of a Book Collector: Reminiscences on Some Old Books and Their Authors*. Claude A. Prance. ISBN 0-933951-30-2. LC 89-12734.

4. *Vision and Revisions: Essays on Faulkner*. John E. Bassett. ISBN 0-933951-32-9. LC 89-14046.

5. *A Rose by Another Name: A Survey of Literary Flora from Shakespeare to Eco*. Robert F. Fleissner. ISBN 0-933951-33-7. LC 89-12804.

7. *Blake's Milton Designs: The Dynamics of Meaning*. J.M.Q. Davies. ISBN 0-933951-40-X. LC 92–32678.

8. *The Slaughter-House of Mammon: An Anthology of Victorian Social Protest Literature*. Edited by Sharon A. Winn and Lynn M. Alexander. ISBN 0-933951-41-8. LC 92-7269.

9. *"A Heart of Ideality in My Realism" and Other Essays on Howells and Twain*. John E. Bassett. ISBN 0-933951-36-1. LC 90-46908.

10. *Imagining Romanticism: Essays on English and Australian Romanticisms*. Edited by Deirdre Coleman and Peter Otto. ISBN 0-933951-42-6. LC 91-36509.

11. *Learning the Trade: Essays on W.B. Yeats and Contemporary Poetry*. Edited by Deborah Fleming. ISBN 0-933951-43-4. LC 92–39290.

12. *"All Nature is but Art": The Coincidence of Opposites in English Romantic Literature*. Mark Trevor Smith. ISBN 0-933951-44-2. LC 93–27166.

13. *Essays on Henry David Thoreau: Rhetoric, Style, and Audience*. Richard Dillman. ISBN 0-933951-50-7. LC 92–39960.

14. *Author-ity and Textuality: Current Views of Collaborative Writing*. Edited by James S. Leonard. ISBN 0-933951-57-4. LC 94-15111.

15. *Women's Work: Essays in Cultural Studies*. Shelley Armitage. ISBN 0-933951-58-2. LC 95-6180.

16. *Perspectives on American Culture: Essays on Humor, Literature, and the Popular Arts*. ISBN 0-933951-59-0. LC 94-14908.

17. *Bridging the Gap: Literary Theory in the Classroom*. Edited by J.M.Q. Davies. ISBN 0-933951-60-4. LC 94–17926.

18. *Juan Benet: A Critical Reappraisal of His Fiction*. Edited by John Baptist Margenot III. ISBN 0-933951-61-2.

19. *The American Trilogy, 1900–1937: Norris, Dreiser, Dos Passos and the History of Mammon*. John C. Waldmeir. ISBN 0-933951-64-7. LC 94-48837.

20. *"The Muses Females Are": Martha Moulsworth and Other Women Writers of the English Renaissance*. Ed. by Robert C. Evans and Anne C. Little. ISBN 0-933951-63-9.

"The Muses Females Are"

*Martha Moulsworth
and Other Women Writers
of the English Renaissance*

edited by

Robert C. Evans and Anne C. Little

LOCUST HILL PRESS
West Cornwall, CT
1995

Library of Congress Cataloging-in-Publication Data

The Muses females are : Martha Moulsworth and other women writers of
the English Renaissance / edited by Robert C. Evans and Anne C.
Little.
   315p.   cm. -- (Locust Hill literary studies : no. 20)
   ISBN 0-933951-63-9 (library binding : alk. paper)
   1. Moulsworth, Martha--Criticism and interpretation. 2. English
literature--Early modern, 1500-1700--History and criticism.
3. English literature--Women authors--History and criticism.
4. Women and literature--England--history--17th century.
5. Moulsworth, Martha--Contemporaries. 6. Autobiography--Women
authors. 7. Sex role in literature. 8. Renaissance--England.
I. Evans, Robert C. II. Little, Anne C. III. Series.
PR2323.M67Z78 1995
821'.4--dc20   95-22413
                                                       CIP

Printed on acid-free, 250-year-life paper
Manufactured in the United States of America

for

Claramae Dunham and Margaret Hockenberry
(with thanks for their love)

and to

Bob, Lisa, and Stephanie Little

Contents

Autobiographical Approaches

Gender Issues: Education, the Muses, and Widowhood

Appendices

Acknowledgments

The editors of any collective effort such as this must feel especially grateful to all the contributors who agreed to participate. We thank them for their generosity, their promptness, their patience, and especially their encouragement at every stage along the way of preparing this book. For similar virtues we also owe a huge debt of gratitude to Tom Bechtle of Locust Hill Press, who has been unfailingly kind, supportive, and tolerant. A better publisher and editor could not be asked for or found. Although his name does not appear on the title page, in many respects this is largely Tom's book.

The editors owe special thanks to Professor Steven May for his early encouragment and assistance; to Alan Gribben and other administrators at Auburn University at Montgomery, who could not have been more supportive; and to our colleagues in the Department of English and Philosophy, who helped in every way possible. Finally, we are especially and enthusiastically grateful to Stephen Parks of the Beinecke Library at Yale University. He has been an unstinting supporter of this project from the very first moment and has been, at every stage, a model of magnanimity.

We are grateful to the various libraries where work on this project was done, including not only the Beinecke but also the Bodleian; the Folger; the British Library; the Public Record Office in Chancery Lane; the Greater London Record Office; the National Register of Archives; the Hertfordshire County Record Office; the Goldsmiths' Library (and its very hospitable, helpful librarian, David Beasley); the Library of Drapers' Hall; the Guildhall Library; the University of London Library; the Rare Books Library of University College, London; and the Public Library of Hoddesdon in Hertfordshire. We thank the Beinecke for permission to publish the photographs of the original manuscript; we thank the Bodleian for permission to publish the transcript of Thomas Hassall's funeral sermon; we thank the London Charterhouse and the Greater London Record Office for permission to publish the transcript of Ane

Lawraunce's letter to Thomas Sutton; and we thank the Public Record Office for allowing us to use the wills of Martha Moulsworth and her three husbands.

In fact, through a very strange coincidence, it was at the Public Record Office that one of the editors made the altogether chance acquaintance of Mr. Ivan Molesworth, a direct descendent of the brother of Martha's third husband. We thank Mr. Molesworth for the help he provided during what seemed a little like an episode from *The Twilight Zone*. Finally, we thank Mrs. V.I. Taylor for her exceptional kindness and hospitality, her patience over the phone, and her willingness to save one of the editors from a long walk in the English rain.

Individually, Robert Evans wishes to thank, as always, Ruth, as well as his family and the many students who contributed so much to the atmosphere of good feelings and goodwill from which this volume has emerged. These include especially Kevin Bowden, Lynn Bryan, Randall Cobb, Phil Festoso, Kurt Niland, Karen Pirnie, Neil Probst, Judy Sims, Hubble Sowards, and Gwen Warde. Anne Little has been a superb friend, colleague, and co-editor. Finally, four other colleagues deserve special thanks and special mention: Jim Barfoot, Ann Depas-Orange, Jan Dudle, and especially Barbara Wiedemann.

Anne Little wishes to thank friend and colleague Robert Evans for offering her the opportunity to work on this exciting project. She also thanks that other Robert for his good-natured support in the midst of his own academic deadlines. She wishes to thank Alan Gribben and Jim Barfoot personally for their encouragement and Susie Paul for the sparkle she brings to life at AUM.

Contributors

Jean R. Brink is Professor of English at Arizona State University. She is the author of *Michael Drayton Revisited* (Boston: G.K. Hall, 1990) and is currently working on a biography of Spenser that will contextualize documentary sources and shed new light on Spenser's life and works. She is also the General Editor for the Garland Encyclopedia on Renaissance women.

Esther S. Cope is Professor of History at the University of Nebraska–Lincoln. Her most recent book is *Handmaid of the Holy Spirit: Dame Eleanor Davies, Never Soe Mad a Ladie* (University of Michigan, 1992). She is currently editing thirty-eight of Davies's prophetic writings for the Women Writers' Project in a volume to be published by Oxford University Press in 1995.

Joseph P. Crowley is an Assistant Professor of English at Auburn University at Montgomery. He holds the Ph.D. in English from the University of North Carolina at Chapel Hill. His publications and research have mostly been in areas of Old English language: dialects, charters, place-names, and interlinear glosses to Latin prayers.

Ann Depas-Orange is Assistant Professor of English at Auburn University at Montgomery. She holds a master's degree from Tuskegee University and is presently completing her doctorate. She has written on American women of color, including Julia Cooper and Maria W. Stewart, and has also written on composition theory. From 1987 to 1989 she held a Bush Foundation Faculty Development Award at Tuskegee University. She is co-editor of a forthcoming collection of student essays on early modern women writers.

Robert C. Evans is the author of four books on Ben Jonson and of various articles on Jonson and other Renaissance authors. With his colleague Barbara Wiedemann, he co-edited *"My Name Was*

Martha": A Renaissance Woman's Autobiographical Poem (1993), the first edition of Moulsworth's "Memorandum." He was recently named Distinguished Research Professor at Auburn University at Montgomery, where he has taught since 1982.

Germaine Greer, Ph.D., is a fellow of Newham College, Cambridge, and the founder, Director, Managing Editor and sole financier of Stump Cross Books, under which imprint she publishes scholarly editions of works by women. So far they have managed to produce *The Uncollected Works of Aphra Behn*, and *The Collected Works of Katherine Philips* in three volumes, edited by Patrick Thomas and others. *The Surviving Works of Anne Wharton* is in preparation and sadly held up for lack of funds to finance the printing which has become exorbitantly expensive.

Isobel Grundy is Henry Marshall Tory Professor at the University of Alberta, Canada. She has published on mainly eighteenth-century topics, including Samuel Johnson and Lady Mary Wortley Montagu, whose life she is now writing. She was one of three authors of *The Feminist Companion to Literature in English: Women Writers from the Middle Ages to the Present* (Yale University Press, 1990) and is now one of a team working to produce a history of women's writing in the British Isles, which will be published both in print and electronically.

Patricia N. Hill is Associate Professor of English at Auburn University at Montgomery, where for more than fifteen years she was department head. Her teaching interests are wide-ranging, and she has written on such topics as religion, myth, Orwell, Wordsworth, and Jung. She was awarded an NDEA fellowship and recently completed a second master's degree (with honors) in religious studies.

Mary Ellen Lamb, Professor of English at Southern Illinois University, is the author of *Gender and Authorship in the Sidney Circle* (University of Wisconsin Press, 1990) and of numerous articles on early modern women writers and Shakespeare in journals such as *Shakespeare Survey*, *Shakespeare Studies*, *English Literary Renaissance*, and *Criticism*.

Anne C. Little is an Associate Professor of English at Auburn University at Montgomery. Although her specialty in American literature has prompted work on such diverse authors as William Faulkner, Flannery O'Connor, and Denise Levertov, she has also written on Ben Jonson and Alice Perrin. She is currently revising a study of the composition of *By Love Possessed*, by James Gould Cozzens, and is co-editing (with Robert Evans and Barbara Wiedemann) *Perspectives*, a compendium of abstracts of critical articles to accompany the study of the short story.

Anthony Low is Professor of English and chair of the department at New York University. Among other works he is the author of *Augustine Baker* (1970), *The Blaze of Noon* (1974), *Love's Architecture* (1978), *The Georgic Revolution* (1985), and *The Reinvention of Love* (1993). His next book has the working title *Umpire Conscience*.

Susie Paul, Associate Professor of English at Auburn University at Montgomery, is the mother of Joseph and Amelia and the author of a book on Faulkner and of articles on various American writers. She teaches composition and American literature and has had poems published in such journals as *Kalliopi*, *Negative Capability*, *Petroglyph*, and *Georgia Review*.

Curtis Perry is a Lecturer in History and Literature at Harvard University. He is the author of recent and forthcoming essays in *Studies in English Literature*, the *Journal of Medieval and Renaissance Studies*, *Renaissance Drama*, and *Spenser Studies*, and is currently preparing a book-length manuscript on Jacobean literature and culture.

Karen Worley Pirnie has an undergraduate degree from Stanford University and a master's degree in liberal studies from Auburn University at Montgomery, where she wrote a thesis on the character Celia in Ben Jonson's *Volpone*. Presently she is completing her Ph.D in the Renaissance Studies Program at the University of Alabama.

Anne Lake Prescott, who teaches at Barnard and Columbia, is the author of *French Poets and the English Renaissance* and a number of articles on Renaissance subjects. Co-editor of the 1993 Norton Critical Edition of Edmund Spenser's poetry, she is completing a book on Rabelais and Renaissance England and, with Betty Travitsky, collecting material for an anthology of early modern English texts by men and women aimed at increasing students' awareness of gender in Renaissance literature.

Neil P. Probst is completing a degree in English literature at Auburn University at Montgomery. He is the co-author of two brief articles on Ben Jonson published in *Notes and Queries* and is compiler of an analytical index to Jonson's *Discoveries* scheduled for publication in the *Ben Jonson Journal*.

Josephine A. Roberts is William A. Read Professor of English at Louisiana State University. Her publications include a book on Sir Philip Sidney's *Arcadia* (1978) and editions of Lady Mary Wroth's poems (1983; rev. 1992) and the first part of her prose romance, *The Countess of Montgomery's Urania* (1994). She is completing her edition of the second volume of Wroth's *Urania*, the unpublished holograph manuscript at the Newberry Library, Chicago.

John T. Shawcross, Professor Emeritus, University of Kentucky, has published on various Renaissance authors, including Spenser, Shakespeare, Donne, and Milton. A forthcoming collection presents an essay on Bathsua Makin and Katherine Philips as additional marginalized authors.

Matthew Steggle is a doctoral student at Oxford University. His research interests include Jonson, Nashe, and the Renaissance reception of Greek Old Comedy.

Eric Sterling (Ph.D. Indiana) is an Assistant Professor of English at Auburn University at Montgomery. He has published articles on Edmund Spenser, William Shakespeare, Edward Albee, and Arthur Miller and has presented papers at numerous scholarly conferences.

Frances Teague is Professor of English at the University of Georgia. She has published four books on various aspects of Renaissance drama. Her essays range widely, including studies of Elizabeth I, Christine de Pizan, Bathsua Makin, and Frances Brooke. Currently she is completing a study of Makin's life and work.

Preface

In the brief period since the first publication, in 1993, of "The Memorandum of Martha Moulsworth," both Moulsworth and her poem have been the subject of increasingly serious and appreciative attention. Her work has been recognized as one of the earliest pieces of autobiography in English, as one of the first autobiographical poems, as one of our best pieces of information about the inner life of an early modern woman, and as one of the earliest and most radical calls in England for educational equality. One reviewer of the first edition termed the poem an "important discovery for Renaissance scholars," but she also "highly recommended" it to undergraduates, graduate students, and faculty in general.[1] David Norbrook (himself a very distinguished Renaissance scholar) stressed the poem's considerable historical value but also called it a text possessing "a degree of formal interest well beyond the documentary."[2] Likewise, another reviewer emphasized the poem's interest not only as an important cultural document but also as a satisfying work of art.[3]

However, not only scholarly reviewers have responded positively to Martha Moulsworth's poem. So have the numerous students who have now encountered the work—including beginning writers in composition classes, beginning readers in sophomore survey courses, more advanced students in upper-level literature classes, and students in masters' and doctoral-level programs. In fact, one of the most gratifying aspects of working with the "Memorandum" has been the opportunity such work has provided to involve students in serious pioneering scholarship focusing on a previously unknown author. For that matter, the whole Moulsworth "project" has been satisfyingly collaborative from the

---

[1]J.P. Baumgaertner, in *Choice* (March 1994): item 31–3653.
[2]See *Notes and Queries* 239.4 (December 1994): 566.
[3]Nancy Gutierrez, in *Sixteenth Century Journal* 24 (1994): 936–37.

start, involving students and colleagues in a genuinely shared (and sharing) effort.

Not only students and teachers, however, have responded to Martha Moulsworth. Since her poem has been featured in at least one state-wide lecture program, it has also been "tested" before widely diverse public audiences. Repeatedly the poem has passed these tests exceptionally well. Here is a voice that seems to speak clearly and engagingly from a distance of centuries, and which seems to speak compellingly to audiences who have no professional interest in early modern culture. As might be expected, the poem appeals greatly to people who have reached (or passed beyond) middle age, but an especially surprising feature of the poem's reception has been the enthusiasm with which young people have responded to the work and its author. Young college-age men, in particular, have routinely expressed admiration for Moulsworth's strength of character and resilient spirit, and one member of an audience memorably summed up Martha's personality by calling her "spunky."

In fact, reviewers, scholars, students, and general readers have all indicated a real desire to learn more not only about Moulsworth's poem but also about her life. When the "Memorandum" was first published, biographical information seemed very hard to come by; in the intervening years, however, an enormous amount of new data has been uncovered. One function of this book, then, is to bring together these biographical facts, but an even more important function is to bring together some of the varied and vigorous responses the poem has so far elicited from its first readers, who include some of the most accomplished critics and scholars of the early modern period. The fact that so many fine minds agreed so readily and generously to participate in this project testifies, we think, to the real merit of Moulsworth's poem, not only as a piece of historical evidence but also as a thoughtfully crafted work of art. Finally, one further function of this volume has been to provide contributors a chance to relate Moulsworth to other significant women writers of her day. Many essayists use Moulsworth as a touchstone for discussing numerous other authors, including such figures as Anne Bradstreet, Margaret Cavendish (the Duchess of Newcastle), Lady Anne Clifford, An Collins, Queen Elizabeth I, Elizabeth Grymston, Lady Elizabeth Langham, Aemilia Lanyer, Bathsua Makin, Elizabeth Melville, Katherine Philips, Mary Sidney (the Countess of Pembroke), Rachel Speght, and Lady Mary Wroth (to name a few).

Ultimately, of course, the book's chief focus remains Moulsworth's poem and personality. In fact, almost everyone—in classes, lectures, letters, and essays—has responded warmly to Moulsworth the person; she seems to have been the kind of human being most people would enjoy meeting and knowing. The editors of this volume therefore have felt privileged to work so closely with Martha and her poem, and they take pleasure in helping to introduce both to an even wider circle of new acquaintances.

Introduction

Anne C. Little

Rarely in the late twentieth century does the literary critic write without first having to consider a body of published scholarship about the work to be discussed. The process usually requires ensuring that one's analysis is original and responding to other relevant ideas. The writers in this volume, however, began with a relatively clean slate. The work they examine, "The Memorandum of Martha Moulsworth, Widdowe," was only recently discovered in the Beinecke Library at Yale, having gone largely unnoticed in the back of a manuscript volume of political documents. The only essays about the poem to be read in preparation for this volume were those which editors Robert C. Evans and Barbara Wiedemann wrote to accompany the poem at its publication by Locust Hill Press in 1993. The possible approaches were therefore almost unlimited.

Soon after the publication of the Martha poem, as the "Memorandum" is sometimes affectionately called, two follow-up volumes were conceived. The first, *The Muses Females Are: Martha Moulsworth and Other Women Writers of the English Renaissance*, now completed, includes invited essays from major scholars in Renaissance literature, history, and women's studies. The second volume will contain essays by winners of an international contest open to undergraduate and graduate students.

Responses to the requests for essays for the first volume were exciting. Within several weeks of mailing the requests, we had received a number of letters, some declining because of previous commitments, but all enthusiastic about the poem and the proposed volume of criticism. By 15 December 1993 we had received our first essay, "Early Modern Women and 'the muses ffemall,'" by Frances Teague, and responses and papers continued to arrive for many months.

We gave no suggestions and set no parameters except page length, but left to the writers all decisions of what to discuss. On the few occasions when submitted abstracts or essays suggested possible repetition, we informed the author of the later entry. The scholars worked for the most part in isolation from each other, trying to flesh out the portrait of the poet, responding to the poem from numerous perspectives, and placing it in various contexts. Now that the essays have been completed, the assembled body of scholarship provides a varied cross-section as each essay illuminates a different facet of the "Memorandum."

When the poem was first published, little was known about Martha Moulsworth's life except what she mentions in the poem. A bookseller's information sheet describing the manuscript states that Moulsworth's father had died in 1580, a surprising biographical detail that seemed erroneous because it contradicts the poem. However, since the poem was published, much information has been found, including confirmation of the date of Moulsworth's father's death. As a result of the first three essays, which explore Moulsworth's biography, one now has a much better sense of the person behind the poem.

In her essay "'Backward springs': The Self-Invention of Martha Moulsworth," Germaine Greer cautions against accepting autobiography as truth because the writer is in fact attempting "to reinvent the self as text." Any effort like Moulsworth's to compress a life into a relatively short poem necessitates choosing details to fit the portrait being created. Drawing on the biographical facts she discovered about Moulsworth's life, Greer contrasts the persona created in the poem—a pious, educated daughter, wife, and mother whose children had all died—to the persona revealed in her will—a generous, motherly woman bequeathing money to other people's children.

Isobel Grundy's essay "Identity and Numbers in Martha Moulsworth's 'Memorandum'" takes another approach to biography. By citing facts found in historical documents and raising questions and offering hypotheses prompted by those records, Grundy demonstrates how biographies come into focus. She offers details about the identity and profession of Moulsworth's father, suggests four Thomas Thorowgoods who might have been Moulsworth's second husband, and names two children who were probably born to Moulsworth. Grundy also compares the "Memorandum" with works by Lady Eleanor Douglas and Elizabeth (Cavendish) Egerton, Countess of Bridgewater, to show how Moulsworth, following a practice common among Renaissance women, uses numerology to demonstrate the order and significance of events in her life and establish her "historical identity."

"The Life and Times of Martha Moulsworth," by Robert Evans, gives a surprisingly full account of Moulsworth, placing her in the life of a London neighborhood (probably Farringdon Within or Bread Street) and in the town of Hoddesdon, north of London, in which she later lived. He draws on the wills of Moulsworth and her three husbands, the sermon preached at her funeral, and a variety of other sources to develop the portrait sketched in the poem. These sources reveal Moulsworth and her three husbands to have been prominent, respected citizens active in civic and religious life, and occasionally involved in an ongoing controversy between two local vicars. Although Moulsworth had lost all her own children by the time she wrote the "Memorandum," she maintained a particularly close relationship with one stepdaughter and her husband and children. The historical documents confirm that Martha was indeed, as the poem suggests, a generous, devout, independent, and intelligent woman.

The six essays and notes in the second group examine the poem as a literary text. Anthony Low's "Martha Moulsworth and the Uses of Rhetoric: Love, Mourning, and Reciprocity" recognizes the poem as autobiography but also places it in the genre of memorial elegy. Low finds Moulsworth's honest expression of mourning innovative at a time when Protestant grief was generally repressed, and he argues for the poem's inclusion in the canon because of Moulsworth's artfulness. Derived from her study of Latin, rhetorical devices like *epizeuxis* ("'And yett, and yett' … [repeated] without intervening matter") enable her to evoke emotion in her reader. Also progressive is her acknowledgment of mutually satisfying married love, which few English poets before Milton recognize.

Surprised that an early modern woman includes marginalia in her poem, Anne Lake Prescott, in her essay "Marginally Funny: Martha Moulsworth's Puns," analyzes the subtle and sophisticated puns outside the text of the poem. The "tell clocke" tolls the hours of Moulsworth's life while acknowledging the contemporary view that the muse of poetry makes one slothful. "Lattin" plays on the meaning of "latten," a base alloy of copper and zinc, and emphasizes the limited value of Latin as a "mariadge metall." Prescott finds unity in the poem through the pun on latten, the "siluar" of widowhood, which Moulsworth finally treasures, and other references to metal and money. These allude to the marriage market and remind the reader that the scholarly world beyond is closed to women.

Mary Ellen Lamb's essay "The Poem as a Clock: Martha Moulsworth Tells Time Three Ways" analyzes how one kind of time depicted in Moulsworth's poems thwarts the other two kinds of time used to structure the poem. The obvious structuring device, linear time, is marked by references to actual dates and events related to Moulsworth's three marriages and ending with her widowhood. A second kind of time, cyclical, contrasts with the first and is measured by days in the Anglican calendar. Within this framework Moulsworth memorializes each husband by mentioning the saint's day on which he died. The third, "meditation-time," is delineated by biblical references which allow her to contemplate judgment day, thus conflating past, present, and future. As she carefully orders time into linear and cyclical patterns, Moulsworth seems confident she will live with all three husbands in a spiritual state in the afterlife. However, her meditations on the biblical texts lead her to envision corporeal resurrection, which poses a dilemma at the end of linear time when she will have all three husbands.

In his note "'The Memorandum,' Sacraments, and Ewelme Church," Matthew Steggle follows the example of critics who have studied George Herbert's *The Temple* and examines Moulsworth's poem through architectural metaphors, which he locates in St. Mary's Church, Ewelme, Oxfordshire. Although Moulsworth was probably baptized in this church during her father's tenure as rector, Steggle chose the church primarily because it is typical of rural Anglican churches during Moulsworth's time. Like the well-preserved church, whose walls are covered with scriptural texts and with the letters "IHS" ("the sacred name of Jesus"), the "Memorandum" contains elements which are both decorative and meaningful. Images which adorn the poem become signs that God has given Moulsworth grace to "dight" her "Inward house," and the poem as a whole becomes a testament to the new stage in her life which she celebrates through the poem: her widowhood.

My note, "'By him I was brought vpp': Evoking the Father in Moulsworth's 'Memorandum,'" questions why an apparently straightforward poet like Moulsworth would exaggerate the influence of her father. Although her father in fact died before she was three years old, she attributes to his teaching the positive aspects of her character as well as her learning of Latin. She could have been motivated by a number of factors, including the desire to supply a respected figure to sanction her education and her writing.

Susie Paul's note, "Martha Moulsworth's 'Memorandum': Crossing the Climacteric," finds Moulsworth's poem to be a guide for those facing the climacteric and old age. Anticipating the strategies offered by women writers in the late twentieth century, Moulsworth takes the steps necessary to move serenely into the last stage of her life. She risks being labeled a crone as she speaks out against inequity by advocating a university for women. She commemorates the men in her life while at the same time letting them go and embracing her own freedom. And, finally, revealing the wisdom of acceptance she has learned with age, she celebrates the "siluar" of widowhood.

"Biblical Resonance in Moulsworth's 'Memorandum,'" by Robert C. Evans and Neil P. Probst, examines the allusions to scripture found in the margins of Moulsworth's poem. The first allusion—"Acts 17:28 &c"—is one of the richest, with its "&c" (*et cetera*) which prompts the reader to look beyond the cited verse. In addition to containing the biblical passage echoed in the poem, this reference sanctions both the writing of poetry and a classical education like Moulsworth's, includes imagery of the precious metals Moulsworth incorporates, stresses the need to prepare for judgment as Moulsworth does, and mentions a woman who embodies the same intellectual and Christian qualities noted in and advocated by Moulsworth. Other complex allusions also send the reader to reexamine the biblical text, which in turn enhances the reading of the poem.

The essays in the third section focus on autobiography and attempt to place Moulsworth's work in the context of that genre. In her essay "'My Inward House': Women's Autobiographical Poetry in the Early Seventeenth Century," Josephine A. Roberts examines Moulsworth's poem against the three most common kinds of women's autobiography during the period: the dream-vision, the mother's legacy, and the epitaph. Although rejecting the form of the dream-vision, Moulsworth, like Aemilia Lanyer and Lady Mary Wroth, borrows elements from that genre to present her "Memorandum." Her poem is also similar to works such as Elizabeth Grymeston's book of advice to her son, but instead of writing for her own children (who she notes are all dead), she writes for children of the future. As Moulsworth remembers her three husbands, the poem becomes a kind of epitaph like those Elizabeth Egerton and Katherine Philips wrote to their sons.

Curtis Perry's "'My muse is a tell clocke': The Paradox of Ritual Autobiography in Martha Moulsworth's 'Memorandum'" reveals how the poem functions as both a ritualistic memorialization of events in Moulsworth's life and a commemoration of those events in her life which are public rituals. In a society which considered eloquence in women to be unchaste, Moulsworth "negotiated" within the tradition of ritual autobiography to find a voice that was acceptable for a woman. While appearing to observe the restrictions placed on women's writing, she managed to do what our more modern conception of autobiography expects. She created an identity as she described her own education and endorsed a university for women. With her acknowledgment that Christians have their being only in Christ, she seems also aware that she can have her being as a woman writer only within a traditional form like autobiography.

Karen Worley Pirnie offers a survey of scholarship in "Research Sources on Seventeenth-Century Women's Autobiography." She summarizes, and sometimes assesses, bibliographical articles, studies which define and discuss autobiography in general and women's autobiography in particular, books containing primary texts, and criticism on clusters of seventeenth-century women as well as individual writers, including Julian of Norwich, Margery Kempe, Margaret Cavendish, and others. As she outlines what has been done, Pirnie explains where Moulsworth would fit into the discussions had she been included, thus implying topics for future consideration.

The last four essays deal with gender issues: education, attitudes about women writers and the muses, and the institution of widowhood. John T. Shawcross, in "'The Muses Females Are': Renaissance Women and Education," discusses the issue of genderfication as it applies to literary critics of today and the newly discovered seventeenth-century works they examine. Shawcross welcomes the retrieval of lost writings by women but suggests less emphasis on the fact that women wrote them and more on their quality as literature. He argues that critics have failed to show the literary merit of works like the psalm translations of Mary Sidney Herbert, the Countess of Pembroke, and the less well-known poems by Anne Bradstreet because of an emphasis on "gender categorizations." Despite the progressive ideas on education expressed by writers like Bathsua Makin and Martha Moulsworth, Shawcross sees reflected in the works of both women the acceptance of more traditional views on female roles and capabilities. Although genderfication continues to be evident today, he sees the seventeenth century as an important transitional period in changing attitudes toward women.

Frances Teague's "Early Modern Women and 'the muses ffemall'" offers Renaissance notions about the muses as one explanation of why so few women of the period wrote and why those who did sought support from other women. Because of the view that inspiration resulted from an erotic relationship between the female muse and the male writer, some women hesitated to write, fearing the label of lesbian or even whore. Martha Moulsworth exemplifies women who adopted another perspective, those who identified with the muses because they were female and consequently felt authorized by the muses to write. The relationship women like Moulsworth found with the muses can also be seen in the networks of mutual support female writers established with other learned women.

"Educating Women and the Lower Orders," by Jean R. Brink, challenges revisionists who doubt that educational opportunities for women increased during the Renaissance. In the mid-sixteenth century women and the lower classes were deemed unsuited for education, but three examples suggest that prejudices against women later began to loosen. Martha Moulsworth demonstrated that a woman of the gentry could be educated, and she herself suggested a university for women. Bathsua Makin was respected for her learning and sought to educate other women as well. Although Richard Mulcaster, the headmaster of Merchant Taylor's School in London, differed from Makin by rejecting education for the poor, he anticipated her by espousing female education as early as 1581.

In her essay "'The Widdowes Silvar': Widowhood in Early Modern England," Esther S. Cope tests the accuracy of some seventeenth-century stereotypes, surveys the various kinds of widows that actually existed, and places Moulsworth in the context of the institution of widowhood. Widows were often depicted as figures of fun or pity because they no longer had men to guide them, and in reality, the "'forlorn' or 'poor' widow" seems to have been fairly common. However, young women frequently remarried to secure their financial position or gain a father for their small children, and some women were able to continue their husbands' businesses, thus making marriage optional. Others, who were seen as "reverend widows," dedicated themselves to a life of piety and/or good works rather than remarrying. After her first husband died,

Moulsworth followed the pattern of the young widows by taking a second husband within a year. Her third marriage is atypical, but her decision not to wed a fourth time allows her to fit into the category of "reverend widow" as she turned her attention toward God. Although the poem offers a rare firsthand look at Renaissance widowhood, Cope finds equally enlightening the portrait of Martha Moulsworth, "widdowe."

Following the essays are several appendices to supplement reading of the poem. Appendix 1 consists of old- and modern-spelling versions of the "Memorandum" as well as annotations and a photographic reproduction of the Yale manuscript. Appendix 2 contains "Transcripts of the Wills of Martha Moulsworth and Her Three Husbands" and a list identifying the persons mentioned in the wills. Both parts of this appendix were prepared by Robert Evans. Appendix 3 includes a transcript (by Evans) of "Thomas Hassall's Funeral Sermon on Martha Moulsworth," and notes to the sermon by Ann Depas-Orange. "More Poems by Martha Moulsworth?," Evans's note found in Appendix 4, raises the question of whether more poems by Martha Moulsworth may exist and offers one example which could be Moulsworth's. Appendix 5 presents "'A Suter for My Sealfe': A Letter, 1610, from Ane Lawraunce to Thomas Sutton," a previously unpublished letter by a contemporary of Moulsworth who shows the kind of spirit that characterizes Moulsworth's poem. The letter was transcribed and edited by Joseph P. Crowley, with an introduction by Patricia N. Hill. Appendix 6 completes the volume with a timeline prepared by Eric Sterling, "Women Writers of the English Renaissance: A Chronology of Texts and Contexts" from 1558 to 1660.

Both editors of the present volume share the excitement generated by the discovery of Martha's poem and the scholars' thoughtful analyses of it which follow here. Although the critics here assembled respond in such diverse ways to Moulsworth's work, the poem is quite rich and offers many other avenues to be explored. We hope the reader will be stimulated to further study of the poem through the essays, notes, and appendices in *"The Muses Females Are."*

Moulsworth or Molesworth?
A Note on Names, Spellings,
and Editorial Principles

Robert C. Evans

Since the original publication of Martha Moulsworth's "Memorandum" in 1993, an extraordinary amount of new information about her life and circumstances has come to light. References to Moulsworth, her husbands, and other relatives occur in numerous surviving documents, and one purpose of this book is to bring together as much of that evidence as possible. One problem, however, immediately presents itself—namely, the well-known tendency (familiar to anyone who has worked with Renaissance manuscripts) for spelling to seem highly capricious, or at least to lack the absolute regularity that modern writers and readers tend to take for granted.

In this case the problem is particularly acute, since our only known surviving manuscript of the "Memorandum" gives its author's name, in the poem's very title, as "Martha Moulsworth," whereas most other contemporary documents (including her will) give the spelling "Molesworth." Moreover, in other contemporary documents the name is spelled in a bewildering variety of ways, including Moulsworth, Moulsworthe, Moullsworth, Mowleswoorthe, Mowlsworth, Molesworth, and even Mullesworth.

The same variety afflicts (or adorns, depending on one's point of view) numerous other names that turn up in the following pages. Martha's will, for instance, speaks of her step-son-in-law as "Marmaduke Rowdon," although the more common spelling seems to have been "Rawdon," as the will itself later makes clear. Similarly, in that will, the spelling of Martha's first husband's last name is given as "Pryn," whereas the spelling given in the poem (and the more common spelling in contemporary manuscripts) is

"Prynne," while in the will of the first husband himself the spelling is given as "Pryne." Similarly, the poem manuscript gives the spelling of Martha's second husband's name as Thomas "Througood," whereas the more common spelling seems to have been "Thorowgood."[1] And, as we have already seen, even within Martha's own will, spelling is anything but consistent. Sometimes, for instance, a name is given as "Edmondes" and sometimes as "Edmonds"; sometimes a person is referred to as "Edward" and another time as "Edmond." Sometimes a name is spelled "Hassell" that was more commonly spelled "Hassall."

None of this, of course, is too surprising. Martha and her contemporaries were living in what was still largely an oral culture— one in which "literacy" was neither as widespread nor as regularized as it can sometimes seem today. As a standard reference source reminds us,

> In Shakespeare's time no standard system of spelling existed in English. Extant manuscripts and letters indicate a total lack of uniformity: a given word was frequently spelled more than one way on the same page. Printed material was somewhat more consistent, but even here the most important determinant in spelling a word was frequently the space or lack of space which a compositor had available in setting up a line of type. Added to this is the fact that the compositors' personal spelling habits were frequently reflected in the text.[2]

E.K. Chambers records eighty-three different spellings of the name "Shakespeare" itself in the fifteenth and sixteenth centuries,[3] and he notes that "the same man's name is often variously spelt in a single document" (2:372). He reports, for instance, that "John Shakespeare [the poet's father] gets at least a score of the forms" used in references to him (Chambers 2:372). Chambers also remarks that the "poet's own spelling ... seems to have been usually Shakspere, sometimes in an abbreviated form, but the main signature to the will is Shakspeare" (2:373). Early printed versions usu-

---

[1] The shorter spelling in the manuscript may simply have resulted from the need to squeeze the name into the available space.

[2] See *The Reader's Encyclopedia of Shakespeare*, ed. Oscar James Campbell and Edward G. Quinn (New York: Thomas Y. Crowell, 1966), 818.

[3] See E.K. Chambers, *William Shakespeare: A Study of Facts and Problems*, 2 vols. (Oxford: Clarendon Press, 1930), 2:371.

ally use the now-standard form of "Shakespeare," yet even this was sometimes printed as "Shake-speare" (Chambers 2:373).

One feels grateful, then, that there seem to be only two basic options to choose from in referring to Martha. One either selects "Moulsworth," the spelling given in our only known manuscript of the poem, or one selects "Molesworth," the spelling given in the will transcribed fourteen years after the poem was completed. After much debate with myself, and after consulting with my collaborators in this volume, I have decided to opt for "Moulsworth" when referring to the author of the poem and for "Molesworth" when referring to that author's relatives (especially her third husband).[4] I hope that this choice can be justified on several grounds.

In the first place, the "Moulsworth" spelling conforms to our only known surviving manuscript of the "Memorandum." Until another, earlier, or more authentic manuscript turns up, there seems some justice in following the spelling given in what is at present our best source. It seems impossible to say (at least for the moment) whether the handwriting in the manuscript was done by Martha herself, or whether it was produced by someone else. If the handwriting *is* Martha's, then the decision to use "Moulsworth" seems especially sound. If the handwriting is that of someone who was taking dictation from Martha, then we can assume that she at least glanced at the finished text and had no objection to the spelling given there. If the handwriting is that of someone copying from Martha's own holograph, then selecting the "Moulsworth" spelling also seems justifiable. Numerous other possibilities can be imagined, all involving different degrees of speculation. However, since "Moulsworth" seems to have been a common and acceptable spelling of Martha's name during Martha's time, there seems no reason to assume that she could not have chosen this spelling herself on occasion.

Moreover, by referring to Martha as "Moulsworth" and her husband as "Molesworth," a wholly accidental benefit will accrue—the benefit of allowing us to distinguish more easily between them in the pages that follow. In fact, it is even just faintly possible that at the time she composed her poem, Martha chose the

---

[4]However, if a contributor to this volume has expressed a strong preference for using "Molesworth" rather than "Moulsworth" to refer to Martha, Anne Little and I have decided to honor the contributor's preference.

"Moulsworth" spelling as a subtle way of asserting her independent identity.

In addition, using the "Moulsworth" spelling has the practical advantage of keeping this volume uniform with the book in which Martha's poem first came into print. Librarians everywhere will probably appreciate such consistency, although they should be advised that the best procedure will be to cross-index Martha Moulsworth as Martha Molesworth. Perhaps in time "Molesworth" will come to seem the preferred spelling, just as today we routinely refer to "Shakespeare" rather than to "Shake-speare," "Shakspere," or "Shakspeare."

Finally, it should be mentioned here that in the essays and documents that follow, the original spellings of all words are used unless otherwise noted. Likewise, original punctuation (or the lack thereof) has also been preserved. One or two essayists have chosen to modernize spelling in some documents they quote, but elsewhere (especially in the appendices and in the long biographical essay), the spellings printed are the same spellings as originally written in the archival sources. Usually these spellings are not difficult to decipher, but in cases where problems seem likely to arise, explanatory notes have been given.

Biographical Approaches

"Backward springs":
The Self-Invention of Martha Moulsworth

Germaine Greer

Renaissance autobiography being lineally descended from the *apologia pro vita sua* by way of the scaffold speech, it is inevitable that a naive reading should regard it as documentary and as a consequence defective if it is not truthful. Yet every writer of autobiography sets out not to explain the self via text but to reinvent the self as text. Literary autobiography is *sui generis* not to be trusted. The extent to which the Martha Moulsworth of "The Memorandum" is a literary construct can only be fully understood when the other texts that comprise the documentation of her life events are compared to her poem, but any reader is at once aware that radical re-invention strategies are in operation. Any autobiographer, let alone a biographer compressing fifty-five years into fifty-five couplets, must select the identifying events and characteristics that will create a consistent image. Moulsworth identifies herself as the daughter of a father rather than a mother and the successful wife of her husbands rather than the unsuccessful mother of short-lived children. In "The Memorandum" Moulsworth chooses to define herself only in her relationships with men as daughter, wife and widow.

If we examine the other important text authored by Moulsworth, namely her will,[1] we must be astonished at the contrast between the "I" of that text and the "I" of the poem. Moulsworth painstakingly lists a series of considerable legacies to a horde of other people's unmarried grandchildren and great grandchildren. The bulk of her considerable estate she left to her stepdaughter, Elizabeth Rawdon, and her children, not only be-

---

[1]For the full text of this document, see Appendix 2 of the present volume.

cause Elizabeth's father had left her "a plentiful estate" which she had enjoyed "these many yeares" but because the Rawdon women had "ever been loveinge and kinde" to her, and "allwaies diligent and careful" of her "both in sicknesse and in health insoemuch" that they had gained and continued to deserve her love, as if Elizabeth had been her "owne childe." She ended: "And I love the said children and grand-children as if they were my own." It is hard to reconcile this fairy godmother with the tight-lipped hero-ine of "The Memorandum of Martha Moulsworth." The question that must be asked is whether the verse medium as understood by Moulsworth demands that she present herself as the object of male attention and place herself in a sober and dignified world as on a glass mountain far above the domestic uproar of women and chil-dren. The poem creates an image of her as the Gentleman's Daughter Who Once Knew Latin. Dear as her plea for a women's university might be to twentieth-century feminists, it is the poem that demands it; when it came to the crunch Moulsworth left noth-ing whatever to any institution of learning, not even to her father's old college, of which she seems fourteen years earlier to have been so proud. She did not stipulate, as many other testators of the same period did, that the sums should be set aside for the legatees' edu-cation.

The rigorous numerical ordering of the poem reveals not only that Moulsworth is, like Anne Bradstreet, "a right Du Bartas girl,"[2] but that she is anxious to impose order upon a disorderly career. A woman who buries three husbands and an untold number of chil-dren and can contemplate taking a fourth husband is a destructive figure. By expressing each year of her life in a neat couplet tagged with biblical echoes, Moulsworth seeks to neutralize alternative interpretations of her story. Her failed child-rearing is compressed into a single couplet:

> I by the ffirst, & last some Issue had
> butt roote, & ffruite is dead, wch makes me sad (ll. 71–72)

Other women writers of the period list their dead children by name, recording the dates of each birth, christening, death and burial; Lady Mary Carey was moved to do this even for a "little Embrio, void of life and feature."

---

[2]The expression is taken from the first introductory poem by Nathaniel Ward, to *The Tenth Muse* (1650); see also *The Works of Anne Bradstreet*, ed. Jeannine Hensley, Foreword by Adrienne Rich (Cambridge, MA: Harvard University Press, 1967), xi–xiv.

> Seven tymes I went my tyme; when mercy giving
> deliuerance vnto me; and mine all liuing:
>
> Strong, right-proportioned, louely Girles, & boyes
> There fathers; Mother's present hop't for Joyes[3]

Moulsworth has no intention of penning an obstetric poem; the children she bore are faceless, nameless "Issue," particularized, somewhat meaninglessly, as "roote, & ffruite." Because the couplet encapsulates her twenty-six-year reproductive career, it sticks in the side of her poem like a thorn; the effect is at first shocking in its callousness and then disturbing, as if its tightness were the tightness of a flinch. If we compare the syntax and connotation of this one couplet with the amplitude of Moulsworth's beginning, with its fanfare:

> Now on thatt day vppon thatt daie I write, (l. 4)

we must be struck by the density of concentration in what is not in the least an off-hand couplet.

In 1632, aged fifty-five, Moulsworth thought of herself as a learned virgin spoiled to no good effect; by 1646 she had transformed herself into a munificent matriarch by adopting her stepchildren and their children and grandchildren as her own. Both stages result from new re-inventions of self.

The self-conscious artifice of the earlier re-invention isolates Moulsworth in a cold solipsistic world in which she is free to indulge a harmless and fairly common kind of self-deception. Before she tells us anything she tells us her age which will be the vantage point from which she will order her life-as-text, then she asserts her submission to the will of God, indicating unmistakably where her religious sympathies lie. At the time of writing her poem Moulsworth was involved in two law-suits brought by the vicar of Broxbourne to whom her second husband Thomas Thorowgood had left a yearly sum for the preaching of six sermons in Hoddesdon chapel.[4] Moulsworth had illegally diverted the money, adding it to the bequest already enjoyed by the preacher of her own

---

[3]"Upon ye Sight of my abortive Birth ye 31th: of December 1657," printed in *Kissing the Rod: An Anthology of Seventeenth-Century Women's Verse*, ed. Germaine Greer, Susan Hastings, Jeslyn Medoff, and Melinda Sansone (New York: Farrar Straus Giroux, 1989), 158–61.

[4]*The Parish Register and Tithing Book of Thomas Hassall of Amwell*, ed. Stephen G. Doree (Hertford: Hertfordshire Record Society, 1989), xxii, 221, 229.

choice. So adroitly did she ply her attorneys that the churchwardens lost heart, dropped the case, and were forced to pay costs. (When the case was brought again after Moulsworth's death the parliamentary authorities found for the churchwardens.) Moulsworth's citation of the New Testament rather than the Old, as well as her use of Nicephorus, identifies her as a member of the Laudian faction. Religious polemic being central to her life at the time of the "Memorandum," it is also central to her life-as-text. Even if there were no documentary reason for accepting the genuineness of this orientation, it is undeniable, because it affects the cast of every line.

Less convincing is Moulsworth's celebration of her father, Dr. Robert Dorsett, the tutor who wrote letters in Latin to his erstwhile pupil, Sir Philip Sidney, in the debased pseudo-Ciceronian style that Sidney despised.[5] Moulsworth, whose three husbands were substantial businessmen, stresses her father's gentle birth and his connection with the land. When Dorsett died intestate the administration of his estate was taken over by a neighbor, his wife renouncing her common-law right.[6] As no entail was involved and no jointure appears to have been owed to Martha Dorsett, we may assume that Robert Dorsett had little more than the living of Ewelme which passed to his successor. We may infer from the fact that when she died less than a year after her husband Moulsworth's mother left her children and all she possessed to the care of her mother and step-father, Helena and Ralph Johnson, that her husband's only substantial connection was with his college.[7] Yet in her poem Moulsworth wishes to give not only the impression that her present wealth is hers by descent from her father, but that her father bequeathed her intellectual riches as well.

---

[5]James M. Osborn, *Young Philip Sidney: 1572–1577* (New Haven and London: Yale University Press, 1972), 312–13. Dorsett's distinguished career at Christ Church College, Oxford, which he entered in 1560, becoming BA in 1565, a canon in 1572, rector of Ewelme in 1574, serving as lecturer in rhetoric and theology, prebendary and treasurer, can be traced in the register preserved in the college library where eleven of his letters to Sir Philip Sidney may also be seen. His untimely death was commemorated by his colleagues and students in a collection of Latin poems to which George Peele contributed (BL. Add. MS 22,583). The living of Ewelme was in the college gift.

[6]PRO Chancery Lane; administration granted to William Palmer of South Stoke, Oxfordshire, relict renouncing.

[7]PRO Chancery Lane, Prob. ii, 63, 108–9.

Robert Dorsett died in 1580, when Moulsworth by her own computation should have been three years old.[8] The parish registers for Ewelme not having survived, the date of birth she gives for herself cannot be verified, but it seems unthinkable that she would use an untruth as the organizing principle of her poem. If the date of birth is true, the claim that Dorsett decked his daughter's mind with learning Latin must be false. The phenomenon is commonplace; every family historian encounters cases of individuals who pride themselves on superior connections that never existed. The claim that Moulsworth had once known Latin, apart from being unverifiable, confers veritable uniqueness; Mary Sidney, the great Countess of Pembroke, sister of the two brothers who learnt their Latin from Moulsworth's father, is not thought to have known Latin, which was less likely to be taught to women in the 1580s than it was when the great queen herself was growing up.

The truth is that any education Moulsworth had, and we know from Hassall's funeral sermon[9] that she read and wrote copiously, she had from her guardians, who are not mentioned in "The Memorandum." The intriguing story of how Dr. Dorsett's daughter came to be married to a substantial goldsmith at the age of twenty-one, when she would have been for the first time "at her own disposal," is not the story Moulsworth wishes to tell in "The Memorandum." In 1632, Moulsworth wishes to present herself as an outsider in the world of business, a gentlewoman among tradesmen. Though Bevill Molesworth was sufficiently substantial a businessman to be able to qualify as a Farmer of the Great Customs,[10] she prefers to identify him as a scion of noble stock. All her life Moulsworth had been the beneficiary of other people's business acumen, but in her poem she prefers to show esteem for rather exiguous lineage and to value herself for lineage. By the time she is drawing up her will she is unashamed to note that all her bequests are destined for the children of members of the business community, even acknowledging a chandler as her cousin. Moreover the piety of her fifties seems to have been driven out by warm feeling towards the extended step-family that had named so many daugh-

---

[8]As Dorsett lived at Ewelme when not in college, and his wife would not have been able to live with him in college, it seems likely that Martha was born and christened at Ewelme.

[9]See Appendix 3 of the present volume; the specific passage occurs at 52v–53v.

[10]*Reports of the Historical Manuscripts Commission*, 80, 1, 296.

ters Martha, revealing the extent of her gossipry (godparenthood) for, in sharp contrast to all three of her husbands, she makes no bequest whatsoever to any church organization. Interestingly, Moulsworth left £5 to her godson, the militant Puritan pamphleteer, William Prynne (1600–1669, *DNB*), a connection of her first husband's whom the author of "The Memorandum" might have been unwilling to acknowledge. As Prynne was Laud's principal persecutor and had recently published a series of libels on him and an account of his trial, we must assume that by 1646 Moulsworth's Laudian sympathies had been eradicated and with them her vision of herself as the gentlewoman who knew Latin before she married businessmen and came down in the world. It is possible, of course, that the terms of her will were entirely composed by the witnesses and executrix, but the great number of personal bequests indicates rather that Moulsworth had been composing her will for many months before the document was officially drawn.

The astonishing contrast between the withdrawn and superior persona of "The Memorandum" and the social and sociable speaker of the will is also at least partly the result of a difference in genres. "The Memorandum" is addressed to no-one; its ironies ("I loue siluar well"; l. 110) are inward smiles not unmixed with bitterness. The woman who dictated her will was addressing the witnesses and her executrix, who represented posterity. The language of will-making is as highly wrought as the language of poetry, but it is a demotic form which even the semi-literate knew how to imitate. Where "The Memorandum" is a document in the construction of self-esteem, the will is the expression of the soon-to-be-annihilated self. It is as open and outward, turned as it were toward the posterity of younger and smaller Marthas, as "The Memorandum" is inward.

Identity and Numbers in Martha Moulsworth's "Memorandum"

Isobel Grundy

Martha (Dorsett) Moulsworth, writing the story of her life in verse on her fifty-fifth birthday, 10 November 1632, presented that story in such a way as to draw out the significance of its details and to make them memorable. With her three husbands and all her children already dead, and wondering how many years were left her, she turned to poetry to vindicate the worth of her life. In commenting on such a work it is almost impossible to separate the critical from the biographical. Nor can I exclude my own biography: I am fifty-five myself as I write about the fifty-five-year-old Martha.

The poem expresses, or perhaps constructs, a healthy sense of self-worth. Baptised within 24 hours of her birth, unmarried till the then late age of twenty-one, she gives reasons for preferring early baptism and late marriage. She praises the biblical character from whom her Christian name derives, and does not mention the famous reproof which Christ addressed to the original Martha. She celebrates her father's spotless fame, his rank and wealth, and his education of her (although she concedes that this did not improve her marriage prospects). All of her three marriages, she says, were loving and fulfilling, and when her husbands died they were fortunate in dying on saints' days, as a reminder that for the Christian the death-day should be celebrated as the first day of eternal life. In keeping with the genre of the poem, she mentions only very briefly her sadness for her dead children. Finally, she praises the state of widowhood. Quite likely she wrote the poem partly to confirm a decision against accepting some prospective fourth bridegroom; it seems also that she wrote it partly to quell some lurking regret for the life of celibacy and study which she had not lived.

The most appropriate response to the poem must surely be to co-operate with Moulsworth's project of making herself remembered. She gives her father's name, and says he was a graduate of Oxford and a Doctor of Divinity. It is therefore easy to identify him: he was Robert Dorsett, B.A. 1565, D.D. 1579. His propertied status may have helped his rapid rise: having entered Christ Church, Oxford, in 1561, he became a Canon there in 1572, and Dean of Chester in 1579.[1] He was also Rector of Winwick, Northamptonshire, from 1572, and of Ewelme, Oxfordshire, from 1574. Ewelme was a place of some distinction, having a palace (long since demolished) which Elizabeth I had received as a gift from her young brother, Edward. Henry VIII had held a Privy Council there; a walnut tree there, in which it was *said* the young Elizabeth used to play, survived till the 1970s.

James I was later to attach the Rectorship of Ewelme to the Regius Professorship of Divinity at nearby Oxford; many later Rectors held high office in the church.[2] Martha Moulsworth's father looked set fair to do this too; but he died on 29 May 1580, almost certainly below the age of forty. He was buried at Ewelme, so this may have been where he lived and where his daughter Martha was born, though her birth is not listed in the International Genealogical Index for Oxfordshire.[3] But the odd thing about his death, in relation to his daughter's poem, is that she was only two-and-a-half when his Latin teaching ended. Who, one wonders, brought her up after that? Did she benefit, as girls too benefited at one or two places at this date, from the endowment of 1437 which employed a priest to give free grammar lessons to boys from the four manors around Ewelme?[4] Her silence suggests that this may have been a part of her story that she was willing to forget.

Martha's first and third husbands were evidently not university men. Her second might be any one of three Thomas Thorowgoods listed as entering Cambridge colleges in 1574, 1579, and

---

[1]Joseph Foster, *Alumni Oxonienses ... 1500–1714*, Oxford and London, 1891.

[2]Peter Renshaw, *A Guide to the Memorials and Brasses of Ewelme Church* (n.p.: n.p., 1987; [unpaginated]).

[3]Parish registers (filmed by the Church of Latter-Day Saints as the IGI) have by no means all survived from such early dates; Martha Dorsett's birth is unrecorded also in the lists for other counties with which her father had known connections.

[4]Kate Tiller and Ewelme Local History Group, *Ewelme History Trail* (n.p.: n.p., 1993), 9–11.

1580[5] (any one of them several years older than she was); or he too might be a man without university education, possibly one of that name christened in London in 1581 (in which case he would be several years younger).[6] It was in London, at St. Mary Magdalene, Old Fish Street, that Thomas and Martha were married, on the date that Martha gives as 3 February 1604, but which was probably, as Robert Evans persuasively argues, 3 February 1605 by modern reckoning.

The IGI, along with its unmistakable corroboration of Martha's second marriage, raises a number of intriguing possibilities. Richard and Martha, infant son and daughter of Nicholas Prynne, were baptised on 13 June 1602 and 15 April 1604 respectively, at St. Matthew, Friday Street. The father's combination of names is unusual; with the little girl's Christian name, it produces at least a strong likelihood that these were our Martha's children. If so, then her baby Martha was posthumous, and she was about five months pregnant when Nicholas died in December 1603, five years, eight months from their marriage. It was only a little over a year "sett on my mourninge score" (l. 54) before she re-married—perhaps in order to have a father for her children.

Her last husband may well have been the Bevill Moulsworth whose daughter Grace was christened at St. Peter, Westcheap, London, in 1587.[7] Although Martha says she and Bevill had at least one child together (whom she must have borne at forty-two or more), the IGI retains no record of it. But there were at least two other Martha Moulsworths in London, each the wife of a Wingfield (or Winkfeild or even Winglefield) Moulsworth, who were extremely prolific. Since one of the earlier Wynfeild's sons was christened Beyvell in 1602, Wingfield was likely a brother of Martha's Bevill. I have been unable to find any evidence of the Moulsworths' descent (mentioned in l. 59) from the Mortimers, a family whose medieval status is reflected in the fact that Edward III claimed the throne by descent from Roger Mortimer, Earl of March. One version of the Mortimer arms shows a bold geometri-

---

[5]John Venn and J.A. Venn, *Alumni Cantabrigienses ... Part I ... to 1751* (Cambridge: Cambridge University Press, 1924).

[6]For fuller discussion of these matters, see the biographical essay by Robert Evans included in this volume.

[7]Another Bevil (son of Robert Mowlsworth), born in 1584, would be too young to be active in the port of London in 1603, as the notes in *"My Name Was Martha"* explain that Martha's husband was.

cal design in blue, silver and gold, whose heraldic description runs: "Or, three bars azure, on a chief gold three pallets between two gyrons azure (*or* of the second), over all an inescutcheon argent."[8]

This last marriage (fittingly, Moulsworth says, her best) made her part of a large family as well as a well-descended one. It was marked by the partners' numerical appropriateness to each other: each was marrying for the third time. This is the kind of coincidence that might still make people say "it was meant"; but Martha Moulsworth's attention to numbers and dates shows that in her world-view it is God's providence, not coincidence, that rules.

Being just 55, she writes one couplet for each year of her age: 110 lines. She carefully numbers the years and months of each marriage, and of the intervals between, and finds a perfect mathematical balance. Her second marriage (the one in the middle), very conveniently took place in the year she passed the age of twenty-seven-and-a-half, exactly half her present total. Just as that year of her age was broken at its mid-point by the mid-point of her life-so-far, she breaks her poem at its mid-point (the 55th line, mid-way in a couplet) with her marginal note about her middle husband. With only slightly less perfect symmetry, her poem divides into three as well. Mathematics do not permit her to do this perfectly: as we used to say at school, three into 110 won't go. However, the poem is laid out in the Yale manuscript so that its pages contain, respectively, 34, 38, and 38 lines.

Her first husband dies on the feast of the first Christian martyr, the first day after Christ's birthday. Her second dies on the day which is, unusually, consecrated to two saints. Her third dies on a day she can plausibly associate with Christ's resurrection, and therefore with the nature of God, which is triune, or three-in-one.

Using numbers to enforce a sense of significance, of things being "meant," was common practice among women writers at this date, as it was among the populace at large. The prophet Lady Eleanor Douglas, addressing "the high Court of Parliament, The

---

[8]C.W. Scott, ed., *Boutell's Heraldry* (London and New York: Frederick Warne, 1950, rev. 1958), 58–59, 164; variant, 157. Modern descendants of Mortimers and Molesworths (the latter probably unrelated to Martha's last husband) have different arms again (Arthur Charles Fox-Davies, *Armorial Families* [Newton Abbot: David and Charles, 1970]). The Mortimer arms are shown as different though related in John E. Cussans, *Handbook of Heraldry* ... (London: Chatto and Windus, 1873), 225.

Honorable House of Commons" in *A Star to the Wise*, 1643, enforces the validity of her first supernatural vision by numbers: in this case the number one, which signifies the unity of God. The word of God, she says, came to her first in "the *first* yeer of [Charles I's] Raign, when His first Parliament called at *Oxford*": to her, "the Daughter of the *first* Peer or Baron, her *first* Husband the Kings [sic] *first* Sergeant ... in *Berkshire*, the first of Shires ... about the end of July; which moneth, named after the *first* Emperour." To publish her vision she "went immediatly to *Oxford*, that *first* University," and the pamphlet in which she published it was in due course burned by a newly-appointed bishop "in his *first* yeer, 1633."

Lady Eleanor is not typical of anything, but rather a law unto herself. But without looking further than the standard anthology of poems by seventeenth-century women, we find two elegies on children which try to make sense of their deaths by finding significance in numbering their few days of life. Elizabeth (Cavendish) Egerton, Countess of Bridgewater, writing in 1656 "On my Boy Henry," says,

> It lived dayes as many as my years,
> No more; wch caused my greeved teares;
> Twenty and Nine was the number;
> And death hath parted us asunder;

and Katherine Philips writing in 1655 "On the death of my first and dearest childe, Hector Philipps, borne the 23d of Aprill, and dy'd the 2d of May 1655," says,

> Twice Forty moneths in wedlock I did stay,
>   Then had my vows crown'd with a lovely boy.
> And yet in forty days he dropt away;
>   O! swift vicissitude of humane joy![9]

The anthology notes that Philips, who married in August 1648, is accurate about the period between then and her son's birth, but that according to her title he lived barely ten days, not forty. She must have intended *either* to give the baby's birth date as 23 March *or* to give his death date as 2 June. Either of these would give him the right number of days of life. If this is the explanation, there is a touching and upsetting discrepancy between the mother's pur-

---

[9]Germaine Greer, Susan Hastings, Jeslyn Medoff, and Melinda Sansone, eds., *Kissing the Rod: An Anthology of Seventeeth-Century Women's Verse* (New York: Farrar Straus Giroux, 1989), 117, 196–97.

poseful effort to find meaning—therefore consolation?—in numbering, and her unconscious reluctance to name the actual date of
birth, or more likely that of death.[10]

In any case, Moulsworth's use of numbers for validation seems
to lie somewhere between the prophet, boldly self-assertive, and
the grieving mothers seeking significance and therefore acceptance. By "telling" the clock of the years (see l. 11), building numbers into her poem and her life, she builds both poem and life in
accordance with the order and harmony which God has built into
the cosmos for the aesthetic pleasure of human beings. In the classical or Pythagorean tradition, the universe was structured on bi-
naries; mathematics stood in opposition to disorder and chaos, as
light stood against darkness—and male against female. In the
Christian or Augustinian tradition, the numerical properties of
things reflected the mind of God; harmony and order were divine,
while "multitude without unity is chaos."[11] For Martha
Moulsworth, a woman who after years of marriage retained her
early love of learning and the Muses, who had an unusually strong
sense of just what opportunities her gender had denied her, numbering the days of her life was a way of insisting that her mind, although female, was no site of flux and chaos. Three marriages,
plotted on a progressive curve, have a shapeliness which a fourth
marriage would debase into a mere crowd. She shows her life and
her poem to be perfectly balanced at the moment of writing: her
life by God, her poem by herself.

Number was, too, as important in history as in theory.
Margaret Cavendish, Duchess of Newcastle, said that she wrote
her autobiography in order "to tell the truth, lest after ages should
mistake"—especially, if her husband should marry a third time
after her death, lest they should mistake which wife was which
and what her historical identity was.[12] Moulsworth (with her several husbands, her dead children, her last husband's earlier wives
and multitudinous relations, some of them sharing her name) must

---

[10]Patrick Thomas, editor of Philips's *Collected Works*, suggests that
"May 2 . . . may be a mistake for June 2" (vol. 1, *The Poems* [Stump Cross:
Stump Cross Books, 1990], 13).

[11]Cf. Christopher Butler, "Numerological Thought" (1, 12, and 24) and
Marie-Sofie Rostvig, "Structure as Prophecy: The Influence of Biblical
Exegesis upon Theories of Literary Structure," in Alastair Fowler, ed.,
Silent Poetry: Essays in Numerological Analysis (London: Routledge and
Kegan Paul, 1970), 32.

[12]*Nature's Pictures Drawn by Fancie's Pencil to the Life* [1656], 390–91.

have felt the likelihood that all memory of her would vanish into that "multitude without unity" which is "chaos." Most of her contemporaries have left no enduring mark even in the parish registers; and the registers, which hide innumerable individuals indistinguishably under the same name, or spell an identical name a myriad different ways, provide a vivid impression of the confusion of multiplicity. Through number, as well as through her verbal skills, her Christian faith, her appreciation of her husbands and her solidarity with her sex, Martha Moulsworth redeems her single, separate identity.

The Life and Times
of Martha Moulsworth

Robert C. Evans

Although her poetic "Memorandum" is likely to remain our most compelling source of information about Martha Moulsworth's life (especially her inner life), a surprising amount of additional biographical data does survive. These data include Martha's will and the wills of her three husbands; a funeral sermon preached when she died (in 1646); and a variety of other material scattered throughout a wide range of sources. From such evidence we can piece together a fairly full account of at least the outlines of her existence and circumstances—the kind of world in which she lived and moved. Thus, in the period since the initial publication of her "Memorandum" in 1993, Moulsworth has gone from being an almost unknown author to being a writer about whom we know quite a bit.

This increase in knowledge has been due to the investigative work of such scholars as Steven May, Isobel Grundy, and especially Germaine Greer.[1] It was Professor May, for instance, who first called my attention (in private correspondence) to a document associating Moulsworth with a small town north of London. This one hint subsequently led to the discovery of a wealth of new material. Similarly, it was Professor Grundy who independently confirmed a suggested date of death for Martha's father (a fact crucial for interpreting the "Memorandum"). (For fuller discussion of this and other details, see her essay in this book.) Finally, it was Dr. Germaine Greer whose own research on Moulsworth's life turned up so much valuable information, particularly the connection be-

---

[1]For more details of this cooperative scholarship, see my article "A Silent Woman Speaks: 'The Memorandum of Martha Moulsworth / Widow,'" *Yale Library Gazette* (forthcoming in 1995).

tween Sir Philip Sidney and Martha's father (who functioned as
Sidney's tutor); some circumstances of Martha's early life (after the
deaths of her parents); and a host of other material relevant to
Martha's marriages and mature existence. (See Dr. Greer's essay in
this volume.)

My own work has independently confirmed the findings or
suggestions of May, Grundy, and Greer while also turning up
some new data, and in this essay I hope to bring together the facts
of Moulsworth's life as we presently know them. These facts
largely support (and greatly supplement) the account of her existence offered in the "Memorandum" itself, but on a highly significant point they seem to differ from the poem. Thus, the poem
seems to imply that Martha's father personally instructed her in
acquiring Latin: "Beyond my sex & kind / he did wth learninge
Lattin decke [my] mind / ... Butt I of Lattin haue no cause to boast
/ ffor want of vse, I longe agoe itt lost" (ll. 29–30; 36–37). However,
the facts now established by Professor Grundy and Dr. Greer make
it almost certain that Moulsworth's father was dead by the time
she was three years old, which makes it unlikely that he could personally have instructed her in Latin except in the most rudimentary sense. What to make of this apparent discrepancy between the
poem and the external data is a difficult question (one discussed
more fully in Anne Little's essay in this volume). Suffice it here to
say that the information about the early death of Moulsworth's father casts provocative new light on her poem.

Other biographical data also illuminate the poem in intriguing
ways. Moulsworth's interest in founding a women's university, for
instance, may have been stimulated by the fact that she lived much
of her life in a small town that was a frequent stopping-point for
students and scholars travelling between London and Cambridge.
She must therefore have had many opportunities to meet and talk
with learned men and to feel, perhaps, the frustration of having
been denied the kind of higher education they could take for
granted. Similarly, new biographical information suggests that
when Moulsworth's poem declares the need "to Maytayne, &
ffight ffor" the Christian religion (l. 86), she herself took this admonition quite seriously; she was a staunch defender, it turns out,
of a particular preacher and his church. Furthermore, the new biographical data help emphasize the loving relations that seem in
fact to have existed between Martha and all three of her husbands,
and the data also reveal much about her material circumstances
and her practical, worldly abilities. Finally, the new materials have

much to tell us about Martha's personality and ideals. In many ways, then, the biographical evidence bears significantly on her poem, but before discussing its relevance it seems worthwhile to review the evidence in chronological order.

Martha's Father, Robert Dorsett

Professor Isobel Grundy and Dr. Germaine Greer were the first scholars involved with the present project to confirm the identity of Martha's father. He was Robert Dorsett, who received his B.A. from Oxford University in February 1564/65 and his doctorate in divinity in 1579. As Professor Grundy notes, he became a Canon at Christ Church College, Oxford, in 1572 and served as "Rector of Winwick, Northamptonshire, from 1572, and of Ewelme, Oxfordshire, from 1574" (Grundy 10). By 1579 he had been appointed Dean of Chester, and he seemed headed for further advancement. Although Martha claims that he owned land at the time of his death on 29 May 1580 (l. 23), Dr. Greer finds little confirmation of this in the surviving records. Yet, as she notes, a great deal of other information about Dorsett's life does survive, especially concerning his connection with Sir Philip Sidney.

Many of Dorsett's letters to Sidney are quoted at length in *Young Philip Sidney*, the exemplary biography by James M. Osborn.[2] Sidney's studies at Oxford began in February 1568 (Osborn 16), and because it was unusual for a boy of his rank even to attend university, he apparently "received extraordinary attention from the Christ Church authorities" (Osborn 19). The fact that Dorsett was selected as one of his tutors therefore speaks well of Dorsett's own character and accomplishments. The later correspondence between Dorsett and Sidney suggests a close relation, and perhaps Dorsett was one of the men who benefitted even at this early stage from Philip's patronage. Thus Thomas Moffett, an old teacher, reported that instead of wasting the funds sent by his

---

[2]See Osborn, *Young Philip Sidney: 1572–1577* (New Haven: Yale University Press, 1972). Dorsett is also mentioned very briefly in Malcolm William Wallace, *The Life of Sir Philip Sidney* (1915; rpt. New York: 19Octagon, 1967), 103 and 165; and in Katherine Duncan-Jones, *Sir Philip Sidney: Courtier Poet* (New Haven: Yale University Press, 1991), 106 and 115. Duncan-Jones also presents evidence indicating that as a very young academic, Dorsett had acted before Queen Elizabeth (37).

relatives, Sidney "'distributed them either frugally for his own uses or more generously for the alleviation of learned men'" (qtd. in Osborn 21). According to Moffett,

> No one was more obliging than he, more courteous, or more agreeable to the souls of the members of the University.... If perchance he met on the street some learned and pious man, you would have said that nothing could have been more loving and more united than they.... [Yet he] did not pour out his love rashly upon everyone, nor did he cleave in never-ceasing love to anyone not like him also in love for virtue.... [He was always] distinguished among the company of all the learned men. In their presence he maintained ... a gravity, joined with modesty.... [Therefore,] how genuinely both the humane, learned race of academicians and the churlish, unenlightened race of townsmen loved Sidney, even as no other one! (qtd. in Osborn 21–22)

Osborn finds Moffett a credible witness, and surely one of the "learned men" who must have been closely involved with Sidney at this time was Martha's eventual father, Robert Dorsett. If Martha later heard stories of her father's links with Sidney, it is little wonder that she speaks of him so glowingly in her "Memorandum." After all, even a man as notable in his own right as Fulke Greville was proud to have his tombstone attest, as one of his accomplishements, that he had been a "friend of Sir Philip Sidney."[3]

The correspondence between Sidney and Dorsett dates from between June 1575 and June 1576. We know of it mainly from surviving Latin epistles from Dorsett to Sidney, but some of these are responses to Sidney's own letters. In one of these Sidney had apparently commended to Dorsett his younger brother Robert, as well as two other young friends of Sidney who were beginning their studies at Christ Church (Osborn 312). The fact that Sidney sent his brother and other protégés to be tutored there suggests that he himself had been pleased with his experiences at Oxford, and the fact that he specifically addressed Dorsett suggests already a close bond between them. Replying to Sidney, Dorsett himself called his old student "beloved Philip" and professed his strong and undying loyalty (Osborn 313), claiming that with Sidney his "spirit has been bound up all my life, and will be until the end" (Osborn 313). Such phrasing suggests that their relationship had

---

[3]See the entry on Greville in the *Dictionary of National Biography*.

already been friendly for some time. The fact that Sidney entrusted his cherished younger brother to Dorsett's care implies his genuine respect for his former tutor.

Little wonder, then, that Martha speaks of her father as "a Man of spottles ffame" (l. 21). The qualities Dorsett praised in others suggest his own values, as when he extols Robert Sidney, saying that "together with a quite polished mind he shows such gentle and moderate ways, combined with a remarkable spirit and such delicate courtesy, that it would require a stony heart not to welcome such a balanced, gentle, and tender nature" (qtd. in Osborn 316). Dorsett seeks Christ's favor in tutoring young Robert, and he promises to apply all his "efforts, care, and industry" to the task (qtd. in Osborn 316). He shows tolerance of Robert's first efforts at Latin (assuring Philip that "'practice will make future [letters] more fluent'" [qtd. in Osborn 316]), and he expresses gratitude to Philip for communicating his "love and benevolence to me on so many occasions'" (qtd. in Osborn 317). When plague threatened Oxford, Dorsett took care to dispatch young Robert to Northamptonshire, where (he promised) the boy would stay "'until God with greater favour will release the city from the plague'" (qtd. in Osborn 369). Dorsett's letters corroborate many of Martha's claims about him; he seems to have been the kind of intelligent, virtuous man whom Sidney could respect. Dorsett was the sort of person who might very well have taken a real interest in ensuring the education of his infant daughter, who was conceived not long after the end of his surviving correspondence with Sidney.

Dorsett obviously saw Sidney as more than an exemplary former student; he was also an increasingly powerful man, and so Dorsett sought Sidney's help in winning patronage for various friends. In fact, Osborn claims that Dorsett was "constantly active in academic politics" (314), and he quotes a letter in which Dorsett pushed the candidacy of a particular aspirant to a high position at Christ Church. Indeed, in a letter dated 24 October 1575, Dorsett sought Sidney's help on his own behalf, and his phrasing again suggests a good deal about his hopes, character, and circumstances in the years immediately preceding Martha's birth:

> ... though I am not all that well furnished with life's necesssities, I shall not strive for anything lest I seem to fall a prey to ambition, which I have always feared as a stain on any virtuous life. Should there, however, be anything of which ... you might find me worthy, I should indeed accept your

favour with the greatest pleasure and gratitude. (qtd. in
Osborn 369–70)

Further evidence of Dorsett's rather modest living conditions
appears in a letter dated 1 December 1575, which begins by
thanking Philip for his "'extreme goodness towards me,'" and
which then goes on to mention that Robert Sidney and his friends
"'will shortly come to Ewelme, where I have a house, albeit a
sparsely equipped one'" (qtd. in Osborn 374). This was probably
the house in which Martha herself was born, and it was apparently
a house that Sidney himself may even have visited. In a letter
dated 17 May 1576 from Ewelme, Dorsett clearly implies that he
had been extended hospitality by Sidney, and now he seeks to return the compliment:

> ... I should like to ask you the favour to let me do for you
> what you have often most magnificently done for me: that,
> whenever you do arrive [in Oxford], you will take the time
> to visit my house, which I should in truth call yours; for
> though it is ill equipped to receive your Excellency, yet I
> have no doubt that you will gladly accept the goodwill of its
> master.... Your Robert is well, as are we, and we most
> earnestly wish you all good health [etc] ... (qtd. in Osborn
> 426)

Once again Dorsett speaks modestly of his house, although this
may reflect more his respect for Sidney than an accurate assessment of his home. In any case, the same letter again suggests the
length and closeness of Sidney's and Dorsett's relationship.
Speaking of Sidney's anticipated visit to Oxford, Dorsett nostalgically recalls the young man's study of letters there—

> I think I can say to your true pleasure as well as your bene-
> fit.... I consider myself happy because it has been vouchsafed
> me to see you flourishing there where you formerly laid the
> shining foundations of your whole life and career, while I
> looked on and wished you the very best of fortune. (qtd. in
> Osborn 425)

Apparently Dorsett even now continued to assist, in various
ways, Philip's interest in learning: Sidney seems to have sought his
advice about teachers of philosophy and Greek, perhaps for his
own instruction (Osborn 416), and Dorsett searched for a book that
Sidney had requested on behalf of Fulke Greville (Osborn 369).
Furthermore, Dorsett purchased a copy of Cicero's *Offices* for

Robert Sidney's use,[4] and he was apparently also serving as tutor to Rowland White, who would later become an important servant of Robert (Osborn 369). It was Robert, of course, who would some-day own the Sidney estate of Penshurst, celebrated in Ben Jonson's famous poem, and one wonders whether Robert or his circle may have had any later contact with Martha, the daughter of his de-voted tutor. In any case, many prominent people were in a position to know of Robert Dorsett and his service to the Sidneys, and Dorsett himself was in an excellent position to tutor his new daughter, Martha. He had the knowledge, the skills, and the con-nections to give her a superb education.

By 1580, however, Dorsett was dead. Martha, at this time, was approximately thirty months old. Any instruction he gave her, whether in Latin or in any other subject, must have been extremely rudimentary. She clearly exaggerates when she says he "brought [her] vpp" in various virtues (l. 27). Perhaps he left detailed in-structions for her upbringing; perhaps he asked his many learned friends to make sure that the girl was properly raised and taught. He could not, however, have taken the kind of active and sustain-ing hand in her education and development that her poem seems to imply. (Nor, apparently, could her mother, who would soon be dead herself; see Germaine Greer's essay in this volume.)

In some ways, Martha's exaggerated claims about her father's direct influence make her poem, if anything, even more fascinating and provocative. What functions, we might ask, did this idealized father figure serve in her life and imagination? What motives prompted her to stress so strongly his alleged impact? These are questions that invite numerous possible responses. For the mo-ment, however, we should turn to the men who had real and un-deniable effects on her life—her three successive husbands.

Marriage to Nicholas Prynne

According to her "Memorandum," Martha married her first husband, Nicholas Prynne, on 18 April 1598, when she was twenty-one. She notes that some people considered this a late age for marriage ("My springe was late, some thinke thatt sooner loue" [l. 51]), but she seems to have been happy with her decision

---

[4]See Millicent V. Hay, *The Life of Robert Sidney, Earl of Leicester (1563–1626)* (Washington, DC: Folger Books, 1984), 24.

("backward springs doe oft the kindest proue" [l. 52]). In fact, she suggests that the marriage to Prynne was, at least to some degree, a free choice rather than an imposed obligation (she says that until she was twenty-one, she "did nott bind my selfe in Mariadge" [l. 50]). Thus, even as a young woman, Martha seems to have displayed the sense of independence later implied in her poem and demonstrated in her subsequent life. In any case, thanks to the research of Professor Grundy, we can be reasonably sure that Martha's first known child with Nicholas Prynne was a son named Richard, who was baptized in the church of St. Matthew, in London's Friday Street, on 13 June 1602. This child is prominently mentioned in Nicholas Prynne's will, and he seems to have been still living at the time his father died.

If we assume a normal nine-month pregnancy, then Richard would have been conceived sometime in the early fall of 1601—that is, more than three years after Martha's first wedding. Whether or not she bore any other children (or suffered stillbirths or miscarriages) during those first few years of her marriage is uncertain. If any earlier children were conceived and died, their loss might have heightened her later desire to leave behind a poetic legacy of her existence. Her poem, after all, implies that any children (including Richard) fathered by Nicholas Prynne were dead by 1632 (ll. 71–72). This would have included a daughter named Martha, whose existence was first reported by Professor Grundy (see her essay in this volume). This daughter was baptized in St. Matthew's church in Friday Street on 15 April 1604—several months after Nicholas Prynne prepared his will (in very late December 1603). Presumably Nicholas Prynne died sometime at the end of 1603 or early in 1604, probably not long before the birth of his new daughter.

Nicholas Prynne's will is our main source of information about his own life and his marriage with Martha; it reveals a good deal about his character, status, and values, as well as his familial, personal, and professional connections. Dated 26 December 1603, during the first year of the reign of King James I, the will describes Prynne as a "Citizen and Goldsmithe of London."[5] The latter fact is especially significant for, as we shall see, Martha's third husband was also a goldsmith. Apparently Prynne was a man of some status in the goldsmiths' company and was proud of this association, since he bequeaths ten pounds "vnto the Company of Goldsmithes

---

[5]For a full text of the will, see Appendix 2 of this volume.

of London to th'intent and for that they shall bringe my Body to buryall," and since he leaves them an additional ten pounds "to make a parcell or peece of plate in remembraunce of me." He leaves ten shillings each to four of the "poore Almes menn of the said Companie whome I will shall beare my Corps to the buriall," and to one of these poor men, James Collins, he leaves an additional forty shillings "to th'ende he shall see that a good Coffin be provided for mee." All these facts suggest that Prynne was not a poor man himself, and that he regarded the goldsmiths' company almost as a fraternity or extended family.

Although religious declarations seem to have been conventional in wills of this period, there seems no reason to doubt Prynne's sincerity. One of his first bequests involves giving and commending his "soule vnto god almightie assuredlie trustinge and believing by the only merritts deathe and passion of Ihesus Christ my Savior and Redeemer to have salvation and free pardon and Remyssyon of all my synnes and eternall lief [sic] in the kingdome of heaven wth the faithefull and elect Children of god." This phrasing, especially the reference to the "elect," suggests that Prynne was not only a devout believer but also a convinced Protestant who held definite Calvinist convictions. Since Martha herself later gave indications of being a firm Protestant who believed in an active approach to preaching the gospel, Prynne's declaration seems relevant to her own life and poem. All three of her marriages, in fact, seem to have involved unions with pious men actively committed to their creed. Prynne, for instance, requests burial "in the parrishe Church of St Mathewe (of wch parrishe I am nowe a parrishoner) in such *Christ*ian sorte and manner" as Martha shall find appropriate, and he is careful to express thanks "for suche temporarie and earthelie goodes as it hathe pleased almightie god of his goodnes to endowe and blesse me w^th." After he arranges for his burial, his very first bequest involves leaving five pounds to John Presse, parson of St. Matthews, and twenty shillings each to Presse's three children—one of whom, as we shall see, would maintain her connections to Martha for decades to come.

Prynne's other bequests give us some sense of the circle of people whom Martha must have known and been friendly with during the years of her first marriage. He leaves sums of various sizes, for instance, to his "Aunte Anne Pryne wyddowe"; to his "Brother Thomas Pryne"; to Thomas Prynne's children; and to his "Brother in lawe Henrie Loftus ... and to [his] Sister in lawe now his [i.e., Loftus's] wief [sic]." Prynne also leaves bequests to his otherwise unidentified "Sister Batten" and to her children (Erasmus, Thomas, and Elizabeth). He leaves money as well to "Mr William Sherston nowe Maior of the Cittie of Bathe" and to Sherston's son Peter. The latter bequests suggest, again, that Prynne must have been a man of some social status. Interestingly, another brother (James Pryne) is mentioned almost near the end of the will, but he receives slightly less money than the brother named Thomas who was mentioned earlier. Whether this placement and the disparity of sums suggest any difference in Prynne's respective feelings toward his two brothers is, of course, impossible to say. It seems interesting, however, that the bequest to James precedes only one other legacy—forty shillings left to "Priscilla Roberts that nurssed my Sonne Richard." This final bequest is intriguing for at least two reasons. First, it implies that Martha, like many financially secure women of her day, was able to employ another woman to nurse (or at least to help nurse) her child. (Perhaps this was because the child was sent outside of London for a period during its infancy—a practice, as we shall later see, that was not uncommon.) Secondly, the reference to Priscilla Roberts is intriguing because Martha herself, in a will drafted many years later, leaves a bequest to a man named Edward Roberts, whom she identifies as her "auncient servant." In addition, an Edward Roberts was one of the witnesses of the will of Martha's second husband, Thomas Thorowgood. If this Edward Roberts was in some way related (as husband? as son?) to the Priscilla Roberts who functioned as a nursemaid during Martha's first marriage, then he may have been a person who knew her throughout most of her adult life.

Nicholas Prynne's references to Martha in his will suggest a loving relationship (as her poem also implies), and his willingness to have this young woman serve as his executrix suggests his confidence in her practical abilities. He twice refers to Martha as his "lovinge wief [sic]," and leaves one-third of his estate "to hir owne proper vse." Another third is left to his "Sonne Richard Pryne and the Childe or Children wherw^th my saide wief nowe goeth," while the remaining third is divided among the various friends, relatives, servants, and business associates already mentioned. Any funds left over from this final third portion are bequeathed to Martha, son Richard, and the child or children Martha was carrying at the time Prynne composed his will. However, if any of the children should happen to die, then their portion, he declares, should revert to Martha, whom Prynne appoints as his "full and sole Executrix." He does, it is true, appoint Henrie Loftus (his brother-in-law) and John Presse (parson of St. Matthew's church) as overseers of the will, and surely Martha would have benefitted from their advice. However, the whole tone of the will suggests that Martha, even in her mid-twenties, inspired the kind of affection and trust that her later husbands and relatives displayed toward her.

In the opening sentences of his will, Nicholas Prynne describes himself as "beinge at this present sicke in bodye but of good and perfect mynde remembrance and vnderstandinge thanks be to almighty god." Certainly he must have been sick enough to worry that his end was near, and when he died not long after composing his will, he left Martha with a young son to raise and pregnant with the daughter who would bear her own name. Nicholas, presumably, was buried (as he wished) in the parish church of St. Matthew in London's Friday Street, not far from St. Paul's Cathedral. Since his and Martha's son Richard had been baptized in the same parish church in 1602, the couple must have been residing in that parish for a good part of their marriage. Prynne's bequests to the church's parson and his children also suggest this, implying that Nicholas and Martha were loyal parishioners. And, since we know that St. Matthew's (now demolished) lay inside the boundaries of a particular ward of London (a ward called "Farringdon Within"—i.e., within the old City walls) we can speculate with some assurance about where, precisely, Martha and her husband and son lived and what their living conditions were like.[6]

Although St. Matthew-Friday Street lay in the ward of Farringdon Within, most of Friday Street itself lay in Bread Street Ward. John Milton was born in the latter ward in 1608; his father was a scrivener there, and Shakespeare himself would later buy property in Farringdon Within (although it is unlikely that he ever lived there). Richard Burbage, the famous actor and theatrical entrepreneur, had set up a private theater (The Blackfriars) nearby in 1596, where companies of boy actors chiefly performed.[7] Thus, if

---

[6]In reporting information about Martha's life in London, I will be drawing on several sources, including Fran C. Chalfant, *Ben Jonson's London: A Jacobean Placename Dictionary* (Athens: University of Georgia Press, 1978); an anonymous but extremely helpful book entitled *The City of London* (London: Times Publishing, 1927); and William Kent, ed., *An Encyclopedia of London* (London: Dent, 1937).

[7]For most of the facts mentioned in this paragraph, see *The City of London*, 47 and 58–60.

Martha and her husband were at all inclined to attend stage plays, they could easily have done so. (Other theaters were just across the river in Southwark.) It seems quite likely, in fact, that Martha was one of those "privileged playgoers" who were among the first audiences of such playwrights as Shakespeare and Jonson, and perhaps her probable attendance at plays helped feed her own literary interests.[8] In any case, her residence in or near Farringdon Within would have placed her in a particularly vibrant and stimulating part of London.

Bread Street had been so named because of its association with bakers; Friday Street was associated with the selling of fish (*City of London* 47). John Stow, in the edition of his famous *Survey* of London published in 1603 (that is, in the same year that Nicholas Prynne composed his will), offers a colorful description of life in Farringdon Within.[9] "Stinking Lane" was one nearby street (Stow 279), and the ward also contained a large "shambles" or flesh-market (Stow 283). Pentecost Lane was filled with various slaughter houses for butchers, and in fact the Butchers' Hall stood within this ward (Stow 283). So did the hall of the Barber-Surgeons (Stow 282), although Paternoster Row was associated with stationers and scriveners (Stow 302). At Newgate market, residents could purchase corn, meal, and other supplies (Stow 307), but garden plots lying along the city wall (Stow 282) made it possible for them to grow and sell food as well as buy it. One source has termed the ward "a dissolute and turbulent quarter which gave much trouble and offence to authority" (*City of London* 58), but the proximity of St. Paul's Cathedral also made it a mecca for visitors from all over London. The famous boys' school at St. Paul's was flourishing when Martha lived nearby, and the Cathedral itself was a favorite meeting place, especially for gossips who strolled up and down the middle aisle. Booksellers had shops in the vicinity, and an open-air pulpit was used by famous preachers late every Sunday morning. Surely Martha must have attended these sermons from time to time, and in fact in 1603 she could have heard a particularly famous and strong attack on women (*Encyclopedia of London* 558).

---

[8]See Ann Jennalie Cook, *The Privileged Playgoers of Shakespeare's London, 1576–1642* (Princeton: Princeton University Press, 1981), which gives a very full portrait of the upper parts of London society during this period.

[9]See *The Survey of London* (London: Dent, n.d.).

The main convenience of living near St. Paul's Cathedral, however, probably had to do with its proximity to Goldsmiths' Hall, with which Nicholas Prynne was associated. In fact, many goldsmiths seem to have lived in this general vicinity, and several famous ones had been buried, like Prynne, in St. Matthew's parish church (Stow 289). Prynne's probable residence in this parish also put him close to Guildhall, the civic center of London and seat of the Lord Mayor and Court of Aldermen. The ward of Farringdon Within, in Martha's time, was overseen by one alderman, twelve members of a common council, seventeen constables, and at least thirty-seven other officials (Stow 307). It seems to have been a lively and bustling place, where Martha could shop for food, see plays, hear sermons, buy books, and make the acquaintance of a wide variety of people from all across the social spectrum. If she had any intellectual curiosity (and her poem clearly suggests that she did), she must have found these early years in London highly stimulating.

Yet Nicholas Prynne's death in late 1603 or early 1604 (during a time of plague) left her suddenly alone, with one small child to care for and another on the way. It hardly seems surprising, then, that her first period of widowhood was also her shortest. She had good practical reasons to desire another mate. If her first marriage had seemed, to some degree, a matter of free choice, her second must have been partly a response to economic and emotional necessity.

Marriage to Thomas Thorowgood

The date of Martha's second marriage can seem confusing. If she married on 3 February 1604, as a marginal note in her poem plainly says, then she would have remarried almost immediately after her first husband's death, while still pregnant with his child. Yet if she did remarry so soon, then none of the subsequent marginal dates she lists would fit the actual chronology of her life. The simplest explanation (and the one that squares best with the later marginal dates she offers) is that in referring to her second marriage, she uses the common Renaissance practice of dating the beginning of the new year (or year of grace) not at 1 January but at 25 March. She later uses the same style of dating when discussing the death of her third husband, and so when she tells us that she married "Thomas Througood" (most commonly spelled "Thorowgood") on 3 February 1604, she actually refers to what *we* would call 3 February 1605 (or, in scholarly writing, "1604/05"). Reading the date as 1605 also makes sense of her claim that after the death of her first husband, "then was a yeare sett on my mourninge score" (l. 54). In other words, she mourned for a year (the customary period) before remarrying.

Martha's second husband, Thomas Thorowgood, was the son of William Thorowgood, a member of the Drapers' Company who "had a large business as clothier in Cheapside,"[10] one of London's largest and most important streets and a center of commercial activity. Cheapside was very close to St. Paul's Cathedral and not far from the parish church of St. Matthew's Friday Street, where Martha and Nicholas Prynne had worshipped. Martha would have had ample opportunity, then, to become acquainted with the Thorowgoods, who enjoyed the same kind of status within the Drapers' Company that Nicholas Prynne enjoyed as a goldsmith. Her first husband was a successful businessman, and so would be her second.

Thomas Thorowgood had received his "freedom" from (that is, full membership in) the Drapers' Company in 1587. He received his freedom "by patrimony"—in other words, as the son of William Thorowgood, who was already a prominent draper.[11] Surviving accounts in Drapers' Hall record William Thorowgood's relations with his apprentices in 1546 (the year he achieved his freedom by apprenticeship), and in 1554, 1555, 1555, 1559, 1564, 1567, 1567 (again), 1568, 1571, 1578, 1580, and 1581. Moreover, the same records also show that children of William Thorowgood (including Thomas) were baptized in 1553, 1554, 1557, 1558, 1561, 1565, and 1566.[12] Thomas, his eldest son (and Martha's future hus-

---

[10]See J.A. Tregelles, *A History of Hoddesdon in the County of Hertford-shire* (Hertford: Stephen Austin, 1908), 160.

[11]See Percival Boyd, *Roll of the Drapers' Company of London* (Croydon: J.A. Gordon, 1934), 182.

[12]All this information comes from the "Register" of the Drapers' Company, kept at Drapers' Hall in London. I thank the librarian there for her very kind assistance. Interestingly, the Register also reports the baptism, on 26 February 1597(98?), of a child named John, son of Thomas Thorowgood, who was baptised at the church of St. Christopher le Stockes. Could this have been a child from our Thomas Thorowgood's previous marriage? Thorowgood's wife is reported to have passed away in February 1597; could she have died in childbirth? Or was this infant

band), had married a woman named Heigham (whose first name was probably Elizabeth) sometime before 1595 (Tregelles 163)— probably in fact before 1592, since their daughter (also named Elizabeth) was nineteen by 1611.[13] Elizabeth Heigham was the daughter of a London wine merchant (Tregelles 163).[14] One daughter, Elizabeth, did survive from this marriage between Heigham and Thorowgood, and this little girl would later grow up to be one of Martha Moulsworth's closest relatives and dearest friends.

By February 1605, when Thomas Thorowgood married the recently widowed Martha Prynne, he had long been a widower himself, his wife Elizabeth having passed away in February 1597 (Tregelles 163). Moreover, his businessman-father, William Thorowgood, had also died (in 1602), leaving Thomas as his chief heir. Thomas inherited most of his father's property, including premises in London (Tregelles 161), and it was presumably in London that he met, courted, and married the twenty-eight-year-old widow, Martha Prynne. Perhaps the marriage was suggested and arranged by members of their respective families, as was often the case. In any event, their household, at least initially, would presumably have included Martha's son (the two-and-a-half-year-old Richard Prynne), her daughter (Martha Prynne, slightly less than a year old), and Thomas's own daughter, Elizabeth (who would have been about thirteen). Of these children, however, only Elizabeth seems to have lived until 1632, the date of Martha's poem. Moreover, that poem tells us that the newly married couple had no surviving children of their own (l. 72). It is easy to imagine, then, the close bond that eventually must have developed between the young, motherless step-daughter and her still rather young step-mother, whose own children would eventually pass away. All the surviving evidence—particularly Martha's will—suggests that her ties with her step-daughter Elizabeth were heartfelt and sincere.

"John" the son of *another* Thomas Thorowgood? No son named John is mentioned in the latter's will, although a nephew so named is mentioned.

[13]See *Allegations for Marriage Licences Issued by the Bishop of London*, compiled by Joseph Lemuel Chester and George J. Armitage (London: Harleian Society, 1887), 1: 328. I wish to thank Ivan Molesworth for help in tracing this source.

[14]As previously mentioned, records at the Drapers' Hall mention the baptism on 26 February 1597 of a John Thorowgood, son of Thomas, but this could have been the nephew later mentioned in our Thomas's will. Many Thorowgoods were drapers.

One of the most significant facts about Martha's new husband was his family's connection with the small town of Hoddesdon, which lay about twenty miles north of London on the main road to Cambridge. It was here that Martha would spend much of her subsequent life, not only as Thomas Thorowgood's mate but also (later) as the wife of another prominent resident, Bevill Molesworth. When Bevill Molesworth died, it was in Hoddesdon that his widow would spend probably the bulk of her remaining days, and it was probably in Hoddesdon that she composed her poetic "Memorandum." Her ties to London would never be completely broken; both her second and third husbands had residences there, and Martha therefore may have lived in the capital off and on for long periods of time. However, with her marriage to Thomas Thorowgood, Hoddesdon would now play an increasingly prominent role in her life. It is thus to Hoddesdon, and to the Thorowgood connection with that town, that we should now turn.

The Texture of Life in Hoddesdon

Much of our knowledge about life in early seventeenth-century Hoddesdon derives from two sources. One of these, *A History of Hoddesdon in the County of Hertfordshire*, by J.A. Tregelles (1908), is one of those incredibly long and detailed local histories that do real credit to both author and publisher, since neither can have undertaken them in the hope of really profiting financially. Our other main source, on which Tregelles himself draws, is the recently published *Parish Register and Tithing Book of Thomas Hassall of Amwell*, thoughtfully edited and introduced by Stephen G. Doree.[15] Hassall's work is valuable not only because it covers the first half of the seventeenth century (exactly the period that interests us here) but also because Hassall himself, as a parish priest, was a major figure in Hoddesdon and a long-time friend, admirer, and protégé of Martha Moulsworth. In fact, it was Hassall who preached Martha's funeral sermon when she died in 1646, and his comments there and in the *Register* provide a wealth of information that both

---

[15]*The Parish Register and Tithing Book of Thomas Hassall of Amwell*, edited by Stephen G. Doree (Hertford: Hertfordshire Record Society, 1989). When citing Doree's very valuable introduction, commentary, and notes, I will refer parenthetically to "Doree." When referring to Hassall's own works I will use the short parenthetical citation "Hassall, *Register*."

supplements and confirms the details presented in her poem. Hassall, Doree, and Tregelles will prove extremely helpful in discussing Moulsworth's life from this point forward, but for the moment they can prove especially helpful in conveying some sense of what it was like to live in Hoddesdon itself.

In his introduction to Hassall's *Register*, Doree reports a wealth of useful information, drawing largely (as everyone must) on Tregelle's indispensable spadework, as well as on Hassall himself. He notes, for instance, that in 1633 (just around the time when Martha composed her "Memorandum"), Hoddesdon consisted of 120 houses with gardens, although the number of total households exceeded this figure (Doree viii). He suggests that in 1634 the population of Amwell, the parish for which Hassall was responsible, was approximately six hundred. However, most of Hoddesdon was actually situated in the neighboring parish of Broxbourne, and it was in this parish that Moulsworth herself actually lived. The division of the town between two parish churches (and thus between two parish priests) was, as we shall see, a major source of tension, as well as a major cause of Martha's active involvement in local ecclesiastical politics.

Hoddesdon in the first decades of the seventeenth century was a small but thriving place. Its location, approximately twenty miles north of London, made it a natural stopping point for travelers commuting to and from the capital, especially travelers connected with Cambridge University. Tregelles notes that Hoddesdon was considered a good rest stop, since no town (apart from Edmonton) was closer to London (101). Thomas Hobson, the celebrated coach driver from Cambridge, passed through Hoddesdon once a week for seven decades, transporting the young Milton as well as hundreds of other travellers (Tregelles 113–14). Numerous inns and alehouses had grown up over the years beside the broad road that cut through the middle of town, and Martha's new family, the Thorowgoods, at one time or another owned a number of these. In 1591, for instance, William Thorowgood, the father of Martha's husband Thomas, bought The Grange inn (Tregelles 117), and Thomas himself owned The White Hind in 1600 (Tregelles 121) as well as The George (Tregelles 123). At various points the Thorowgood family was also connected with such other inns as The Cock, Thurgoods, Laurel House, The Falcon, and The Maidenhead (Tregelles 117–34). Many of these establishments (like such other inns as The Dolphin, The Two Brewers [later The Five

Bells], The Vine, The Bull, The Black Lion [later The Salisbury Arms], and The Swan) brewed their own beer (Tregelles 117–34).

Martha must have had something to do with running her husband's inns, and the mere fact of living in Hoddesdon would have given her a chance to meet and talk with numerous students and teachers connected with Cambridge, one of the two universities for men she mentions in her poem (l. 33). Many interesting people must have stayed in Hoddesdon while making their way between Cambridge and London.

At least twenty-eight inns or taverns were operating in Hoddesdon in 1595 (Tregelles 263–65), and The Bull, Black Lion, and Swan each had huge timber sign beams (more than forty feet wide) spanning the width of the highway, including the foul ditches (measuring, on the east side, four feet wide and three deep) that ran along both sides of the road (Tregelles 101; 129–30; 155). Residents crossed the ditches over gangways, and tenants with houses or businesses facing the ditches were expected to clean and maintain their individual portions. Cross ditches drained the main ditch into a nearby marsh, but during dry spells conditions became especially unsanitary—a problem exacerbated, no doubt, by the fact that residents threw trash onto the road (although disposing of carrion in this way was prohibited; Tregelles 101; 368). Such litter was meant to be trodden down (and thus processed for composting) by the heavy pack horses, saddle horses, and caravans of carriages that regularly passed through town (Tregelles 101; 155; 368; 378).

When plague hit Hoddesdon in 1603, its victims included two entire families (Tregelles 369), and plague and other sicknesses were never entirely remote threats (Tregelles 240; 337). In 1625, the plague hit especially hard again, killing twenty-two people in just a few hours; many were buried on the same day they died (Tregelles 378). Even so, Hoddesdon was considered a much healthier place in which to live than London, and this helps account for the fact that Martha's last two husbands, who were prominent businessmen in the capital, also had homes in Hoddesdon and lived there for much of each year. Few of the London businessmen with homes in Hoddesdon could commute back and forth daily, so they tended to have residences in both places. Nonetheless, their city wealth gave them a special prominence in the small town, and Martha clearly enjoyed great status there.

Hoddesdon's proximity to London and its general reputation for healthy living conditions helped create another industry besides inn-keeping: Many infants from the capital (especially from Christ's Hospital) were sent to Hoddesdon to be nursed (Tregelles 372; Doree xi), and the poorer women who tended to live in Thomas Hassall's parish of Amwell were particularly likely to serve as nurses (Doree x). Many residents, especially widows, took care of more than one child at once (Doree x), and in the course of thirty-five years, nursing children made up almost ten percent of all the burials Hassall recorded in his *Register* (Doree x). It seems unlikely that Martha ever had to serve in this capacity; in fact, if her earlier experience in London with her son Richard Prynne provides any clues, her own children were probably nursed by others. Yet for many of her neighbors in Amwell parish, nursing was an important source of extra income in an economy that was generally rooted in poorly paid agricultural work (Tregelles 348–54). Corn, hay, cattle, sheep, and pigs were widely raised (Doree x; Tregelles 89–90), and numerous common fields, ranging in size from three to fourteen acres, surrounded the town (Tregelles 88–91). Many of these bordered meads and also marshes running down to the River Lea, which lay not very far to the east (Tregelles 92–93). Ancient forests filled with oaks stretched into the distance, and these woods were favorite hunting grounds for such luminaries as the aristocratic Cecil family and also King James.

A real possibility exists that Martha could have come into close contact with royalty while living in Hoddesdon. Shortly after James's accession in 1603, the Privy Council ordered the construction of bridges to facilitate the king's movements while hawking and hunting deer nearby, and one bridge, called His Majesty's Great Bridge, was prohibited to common people (Tregelles 104). Queen Elizabeth had visited the nearby Cecil estate of Theobalds at least a dozen times during her reign, and when she died, James passed through Hoddesdon in May 1603 on his way to London, later returning to the area many times (Tregelles 113). Since Martha was a leading resident there during her marriages to Thomas Thorowgood and Bevill Moulsworth, it seems quite likely that she would have had some contact with the king. H.F. Killick reports that James often visited the house in Hoddesdon of Marmaduke Rawdon, Martha's future son-in-law, with whom the monarch apparently frequently consulted.[16] Martha's status and family connections, in London but especially in Hoddesdon, therefore make it likely that at various points she would have been in James's presence.[17] She would have had contact, then, not only with students and teachers from Cambridge but also with the courtiers of a king who prided himself on his devotion to learning.

The state of learning in Hoddesdon itself was not particularly strong. The Thorowgood family had been instrumental in trying to found a grammar school in the town in 1561, and in fact William Thorowgood, Martha's father-in-law, later wrote a history of the school and its finances (Tregelles 238–41; 328). However, when plague struck in 1578, many supporters of the school seem to have fallen victim, and apparently it ceased functioning in 1595 (Tregelles 242). Education of some sort must have gone on, and perhaps one of Martha's incentives for reading as widely as she apparently did was to help with the instruction of her own children and, later, her numerous grandchildren. In any case, it seems fitting that her daughter-in-law's house, in which the learned and devout Martha undoubtedly spent much time, would by the nineteenth century become first a girls' school and then a convent for nuns.[18]

When living in Hoddesdon, Martha would have been able to engage in varied activities. She undoubtedly spent much time at church—either at the small chapel in Hoddesdon itself (where Hassall often preached) or at the larger parish church of Broxbourne, a mile or so south of the town. When not in church,

---

[16]H.F. Killick, "Memoirs of Sir Marmaduke Rawdon, Kt. 1582–1646," *Yorkshire Archaeological Journal* 25 (1919): 315–30, esp. 318.

[17]For an account of James's travels in the vicinity throughout his reign, see Alan Thomson, "Progress, Retreat, and Pursuit: James I in Hertfordshire," in *Hertfordshire in History: Papers Presented to Lionel Munby*, ed. Doris Jones-Baker (Hertford: Hertfordshire Local History Council, 1991), 93–107. Sue Garside, in her book *Hoddesdon Highlights: An Introduction to Interesting People and Places* (Hoddesdon: The Book Centre, 1988), reports that a special "summer house" was built as an annex to Rawdon House so that smokers could go there to indulge their habits when the King (who hated tobacco) was visiting the house itself (16). Garside's book prints a color photograph of Rawdon House.

[18]For an entertaining brief account of the house's fortunes over the years, as well as for other useful information about its environs, see E.W. Paddick, *Hoddesdon: Tales of a Hertfordshire Town* (Hoddesdon: Hoddesdon Urban District Council, 1971).

she may have visited the busy market in the village center, which was famous for its malt shops and for its tall market cross (Tregelles 246). Permanent stalls, occupied by such tradesmen as butchers and fishmongers, competed with numerous temporary structures, and in fact by the mid-sixteenth century the Hoddesdon market had become so thriving that baillifs in the larger nearby town of Hertford unsuccessfully tried to have it shut down (Tregelles 245). Competition from barges had more success in diverting commercial traffic away from Hoddesdon (Tregelles 247; 338–39), but the market never ceased to be lively. The town must have seemed an inviting place to settle, and various steps were taken to prevent indigent persons from taking up residence there (Tregelles 340–43). Market stalls, for instance, were not to be used as living spaces, and although almshouses existed, an influx of needy (and potentially disruptive) persons was discouraged. Tregelles suggests, however, that "decent" people, even if poor, were allowed to immigrate (340), and, as we shall see, Martha and her extended family (the Thorowgoods, Molesworths, and Rawdons in particular) seem to have had some interest in helping the poor. They also took an interest in promoting local religious life, and in general they seem to have regarded themselves as the town's benefactors. Certainly they were among its leading citizens.

Married Life in Hoddesdon with Thomas Thorowgood

By 1605, when the newly married Martha Thorowgood probably first came into close and extended contact with Hoddesdon, only three of the town's houses were made of brick (Tregelles 153), and one of these was probably owned by her husband Thomas. His prosperous family had had long and varied connections with the town and were related by marriage with many of its other leading citizens (Tregelles 131; 144; 150–51; 158–63; 247; 322; 339; 355; 360; 374). By the mid-sixteenth century the Thorowgoods had become the wealthiest family in the immediate area (Tregelles 322), and when William Thorowgood (Thomas's father) died in 1602, he left bequests providing for the distribution of bread and beef to the town's poor. Moreover, he also endowed a series of sermons designed to promote the Protestant faith (Tregelles 274–75). William Thorowgood was, evidently, a convinced Protestant with no sympathy for Catholicism (Tregelles 161), and he seems to have felt a personal dislike for John Spencer, the vicar of his own parish church of Broxbourne. His will specified that Spencer should not receive any of the money left to endow the series of sermons (Doree xx).

Thomas Thorowgood apparently shared his father's dislike of Spencer and of subsequent vicars of Broxbourne, whom he may have considered insufficiently committed to Protestant reformation and to preaching (Hassall, *Register* 203–4). In any event, he turned his patronage to Thomas Hassall, the young vicar of the neighboring parish of Amwell. Hassall, who would develop a long and apparently close relationship with Martha and who would eventually preach her funeral sermon, considered Thomas Thorowgood his "very good friend," and it was Hassall whom Thorowgood selected to preach the series of endowed sermons (Hassall, *Register* 203–4; 227–28). When Spencer's successor objected to allowing Hassall to preach at the Broxbourne church, Thorowgood transferred the sermon series to a small chapel in the middle of Hoddesdon itself, and other members of the extended Thorowgood family helped endow still another series of twice-monthly sermons for Hassall to preach there (Hassall, *Register* 204). Thus, from the time Martha arrived in Hoddesdon, and for many years afterward, her new family was at the center of religious contention in the community and had the support of many of the town's other most influential citizens. Although the Thorowgoods were members of the Broxbourne parish, they tended to favor Hassall (of Amwell parish), and they promoted his efforts to make the Hoddesdon chapel a center of community religious life (Doree xv; xviii; xx–xxii). Martha herself would eventually become personally involved in the conflict between the competing ministers— a fact that sheds interesting light on certain passages in her poem. The strong religious beliefs the "Memorandum" implies seem to have been sincere.

Various vicars of Broxbourne, frustrated by the support attracted by Hassall, sought to discourage their parishioners from attending his sermons, and tensions lasted for decades (Hassall 204– 7). The successful resistance offered by Thomas and Martha suggests their commitment, influence, and strong sense of involvement with Hoddesdon. Although he probably spent a good deal of time in London, Thomas Thorowgood evidently considered himself first and foremost a citizen of the much smaller suburb; when, on 16 March 1610/11, his daughter Elizabeth (Martha's stepdaughter) applied for a marriage license, both she and her father listed themselves as residents of Hoddesdon.[19] The young girl who had been thirteen when her father had remarried was now a nineteen-year-old young woman who had probably already developed the close attachment to her step-mother that seems to have lasted throughout their lives. Martha and Thomas apparently had no children of their own, and Martha's two children from her first marriage (Richard and Martha Prynne) were dead by 1632, and perhaps much earlier. Moreover, since the only child of Martha's third marriage would not long survive, her longest and apparently deepest attachment to a child was with the daughter of her second husband. Elizabeth Thorowgood (as Martha would say in her will) received and returned the kind of affection that made her seem like Martha's own daughter.

Elizabeth's first and only husband, Marmaduke Rawdon, is called in the marriage application a bachelor and clothworker, aged 29, of the All Hallows Barking parish church in London, described by one modern source as "one of the oldest and most interesting of our London churches" and as "the burial place of many who lost their heads" on Tower Hill, near the famous Tower of London (*City of London* 65). The hall of the Clothworkers' Company was also nearby, and since Thomas Thorowgood was a draper and his new son-in-law a clothworker, it is not hard to imagine how Rawdon came to know the Thorowgood family. Elizabeth must have seemed a very eligible bride, and Rawdon himself must have seemed very promising as a son-in-law and husband. He had been a successful merchant in France and had developed what H.F. Killick calls "extensive foreign connections" (315). When he returned to London in 1610, he settled in Water Lane, off Great Tower Street, where he eventually established himself as a pillar of London society, becoming a master cloth-worker; a captain of the trained bands of volunteer soldiers; a master of one of the London hospitals; a benefactor of various London churches and of the Clothworkers' Hall; a member of the Municipal Corporation of London; a trusted advisor of King James, King Charles, and their mutual favorite, the Duke of Buckingham; a member of Parliament; and, finally, a leader of royalist troops dur-

---

[19]See *Allegations for Marriage Licences Issued by the Bishop of London*, compiled by Joseph Lemuel Chester and George J. Armitage (London: Harleian Society, 1887), 1:328.

ing the Civil War (Killick 318; 327; Tregelles 165–66).[20] This last
service, on top of all of his other accomplishments, led to his being

---

[20]See Also F.W. Allington, "Sir Marmaduke Rawdon," *East Herts
Archaeological Society Transactions*, 4.1 (1908–09): 113–16, esp. 113. More information about Rawdon, his wife, and their children is contained on page
189 of *The Visitation of London Anno Domini 1633, 1634, and 1635*, ed. Joseph
Jackson Howard (London: Harleian Society, 1883), which prints the following data:

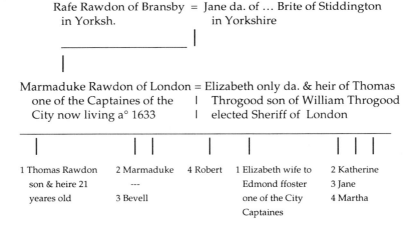

Rawdon

Tower Ward

Theise Armes & Creast are exemplified vnder
the hand & seale of the learned Camden
Clarenceux to Marmaduke Rawdon of London
dated 20 Sept. 1618, 16 Jacobi Regis

Rafe Rawdon of Bransby   =   Jane da. of … Brite of Stiddington
   in Yorksh.   in Yorkshire

Marmaduke Rawdon of London = Elizabeth only da. & heir of Thomas
  one of the Captaines of the | Throgood son of William Throgood
  City now living a° 1633 | elected Sheriff of London

1 Thomas Rawdon	2 Marmaduke	4 Robert	1 Elizabeth wife to	2 Katherine
son & heire 21	---		Edmond ffoster	3 Jane
yeares old	3 Bevell		one of the City	4 Martha
			Captaines	

Marmaduke Rawdon, then, had apparently had a pictorial representation prepared of his coat of arms; this process was known as exemplification. The process had been supervised by the famous scholar William
Camden, who held the title of Clarenceux—the chief heraldic official. The
exemplification was dated 20 September 1618, the sixteenth year of the
reign of King James I. The family tree tells us about Marmaduke Rawdon's
parentage, his marriage to the daughter ("da.") of Thomas Thorowgood,
and the four sons and four daughters who had been born to them by 1633,

knighted (in December 1643) by Charles I, and when Rawdon died in 1646 (the same year as his step-mother-in-law, Martha Moulsworth), he was considered a hero of the royalist cause (Allington 115). Through him Martha broadened even further her already wide and influential social circle.

Rawdon's ties to London were obviously strong, but his ties to Hoddesdon became more and more firm as time went by. During their years of marriage, Elizabeth bore him eighteen children, for whom Martha seems to have felt strong affection (especially for some of the girls).[21] By 1632, when Martha had no children of her own, she had an abundant number of step-grandchildren, and it was perhaps the ever-expanding size of his family that led Marmaduke Rawdon to construct, in Hoddesdon, what is still perhaps the town's most famous building. Originally called Hoddesdon House but for centuries since termed Rawdon House, it is a superb example of Jacobean architecture (Tregelles 144). It was constructed in 1622, and, according to John Alfred Hunt, its style was influenced by nearby Hatfield House (1611), the country home of the powerful Cecil family (earls of Salisbury).[22] Huge for its day and built with expensive, attractive, and innovative red brick, it boasted an intricately carved oak staircase, a gallery cupola providing a vast view of the surrounding countryside, a large and attractive garden, a broad front hall, a chamber for guests, a long gallery at the head of the impressive staircase, and a ground floor paved with black and white marble squares (Hunt

---

when the visitation (i.e., survey or inspection) was conducted. Apparently at this time, Rawdon was officially a resident of London's Tower Ward (which is near, but does not include, the Tower of London).

[21]For the figure of 18 children, see Killick 328. See also the biography of Rawdon printed in E. Hailstone, ed., *Portraits of Yorkshire Worthies*, 2 vols. (London: Cundall, 1869), Vol. 2 (no page), and also the biography printed in Robert Clutterbuck, *The History and Antiquities of the County of Hertford*, 3 vols. (London: John Nichols, 1821), 3: 74–75. As will be mentioned in greater detail later, Marmaduke Rawdon benefitted Hoddesdon by constructing an aqueduct that brought water to a fountain in town. A poem celebrating this benefaction wittily begins, "Twas nott for want of Children thou didst frame / this aquaduct to eternize thy name...." The author of this poem may have been Edmund Parlett, who served for a period as vicar of Broxbourne. See British Library Additional MS 18,044, fols. 78r–78v.

[22]See John Alfred Hunt, "Rawdon House, Hoddesdon," *East Herts Archaeological Society Transactions* 2.1 (1902): 11–17, esp. 11.

11–14; Tregelles 152–53). As mentioned earlier, by the late nine-teenth and early twentieth centuries, the house had served succes-sively as a family residence; a school for girls; and a Catholic con-vent. Today it houses law offices (Hunt 15–16). In Martha's time, however, it was the center of comfortable life in Hoddesdon, and in her later years she must have spent much time there. Certainly her connections with Marmaduke and Elizabeth Rawdon were never ruptured, and in fact they seem to have grown more and more intense as the years went by.

Surely this must have been true in the period immediately fol-lowing Thomas Thorowgood's death. His will, dated 24 October 1615, was proved or probated less than a month later, and so for the second time in her life, Martha was again a widow. Her time as the wife of Thomas Thorowgood had lasted (as her poem tells us) for ten years and nine months, and for almost another four years she would remain unmarried. Presumably she continued to live primarily in Hoddesdon, which was also the residence of Bevill Molesworth, the man who would become her third husband. Her financial and social status as Thorowgood's widow would have made her an attractive bride for purely practical reasons, apart from her qualities of character. Thorowgood's will provided for her comfortably, and his will is also a highly useful source of in-formation about the details of her second marriage and the ex-tended family of her second husband.

Thorowgood opens his will by defining himself as a "gent[leman]" who, despite "beyng visited by the hand of god and vnder the Arrest of bodilie sicknes," is in "mynde and vnderstand-ing well setled and resolued by gods greate mercy" (see Appendix 2). His commitment to his faith, already demonstrated by his part in the feuding between the vicars of Broxbourne and Amwell, is made explicit in his will, which bequeaths his "Soule and better parte to hym my Creator and Redeemer whose I whollie am." He describes himself as "holding fast by that guifte of faithe which he hathe bestowed vppon me the assurance of his grace and mercy in the free and full pardon of all my sinnes thoroughe the alone and all sufficient meritt and mediacion of Jesus Christ." The phras-ing here, especially the references to the gift of grace and the all-sufficient merit of Christ, suggests a strongly Protestant faith, while subsequent phrasing anticipates language also used in Martha's "Memorandum." Thus Thorowgood says that through Christ he expects to "obteyne eternall life and an Inheritaunce *amongest the Saintes* [italics added] in the Caelestiall kingdome which assurance I haue euer held by gods grace" (see "Memorandum," l. 74). Similarly, other phrasing from his will, although conventional, also seems echoed in her poem, as when he speaks of how "god shall call me to rest in the common bed of corruption to the generall resurrection of the iust" (see "Memorandum," ll. 95; 99). His emphasis throughout the will involves thanking God for the grace he has already experienced and expects to receive.

When it comes time for Thorowgood to dispose of his worldly goods, he says that he does so "by the permission of my good god & the free assent of Martha my wife." These goods apparently included those that came to him "by waye of Dower of Ioynture"—that is, through his marriage to her. He also mentions "certaine Tenements without Algate in London" which once belonged to his father. Aldgate was one of "the seven main gates in the old City wall" (Chalfant 29), located on the eastern side of the capital, not far from the Tower of London. Whether Thomas and Martha Thorowgood ever occupied these "tenements" is unclear, but in the will they were left to "Elizabeth my daughter wife of Marmaduke Rawdon of London and the heires of her bodie law-fullie begotten." To his daughter Elizabeth, Thomas Thorowgood also left "a certain Mesuage or Tenement in Hodsdon aforesayed commonlie called or knowne by the name of the white Hynde," perhaps an inn or tavern. Furthermore, to Elizabeth he also bequeathed approximately five acres of meadow ground near Hoddesdon; "three guilt potts of silver plate and one silver salt suteable which were my fathers"; and her choice of "all the houshold stuffe remayning in the house which was her graundfather Highams [i.e., the father of his first wife] of all kyndes." Here as before, Thorowgood is careful to specify that he exercises such generosity "by my Wifes willing assent."

Thorowgood's will also instructs Martha, his executrix, to give one hundred pounds to his son-in-law, Marmaduke Rawdon, as well as "three parcell guilte broade Bowles of silver plate which were my ffathers" to Thomas Rawdon, Thorowgood's grandson, "as a remembraunce of my loue to hym." Bequests of varying amounts are left to three sisters (Sara Goughe, Elizabeth Rowley, and Mary Downes), to one brother (or perhaps brother-in-law: Humfrey Downes), and to one cousin and his wife (William and Sarah Lewin). These bequests were intended to be used toward the purchase of rings "in remembraunce of my loue." Most interesting, however, is the bequest to "my sister Anne Lewin widowe," who was to be paid five pounds a year by Martha (in two equal portions) for as long as she and Martha lived together. Thus for a time, at least, after and perhaps even before Thorowgood's death, Martha seems to have shared a house with her widowed sister-in-law. It would be fascinating to know how they got along, how they spent their time, and whether they shared similar interests.

Also remembered in Thorowgood's will were the poor of Hoddesdon as well as Thomas Hassall, the vicar of Amwell (who was to be paid "so longe as he contineweth his vsuall exercise of preaching at Hoddesdon Chappell" and who was also given an extra sum to preach at Thorowgood's funeral). Even the cantankerous vicar of Broxbourne, if he agreed to allow Hassall to preach the funeral sermon in his church, was to "haue such fees as are due to hym." In death as in life, then, Thorowgood remained a champion of Hassall—just as Hassall would remain devoted to Thorowgood's widow and descendants.

Finally, Thorowgood instructed that all his land should, after the death of his wife Martha, be inherited by his daughter Elizabeth and her lawfully begotten heirs; and he specified that if Elizabeth should not survive, the property should be divided between "Marmaduke Rawdon my sonne in lawe" and "William Lewyn and William Downes my neiphues" (an instruction that suggests strong feelings for Rawdon). Everything else was to be left to "Martha my wife whome I ordayne and make of this my last will and Testament full and sole executrix." Unlike the will of Nicholas Prynne (Martha's first husband), this document appoints no overseers to help the widow discharge her responsibilities. By the time Thomas Thorowgood died, Martha was thirty-four years old, and she must have seemed quite capable of managing affairs by herself.

Thorowgood's will was witnessed by Thomas Luther and Edward Roberts. Perhaps Roberts was in some way related (as son? as husband?) to the Priscilla Roberts who had nursed Martha's first-born child; he certainly seems to have been the same Edward Roberts whom she would later describe in her own will as an "ancient servant." The fact that she and Thomas Thorowgood had no children of their own can be explained in any number of easily imaginable ways, but their childlessness probably made the impact of his death all the more powerful. Yet she was now part of a large and apparently loving family, and also a resident of a town small enough to be close-knit. One citizen of that town, Bevill Molesworth, would eventually become her third husband.

Marriage to Bevill Moulsworth

Like Martha's first husband (Nicholas Prynne), Bevill Molesworth was a goldsmith, and by the time he married Martha in 1619 he had achieved very prominent status in his profession. His gravestone suggests that he was born in approximately 1554, so he would probably have been about sixty-five at the time of their marriage, when Martha was about forty-two. To marry at his age and father a child would have been accomplishments in themselves, but Molesworth always seems to have been energetic. Traces of his life survive from years before he married the widowed Martha Thorowgood, and these traces suggest a good deal about his various occupations and social status. Like Martha's first two husbands, he seems to have been an enterprising and successful man of business who spent much of his time in London. Herbert C. Andrews argues that Molesworth came from Northamptonshire stock and identifies him as the third son of John Molesworth of Helpeston.[23] By the latter half of the sixteenth century Bevill seems to have become a member of the Goldsmiths' Company; records at Goldsmiths' Hall show that he was an apprentice of Nicholas Wheeler, who presented him for membership in 1573 (at the age of nineteen).[24]

Molesworth himself, who eventually became a master goldsmith, is linked with apprentices in the Company records for the years 1582, 1584, 1586, 1588, 1593, and 1614 (*Apprentice Book*). He served as a Company warden—an eminent office—in 1603/04, 1605/06, and 1607/08, and in 1613/14 he served as prime warden (an especially significant position; *Apprentice Book*). In the spring of

---

[23]See Herbert C. Andrews, "Sidelights on Brasses in Hertfordshire Churches," *East Herts Archaeological Society Transactions*, 11.2 (1941): 113–27, esp. 126.

[24]See Volume 1 of the *Apprentice Book*, kept at the Library of Goldsmiths' Hall, London. Subsequent parenthetical references to this 4work will cite simply "*Apprentice Book*." I am most grateful to the Librarian, David Beasley, for his very generous assistance and hospitality.

The *Apprentice Book* mentions two other persons named Bevill Molesworth, who were apprenticed in 1609 and 1617 respectively. Both references give the father's name as Robert Molesworth. Perhaps these were nephews or other younger relatives of our Bevill. In any case, they should not be confused with our Bevill, who was already by this time very well established in the profession.

1611 (aged fifty-seven) he was one of sixteen of "the most honest, skilfullest, and best reputed gouldsmithes" selected to participate in the annual "trial of the pix"—a procedure which tested the weight and purity of the kingdom's gold and silver bullion. In that year, unusually, King James himself personally participated in the event, and Molesworth and his colleagues had an actual audience with the monarch.[25] Everything suggests, then, that Molesworth enjoyed high standing in (and long ties with) the Goldsmiths' Company.[26] He would thus presumably have known Martha's first husband, Nicholas Prynne, and he may even have known (or at least known of) Martha herself years before they married.

This is especially likely because Molesworth seems to have lived in the same general area of London (not far from the Goldsmiths' Hall) in which Martha and her first two husbands also had residences. A record from 1591 describes Molesworth as a "citizen and goldsmith of London" and shows that he purchased a brew house called The Red Lion in the High Street of Southwark, in the parish of St. Savior's—just across the river from the Tower of London.[27] Like Thomas Thorowgood, then, Molesworth seems to have had some experience as the owner and operator of a tavern or inn. On 26 November 1611 Bevill Molesworth, identified as a goldsmith, was one of several men who nominated Brian Ianson, a draper, to serve as an alderman for London's Bread Street Ward (which included the parishes of St. John Evangelist and St.

---

[25]See John Nichols, *Progresses, Processions, and Magnificent Festivities of King James the First*, 4 vols. (London: J.B. Nichols, 1828): 2: 420–21. I discuss this incident in more detail in my article "A Silent Woman Speaks" in the *Yale Library Gazette* (forthcoming 1995).

[26]On the Goldsmiths' Company in general, see for instance Sir Walter Sherburne Prideaux, *Memorials of the Goldsmiths' Company*, 2 vols. (London: Eyre and Spottiswoode, 1896); J.F. Hayward, *Virtuoso Goldsmiths and the Triumph of Mannerism, 1540–1620* (London: Sotheby Parke Bernet, 1976); Sir Charles James Jackson, *English Goldsmiths and Their Marks* (1921; rpt. New York: Dover, 1964); and Christopher Lever, *Goldsmiths and Silversmiths of England* (London: Hutchinson, 1975).

[27]Cited by Leslie Hotson in *Shakespeare versus Shallow* (1931; rpt. New York: Haskell House, 1969), 250. I owe this reference to an altogether accidental encounter with Ivan Molesworth, a descendant of Bevill's brother, in the Public Record Office! I thank Mr. Molesworth for his assistance and generosity.

Margaret).[28] The fact that Molesworth functioned in this way suggests that he had not only some connection with Bread Street Ward (which was very close to St. Paul's Cathedral) but also some social eminence there. Similarly, on 24 January 1612 Molesworth was a nominator of Francis Evington, a merchant tailor, to serve as alderman in the adjacent Cordwaines Ward, which contained the parishes of St. Antholin and St. Mary Aldermary (Beaven 116). He presumably lived, then, within easy walking distance of the same neighborhoods in which Martha's earlier husbands and relatives also owned property. It is very possible, and indeed very likely, that he and Martha shared a number of acquaintances and friends.

When, exactly, Molesworth established a residence in Hoddesdon is unclear. Authorities agree that he owned a property there called Bradshaws (subsequently Harveys), at the south end of town, but they do not specify the date at which he acquired it (Tregelles 116, 276; Andrews 124).[29] Its location was quite close to the site of Rawdon House, the famous structure built by Martha's son-in-law Marmaduke (husband of Elizabeth Thorowgood). A document from 1603 suggests that Molesworth already had some connections with Sir Robert Cecil (one of the most powerful men in the kingdom), whose family owned vast properties near Hoddesdon, and so perhaps Molesworth's connections with the town were long-standing.[30] Certainly his will (to be discussed later) suggests that by 1630 he considered Hoddesdon his home, and it seems reasonable to suppose that he was already connected with the town in some way during the years that Martha Thorowgood lived there. In any case, after the death of Thomas Thorowgood (Martha's second husband), the aging Bevill Molesworth would have had ample opportunity to meet and court the middle-aged widow, whether in London or in Hoddesdon itself.

Molesworth seems to have made quite an impact on his new wife, whom he married on 15 June 1619—three years and eight

---

[28]See Alfred B. Beaven, *The Aldermen of the City of London* (London: Eden Fisher, 1908), 1: 49. Hereafter I will cite this source as "Beaven."

[29]For more on this property, see H.F. Hillyar, *The Chronicles of Hoddesdon from the Earliest Times to the Present Day* (Hoddesdon: Thomas Knight, [1948]), 76.

[30]See Great Britain, Historical Manuscripts Commission, *Calendar of the Manuscripts of the ... Marquess of Salisbury*, part XV (London: HMSO, 1930), 362–63. The text of this document is reprinted in *"My Name Was Martha,"* 10–11.

months after the death of Thorowgood. In her "Memorandum" Martha describes Bevill as "a louely man, & kind" (l. 57), and she particularly comments on his physical attractiveness ("such comlines in age we seldome ffind"; l. 58). Considering that he was sixty-five when they married and seventy-seven when he died, her words seem quite a compliment. She discusses him in a wealth of detail not accorded her first two husbands (natural enough, considering that he had been dead less than two years when she wrote her poem). She claims that he was descended from the ancient Mortimer family and that he bore their arms, and she also tells us that (like her), he had been married twice before. Their marriage lasted for eleven years and eight months, during which time they seem to have had at least one child, who apparently died young. Martha affectionately says of Bevill that there "was neuer man so Buxome to his wife" (l. 65), and she tells us that "wth him I led an easie darlings life. / I had my will in house, in purse[,] in Store," then asks, "what would a women old or yong haue more?" (ll. 66–68) At the time she composed her "Memorandum" she was still (she claims) weeping at his loss. Their relationship seems to have been one of the most satisfying chapters in her long and generally satisfying life.

Near the end of their time together, Bevill Molesworth's seventeen-year-old daughter, Elizabeth, became engaged to marry Francis Lucy, a twenty-eight-year-old bachelor living at Lincoln's Inn, one of London's famous Inns of Court. An application for a marriage license, turned up by Professor Steven May, lists Hoddesdon as the residence of both Elizabeth and her father; the marriage itself was to take place at St. Edmund's church in London's Lombard Street.[31] This location was approximately midway between St. Paul's Cathedral and the Tower of London—in other words, in an area of London that Martha and all of her husbands would have known quite well. Interestingly, then, Martha had two step-daughters named Elizabeth. One was the daughter (from a previous marriage) of Thomas Thorowgood; the other was the daughter (from a previous marriage) of Bevill Molesworth. Of

---

[31]The text of the application reads as follows: "Francis Lucy, Esq. of Lincoln's Inn, Bachelor, 28, & Elizabeth Moulsworth, of Hodsdon, Herts., Spinster, 17, da[ughter]. of Bevill Moulsworth of same, Esq., who consents: at St. Edmund's Lombard St." See *Allegations for Marriage Licences Issued by the Bishop of London*, compiled by Joseph Lemuel Chester and George J. Armitage (London: Harleian Society, 1887), 2: 200.

the two, Martha seems to have felt (at least at the end of her life) the strongest attraction to the first Elizabeth, the little girl who had first come into her family in 1605, at the age of thirteen, when Martha married Thomas Thorowgood. It is Elizabeth Thorowgood Rawdon and her children who eventually inherited the bulk of Martha's estate, and it is that Elizabeth about whom Martha has so many tender things to say in her will. Despite the fact that Elizabeth Molesworth was even younger (approximately six) when her father married Martha, her own bond with her step-mother seems not to have been as intense. Perhaps this is merely because she was not as physically close to Martha after Elizabeth's own marriage to Francis Lucy of London.

Not long after his daughter married Francis Lucy, Bevill Molesworth died. Martha's poem specifies the date—24 February 1630/31. On the 17th of that month, Molesworth had completed his will, describing himself as being "weake in bodie with age and sicknes accordinge to the Common condicion of nature, yet enioyinge the freedome of spiritt in vnderstandinge and memory by gods gratious goodnes" (see Appendix 2). He was motivated to compose his will, he said, partly for "feare" and "for the better quietinge of my minde," and he declared that since his "first care" was

> to make my peace with God through the mediacion of Jesus Christ whom as I acknowledge mine onely redeemer, soe I seeke none other Mediator or Saviour, by his only merritt and mediacion desireing and expecting free pardon of all my sinnes, soe that my soule being quitted from the guilt of originall and accuall sinnes maie enioye that happines in his heavenly kingdome by him purchased and promised to all the elect.

The word "elect," especially, suggests that Molesworth was, like Martha's other husbands, a strongly committed Protestant (even a Calvinist), and other evidence will support this conclusion. Yet the will also suggests much else about his relationships and character. He commits his body, for instance, to the "Comon Purgatory of the earth" and specifies that it should be buried "in Broxburne Church vnder that stone where my deare sonne Bevill Molesworth lyeth." Evidence to be discussed later strongly suggests that this was the child Martha bore him, and apparently father and son were indeed buried together in the church's center aisle, where the inscribed gravestone, bearing a brass coat of arms, is still visible. The elder Bevill Molesworth hoped to rest there "vntill the generall resurrection of the iust, wch I most assuredly beleeve." Once again, the will of one of Martha's husbands anticipates phrasing used in her own poem (see ll. 94-99).

Molesworth's first bequest was ten pounds to be distributed at his burial "to the poore of the Towne of Hodsden in the parishes of Broxburne and Amwell." The money was to be handed out "with indifferent respect to the necessitie of the persons in either parish by the ioynt care and discreccion of the Ministers Churchwardens and Overseers for the poore then beinge, of both the said parishes indifferently." Since tensions between the two parishes and their vicars were continuing, Molesworth's bequest can be seen in one way as an effort to make peace, but it can also be seen as an affirmation of Thomas Hassall, the vicar of Amwell, who in fact served as one of the witnesses of Molesworth's will. Nevertheless, Molesworth also left fifty shillings a year (from rent derived from various poor houses in Broxbourne parish) so that the vicar of Broxbourne and his successors might preach a commemorative sermon each year on the Sunday following Molesworth's date of death. The vicar himself was to receive twenty shillings per year for this service. Any poor persons of the parish who happened to be present at the sermon were to divide another twenty shillings, and the remaining ten shillings per year were to be used to maintain the condition of the rental properties themselves, as well as the condition of "the pavements in the Church about the said stone, vnder which my body shall lye buried."

Rental income from tenements Molesworth leased in London, in the neighborhood of the Old Exchange, were left "vnto Martha my wife duringe her naturall life And after her decease vnto my daughter Grace the wife of Thomas Hill of London Gentleman." Grace Hill, then, was another of Martha's step-daughters, while Thomas Hill was another of Martha's sons-in-law by marriage. Grace and Thomas apparently had a son named Bevill, who was to inherit the London properties after the deaths of his parents. (Interestingly enough, Martha would later fail to mention any of the Hills in her own will; had they been inattentive, or had they all died by then?) Molesworth was careful to specify, however, that some other of his properties had been contracted to Francis Lucy, his new son-in-law, and that if Grace or Bevill Hill should legally resist Lucy's right to those properties, then the London properties should descend to Lucy after Martha's death. The mere fact that Bevill Molesworth felt the need to anticipate this possibility may suggest something about the character of his daughter Grace.

Molesworth's will also implies a close connection between Martha's third husband and the family of her second. Thus Molesworth leaves various lands surrounding Hoddesdon to Martha but specifies that after her death they should pass to Marmaduke Rawdon, his neighbor and Martha's son-in-law by marriage. Other properties in the parish of Lewsham, county Kent, were also bequeathed to Martha, but Molesworth took care as well to leave five nobles yearly to be distributed to the poor there, minus ten shillings to pay the parish vicar for an annual commemorative sermon. After Martha's death, any other properties in Lewisham were to descend to Grace Hill, Bevill's daughter, and then to Bevill Hill, his grandson. Finally, Molesworth disposed of the "residue of all my goods and Chattells whatsoever and wheresoever not otherwise disposed (my debts being paid funerall rights decently performed &c)." All this "residue" he "fully and whollie" gave and bequeathed "vnto Martha my wife whom I alsoe do constitute & ordaine of this my last will and testament full and sole Executrix." Just as he seems to have given her broad autonomy during their married life, so he seems to have fully trusted her to administer his estate wisely after his death. Molesworth's will was witnessed not only by Thomas Hassall but also by William Kinge and Sara Lowin. Perhaps this latter was the same "Sarah Lewin" mentioned in the will of Thomas Thorowgood.[32] If so, then the connections between Martha's second and third families seem even stronger than they had already appeared.

Bevill Molesworth's grave still occupies a prominent place in the Broxbourne parish church. It lies at the intersection of the main aisle and a main crossing aisle; partly for this reason, the grave's inscriptions have been worn down over the centuries. The date of burial ("27 Febru: 1630") is still visible, and the brass shield of arms shows up when rubbed. Almost indecipherable, however, is a poem inscribed on the stone:

> Now seaunty seaun yeares past (myne only Sonne)
> I'me come vnto thee my lifes glasse is runne
> Thou hadst the shorter I the longer howre
> Both equall now I hope th'eternall power

---

[32] A "William King, gentleman" is mentioned in a record dated 1647 and having to do with Hoddesdon; see William Le Hardy, ed., *Hertfordshire County Records: Calendar to the Sessions Books … 1619 to 1657* (Hertford: Charles E. Longmore, 1928), 378. A William King also turns up in Hassall's *Register* (see 111, 224).

For Christs blood shed will rayse out of this dust
Our flesh to resurrection of yᵉ Just.

This poem, which reads more smoothly when some light
punctuation is added, could just possibly have been written by
Martha Moulsworth. The last line echoes phrasing from her husband's will and anticipates phrasing from her own later
"Memorandum," and writing an epitaph on her husband (and presumably on her own young son) would have been a fitting outlet
for the poetic impulses she obviously possessed. The possibility of
her authorship is discussed in more detail elsewhere in this volume (see Appendix 4); other possible authors include Edmund
Parlett, the vicar of the Broxbourne church, or even Bevill
Molesworth himself, who may have written the poem in anticipation of his death, just as he carefully instructed in his will that he
be buried with his son. In any case, the epitaph provides very
valuable information about Molesworth's age at his time of death,
and it also indicates something about his attachment to members
of his family and his sustaining religious beliefs. With the death of
her third and apparently most beloved husband, Martha
Moulsworth's life had now entered a new and final phase. For the
rest of her years she would remain the widow Molesworth.

Martha's Final Years in Hoddesdon

At the time of Bevill Molesworth's death in February 1630/31,
Martha was already in her early fifties. She had been orphaned
while still an infant, had been married three times, had buried all
her husbands, and had outlived the children of her first and third
unions. Her life had not been easy, but she was financially comfortable and was apparently a well respected and prominent
member of her local community. Her life up to this point had been
complex and eventful, but she still had another fifteen years to live.
These final years would prove, in some ways, to be among her
most memorable. She would compose her autobiography, would
find herself (twice) in court, would see civil war descend on her
country, would witness that war's effects on her own town and
property, would learn of the hero's death of her distinguished son-
in-law, and would shortly thereafter die herself, with the conflict
still raging and her family's fortune and social standing threatened. The poem she could have written at the end of her life might

have been substantially different in tone from the "Memorandum" we now possess.

Much of our most valuable information about her final years comes from Thomas Hassall, the vicar of Amwell parish, who seems to have been a close friend of Martha for decades. In 1611 he had in fact married one of the minister's daughters remembered in the will of Martha's first husband, Nicholas Prynne (Doree xviii), and it is even possible that Martha (who must have known the bride) had had a hand in introducing the couple. In any case, Martha and the vicar had much else in common. Hassall was only four years older than she, and he had already been serving as vicar of Amwell since 1600 (Doree xviii). He would thus have been one of the first persons to welcome the newly married Martha Thorowgood to Hoddesdon when she arrived there sometime after 1605, and the friendship that probably began at that time persisted until the end of her life. They both had lost spouses and children to death (Doree xix); they shared an interest in poetry (in 1598 Hassall had published verse praising the poems of Michael Drayton [Doree xv–xvi], and he would continue to write poems for years to come); they shared a strong interest in religion (in 1621 Hassall composed a 23,000-word Latin poem dealing with the Bible [Doree xix]);[33] and they shared a mutual interest in seeing the gospel propagated through preaching. It was this latter interest that brought them both into conflict with successive vicars of neighboring Broxbourne parish—the parish of which Martha was technically a member.

The roots of this conflict have been mentioned already. Hassall, whose parish was poorer, nevertheless struck many of the most influential residents of Hoddesdon as a more capable preacher than the various vicars of Broxbourne (some of whom also seem to have labored under the handicap of being touchy and disagreeable). The vicars at Broxbourne tended to resent Hassall's influence over some of their parishioners; they even went so far as to prohibit or impede members of their church from attending his sermons. Their attitudes and actions backfired, however, causing many members of the Broxbourne parish—including the Thorowgoods, Rawdons, and Molesworths—to side with Hassall.

---

[33]British Library Additional MS 18,044 contains a poem by Hassall in tribute to Marmaduke Rawdon. It begins, "My muse was falne a sleep thou bidst it wake / halfe sleeping and half wakinge thus she spake ..." (fol. 101v).

The fact that the small but very convenient chapel in the center of Hoddesdon lay technically within the boundaries of Hassall's parish (closer to most residents than either parish church) gave Hassall an advantage in the competition, and he took every opportunity to improve the chapel and make it a center of the community's religious life.

In this he had an ally in Thomas Thorowgood and especially in Martha, and in fact Stephen Doree writes that "there grew up a strong bond between between [Hassall and Martha] which developed over many years and which enabled Hassall virtually to annexe Marmaduke Rawdon as his patron, advertising the fact on the external wall of the chapel" by having the Rawdon motto engraved there (Doree xxii). Martha seems to have admired Hassall for numerous reasons, and given their many common interests, it is easy to imagine him as her closest intellectual friend and advisor, especially after Bevill Molesworth's death. Certainly he would have been capable of appreciating and encouraging her interest in poetry, and they may well have served each other as sources of books, conversation, and mental stimulation. She was probably a regular attendant when he preached at the chapel, especially since his sermons were funded in part by bequests she administered.

Not long after Martha composed her poetic "Memorandum," the religious tensions that had been simmering in her community for many years came to a boil. According to Hassall's account, in 1633

> Mr Parlet, vicar of Broxborne, began a combustion in the towne of Hoddsden, quarrelling [i.e., legally challenging] the lecture at the chapell as derogatory to his honor and right as vicar of Broxborne.... After some contestation, he caused the churchwardens to sue Mistress Martha Molesworth, widdoe, executrix to Mr Thomas Thorogood, deceased, in the Commissary's court at Starford for the sayd legacye of 40 shillings for 6 sermons, but in the end they lett fall theyr suit and payd her costs. Then he preached at his parish church in the afternoones [at] the tyme of my lecture, forbiddinge his parishoners to repayre to the chappell under payne of presentment [i.e., proceedings in the archdeacon's court], with divers other insolencyes in this kynde. Hence grew much unquietnes in the towne, parts-taking and unkindnes amongst frends and neighbours. (Hassall, *Register* 221)

A later account by Hassall is even more vivid and full of helpful detail, especially concerning Martha's feisty response:

Mr Parlet claymes the 40 shillings a yeare due to hym as vicar of Broxborne, pleads his owne worth, quarrells his parishoners for goinge to the chappell, takes occasion to shewe his stomach against Captayne Rawden and other of my frends [and] in the end falls to a playne suit with Mistress Molesworth, uppon whome he serves 2 processes at one tyme, one to appear at Starford before the commissary to answer to the churchwardens in a plea concerning Mr William Thorogood his legacy of 40s for the six sermons, the other to appeare at London before the judge of the Arches to answer to hymself in a case of detention of tythes pretended. *She appears to both and held hym so close to it beyond his expectation that she made him repent his rash undertaking*. The busines at Starford was soone ended and the churchwardens soone wearyed, who finding theyr error wherunto he had led them, let fall theyr suite, and so were dismissed, payinge costs.

His personall suit against her for tythes held longer and cost more monye, for he owed her more than shee did hym in mony which shee had lent hym and had yearly accounted with her for the same and sett of so much for tythes. Yet he trusted by a trick in lawe to have gotten the suite against her, because, we say, stoppage [i.e., deduction] is no payment. *But in this also shee so well plyed her advocates* and they so closely followed her cause (findinge it to be just, and *shee havinge good cards to shew for it more than Mr Parlet was aware of*) that here also he was glad to lett fall his suit, and, after he had long wasted and wearyed hym self and her, to offer tearmes of peace and to labour reconciliacion which, by the mediation of frends, was effected, the suit ended and they reconciled May 17, 1634. (Hassall, *Register*, 228–29; italics added)

The italicized passages in this account speak volumes about Martha Moulsworth's character, reinforcing many impressions conveyed by her poem. The strength, determination, and cleverness the "Memorandum" implies are also obvious here, and the incidents recounted by Hassall lend special point to the poem's vow "to Mayntayne, & ffight ffor" the Christian religion (l. 86). It would have been easy enough for Martha to back down when challenged by Parlett. That she did not acquiesce tells us something about her resoluteness (and perhaps about her personal dislike for the Broxbourne vicar), but surely she must also have seen the fight as a test of devotion to her personal religious convictions. Hassall apparently struck her as the better minister, and her loyalty to him never abated. In fact, it would eventually lead her heirs into legal squabbles again after her death, and in the mid-1650's a court would decide that Martha had been so loyal to Hassall that she had violated the terms of Bevill Molesworth's will by paying Hassall monies that rightfully belonged to his rivals (Doree xxvi).

For the time being, however, it was Martha who emerged triumphant in court. The balance that seems to have been so strong a part her character also seems reflected in the ultimate outcome of these disputes with Parlett. Although Hassall tells us that the conflict stirred up by "Mr Parlets quarrelsome spirit" had "bred many trobles and great unkindnesses amongst some who had long been frends" (Doree 229), Martha seems to have been uninterested in fighting for fighting's sake, and she proved capable of reconciling sooner than many others might have. Before long, however, with the start of the Civil War, she would witness conflict on a scale that dwarfed the minor skirmishings in Hoddesdon. There seem, in fact, to have been few doctrinal differences between the competing vicars. Hassall, by all accounts, was a conventional Protestant who believed in preaching the word but who had little truck with more radical notions, and in fact he apparently became increasingly conservative as he aged. When war did break out, Hassall sided with the royalists, as did Marmaduke Rawdon, his family, and (presumably) Martha herself.

In the meantime, though, life in Hoddesdon seems to have been both peaceful and pleasant. By the end of 1632 Martha had decided against remarrying, and so her remaining years would increasingly center around her ties with her stepchildren and in-laws, particularly her stepdaughter Elizabeth Thorowgood Rawdon, who gave birth to ten sons and six daughers (Killick 328). Elizabeth now presided over the largest and most impressive home in town, and Martha must have spent many hours there, playing with and perhaps even helping to educate her increasingly numerous grandchildren. (One of these, a boy named Bevill, led a particularly bedevilled early life.)[34] She was the widow of two of

---

[34]A valuable but unpaginated manuscript held at the Hertfordshire County Record Office, MS 79959X, contains "A Brief Relation of ye Antient famely of the Rawdons...." Near the rear of the volume occurs the following account of young Bevill Rawdon; I cannot resist quoting from it: "Bevill the 8th son of S[r] Marmaduke Raudon & / Dame Elizabeth his Wife, was borne in London / the 22th of March 1629 & sent to Hodsden to be / Nurst, whose Nurse though she had a very large / allowance did wilfully endeavour to starve him, / Soe he being very leane & not thriving when

Hoddesdon's most prominent citizens (Thorowgood and Molesworth) and the stepmother-in-law of its greatest living benefactor,
Marmaduke Rawdon. It was Rawdon who helped promote construction of an imposing market house in 1634 (Tregelles 248; Killick 328), and it was he, too, who had already built a conduit, more
than a mile long, leading into the town. This delivered fresh water,
at a rate of a gallon a minute, from a sculpted fountain shaped to
represent the Samaritan woman (Tregelles 284; Hunt 15–16; Killick
327), and it remains a local landmark.[35] Furthermore, his support
of Hoddesdon chapel was crucial to Thomas Hassall (Killick 328).

Marmaduke Rawdon was a highly successful and influential
man. His house in Hoddesdon had been visited often by King
James, and he also seems to have been popular with Charles I
(after 1625 the new king), with Buckingham (the favorite of both
kings), with Phillip, Earl of Pembroke (Charles's Lord
Chamberlain), and also with the people of London, whom he
served as a captain of the militia (Killick 318–19).[36] When a young

---

he / was neer a yeare old, S[r] Marmaduke brought an / eminent D[r] from
London, to see what his distemper / was, who when he had well viewd
him, told them he / was Starued, w[ch] they could not beleive the Nurse /
not having onely a large Sallary / for Nursing him, but also a constant allowance / of New Milk every day, & victuals sent hir from S[r] /
Marmadukes house, by the D[rs] perswasion he was /sent to another Nurse,
& then they found it true, / for he then having his reasonable allowance of
/ Meat did thrive very well, & is now a proper stout / Man, but rather
leane then otherwaies. / This Nurse had Nurst 7 of S[r] Marmadukes
Children / & what should move hir to this (except it were by / Instigation
of the Devill) is not knowne, onely she / confest She had an Intent to have
Starved him / & it troubled hir much vpon hir death bed. / Being taken
from his second Nurse he was brought / vp at his ffathers house till he
was about 8 yeares / of age, & then was sent to the free schoole att /
Bishop Stortford, where he was boarded at the Mother / in Lawes of the
Schoole M[rs] who went about to Starve / him the Second time (as if he had
been borne / vnder a Starving Planet), he having such a Short / allowance
that in Summer time he was glad to / make vp his Svpper wth Crabs &
apples & what / trash he could get, & he durst not complaine, the /
woman threatning if he did that hir son in Lawe / should whip him, but
this was discoverd by his / looks, & he removed to another place, where
he / was well vsed, & liued there at Schoole neer 7 years / & then was
brought from thence, & sent to Lixborne / in Portugal, where he was bred
a Merchant, learnt / the language, & staid there about 4 years...."

[35]E.W. Paddick discusses the fountain and prints a photograph in
Hoddesdon: Tales of a Hertforshire Town (103–5).

relative instructed a tailor to buy him the best clothes he could find
for the money, Rawdon is supposed to have commented (smiling),
"I commend you, nephew; winn gold and weare gold" (Davies 25).
He has been described by one biographer as "affable to all men"
and as

> a great compounder of differences, who could not endure to
> see any in his own family or the town where he lived. He
> loved to see all things gentle and noble about him; his house
> was governed with much order and little noise. He liked to
> see handsome people about him and that they should be
> well dressed. He was a great friend of good horses, and often
> said that he that sold him a good horse, though he paid him
> his full price, yet he would be his friend as long as he lived.
> When he had leisure, which was but seldom, his recreations
> were the artillery garden, a bowling green, and a game at bil-
> liards—then called tables. (Allington 116)

A contemporary account described his house in Hoddesdon as "a
place of much recreation" (Killick 319), and another contemporary
manuscript describes the celebration Rawdon put on to welcome
his sons, as well as his nephew and namesake (usually called
Marmaduke Rawdon of York), during a visit to Hoddesdon.
According to this source, Rawdon

> made att his howse att Hodsden a greate feast, to which was
> invited the Earle of Salisbury and his Countesse, the Lord
> Cranborne his son, with the rest of his [i.e., the earl's] sons
> and daughters, the Lord Norris, and severall other persons
> of honor, where thir was all the varieties that England could
> afford, for viands and severall sorts of wines, and cost, as I
> was informed, one hundreth and fortie pownds. (Davies 24)

This feast, which occurred in the summer of 1638 (Tregelles 381;
Hunt [15] mistakenly says 1631) was probably attended by Martha;
in any case, it shows the kinds of social circles in which she occasionally moved. Although she may have felt disadvantaged in
some ways by having been born a woman, in other ways her life
was rather privileged. Her link with Marmaduke and Elizabeth
Rawdon seems to have been close (they named one son Bevill and
one daughter Martha), so that even after the death of her third

---

[36]See also Robert Davies, ed., *The Life of Marmaduke Rawdon of York*
(London: Camden Society, 1863), 25. Marmaduke Rawdon of York should
not be confused with Marmaduke Rawdon of London, Moulsworth's son-
in-law and uncle of his namesake from York.

husband she was not entirely alone. She was part of a world that must have seemed reasonably happy and secure.

Within a year of the feast at Rawdon House, however, war had erupted between Charles I and his Scottish subjects, and the march toward civil war in England itself had begun. In 1639 Maramaduke Rawdon was still popular enough in London to be selected an alderman (an office he refused) and also a lieutenant colonel for the city. However, as more and more people there began to side with Parliament against the king, Rawdon resigned his commission, and when he refused entreaties designed to win him over to the parliamentary side, he began to be suspected. To forestall arrest he returned to Hoddesdon, and eventually (in March 1643) he presented himself for service to the king at Oxford. He raised a regiment at his own expense, and he showed fierce determination in withstanding several parliamentary sieges in Hampshire. For such service he was knighted by Charles in December 1643, but by April 1646, after further successful service, he was overcome by illness and died. His parliamentary enemies, hearing of his funeral, supposedly fired a mortar at the church. This damaged his fresh grave but missed (by fifteen minutes) killing any of his mourners (Allington 115–16; Killick 330).

Meanwhile, Hoddesdon itself did not escape the effects of the war. King Charles had passed through the town several times in 1641, and came through for one last time in 1642 (Tregelles 381). Hoddesdon as a whole tended to side with the Parliament (Tregelles 382), but everything suggests that Martha Moulsworth and her closest family and friends remained loyal to the king.[37] In 1643 property in Hoddesdon belonging to Moulsworth was burned (although whether directly as a result of the war is unclear; see Tregelles 278), while property there belonging to Marmaduke Rawdon was plundered and confiscated, since Rawdon was con-

---

[37]The funeral sermon on Martha Moulsworth is bound with a similar manuscript sermon on Marmaduke Rawdon preached by his chaplain, John Joanes (Bodleian Library MS. Don g. 9, fols. 1r–27v). At one point Joanes says, concerning Rawdon's "Religion," that "Hee dyed / in the same wherein hee / was Baptized, a true / sonne of y^e Church of England / not adhering eyther to the / right hand, or to the left, / neyther to y^e superstitions / of the Romish Church / Nor to the Scismes, and dis= / sentions of this" (fols. 25v–26r). According to Joanes, "None reapes any / aduantage by his [Rawdon's] death / but the Kings Enemyes" (fol. 26r).

sidered a traitor to the Parliamentary cause (Killick 328).[38] By the
time of his death in the spring of 1646, dark changes had come
over his life and over the lives of those he loved. When Rawdon's
son, also named Marmaduke, visited his father's home in
Hoddesdon not long before the elder Rawdon's death, he found
his mother (Elizabeth Rawdon, Martha's stepdaughter)

> in good health and in a hearty condition though she had
> been sadly used by the Parliamnts. soldyers who had plun-
> dered her of all she had leaving onely but one bed and a lit-
> tle furniture in hir owne Chamber soe that she had not a bed
> to lay hir Children on. Soe he lodged at his grandmothers
> who lived then in Towne though before the plunder few
> houses in Hartfordshire were better furnished. (qtd. in
> Tregelles, 173)

The grandmother mentioned in this account was presumably
Martha, by this point in her late sixties, who seems not to have
suffered to quite the same degree as her stepdaughter's family. In
fact, records of a tax assessment levied in 1645 (and designed, ironically, to support the parliamentary forces) suggests that she may
even have been the wealthiest resident in town. Her lands were assessed at a value of £60, but her "goods" were assessed as being
worth £1200—far more than those of anyone else listed (Tregelles
383). Tregelles suggests that the "£1200 must have meant a great
store of family plate" (383n), but whatever the explanation,
Martha's final years were not spent in destitution. As we shall see,
her will alone suggests the size of her estate.

Final Days

When Marmaduke Rawdon died in April 1646, his extended
family lost perhaps its leading male. Then, within months of her
son-in-law's death, Martha, the family matriarch, also passed
away. Her will, dated 19 July, testifies to the size of her fortune, the
breadth of her connections, and the depth of her generosity and affection (see Appendix 2). She describes herself as a "widowe
weake in bodie, yet by gods goodnes of good understanding and

---

[38]John Joanes, in his funeral sermon on Marmaduke Rawdon, claims
that the latter "neuer / serued his Maiestye / for any priuate ends / for
any sinister respects, / to aduance a fortune, / which he much impayred /
by it." See Bodleian MS Don. g. 9, fol. 26v.

of sound memorie" and declares that one motive for the composition of her will is the "better quieting of my minde." She bequeaths her "Soule both in life and death into the mercifull handes of Almightie God my creator who gave it mee," and she commits her body "to the'arth from whence it came to be decentlie buried at the discretion of my executrix," her stepdaughter Elizabeth Rawdon. Elizabeth had been with her from the time (more than forty years before) when Martha had married Elizabeth's father, Thomas Thorowgood. Apparently the love between the two women became ever more intense over the years; Martha speaks of Elizabeth with extreme affection in her will. The little girl she had helped raise had now become not only a matriarch herself but also one of the most important persons in the old woman's life.

Martha's first legacies, however, are left to a number of relatives who have not been previously mentioned—"the children and grandchildren that are vnmarried nowe of my loveing kinsman Symon Edmondes of London Alderman." Contemporary records suggest that Edmondes was a merchant who (like Marmaduke Rawdon) was involved in overseas trade; in June 1640, when he was serving as a sheriff and had been nominated as a burgess (or alderman), he had been granted a coat of arms.[39] Martha's emphasis on Edmondes and his family shows that despite her many years in Hoddesdon, she had never lost her early connection to important persons in London, and in fact her legacies to Edmondes and his descendants were supposed to be paid out of money owed her (by a William Parnell) in connection with property near the capital. From these funds she left £150 to Symon Edmondes (the alderman himself) to be distributed as follows: £20 to Symon Edmondes, eldest son of the alderman; £20 to Thomas Edmondes, the second son; and £20 each to Elizabeth Edmondes and Sarah Edmondes, presumably either children or grandchildren of the alderman. From the remaining funds, £10 pounds each were to go to two couples: "Hugh Wood the sonne of my cozen Hugh Wood and Martha his wife" and "Christopher Parke the sonne of my Cozen Christopher Parke and Anne his wife." None of these names turns up in the standard sources on Hoddesdon history, so perhaps

---

[39]See various volumes of the series Great Britain, *Calendar of State Papers ... Domestic* (London, HMSO), in particular for the years 1636/7 (345: 412), 1640 (456: 291). References to this series will hereafter be cited parenthetically as "*CSPD*," plus the appropriate year, volumes, and page numbers.

these relatives were directly related to Martha by way of her long-deceased father or mother, or perhaps they were related in some way by her distant first marriage to Nicholas Prynne. Her use of the terms "kinsman" and "cozen" suggests a relation by blood rather than marriage, and if the Edmondes, Park, and Wood families were indeed related to either of Martha's parents, then we might have some further clues for tracing her very early history.

The monies remaining from the original £150 bequest were "to be disposed of by my said kinsman Alderman Edmondes amongst his other children (which to my remembrance I haue not seene) as he shall thinke fitting." The phrasing here is intriguing, suggesting either that Edmondes had had new children recently, whom Martha (perhaps because of the war) had not had a chance to meet, or that other, older children of his had not been as attentive to her as their siblings. The fact that these "other children" are not mentioned by name can support either interpretation, but if the latter reading is correct, then the will shows that Martha was capable of recalling the neglect (as well as the affection) of her relatives. Any monies left over from the disposition of the property near the capital was to go, like much else in her will, to her stepdaughter, Elizabeth Rawdon.

It is to Elizabeth's children that Martha now turns, but not before mentioning a relative linked to her by her very first marriage. She leaves £5 sterling to "william Pryn of Lincolnes Inn" in London, "hee being my husband Pryns godson and mine." As Germaine Greer has suggested, this was almost certainly William Prynne the famous puritan pamphleteer and parliamentary leader, who had lost his ears during the 1630s for seeming to criticize the king, queen, and bishops. His cheeks had also been branded with the letters "S.L." (seditious libeller), and he had been imprisoned and stripped of his membership in Lincoln's Inn (among many other punishments). However, with the coming of the civil war, Prynne was regarded (at least for a while) as a hero by the parliamentary side, and he was granted the right to reside again at the Inn. But he soon proved less radical than some other parliamentarians; he was a firm advocate of Presbyterianism and therefore resisted more independent sects and more democratic political reform. He sought peace with Charles, opposed the eventual trial of the king, helped facilitate the restoration, and was rewarded with new status when Charles II took the throne. This, of course, was years after Martha remembered him in her will. At the time she died, Charles I was still living, and Prynne was (as usual) in the thick of politics and pamphleteering. By this point he had actually become an opponent of the more radical changes sought by others, and he remained as sure of his correctness now as he had always been before.[40] He and his godmother seem to have shared, if nothing else, a similarly resolute character. Knowing that the fiery Prynne was related to Martha casts an intriguing light on the social radicalism implied by her call for a women's university. If she needed a stimulus to independent thinking, she could have found it in Prynne—or perhaps any such influence flowed at least as much in the other direction.

After remembering Prynne, Martha next turns her attention to the Rawdons, direct relations of Sir Marmaduke, the recently dead royalist hero. To his son Marmaduke she leaves one hundred pounds. To another son, Bevill Rawdon (almost certainly named after her husband Bevill Molesworth), she leaves two hundred pounds, and to a third son (Robert) she leaves another two hundred. To Marmaduke Rawdon (her step-great-grandchild), the son of Thomas Rawdon (her step-grandchild), she leaves another £200 but provides that if the littlest Marmaduke should die before reaching the age of seven, his father Thomas should inherit the money. She gives £5 "to my cozen Thomas Willys of London Chaundler" (i.e., candlemaker) and £3 to "my cozen Anne fforster widowe." Furthermore, to the otherwise unidentified Martha Henne she leaves a "parcell of table lynnen" for which Moulsworth had lent ten pounds to Henne's father. Another Martha, however, makes out much better. Moulsworth bequeaths "to Martha Rowdon daughter of my executrix, one thousand poundes of lawfull money of England." This is by far the largest specified bequest in her will, and it seems both intriguing and significant that she leaves it to a grand*daughter* named after herself. At the time of Martha Moulsworth's death, her namesake (born in 1622) would have been about 23 years of age, so perhaps the huge bequest was a contribution toward her dowry.

---

[40]For details of Prynne's life see, for instance (in addition to the entry in the *Dictionary of National Biography*), Ethyn Williams Kirby, *William Prynne: A Study in Puritanism* (Cambridge, MA: Harvard University Press, 1931) and William M. Lamont, *Marginal Prynne 1600–1669* (Toronto: University of Toronto Press, 1963). Kirby touches on Prynne's links with William Sherston, the mayor of Bath who is mentioned in the will of Nicholas Prynne, Martha's first husband (see 4, 139, 156). On Prynne's political views in the period preceding the composition of Moulsworth's will, see Kirby 51–84, esp. 77. For a different emphasis, see Lamont 49–118.

Martha also remembers several step-great-grandchildren, including Elizabeth and Martha Forster, daughters of her grandson-in-law Edmond Forster (the husband of Elizabeth Thorowgood, daughter and namesake of Martha's own step-daughter). The girls receive £150 each, while their brother Edmond is left £200.[41] Interestingly, Martha's step-granddaughter Elizabeth, wife of the elder Edmond Forster, is not mentioned in the will—a fact suggesting that she may have been dead by this time, especially since Moulsworth singles out her husband for several references. If Elizabeth had indeed died by 1646, this would also help to explain the size of the massive bequest to her still-living sister, Martha. In any case, the remaining bequests (except for one) are somewhat more modest but are in some ways more revealing. Thus Moulsworth leaves "to Edward Roberts my auncient Servant" a monthly pension of four shillings for the rest of his life. Her concern to provide for Roberts, who had been a witness to the will of Thomas Thorowgood and who may even have been with Martha since the days of Nicholas Prynne, speaks well of her loyalty. However, to her stepdaughter Elizabeth Lucy (the daughter of Bevill Molesworth) she leaves only her "gold ring with five Diamonds in itt," and to Elizabeth Lucy's daughter Martha (Martha Moulsworth's granddaughter and probably her namesake) she leaves simply "my greate chaine of gold." Perhaps these bequests had great sentimental value, but it is hard to resist the impression that Martha Moulsworth's connections with the child and grandchildren of her third husband were less intense than with the child and grandchildren of her second.

One of the latter grandchildren, for instance (Edmond Forster, who had already been mentioned previously), is given a further bequest of ten pounds, and the same amount is left to William Bowger [?] and Henrie Crewe, whose relationships to Martha are unspecified. However, Martha's step-daughter Elizabeth Thorow-

---

[41]In British Library Additional MS 18,044, an "Edmund fforster" (presumably the elder of the two just mentioned) is listed as the author of a poem commemorating the death (in 1646) of Sir Marmaduke Rawdon. The poem is written in Latin, then translated into English prose, then translated into English verse; see fols. 74v–78v. This manuscript contains other verses written by members of Martha Moulsworth's circle of family, friends, and acquaintances; it testifies to their interest not only in reading poetry but in writing it. Many of the verses in this manuscript are written in Latin, and many are unattributed. For more on this manuscript, see Appendix 4.

good Rawdon and her family are celebrated in a long and heartfelt passage that brings the will nearly to its close. Once again, as in her "Memorandum" itself, we have evidence of Martha's capacity to generate and reciprocate intense affection:

> The rest and residue of all my goodes, chattells, debts, Iewells, plate, money, lands of inheritance, fee simple, and Coppiehold I give and bequeath vnto my daughter in lawe Dame Elizabeth Rawdon al*ias* Elizabeth Rowdon al*ias* Thorowgood, whome I doe hereby make and ordaine full and sole executrix of this my testament and last will And I doe hereby intimate declare and publishe that the reasons which doe enduce and cause mee to be so liberall and beneficiall vnto my said daughter in lawe Rowdon, and to her children, and grandchildren before named in bestoweing the most part of my estate on them, and giveing my inheritance as aforesaid are as followeth That Thomas Thorowgood my late deceased husband, and ffather of the said Dame Elizabeth Rawdon left mee a plentifull estate of chattles and landes and other hereditaments, which I have enioyed thees manie yeares, And for that *the said Dame Elizabeth and her said children, and grandchildren have ever bene loveing and kinde vnto mee and allwaise diligent & carefull of mee both in sicknes and in health, in soe much that shee and they have gayned and deserve my love, and I doe love her the said Dame Elizabeth as if shee were my owne child, and I love the said children, and grandchildren as if they were my owne* [italics added]

The italicized passage, which consists of what were probably among Moulsworth's last written words, helps illuminate her character and life. The woman whose own children had all predeceased her now found herself surrounded by a large and loving family, full of children, grandchildren, and great-grandchildren who apparently cared for her deeply. Elizabeth, who had been a young girl when Martha first became her step-mother more than four decades before, was now herself a mother and grandmother, whom Martha loved "as if shee were my owne child." In the fourteen years since Bevill Molesworth's death, Martha had remained a widow, just as she had vowed in the closing lines of her "Memorandum." But she had not remained alone, unloved, or unloving. By the time her will was proved in October 1646, she had lived a full, rich, and enriching life and had left the kind of legacies no will can convey.

Death and Remembrance

It was Thomas Hassall, appropriately enough, who preached the sermon commemorating Moulsworth's funeral. She had been his friend and supporter in life, and now he would eulogize her in death (see Appendix 3). The written version of his sermon, dedicated to "Dame Elizabeth Rawdon" and given to her as a memento (31r), speaks of how deeply he stands indebted "to the happy memory of our deare freind decease'd (who in her lyfetyme made her house as myne)," even as he also thanks Elizabeth herself for her "manyfold fauours (who haue made mee as one of your owne family)" (31r). Both passages suggest a long and intimate relationship between the vicar and two of the most important families of his community. (In fact, Hassall calls Moulsworth and the recently-dead Marmaduke Rawdon the "two principall pillours of these two Houses"; 31v). For decades Hassall would have been one of Martha's contacts with the world of books and ideas she so obviously valued. A poet himself, he may have helped encourage her to write her "Memorandum," and (as we shall see) phrasing from his sermon suggests that he may even have read it.

Hassall's sermon was preached on "Weddensday being October the 28th 1646 Being the feast of Simon and Jude" at "Hodsdon Chappel" (33r). It seems fitting that these last words commemorating Moulsworth were preached at the chapel that she and her family had done so much to nurture, and it seems fitting, too, that the sermon was preached on the feast day of Jude and Simon, two saints prominently mentioned in Martha's own "Memorandum" (ll. 81–88). It was a day recently ordained for fasting (as Hassall mentions; 34r), and so we can imagine that the congregants were especially conscious of the solemnness of the occasion. Hassall speaks, he says, both "to expresse our losse" and "to reuiue our Comfort" (34r).

Most of the sermon is given over to exposition of a scriptural phrase (from Luke 10:42)—the idea that "One thing is necessary" (34v). Appropriately enough, these words come from Christ's own comments to the biblical Martha—the same Martha whom Moulsworth mentions in her "Memorandum" (36v). In a long and learned sermon, logically constructed and filled with Latin quotations, Hassall expounds on this key notion of necessity in a manner that gives a real taste of the preaching style that so impressed Moulsworth's extended family. Death, he argues, is one of the things necessary to all humans, and it is therefore also necessary that we consider death in all its complexity (35v–36r). There is even a touch of humor in his remarks that we generally prefer to consider the theoretical rather than the practical implications of death ("we had rather see it well noted by others; then experimented in our selues"; 37r), and in fact the sermon as a whole is rich in its combination of different textures and tones, as when Hassall slyly remarks that if it "were but conuenient only, and not necessary to dye wee could be content to dispence with it for euer" (37r). Hassall even touches delicately on contemporary political issues, doing so in ways that suggest (as one might have expected) some sympathy with the royalist cause.[42]

For the most part, however, his sermon sticks to a non-controversial exposition of fundamental Christian truths. Thus he argues that it is first essential for persons to remember that they must necessarily die; then to remember that they must necessarily prepare themselves for death; and finally to remember that they must necessarily consider their fates following death (41r). The sermon elaborates on each of these points in turn. It attacks sin as the ultimate cause of death (42r–43r) and emphasizes the mental and physical sufferings involved (43r–43v). Hassall stresses the necessity of a person sending a good testimony before him, carrying a good conscience with him, and leaving a good report behind him (44v), and he argues that "It cannot be an evell death, wch followes a good lyfe" (44v). At the same time, he stresses the torments of a bad conscience, and he does so in ways that may have seemed to carry definite political overtones for his contemporary audience:

> Thow therefore y^t pleadest so much for libertye of Conscience, and holdest it for so great a tyranie for any man

---

[42]At one point, for instance, Hassall remarks, "I stand not heere to dispute the Question eyther of Monarchy, or Monopoly though some are of opinion that there is a Vnum necessarium in both these, In the one, for security of State policy; In the other, for restraynt of Popular Libertye" (40v). Hassall thus manages to express an opinion even while claiming that he has no interest in doing so. Later he is even more explicit, referring to the current "Licentiate tymes," when it has become common "To call Euell good, and Good euell, Darkeness light, and Light darknesse; Bitter sweete, and Sweet bitter wherein men are wise in their owne eyes, and prudent in their owne opinions." He claims that the "new Vertue, and new Piety, is to speake euell, and doe euell, to ye most eminent, and excellent things, and persons, both in the Church, and in the Commonwealth" (49v–50r).

to insult ouer thee, or giue lawes to thy tender Conscience;
play not the Tyrant with thyne owne Conscience.... (46v)

Here as elsewhere Hassall implies his skepticism about the ideas
advocated by the most extreme Protestants of his day.

Only near the end of the sermon does Hassall turn to the topic
that most interests us here—Martha Moulsworth the individual. In
fact, his phrasing even suggests that Moulsworth herself specified
that he should preach at her funeral ("being by her dying vote [or
"note"?] desyned to this duty"; 48v). If this was so, then her choice
suggests again the esteem in which she held him. Hassall, in turn,
declares his loyalty to her ("to whose living desert, I owe so much,
and can paye so little"; 48v), and he stresses the length of their relationship: "I knowe it will be expected I should speake much of her,
being of so longe acquaintance wth her (for I see not that face in all
this Assembly, wch hath knowne her longer then my selfe)" (48v).
During all those years, he declares, she always showed him kindness, and although the occasion of his words must always be remembered when judging their veracity, his sermon nonetheless
seems sincere in extolling her friendliness. Thus he depicts himself
as being

> during all that tyme so much obliged to her, (that the reality
> and Constancy of her fauours to mee, may neuer bee forgot-
> ten) And, which is more, That In all this tyme of our so long
> acquaintance (I speake it to Gods glorys) As there neuer was
> any break of vnkindnesse betwixt vs: so neuer any occasion
> for which I might haue wished, I had not knowne her (49r)

The image of a good and decent woman that emerges from Moulsworth's "Memorandum" seems confirmed by Hassall's sermon,
and in fact the sermon both supports and supplements the poem
on many specific points.

Of Martha's time in Hoddesdon, Hassall reports that "She was
no stranger in this place, hauing liued heere the better half of her
tyme; and that part which might best speake her" (49r). This
phrasing suggests that although she spent time in London and
elsewhere, her residence during most of her mature years was the
small town where she died. Hassall stresses her exemplary character, emphasizing her "Integrity, Iustice, Pietye, and well formed
Charitye" and claiming that "shee liued many yeares without
Scandall; and dyed without a Curse" (50v). Ironically, in fact, he
remarks that because her "manner of lyfe and conuersation is so
well knowne to all, … it were but a wast of tyme to repeat it to

you" (49v). Thus our desire for detailed knowledge of her life is defeated by the fact that so many of Hassall's original auditors already knew her so well.

Nevertheless, Hassall does provide some new information about her, and he also confirms some of the claims made in her own "Memorandum." In fact, that poem may conceivably have been one of his sources, since at points he seems almost to echo it. At the very least he seems to be echoing stories he had heard from Martha or her relatives, and so his account has the added interest of being offered by someone who was in a position to question her about her early life. He tells us, for instance, that "Her Byrth was generous[,] descended from honest parents, well knowne and respected in their tymes, and places. The worshipfull House, and Name of Dorsett" (50v). He furthermore reports (in phrasing highly reminiscent of the poem) that "Her Education [was] in such thewes [customs, manners], as were most propper, and commendable to her Sexe yea euen to Arts and Letters" (51r). Interestingly, however, he does not attribute this education specifically to her father (as the poem does), and in fact he provides new information about her early circumstances, noting that Martha, "though left as an Orphane, to the care of others (her parents dijng, whilst shee was yongue) ... receiued the benefitt of her Education from others ..." (51r). This claim is important, since it shows that in spite of her poem's phrasing (which might seem to exaggerate her father's personal role in educating her), the more complex truth about her education was something she must have discussed with Hassall or with members of her family. It was a fact Hassall could mention in an off-hand way and expect to be understood.

If the poem, then, seems at all misleading when it speaks of her schooling, it is probably not because Martha had any desire to hide the true nature of her early education or to overstate dishonestly her father's role. Rather, the tribute she pays her father may reflect stories she had heard about his pride in his new daughter, just as her somewhat embellished account of him may reflect her own pride in having been a child of Sidney's tutor. Perhaps he taught her some "baby Latin" before he died, or perhaps he left detailed instructions for her education or a bequest to pay a tutor for her. Any of these possibilities would help explain her claims in the "Memorandum" about his role in schooling and raising her. Her father, simply as Sidney's tutor, must have loomed large in stories she heard as a child, and it is therefore not surprising that he also figures so prominently in her poem. In any case, Hassall makes it clear that however Martha acquired her learning, she was active in sharing it. He remarks that "as shee receiued the benefitt of her Education from others so she thankfully communicated the same blessing to those, who beinge not her owne, were by mariage of their fathers committed to her tuition" (51r). She must have had an active hand in tutoring many of the grown children who now sat among her mourners, including her executrix, Elizabeth Thorowgood Rawdon. Perhaps she even helped educate her numerous step-grandchildren. In any case, Hassall's words suggest that Moulsworth's remarks in the "Memorandum" about the need for a women's university reflect her own experience as an educator who had herself taught girls but who could teach them only to a limited extent.

Hassall's next comments, concerning Martha's marriages, again suggest that he had access to her poem; some of his phrasing almost seems to echo the "Memorandum." He tells us, for instance, that "Her Mariage beginning in the Pryme of her yeares was noteworthy, hauing had three Husbands, all louing to her, and beloued of her; so that shee would many tymes saye They were all so good, that she knew not which was the better" (51v). Thus the poetic claims of marital bliss she had made fourteen years earlier were claims she apparently never abandoned, and although Hassall's positive comments are certainly appropriate to his commemorative occasion, they also seem to reflect Martha's deepest feelings. What is missing from the sermon, however, is any hint of the ambiguity and complexity that make the "Memorandum" itself so fascinating, especially in its ambivalent comments on marriage.

Hassall gives us an almost wholly positive picture of Martha's married life, conveying no hint of the frustrations or aspirations her poem expresses. Moulsworth herself had lamented the limited educational opportunities available to women, had proposed a specific and even radical remedy, and had depicted marriage, to some degree, as an economic arrangement. Hassall, however, conveys none of these notes, and in fact his summary comment depicts a virtuous but also somewhat conventional, domesticated woman: he views her life as "a patterne of Modesty, Discression, Hospitality, Frugality to others of her Sexe who neyther in Youth, nor Age neede to scorne her Example" (51v). The Moulsworth who could propose a women's university, or boast about the intellectual capacities of women, or reflect wryly on the marriage market, or allude to sexual pleasures, or fight and beat a vicar in court, is altogether missing here. Partly, of course, such omissions simply reflect Hassall's decorous sense of his occasion; he was, after all, preaching a funeral sermon. Yet the fact remains that the picture he offers of Moulsworth's life is far less complex than the one we get from her poem. If the "Memorandum" had not survived, and if our only source of information about her life were Hassall's sermon, it would be easy enough to view Moulsworth as a "model" Renaissance woman, rather than as one who had begun to break the mold.

Even so, Hassall's sermon is extremely helpful in giving us some sense of Martha's final months and days. Apparently her health had begun to deteriorate, causing suffering but also giving her one last opportunity to display the strength the "Memorandum" implies:

> The hand of God pleased by a tedious, and paynefull sicknesse (which in all her former dayes shee had not bin acquainted wth) to make her weary of lyfe, and better prepared for death And, in trueth, it moued many tymes a mixt passion of sorrowe, and ioye in her visiting freinds, to heare, and see how patiently she indured, how earnestly she desyred her dissolution. (52r)

Hassall praises her for having "skillfully practized" the "Arte of dying well" (52v), and he memorably describes how

> during the tyme of her restraynt being vnder ye Blackrodd of this her Visitation shee sought to deceiue the tediousnesse of solitude, and sicknesse, with reading good Bookes, her constant Companions and faythfull Cownsellers;
>
> And withall, so discreetely she ordered her studyes, that they might not seeme tedious. Mixing Ciuell, wth Ecclesiasticall Historyes, and in both finding concurrences with the present tymes (52v–53r)

Even or especially near her end, then, Martha seems to have found sustenance in books and learning, and Hassall seems to express a whole community's pride in her desire for knowledge. Admittedly the knowledge he praises is not the sort hinted at in the "Memorandum" (the kind that would permit women to compete with men and even surpass them); rather, it is the kind of knowledge that helped make Moulsworth an exemplary Christian woman. Yet Hassall's words nevertheless suggest that Martha never lost her love of books or her desire to cultivate her mind, and his final quoted comment even implies that she never ceased applying her knowledge to her immediate, contemporary circumstances. She read history, in other words, not merely with the eye of an antiquarian but with a desire to make sense of her own life and era. Hassall's words may even hint that she attempted to make political sense of her highly unsettled "present tymes."

Certainly his next words confirm an impression also conveyed by the "Memorandum"—that Moulsworth was an attentive reader of scripture. "That Booke of Bookes, the Holy Bible" (he says) "was neuer long from her; attended with some other Handmayds tractats of piety, healpes to Deuotion" (53r). The careful reading of God's word that allowed her to echo the Bible so frequently in her poem was a practice, then, that continued until she died, and Hassall also suggests that Moulsworth consumed secondary devotional literature as well. Even more interesting, however, is his ensuing assertion that she did not merely read but also wrote, and that she wrote not simply to record her knowledge but to share it with other readers:

> And, both to healpe her owne memorye; and to communicate the frute of her studyes to others she had lyinge by her pen, Inke, and paper wherewith she noted such matters as were of spetiall consequence, quoting the places, to commend them to others.
>
> But she hath now taken her leaue of vs, and of all these; leauing vs, and all these behynd her; to the increase of our sorrowes, who are parted from her But to the comfort of her owne soule, wch doutlesse hath caryed ye quintescence of those Collections wth her. (53r–53v)

These words give us firm grounds for believing what we might easily have assumed: that other writings besides the "Memorandum" flowed from Martha's pen. Many of her writings, apparently, took the form of notes from books she read, and many of those notes apparently survived her. Their subsequent history raises a tantalizing but at this point unanswered question; no record of them seems to exist, at least in the likeliest archives. It is not difficult to imagine, however, that the "Memorandum" was not Moulsworth's only poem or her only piece of creative writing. Her reading seems to have been a stimulus to her own thought, and so the real possibility exists that she was the author of a much larger body of work than the one poem we now possess. She may indeed, in Hassall's words, have "caryed ye quintescence" of her reading with her when she died, but she apparently also left a great deal of writing behind.

Aside from her will and the "Memorandum" itself, Hassall's sermon is at present our fullest record of Martha Moulsworth's life. Other poems and other evidence may exist, merely waiting (like the "Memorandum") to be found. Yet even if no other records turn up, we now have enough to form a distinct impression of this woman's qualities, conduct, talent, and intelligence. Thanks to Hassall we can indeed see her life as "a patterne of Modesty, Discression, Hospitality, [and] Frugality" (51v). And thanks to the "Memorandum" we can also see it as so much more.

The Poem Itself

Martha Moulsworth and the
Uses of Rhetoric:
Love, Mourning, and Reciprocity

Anthony Low

Martha Moulsworth's "Memorandum" is a poem of love and remembrance. After autobiography or confession, its primary genre—that is, its human end or purpose—is memorial elegy. But within that broad genre love plays an important part: both as present longing, which Moulsworth reveals for her departed father, husbands, and children, and as past affection, which she felt for them while they were still alive. One of the chief structuring principles of the poem is provided by temporal passages in Moulsworth's life, large patterns of time marking births, marriages and deaths. The marginal dates Moulsworth supplies in connection with her three husbands must be marriage dates. If we use her figures in our calculations, we find that her three husbands died on the Feast of St. Stephen, December 26, 1603; the Feasts of Sts. Jude and Simon, October 28, 1615; and the Feast of St. Matthias, February 24, 1630/31—about a year and nine months before her poem was written.[1] Moulsworth makes a particular point about the deaths of her husbands on saints' days:

> My husbands all on holly dayes did die
> Such day, such waie, they to the Saints did hye
> This life is worke-day even att the Best
> butt christian death, an holly day of Rest. (ll. 73–76)[2]

---

[1] The dates are old style, so the marriage to Thomas Througood [Thorowgood], given in the poem as February 3, 1604, would be 1605 new style.

[2] This and subsequent citations are to Martha Moulsworth, *"My Name Was Martha": A Renaissance Woman's Autobiographical Poem*, ed. Robert C. Evans and Barbara Wiedemann (West Cornwall, CT: Locust Hill Press,

Moulsworth is playing here on the idea taken from commentaries on Genesis and the hexameral literature that time and history are like the six days of creation (when God worked) but that the after-life is like the seventh day (when he rested).[3] Herbert's "Sunday" plays on these connections between work days and ordinary life, Sundays and eternity. But Moulsworth applies the popular analogy to saints' days, not to the Christian sabbath, as one might normally expect. At the time that the poem was written (1632) differences of opinion about holy days were especially strong and contentious.[4] Puritans and those who considered themselves Reformist were very keen to abolish saints' days and even Christmas from the calendar. Because Moulsworth not only finds providential significance in the deaths of her husbands on feast days but incorporates that fact into a devotional trope, it is clear that her religious sympathies are high-Church or Laudian.

She is, however, a good Protestant Anglican who obeys the strict injunction in the Thirty-Nine Articles against praying for the dead. She mourns and memorializes her loved ones by writing her poem, but she does not seek to influence their fate. Memorialization or commemoration—a process suggested by her title[5]—was the chief authorized response to the death of loved ones in the Anglican communion. That she also allows herself to mourn—openly, naturally and without signs of inward conflict or self-rebuke—is more significant historically than it may seem to modern readers. As G.W. Pigman has shown, at the Reformation English Protestants took a rigorist approach to mourning the dead. Their theology (based on 1 Thessalonians 4:13–14) instructed them to scold those who grieved and to repress their own grief rather than express it naturally.[6] A repressive attitude toward what we would

---

1993). When quoting from Moulsworth and other early writers, I silently expand contractions, regularize *i*, *j*, *u*, and *v*, and change initiall *ff* to *f*.

[3]The most prominent and popular hexameral work in Moulsworth's time was *The Divine Works and Weeks* of du Bartas, translated by Joshua Sylvester, published in 1605 and often reprinted.

[4]See David Cressy, *Bonfires and Bells: National Memory and the Protestant Calendar in Elizabethan and Stuart England* (Berkeley: University of California Press, 1989).

[5]Latin *memorandum*, "to be remembered" or "important things that must be remembered."

[6]See G.W. Pigman III, *Grief and Renaissance Elegy* (Cambridge: Cambridge University Press, 1985). Although Pigman does not make the point, repression of mourning, like the repression of prayers for the dead, re-

consider to be the natural work of mourning is still dominant in Ben Jonson's poetry as late as his "Elegie on my Muse," written for Lady Venetia Digby who died in 1633. Among pioneer poems of mourning that broke free from the prevailing rigorist temper of early English Protestantism were Milton's "Lycidas" and Henry King's "The Exequy," both written for persons who died in 1638. Although Moulsworth does not vent her sorrow at length, nevertheless it is unusual for her to have written—as early as 1632—a poem that expresses grief naturally and without self-rebuke. In this respect, "The Memorandum" was somewhat before its time in the development of English elegy.

There are other things to admire about her poem. A good poet is a skillful poet, a master of words and of rhetoric. To say as much is at once to state the obvious and yet to violate certain rigid modernist and postmodernist shibboleths commonly enforced in today's academic community. Aren't sincerity and authenticity, self-display and representation of one's ethnic or gender group, more important than any amount of technical skill? Or to put it differently, aren't all texts equal, as the New Historicists and cultural materialists argue—whether they are poems, journal entries, or recipes? Isn't literature, as a form distinct from other writing, dead? I hope readers will be inclined to answer these questions negatively; because if we who profess and love literature refuse to stand up for poetry as something different and intrinsically worth reading, who will? Not the bankers, media entrepreneurs, or politicians.

It is a real pleasure to encounter a previously unknown poet, also a woman, and to find that she is a first-rate writer. It is not plausible to pronounce someone a major poet on the basis of a single poem. If all of Henry King's poems were as good as "The Exequy," he would be a major poet; but they are not. If a body of poems as good as "The Memorandum" were to turn up, then Martha Moulsworth would have some claim to be a major poet. Certainly "The Memorandum" is more than a historical curiosity; it belongs in the major anthologies on the basis of its poetic quality.

That is easy enough to say; but how does one demonstrate it? To begin with, we must remember what all good writers in the Renaissance knew from their elementary schooling. Real poetic skill

---

sulted from the abrupt elimination of Purgatory, so that the souls of the dead were thought to go immediately to heaven (where tears were inappropriate) or to hell (too awful to contemplate).

is not empty formalistic virtuosity, but uses compressed technical means to speak to human reason and emotions and direct them toward significant ends. The main source of poetic skill in the earlier seventeenth century was rhetoric, taught in the schools almost entirely in Latin and therefore available mainly to men. As Walter Ong has argued, Latin was the father tongue, which schoolmasters taught young boys almost exclusively.[7] Learning one's way in the Latin trivium and in the ancient culture that accompanied it involved pupils in all the rituals that anthropologists have identified with rites of passage into manhood, including difficulty, strict discipline enforced with corporal punishment, and admission of those who succeed into the community from which the uninitiated (in this case those who know only the vulgar language that babies learn on their mothers' laps) are excluded. Some prominent women, such as Queen Elizabeth and the Countess of Pembroke, knew Latin. But their accomplishment was probably as rare even among upper-class women as it was common among educated men. That was one reason there were so few women poets in the Renaissance; most women lacked the technical skills drilled into men from their earliest schooldays.

Moulsworth affirms that her father decked her mind with "learninge Lattin" (l. 30). Although his personal role may not have been as important as she seems to imply, her phrase nevertheless suggests a process as well as a body of knowledge. She has, she says, forgotten the use of the Latin language; but not, on the evidence of her poetry, the habits of mind and technique that accompanied it. Her use of classical rhetoric is very skillful. She seems not only to have been educated in the language but to have received a thorough grounding in the trivium, which she uses with the subtle finesse characteristic of the best poets of her time.

Although "formalist" criticism is not popular these days, Moulsworth deserves praise for her skill. We sometimes forget that, as Brian Vickers has often pointed out, rhetorical techniques are a means of expressing real emotions and evoking them in the reader.[8] Take, for example, the emotional climax of the passage in

---

[7]Father Ong mentioned this idea as a work in progress when he spoke to my class at New York University about 20 years ago; unfortunately I cannot find the written version.

[8]See, e.g., his recent summary, "Rhetoric," in *The Cambridge Companion to English Poetry: Donne to Marvell*, ed. Thomas N. Corns (Cambridge: Cambridge University Press, 1993), 101–20.

which Moulsworth describes her love for her third husband. This is, as it happens, one of the places where she takes elegy in its new direction by the unrestrained and seemingly natural expression of her grief:

> Two years Almost outwearinge since he died
> And yett, and yett my tears for him nott dried.
> I by the first, and last some Issue had
> butt roote, and fruite is dead, which makes me sad.
>
> (ll. 69–72)

"And yett, and yett," which imitates the catch of grief, is an instance of *epizeuxis* (repetition of a word or phrase without intervening matter), a rhetorical device properly used to express strong emotion.[9] Vickers gives as an instance Herbert's repetition of the phrase "my God" in "Sighs and Groans":

> Thou art both *Judge* and *Saviour, feast* and *rod*,
> *Cordiall* and *Corrosive*: put not thy hand
> Into the bitter box; but O my God,
>   my God, relieve me!

Herbert's repetition marks an intensification of his grief and remorse. Other typical instances are provided by George Puttenham, in his *Arte of English Poesie*:

> Ye have another sort of repetition when in one verse or clause of a verse, ye iterate one word without any intermission, as thus:
>
> *It was Maryne, Maryne that wrought mine woe.*
>
> And this bemoaning the departure of a deere friend.
>
> *The chiefest staffe of mine assured stay,*
> *With no small griefe, is gon, is gon away.*
>
> And that of Sir *Walter Raleighs* very sweet.
>
> *With wisdomes eyes had but blind fortune seene,*
> *Than had my loove, my loove for ever beene.*[10]

All these writers, including Moulsworth, use the device for essentially the same purpose: to express strong emotion involving loss and sorrow. The expert poet knows when to use such a scheme or "figure Auricular." But "Vulgar" rhymers, Puttenham remarks, fail to observe the vital connection between means and end. Therefore their "repetitions be not figurative but phantastical, for a figure is

---

[9]Vickers, *In Defense of Rhetoric* (Oxford: Clarendon Press, 1988), 338–39.

[10]*The Arte of English Poesie* (London, 1589), fol. 167.

ever used to a purpose, either of beautie or of efficacie."[11] One may add that, although it takes a classical humanist education to learn how to use all of these technical devices of rhetoric, which run into the hundreds, it does not take such an education for a reader to respond to them emotionally. The orator is trained; her auditors need not be. In each instance of epizeuxis I have cited, the responsive reader will notice that an emotion is *evoked* by the figure in question. When used in consonance with linguistic meaning, the connection between figure and emotion is not arbitrary but natural. One might reasonably extend T.S. Eliot's "objective correlative" from the images and tropes to which he applied his term to the verbal patterns and schemes of Renaissance rhetoric.

One of the most notable figures Moulsworth uses is *antimetabole* or "the Counterchange." As Puttenham defines the term: "Ye have a figure which takes a couple of words to play with in a verse, and by making them to chaunge and shift one into others place they do very pretily exchange and shift the fence."[12] Although Vickers calls this a figure of "vehemency or distress,"[13] it can also be used for other purposes. By its very nature it is a figure of balance and exchange, so it can become a figure of reciprocity and of mutuality, which is the way Moulsworth characteristically deploys it:

> Thrice this Right hand did holly wedlocke plight
> And thrice this Left with pledged ringe was dight
> three husbands me, and I have them enjoyde
> Nor I by them, nor they by me annoyde
> all lovely, lovinge all, some more, some lesse
> though gonn their love, and memorie I blesse. (ll. 43–48)

The result of her repeated use of antimetabole is to emphasize the interchange of agency. She loved her husbands; her husbands loved her. So neither husband nor wife is reduced to a passive object. There is mutuality and reciprocity in their love, as also (Moulsworth discretely implies) in their sexual pleasure. Robert C. Evans notes that "enjoyde" "simultaneously suggests physical, emotional, and spiritual satisfaction"[14]—a satisfaction in which both husband and wife are equal participants.

---

[11]Puttenham, fol. 168. The first quotation is taken from Puttenham's concluding table of contents, "The names of your figures Auricular."

[12]Puttenham, fol. 174.

[13]Vickers, "Rhetoric," in *The Cambridge Companion*, 110.

[14]Moulsworth, 22.

Here, too, Moulsworth is an innovator. Mutuality and reciprocity did not come naturally to male Renaissance love poets, who were for the most part obsessed by Petrarchan and courtly love conventions. Affectionate mutuality was far from being a historical novelty, but it is not often to be found in English love poetry of the sixteenth and seventeenth centuries.[15] Contrary to a number of studies on the subject, the reinvention of mutual, reciprocal love was not specific to Puritans, so in that respect it is not surprising to find that Moulsworth, who as we have seen was Laudian in her religious sympathies, participated in the spirit of its redefinition. Once more she was somewhat before her time. Not until Milton's *Paradise Lost* gained broad cultural ascendancy was mutual married love of this kind firmly established in English poetry. In our age, which is especially nervous about fathers and suspicious of patriarchy, the pendulum has swung back the other way, and it may be hard for us to sympathize with Moulsworth's refusal to replace the traditional submission of women and wives with a compensatory craving for dominance or for individual autonomy. Yet her calm and generous granting of equal agency to both partners in marriage provides an admirable model, which the male poets of her time would have done well to imitate—and we as well.

The obvious analogy to Moulsworth as she describes herself—an apparent instance of art anticipating life—is Chaucer's Wife of Bath. She too was a much-married feminist who advocated resistance to male dominance but found that reciprocity in love, as realized in her last marriage and partly exemplified by her tale, was equally important. Although Moulsworth lacks the Wife of Bath's feisty contentiousness, the resemblance between them may still remind us that, as a poet, Moulsworth shares with the Wife's creator Chaucer some of his ability to write realistically about intimate matters of love, sexuality, and human relations without undue fuss, guilt, or prurience. Since "The Memorandum" remained in manuscript until 1993 and apparently did not circulate widely, it could not have had a direct effect on the development of English elegy or love poetry. That is too bad, because in many ways it is an innovative work, which embodies its innovations in a rhetorical language of admirable power and skill.

---

[15]See Anthony Low, *The Reinvention of Love: Poetry, Politics and Culture from Sidney to Milton* (Cambridge: Cambridge University Press, 1993).

Marginally Funny:
Martha Moulsworth's Puns

Anne Lake Prescott

Martha Moulsworth, as her editors well show, was an unusual woman, all the more so because her pronounced sense of individuality accompanies an equally pronounced impression of balance and poise. Her independence of mind, I think, may explain two unusual aspects of her manuscript: her margins contain self-reflexive remarks, not merely bits of information or scriptural citations (important though those are), and both remarks incorporate urbane puns with implications that further ironize, although I doubt they seriously undermine, the main text. The first note, next to line 7, says, "my muse is a tell clocke, & echoeth everie stroke wth a coupled ryme so many tymes viz 55." The second, next to some lines on her now largely forgotten Latin, says "Lattin is nott the most marketable mariadge mettall."[1]

I will explore these two jests in a moment. It should be said first, though, that Moulsworth was unusual as a woman writing a completed text incorporating marginal commentary on itself. Marginalia have attracted attention recently because of the significance they seem to have for concepts of authorship or authority, for reception study, for the impact of printing.[2] The permutations

---

[1]I quote *"My Name Was Martha": A Renaissance Woman's Autobiographical Poem*, ed. Robert C. Evans and Barbara Wiedemann (West Cornwall, CT: Locust Hill Press, 1993), 4–5. I have modernized *u/v*.

[2]See, e.g., William W.E. Slights, "The Edifying Margins of Renaissance English Books," *Renaissance Quarterly* 42 (1989): 682–716, who provides a taxonomy; Laura Kendrick, "The Monument and The Margin," *South Atlantic Quarterly* 91 (1992): 835–64, who relates glosses to varieties of authorship in the late Middle Ages; and Evelyn B. Tribble, *Margins and Marginality: The Printed Page in Early Modern England* (Charlottesville: Uni-

and possible effects of marginalia are many, especially since what is printed or handwritten in the margins of texts can be by the author, the printer, a third party (real or feigned for the occasion), or the reader. Since nonauthorial marginal commentary in printed books was most often applied to classical or religious works, it has been argued that for an author to include a paratextual apparatus or even mere citations and directions was to create the suggestion of authority, of authorship, of weightiness.[3] Spenser's *Shepheardes Calender* and some of Ben Jonson's masques are among the most often cited examples, problematic though they might be in many regards. For the margin to comment humorously on the main text sets up yet other tonalities, as witness the sidenotes that someone, probably Erasmus, contributed to More's *Utopia*. To joke about one's *own* writing, to divide oneself between the already urbane narrator of a story in the page's middle and an even more dryly observant commentator looking in from the outside spaces is indeed remarkable. Although not unprecedented, the performance (so far as I know, but we probably need more study of the matter) is particularly astonishing in a text by a woman.

It also is noteworthy that Moulsworth's textually self-conscious marginal comments are such good puns. In their daily lives early modern women doubtless had as sharp a sense of the ridiculous as those of our own day and as lively wits. Still, if with exceptions, the dominant tone of women's writings was not satirical.[4] What makes Moulsworth's jests so attractive, I think, is the impression they give of an irrepressible humor that itself derives from a sense of distance from the self, from the divided perspective that

---

versity Press of Virginia, 1993). Moulsworth's text was not printed (until now), but differences between print and manuscript matter less than those among commentary on someone else's work, the citation of authorities in one's own margins, and the presence of ironic remarks about one's own text. I thank Professor Heidi Brayman, who is completing a dissertation on paratextual matter, for discussing such issues with me.

[3] The effects can be ambiguous, though, for author(itie)s in the margin, protecting the text (and perhaps an increasingly imperial self) like the ranks of some Praetorian guard, can compete with the author for authority: the guards endanger the emperor. For the example of Ben Jonson and his margins, see Tribble.

[4] I do not mean to homogenize women's writings in Renaissance England or exaggerate their piety. Rachel Speght and Amelia Lanier are invigoratingly argumentative and Mary Fage's taste for the politics of wordplay is shown by her long parade of flattering anagrams, *Fames Roule* (1637).

wordplay at least momentarily requires. All puns are stereoscopic. They had, furthermore, long been the topic of analysis and advice. Moulsworth, that is, uses a rhetorical trope described in books that her father would have known and that perhaps she read too. Cicero himself says that "Puns [*ambigua*], based on words and not on things, are especially clever," being if not laughter-provoking then "evidence of sophisticated literary ability." And, he adds later, "Such wordplay [*ambiguum*] in itself wins great commendation, ... because to be able to change a word's force into something other than the usually accepted sense seems to indicate a man of ingenuity [*ingeniosi*]" (*De Oratore* II.II.lxi.252, 254). Even those who did not read Cicero would have found such notions in the second book of Thomas Wilson's *Arte of Rhetorique* (1553), which ends with many pages on rhetorically useful jesting, including wordplay.

Moulsworth's humor, then, is not only a matter of self-deprecating charm and native wit; her equivocations were facilitated by the rhetorical tradition in which her father had been trained, her culture's love of wordplay, and the healthy indifference to regular and regulated orthography. With its spelling still unsettled and unpoliced by parents, teachers, and editors, early modern English came to its users pre-punned and thus even more slippery than in our own time. Really good intentional puns, though, usually have resonance, like Hamlet's remark that his uncle is "a little more than kin but less than kind" or like the ambiguity with which the dying prince comments on what comes next: "The rest is silence." Moulsworth's first marginal pun, her dry allusion to her "tell clocke" muse, also has poignant, if less tragic, significance.[5] As the note by Evans and Wiedemann says (citing the *OED*), a "tell clocke" is one who watches the hours pass on a clock and hence passes the time "idly." This, in an age and class stressing work, perhaps especially for housewives, is no light matter: a common indictment of poetry was that it derives from and encourages sloth, that the muse makes work for idle hands. But *this* "tell clocke" and hence contemplative muse leads an active life as well, for in fact she echoes the passing years and their labors, the marriages and

---

[5]The note is one of the few I have seen in which a poet explicitly directs our attention to numerical patterning. Many scholars, myself included, believe that Renaissance writers were fascinated by such structures (imitating in human words the cosmos God had ordered "in measure, nomber & weight" [Wisdom 11.17]), but clear extra-textual evidence is hard to find.

deaths, the gains and losses. From one point of view, the muse is idle as she stares at the clock, but in the pun she is also the clock itself, tolling her "coupled" rhymes and enabling Moulsworth to record the "couples" that time created and then, through its "strokes," undid. So the muse that many in her culture thought a wastrel and slack-off, is also—as befits a daughter of Memory—monitory and commemorative. The note's own little gesture toward verse (jingling "ryme" with "tymes") meanwhile adds to the mischievous mixture of signals.

Moulsworth's remark in the margin next to her report that her father had encouraged his young daughter to learn Latin is even subtler. Through neglect, she has largely forgotten what she was taught: "Butt I of Lattin have no cause to boast / ffor want of use, I long agoe itt lost" (ll. 37–38). Had she had no better dowry than Latin, she adds, "I might have stood a virgin to this houre" (l. 40). Evans's analysis of this passage brings out its balance of humor, resignation, and resentment; he does not, though, make anything of the margin's pun on "Latin."

Renaissance readers coming on the statement that "Lattin is nott the most marketable mariadge mettall" would have certainly recognized and probably enjoyed Moulsworth's wry humor, for this is a pun with multiple overtones. "Latin" is of course the learned language more useful to scholars than to wives; compared to gold and silver, it was—and is—not likely to figure among a young woman's assets in the cultural work of snaring a husband. But "latten" is also a metal alloy, a yellowish mixture of copper and zinc. Little mentioned in our own age, it is not among the precious metals and indeed can be contrasted with them, as when Chaucer says of the sun in the "colde, frosty seson of Decembre" that "Phebus wax old, and hewed lyk laton, / That in his hoote declynacion / Shoon as the burned gold with stremes brighte."[6] Moulsworth was not the first to pun on *Latin* and *latten*. In Thomas Tomkis's *Lingua* (1607), a lively if misogynist academic comedy, all Five Senses accuse Lingua (the tongue, that is, and the play's only woman) of having "made Rhetorique wanton" and reduced "Logicke to bable." Common Sense agrees, saying of her macaronic "Gallemaufry" of words: "I am perswaded these same language makers have the very quality of cold in their wit, that freezeth all Heterogeneall languages together, congealing English Tynne,

---

[6]"The Franklin's Tale" (1244–47), in Chaucer's *Works*, ed. F.N. Robinson (Boston: Houghton Mifflin, 1957).

Graecian Gold, Romaine Latine all in a lumpe" (III.5). The pun must have once been common in schoolrooms and universities.

Moulsworth's immediate point, of course, is that scholarly learning does not get a woman as far in the social world of marriage alliances as does money; the subtler implication—one enforced by the pun's ironic setting of Latin with/against latten—is that academic learning is not a precious metal at all. Latin is not gold and cannot be traded for gold—or a husband. The pun regenders an old grievance, although the tone is cheerful. Yet there may also lurk somewhere in the sly remark a hint that although on the marriage market Latin is merely latten and of no interest to suitors, including presumably those she took in marriage, it is by that same token outside the marital buying and selling system. Latin, precisely because the larger society considers it an inferior metal (yellowish, not glistering), belongs to the same university world that Moulsworth so astonishingly thinks should be open to women, the world of "witt, and tongs" (l. 35).

Moulsworth says she has lost the "use" of Latin, although in one regard (from a Utopian point of view, for example), latten has more practical "use" than gold. In context, the word "use" itself has resonance, for metal coins may be put to "use" by usurers or, more positively, by the good servant in Christ's parable of the talents (Matthew 25). Enjoined by God himself to multiply, husbands and wives can even put themselves to "use"; thus in a sonnet recalling the parable, Shakespeare urges his young friend toward fatherhood for the sake of giving a good account of his "treasure" and his "beauties use." And, as Marlowe's sophistical Leander argues when trying to talk Hero into bed: if rich ore is not "us'de" it might as well be the "basest mold," whereas "being put to lone, / In time it will returne us two for one."[7] Although Moulsworth has lost the "use" of Latin, she has something better than latten—gold and her body in marriage—to put to use. Yet to lose something for "want of use" reinforces, in its irony, the hint of regret and nostalgia—even, just maybe, of guilt—in this part of the poem and bears with it, gently, a reminder that no matter how kind, loving, and sexually pleasing her husbands were to her, they did not encourage the intellectual "use" of what must have seemed to them an inferior and useless coinage, at least in a wife. Latin/latten is the forgotten and buried talent.

---

[7]Sonnet 2; *Hero and Leander* I.232–36, in *Elizabethan Minor Epics*, ed. Elizabeth S. Donno (New York: Columbia University Press, 1963).

The pun also contributes to the poem's impression of tightness, of controlled cross-reference, for Moulsworth makes other metallic and monetary allusions: the spousal exchange of rings, the corrupt custom of selling gentility, her access to her husband's purse, and the use of several words with secondary economic meanings like "score" and "number" (ll. 55; 62). Above all, there are the last lines: "the Virgins life is gold, as Clarks us tell / the Widowes silver, I love silvar well." She is now, in her mid-fifties, neither a golden virgin nor a latten scholar but a silver widow—with gray hair, one supposes. The "clarks" themselves, confusingly, sound like those Catholic clerics whom Chaucer's Wife of Bath defies in her prologue by saying she is content to be a serviceable vessel made of "tree," not a virginal one "al of gold" (99–101). Protestant "clarks" like Moulsworth's father usually held a different view of the comparable merits of virginity and marriage. At least Moulsworth thinks she has become silver, not wood. Her smiling remark that she likes that metal is gendered in several senses: it is modest, like a good wife, and feminine in the taste it implies: any alchemist, metallurgist, or astrologer knows that gold is solar, radiant, and male, while silver is lunar, mediating, and female. An expression of taste, the statement "I love silvar well" is also an affirmation of identity: transmuted by the very years that her muse has both watched and told, she has lost her learned Latin and her virginal gold, but she is still of nobly female metal (and mettle) all the same. Sterling, we might call her.

The Poem as a Clock:
Martha Moulsworth Tells Time Three Ways
Mary Ellen Lamb

The autobiographical project shaping "The Memorandum of Martha Moulsworth, Widow" shares a distinctive feature with the project attempted within the diaries of Lady Anne Clifford, written roughly during the same period. Both Clifford and Moulsworth respond to a problem in self-definition created within their marriages by constructing two competing versions of themselves according to two competing versions of time. As a way of mediating the conflicts in her self-definitions caused by her marriages to three husbands, Moulsworth arranges the events of her life along two competing versions of time: a linear model beginning with the author's birth and ending with her widowhood, and a cyclical model drawn from the *Book of Common Prayer*. In her diaries, Anne Clifford also employs differing time-frames to defend her claim as an aristocrat to inherit land in opposition to both her husbands, who demanded that she relinquish her claim for a settlement offered to be paid to them. To her current obligation as a wife to obey her husbands during her lifetime, Clifford juxtaposed her long-standing obligation as an aristocrat to her ancestors to pass down her land to her future heirs.

While the problems in self-construction are different for Clifford and Moulsworth, the strategies of using opposing time-frames are similar. This similarity, within autobiographical writings by two women of such different classes and marital experiences, suggests the flexibility of self-definition possible to women in the early seventeenth century. This flexibility is gained not by appealing to feminist discourses, however, but by adapting conservative discourses already present within the period.

As Robert C. Evans has demonstrated, "Time—its passage, pains, joys, and triumphs—is one of the most obvious organizing themes" of "The Memorandum of Martha Moulsworth."[1] Identifying the poem as a record of its author's life to posterity, the title of the poem expresses an acute consciousness of the passage of time. The poem's first line foregrounds the time of composition as crucial to its content: "The tenth day of the winter month Nouember," which is in fact the author's birthday. The marginal note beginning next to line seven goes even further: the poet's "muse is a tell clocke" and "euerie stroke" is told by a "coupled ryme" so that the poem consists of fifty-five couplets, one for every year of the author's age. The arrangement of this poem/clock reveals that Moulsworth structured her life in terms of her marriages; in fact, page breaks in the manuscript coincide with its division into thirds (or almost thirds) corresponding to the three periods of Moulsworth's life: before her marriages, during her marriages, and after her marriages.[2]

This essay explores the function of the strict numerical ordering of this poem/clock within a larger autobiographical project. Like other autobiographical writings, "The Memorandum" resolves, or attempts to resolve, a problem in the author's construction of a coherent self. In Moulsworth's case, "The Memorandum" mediates an issue arising from her primary construction of her self as a woman who has been married three times. From this autobiographical project emerges a complex meditation on various forms of time.

Moulsworth comes to terms with her identity as a thrice-married woman by arranging the events of her life along two versions of time: a linear model beginning with the author's birth and ending with her widowhood, and a cyclical model drawn from the *Book of Common Prayer*. Both of these versions separate her relationships with her husbands into discrete chronological units. But neither model resolves the threat posed by an additional version of time, explicit in her reference to the resurrection near the end of the poem and implicit in the Biblical citations in the margins. Moulsworth poses this threat by asking, "wch of theis three" shall

---

[1] See *"My Name Was Martha": A Renaissance Woman's Autobiographical Poem*, ed. Robert C. Evans and Barbara Wiedemann (West Cornwall, CT: Locust Hill Press, 1993), 13.

[2] Isobel Grundy, in her essay "Identity and Numbers in Martha Moulsworth's 'Memorandum'" (printed elsewhere in this collection) observes that a marginal note on Moulsworth's middle husband further divides the poem into halves.

she call "husband" at the end of time? (ll. 98–99) While she notes that to ask this question is "vayne" and "prophane" (l. 97), this question still has entered the text.

The apparent easiness of Moulsworth's solution, that after the resurrection she and her husbands will live together as angels without "wedlocks bonds" (l. 102), is not consistent with her determination to refuse to remarry in the "Meane tyme" (l. 103), as she calls her widowhood. One reason for her resolution is based in her positive experiences with her husbands: what husband could be "A Better" (l. 107) than these? But the other reason to remain a single widow contradicts her representation of the afterlife as lacking marital bonds. Her image of her marriages as a "threefold cord" (l. 105) which may be broken by a fourth knot expresses a sense of herself as simultaneously married to all three husbands even in the afterlife. The Biblical texts cited in the margins suggest that this issue is not limited to a future apocalyptic moment. Time also collapses in the poem's use of these Biblical texts, as the poem conflates past, present, and future. These citations create an alternative sense of time, through which the second coming is already occurring, and has always already occurred, to create a chaotic subtext which thwarts the apparent order so painstakingly imposed by this poem that is also a clock.

Linear Time

The fifty-five couplet form of "The Memorandum" is an apt vehicle for expressing the linear time of the author's fifty-five years. Page breaks in the manuscript coincidentally divide these years into three self-contained consecutive units. Covering the period before Moulsworth's first marriage, the first unit includes conventional biographical information: her birthday; her baptism at one day's age and her baptismal name; her father's lineage, vocation, and education; and his role in her education.[3] This section concludes with a clarion call to support women's education through the creation of a university for women. This proto-feminism is confined, however, to the pre-marriage portion of Moulsworth's poem; the second portion, which covers the periods of

---

[3]In her essay elsewhere in this volume, Isobel Grundy notes that Moulsworth's father died when she was only two-and-a-half; this represents an interesting discrepancy in the poem.

Moulsworth's marriages, begins by stating the incompatibility of women's learning and marriage. She has lost her Latin "ffor want of vse" (l. 38) and, as the marginal notation makes clear, "Lattin is nott the most marketable mariadge mettall." The implicit confinement of learning, including the reading and perhaps the writing of poetry, to the temporal phase before marriage becomes explicit as, no longer a virgin, she must bid the "virgin Muses," as well as her "virgin life," "ffarewell" (l. 42).

The second portion of Moulsworth's poem is most like a "Memorandum" in its meticulous recording of the exact dates of her weddings and the lengths of her marriages. She expresses and then allays anxiety about being behind schedule in marrying her first husband at the age of twenty-one ("My springe was late"; l. 51). Less conventional is her recording of her mourning periods in terms of years and months. In much of this middle section, however, Moulsworth describes her third husband, who is clearly her favorite, and she constructs her marital experience according to a linear narrative of her progress in her domestic life. She devotes many lines to describing Bevill Molesworth: his unusual "comlines in age" (l. 58); his lineage from the Mortimers (l. 59); his kind and "Buxome" treatment of her, giving her "an easie darlings life" with her "will in house, in purse in Store" (ll. 65–67). As Evans notes, her description of Molesworth's death is "far more elaborate, vivid, and emotional than her description of her first two husbands' passings" (30). As fits this clock-poem, Moulsworth expresses her emotions in terms of time: this "second spring" of her marriage, "to soone awaie it hasted" (l. 64); and, as Evans has remarked, her line "And yett, & yett my tears ffor him nott dried" (l. 70) underscores "both Moulsworth's sense of pain and her surprise that her pain continues to be so intense" (27) for two years after his death. Especially following her expression of grief for her third husband, her allocation of only two lines to her deceased children, described as "some Issue" (l. 71), seems disturbingly brief; but rather than absence of feeling, this brevity probably indicates that they were peripheral to the autobiographical project of this poem, to puzzle out her marital, rather than her maternal, identity. This project also explains her evident satisfaction that her third husband had also been married two times before: "Third wife I was to him, as he to me / third husband was, in nomber we agree" (ll. 61-62).

Cyclical Time

The third section, which covers the period of her widowhood, records Moulsworth's means of memorializing her three husbands according to the saints' days on which they died, according to the church calendar of the *Book of Common Prayer*.[4] Moulsworth's extended descriptions of these saints' days represent these conjunctions as more than coincidence. Moulsworth's means of memorializing her husbands folds them into a larger devotional experience designed to encourage communicants to relive core events of the life of Jesus and the early church according to the church calendar. Ideally, Anglicans were to experience every year the anticipation of advent, the joy of Christmas, the repentance of Lent, the triumph of Easter, the inspiration of Pentecost not as history but as a present, sacramental reality of import to their individual lives. Similarly, the annual remembrance of the saints was to make them alive spiritually within the memory of the individual believer. Thus, the association of Moulsworth's husbands with specific saints' days shaped the way her husbands were to be remembered, distinguishing them (in theory) not according to their own lives or characteristics, but according to their placement within Moulsworth's annual spiritual journey. Thus, on St. Steven's day, which immediately follows Christmas, Moulsworth remembers that "the morrowe after christ our fflesh did take," her first husband "did his mortall fflesh fforsake" (ll. 79–80). On the day of St. Jude/St. Simon, her memory of her second husband strengthens her determination to fight for her faith. St. Matthias' day renews her memory of her third husband with consolations of spring and the resurrection.

While Moulsworth gives the appearance of following the church calendar, in fact she manipulates it so that St. Matthias day (February 24) appears after St. Jude/St. Simon's day (October 28). Moreover the connection between St. Matthias day, spring, and the resurrection is very tenuous. February is still a winter month in England, and the church celebrated Easter no earlier than late

---

[4]Saints' days are recorded in *The Book of Common Prayer 1559: The Elizabethan Prayer Book*, ed. John E. Booty (Charlottesville: University Press of Virginia, 1976), 29-32; their dates can be determined from tables on pages 37, 45, and 47. I see no evident connection between Moulsworth's poem and the prescribed readings and collects.

March, and often in April.[5] Her distortions of the church calendar make visible the outlines of her own project: to superimpose the deathdates of her husbands on the birth, works, and resurrection of Jesus, in such a way that the body of her last husband "Shall ffeele A springe, wth budd of life, & Breath / And Rise in incorruption, glorie, power / Like to the Bodie of our Sauiour" (ll. 94–96). This hope does not proceed naturally from the coincidence of his death with St. Matthias day. It proceeds instead from her own desire, whose sexuality is encoded in the image of his reviving "budd of life" (l. 94). Her evident wish to enjoy the body specifically of her third husband at the end of time gives special point to her "prophane" questions as to which man she should call husband at the resurrection.

Meditation-Time

Biblical citations in the margins introduce what I will call "meditation-time" into Moulsworth's "Memorandum." Like the memorializings in the church calendar, the practice of meditation conflates past and present, so that past events such as Christ's birth and crucifixion are perceived as present realities, eliciting appropriately intense emotions from the practitioner to yield specific spiritual fruits.[6] Various citations in Moulsworth's "Memorandum" point readers not to the past, however, but to the future day of judgment. These conflate the present and the future, to reveal future events as already implicit in the present. The subtext set up by these citations creates "The Memorandum" as more than a memorial to Moulsworth's husbands. These citations record her sense of her husbands as part of her present reality not only as persons from her past, but also from her future.

The centrality of meditation-time is implicit in Moulsworth's construction of her poem as a clock, where she cites Acts 17:28. In this verse, Paul attempts to convert the Jews by claiming God's presence in believers: "For in him [God] we live, and move, and have our being; as certain also of your own poets have said, For we

---

[5]A calendar for Easter days from 1559-1588 is included in Booty, ed., *The Book of Common Prayer*, 35.

[6]Material on meditation is taken from Louis Martz, *The Poetry of Meditation* (New Haven: Yale University Press, 1954).

are also his offspring."[7] As applied to a clock, this text conflates the linear time recorded in Moulsworth's fifty-five couplets, one for each year, with the timelessness of a life in God, which collapses differences in time and place. This conflation anticipates a more concrete collapse of linear time into meditation-time on earth in the second coming announced by St. Paul three verses later in this passage.

The marginal citations widen Moulsworth's conventional meditation on the meaning of her name to an apocalyptical level. Rather than following the housewifely example of the Biblical Martha, who attended to Jesus's bodily needs rather than listening to his words, Moulsworth internalizes the Biblical scene of composition so that she prepares her soul as her "Inward house" fit to entertain Christ as her guest:

> ... Martha tooke muche payne
> our Sauior christ hir guesse to entertayne
> God gyue me grace my Inward house to dight
> that he wth me may supp, & stay all night
> (ll. 17–20)

In this context, Christ's knocking signifies the immediacy of the end of time. Those who admit Him will sup with Him in heaven; those who deny Him will be relinquished to hell. This passage gives Moulsworth's desire to "supp" with Christ in her soul a time-frame that is simultaneously present and future, linear and apocalyptic.

While Evans aptly emends Luke 10:14 to Luke 10:41, which recounts the Martha story, the context of the final judgment makes some sense of the citation from Luke 10:14. Like the verse from Revelation, this verse also conveys the necessity of admitting and feeding Christ, in the person of his apostles. In Luke 10, Jesus instructs his disciples to enter and to eat the food of cities which receive them. For those cities which do not receive them, they are to wipe away even their dust. The cited line depicts the consequences of their actions to these inhospitable cities: "But it shall be more tolerable for Tyre and Sidon at the judgment, than for you." Taken with the citation from Revelation, the application of Luke 10:14 to the meditation of Martha becomes clear. Those who do not admire and feed the Christ within their "Inward house" are damned, along with the peoples of Tyre and Sidon.

---

[7]All citations are taken from *The Holy Bible in the King James Version* (Nashville: Thomas Nelson Publishers, 1984).

Like the Martha passage, Luke 24:29 describes inviting Christ to supper; like the other cited passages, this one also takes place after the resurrection. After dismissing the news of the risen Christ as told by Mary Magdalene and Mary the mother of James, two of the apostles met a stranger (who was really Christ) at Emmaus. After they explained what had happened, he "expounded unto them in all the scriptures the things concerning himself." Luke 24:29 conveys their invitation to this stranger to share their meal: "But they constrained him, saying, Abide with us: for it is toward evening, and the day is far spent. And he went in to tarry with them." As He broke bread, they recognized Him, and He vanished. This passage resonates with the meditation on Martha, deepening and extending its significance. Inviting Jesus to sup with her, Martha becomes like the apostles, honored with the presence of the risen Christ.

After the next marginal citations, which explain the saints' day of St. Jude and St. Simon as a time to "contend for the faith," the final spate of citations occurs near the end of the poem. In these citations, the apocalyptic time-context implicit in the earlier citations has become explicit. In these passages, however, Moulsworth applies scriptural verse to predict the wholeness of the risen bodies of her husbands, and in particular of her third husband, rather than to the state of her own soul. Imagining the experience of the coming resurrection, Moulsworth draws on Corinthians 15:42 to verify her understanding that mortal bodies (and especially the body of Bevill Molesworth) will be "raised in incorruption." She uses Philippians 3:21 ("Who shall change our vile body, that it may be fashioned like unto his [Christ's] glorious body") to confirm her knowledge that the body of her third husband will be revived "like to the Bodie of our Sauiour" (l. 96). According to meditation-time, this imagined future is already implicit in the present. In a sense it has already happened, and according to her poem, it should be remembered every St. Matthias day.

But according to linear time, as opposed to meditation-time, the second coming has not yet occurred and will not occur until a specific date, when the heavens open and time ends. It is in linear time that Moulsworth's dilemma surfaces; for the bodies of all three of her husbands, not just her third one, will then be resurrected. Her easy solutions, drawing on Matthew 28:18 (which conveys the foolishness of vain questions) and Matthew 22:30 (which denies the presence of marriage bonds in heaven), do not seem to resolve the issue. As represented earlier, she is still the possessor of a "threefold cord" of marriage knots (l. 105). All she can do in this "Meantyme" is to avoid a fourth knot, and to hope for the best. Her final couplet, which affirms her preference for the life of a widow, whose "silver" is less valued within her culture than a virgin's life of "gold," poses no solution at all. It only suggests that she accepts her dilemma with cheerful resignation.

"The Memorandum," Sacraments, and Ewelme Church

Matthew Steggle

Considerable work has been done in recent years, notably with reference to *The Temple* (written by Martha Moulsworth's contemporary, George Herbert), upon the ways in which devotional poetry can be informed by architectural metaphors.[1] I hope to apply these techniques to Moulsworth's "Memorandum," using St. Mary's Church, Ewelme, Oxfordshire, the church in which Moulsworth was probably baptized and of which her father was rector at the time of her birth, to inform a reading of the poem.[2] This is not a crudely biographical reading: Ewelme church is merely selected as a representative example of the rural Anglican church as Moulsworth would have known it.

St. Mary's Church, Ewelme, Oxfordshire, was built in the first half of the fifteenth century by William de La Pole and his wife Alice, grand-daughter of the poet Chaucer. As part of the same benefaction a school and almshouses were also given, and the complex now dominates the center of this small Chilterns village. Thanks to the intervention of a local colonel, the church was fortunate enough to escape the misfortunes that befell most of the

---

[1]See Stanley Fish, *The Living Temple: George Herbert and Catechising* (Berkeley: University of California Press, 1978), and, more recently, Harold Toliver, *George Herbert's Christian Narrative* (Philadelphia: University of Pennsylvania Press, 1993) and Christopher Hodgkins, *Authority, Church and Society in George Herbert* (Columbia: University of Missouri Press, 1993).

[2]Germaine Greer supports the assumption that Moulsworth was baptized in this church; see her essay in the present volume.

parish churches of England in the course of the Civil War.[3] Neither has it suffered any major developments or expansions. As a result it is still in much the same condition as it was when the author of "The Memorandum" was born in 1577.

The state of preservation is so good that the church even retains the Vulgate texts painted in "black letter" script (*Guide* 5) directly onto the plaster of the walls, texts which—like the stained glass—fulfill the dual function of ornament and didacticism. Texts from the Vulgate run around the top of the walls as a frieze in the St. John Chapel on one side of the main altar, walls which are themselves diapered (painted repetitively) with the monogram IHS, the sacred name of Jesus. (This was restored in 1843, but the restoration "is said to follow the original design"; see Sherwood and Pevsner 597.) Such ornament came to seem conservative and old-fashioned by the standards of the more militant forms of Elizabethan Anglicanism. Some institutions eager to prove their Protestant credentials at this period—notably Trinity College, Oxford—were going to some lengths to conceal ornament based on the sacred name of Jesus. But at Ewelme, it survived unmolested, and the Name of Jesus is repeated again and again upon the walls.

Most striking of all is the inscription around the East window. The current East window is Victorian, and it is not clear now what its predecessor portrayed; but the inscription around the East window is a survival. The plaster is painted with a text that snakes decoratively around the arch of the stone frame, forming literally a context for the glass. The text is Matthew 1:21, words spoken by the angel instructing Joseph how to name Mary's son: "Et vocabis nomen eius Jesum; ipse enim salvum faciet populum suum a peccatis eorum" ("And thou shalt call his name Jesus for he shall save his people from their sins").

The Name of Jesus covering every surface of the walls of the side chapel; the name of Jesus given emblematic pride of place above the altar: Moulsworth is in a tradition in which naming is of critical importance.

Also important is the relation between language and structure. In Ewelme church, these texts painted onto the walls are given an almost architectural function. They constitute the walls and frame the window. Likewise, Moulsworth's poem (which in a far more

---

[3]A full description can be found in *Guide to St Mary's Church, Ewelme* (n.p., 1993) and in *The Buildings of England: Oxfordshire*, by John Sherwood and Nicholas Pevsner (Harmondsworth: Penguin, 1974), 595–600.

literal sense is an edifice made from words) plays with the relation between ornament, meaning, and structure.

First of all, it can be shown that Moulsworth's copious Biblical references are all to be seen in the context of a practicing church. The best demonstration of this is in her treatment of the "holly dayes" on which her husbands died (l. 73). These dates are not scriptural: they are dictated by the rhythms of the Church, and it is to the feasts of the Church that Moulsworth relates their deaths. Thus the death of the third husband at the beginning of spring is related both to St. Matthias and to the seasonal changes at his feast-day. This is a poem rooted not in scripture, but in scripture as revealed through the Church.

Moulsworth begins her account of her life with her baptism at the age of one day old, baptism being the sacrament which confers one's name. Traditionally, as Ewelme exemplifies, the font is to be found at the entrance to the church, since baptism is a rite which permits one to become a member of the Church. (The alternative, as Moulsworth says, was to remain in a state of original sin: baptism should be no optional rite arranged for state, but an act of spiritual urgency; ll. 11–16.) Her concern is to show this sacrament establishing her dual status as a product of earth and of the divine, as "the daughter / of earthly parents, & of heauenlie ffather" (ll. 14–15). Similarly, Joseph is told of the dual nature of Jesus in Matthew 1, the naming of Jesus commemorated in the text above the East window at Ewelme: "Thou shalt call his name Jesus: for he shall save his people from their sins." The naming also defines Jesus' role.

Similarly, the poet's baptism is the ceremony which, in defining her name, or at least the part of it not subject to the vicissitudes of marriage, defines too her role:

> My Name was Martha, Martha tooke much payne
> our Sauiour christ hir guesse to entertayne
> God gyue me grace my Inward house to dight
> thatt he wth me may supp, & stay all night (ll. 17–20)

The submerged metaphor here—of her life as a physical structure, an "Inward house"—is one that parallels Herbert's imagery of the Temple. Stanley Fish traces how catechism, in Protestant thinking of the time, was figured as the building of a spiritual temple;[4] but here, appropriately, the fabric of the temple is already complete,

---

[4]See *The Living Temple*, 54ff.

and all that remains to work on is the ornamentation. The ambiguous word "house" covers both the spiritual temple and the humbler "dwelling" in the sense of the private home in which the Biblical Martha entertained Jesus.

Another usefully ambiguous word in these lines is "dight," recurring—again as a rhyme-word—to describe Moulsworth's wedding-ring at l. 44. Both times, then, Moulsworth uses the word to describe an act (ostensibly) of decoration that is really an act with a significatory value. Moulsworth is imaging her life as a church, decorated with signifying ornament that is more than mere decoration because it has a teleological purpose: to induce Christ to stay with her. Thus in ll. 17–20 we see a combination of naming imagery with imagery of text and structure.

Moulsworth's father (carefully named in l. 22) makes his appearance "in scarlett Robe" (l. 26): a robe which, like Moulsworth's wedding-ring, is both ornamental and meaningful, since it defines his role. The robe is a badge of office as well as an item of apparel. Similarly, when Moulsworth claims that her father "did wth learninge Lattin decke [her] mind" (l. 30), yet another ambiguity of the relationship between ornament and meaning is invoked. The interior of Ewelme Church provides another reminder that whatever the uses of Latin as the language of classical literature and international communication, its most conspicuous everyday use was as the language written on the walls and the monuments of churches. At any rate, what matters is that learning itself is figured as an ornament, while at the same time being a tool for comprehension.

From baptism at the font, we move up the aisle to marriage at the altar, as Moulsworth outlines her three husbands, naming each one in a marginal note. The third—who receives the most attention—is located with reference not so much to his name but to his coat of arms, which Moulsworth stresses is not bought with "Heraulds fee" but is genuinely his own (l. 60). As the interior of Ewelme church forcibly reminds one, this is no dead metaphor to people of the Renaissance: the tombs in the chapel (most notably that of De La Pole's father-in-law, Thomas Chaucer) are covered with heraldic insignia whose purpose, like the Latin texts on the plaster, is at once decorative and significatory. The genealogical evidence provided by them identifies the people involved as precisely as naming would.[5]

The metaphor lying behind the baptism, the ring, the robe, the decorations of her "Inward house," and even the heraldic arms is the concept of a sacrament. To quote the famous definition from the *Book of Common Prayer*, a sacrament is "an outward and visible sign of an inward and spiritual grace given unto us, ordained by Christ himself as a means whereby we receive the same, and a pledge to assure us thereof."[6] All the components of the "Memorandum" listed above, apparently ornaments, prove to be tokens signifying some sort of inner grace. In the case of heraldry, it is merely one's ancestry that is guaranteed; the giving of rings is the token of marriage; the robe is conferred upon a graduate as he gets his degree. (Obviously the robe and the arms are sacramental only in a secular sense.) Baptism is a sacrament in the true sense of the word, one of the two specified in the *Book of Common Prayer*. In a slightly more complex way, the decoration of Moulsworth's "Inward house" is a sacramental matter too. The act of decoration is not entirely a voluntary decision on her part: by writing, "God gyue me grace my Inward house to dight" (l. 19), she concedes that she needs inward and spiritual grace to achieve that end. Such grace must be given to her, just as is specified in the already-quoted definition of "sacrament" from the *Book of Common Prayer*. Divine approval and the successful ordering of the "Inward house" are so inextricably linked as to be two sides of the same coin.

And this, of course, is the connection with the texts at Ewelme. Figured as decorative patterns, they are nevertheless sacramental: specimens of things ordained by Christ, signs of grace which also are a means to deliver that grace, and a pledge of it.

Moreover, the poem itself has certain features in common with these texts. Shaped to fit a purely formal and artistic requirement, in its fifty-five couplets, it nonetheless is a statement of faith, and a performative act, a vow of widowhood. The poem itself becomes, I would suggest, a quasi-sacramental token of that state. She names (and hence defines) herself as "Widdowe" in the title, and the

---

[5]See E.A. Greening Lamborn, "The Arms on the Chaucer Tomb at Ewelme," *Oxoniensa* 5 (1940): 78–93.

[6]See "The Anglican Catechism, 1549," in Vol. 3 of *The Creeds of Christendom*, ed. Philip Schaff (1877; rpt. Grand Rapids, MI: Baker Book House, 1966), 521.

poem is an affirmation of widowhood, a token not to be forgotton ("memorandum") of this state as a way of life. This is why it is significant that the poem is explicitly dated to her birthday and hence to the anniversary of her baptism: this poem is figured as a ceremony that baptizes her into a new state.

"By him I was brought vpp": Evoking the Father in Moulsworth's "Memorandum"

Anne C. Little

In the "Memorandum" Martha Moulsworth devotes 10 of her 110 carefully structured lines to her father while barely alluding to her mother as one of her "earthly parents."[1] Moulsworth establishes her father's reputation ("a Man of Spottles ffame" [l. 21]), his heritage ("of gentle Birth" [l. 22]), his wealth ("He had, & left lands of his owne possession" [l. 23]), his occupation ("of Leuies tribe" [l. 24]), and his education (at "his Mother oxford" [l. 25]). Four of the ten lines deal with how her father raised her, particularly the education he provided:

> By him I was brought vpp in godlie pietie
> In modest chearefullnes, & sad sobrietie
> Nor onlie so, Beyond my sex & kind
> he did wth learninge Lattin decke [my] mind (ll. 27–30)

Despite the apparently straightforward message of these four lines, Moulsworth, who was born in November 1577, was only two and a half years old when her father died, a fact which challenges the claim that her father taught her and prompts the query of why a woman who seems so forthright in her autobiography would distort a verifiable fact, especially one her contemporaries (her only intended readers?) might know.

Robert C. Evans, who came upon the poem in manuscript, first learned that Moulsworth might have altered the facts about her father's influence on reading the date given as her father's death in

---

[1] *"My Name Was Martha": A Renaissance Woman's Poem*, ed. Robert C. Evans and Barbara Wiedemann (West Cornwall, CT: Locust Hill Press, 1993), 4–8. For the quoted phrase, see l. 15.

the bookseller's information sheet catalogued with the poem at the Beinecke Library. However, because the sheet contradicted the poem and thus seemed inaccurate, he opted not to mention the discrepancy until it could be resolved.[2] Since the poem was published, Professors Isobel Grundy and Germaine Greer have confirmed the bookseller's date: Moulsworth's father was in fact the Robert Dorsett who died in April 1580, thirty months after Moulsworth's birth.[3] Obviously, then, the father who "brought vpp" his daughter is, as Evans states, "a creation of her own imagination, her invention,"[4] but the question of why she altered this important detail about her life teases the mind.

The first possible explanation is that Moulsworth speaks figuratively. In writing her autobiography, a daughter might naturally be inclined to acknowledge the education provided by a legacy from her deceased father or attained because he had left instructions before his death for her to receive it. But Moulsworth's language in the "Memorandum" implies an active father: "By him I was brought vpp ... he did ... decke [my] mind" (ll. 27; 30). Here Moulsworth does not allude to what her patrimony had provided but instead clearly evokes the actions of a living father.

Moulsworth may wish, as Evans suggests, to recognize her father's pride in her or his talent and reputation as Sidney's teacher, even though he had not actually taught his daughter. Moulsworth's account may even have some truth to it because her father could have taught her some Latin words when she was very young or left instructions about what and how she should be educated.[5]

Moulsworth could also be speaking figuratively in another way. Her reference to her father's role in her life may be the acknowledgement of an aspect of her own nature: her animus, or what Jung calls "the male personification of the unconscious in

---

[2]Robert C. Evans, "A Silent Woman Speaks: 'The Memorandum of Martha Moulsworth, Widdowe,'" *Yale University Library Gazette* (forthcoming in 1995).

[3]See (in this volume) Isobel Grundy, "Identity and Numbers in Martha Moulsworth's Memorandum," 10; and Gremaine Greer, "'Backward springs': The Self-Invention of Martha Moulsworth," 6.

[4]See Evans, "A Silent Woman Speaks" (forthcoming in 1995).

[5]Evans, "The Life and Times of Martha Moulsworth" (in this volume), 69. Germaine Greer has identified Moulsworth's father as Sidney's tutor. See her essay in this volume, 6.

woman."[6] Rather than admit she was compelled by something inside herself, Moulsworth might have offered a cryptic label or concealing image, a "father," to explain how she developed the qualities she claims or acquired the knowledge generally reserved for men.[7]

Isobel Grundy implies a possible explanation of why Moulsworth might have attributed her learning to her father by saying Moulsworth's "silence" about who did teach her "may have been a part of her story that she was willing to forget."[8] If she attained her education in an unpleasant or painful way, naming her father could be a way of diverting attention, her own or that of others, away from the source of the memories to be suppressed. Germaine Greer, on the other hand, sees all autobiography as an attempt "to reinvent the self as text."[9] Moulsworth's will suggests she inhabited a world filled with children (albeit not her own), but the self she presents in the "Memorandum" is identified by her relationships to men. The creation of herself as a woman taught by her father is one of several ways Moulsworth "present[s] herself as the object of male attention and place[s] herself in a sober and dignified world as on a glass mountain far above the domestic uproar of women and children."[10]

Other possible explanations of Moulsworth's motives also come to mind. With the description of her father's reputation, heritage, wealth, occupation, and education, Moulsworth establishes herself as the daughter of a respected man. At a time when women had little identity of their own, Moulsworth appropriates the qualities and accomplishments of her father to suggest her own worth. Being raised by such a man as the father she describes elevates her own status.

By focusing on herself as her father's daughter rather than her mother's, Moulsworth also places herself within the male tradition where knowledge is passed from father to son. As a participant in that long-established process, she becomes the equal of men, no ordinary girl, but one educated "Beyond my sex & kind" (l. 29).

---

[6]Carl G. Jung, et al., eds., *Man and His Symbols* (Garden City, NY: Doubleday, 1964), 189.

[7]I am grateful to my colleague Professor James Barfoot for suggesting this idea.

[8]Grundy, 10.

[9]Greer, 3.

[10]Greer, 4.

Because she is a daughter, however, she is also outside or above that tradition in another sense. For a father to teach a son is customary, but for a father to teach a daughter is extraordinary.

As a woman of her time, Moulsworth probably also felt the need to establish her credibility as a writer. By inventing a father who had taught her Latin, Moulsworth "proves" she has had the education which would provide the rhetorical skills needed by a writer, and in fact the poem lends credence to her claim. As Anthony Low demonstrates in his essay "Martha Moulsworth and the Uses of Rhetoric: Love, Mourning, and Reciprocity," she quite skillfully employs the devices learned through the study of Latin.[11] But why could she not simply claim to have the education she obviously has had without inventing a father to provide it? One possible reason is that his having taught her endorses or sanctions her education. A woman instructed by a man, especially her father, is less threatening than one with the spirit or drive to acquire an education on her own. Furthermore, for such a respected man as her father to have been involved makes the notion of a learned woman more palatable.

Moulsworth's "Memorandum" anticipates the strategy of Anne Bradstreet's "The Prologue," published in 1650.[12] Bradstreet creates the persona of a modest woman who acknowledges her inferiority to male poets in order to deflect the criticism she expects as a woman writer: "A Bartas can do what a Bartas will / But simple I according to my skill" (ll. 13–14). Despite her self-deprecation the Bradstreet evident beneath the persona is a woman of wit, confidence, and surprising directness who knows her critics: "If what I do prove well, it won't advance, / They'll say it's stol'n, or else it was by chance" (ll. 31–32). The ironic contrast between the two views of Bradstreet is similar to that between the two depictions of Moulsworth.

Moulsworth creates the persona of a pious, modestly cheerful, and sober woman to deflect the criticism she foresees as a female poet. Except for the Latin, her father has raised her as society would have wished. And she makes sure the reader notices the lines in which these traits appear. In a poem of fairly regular iambic pentameter, these are among the few iambic hexameter

---

[11]Low, 80.

[12]Bradstreet, *The Works of Anne Bradstreet*, ed. Jeannine Hensley (Cambridge: Belknap Press of Harvard University Press, 1967), 15–16.

lines. In fact, the phrasing makes them sound almost like four trimeter lines, an even sharper break in the pattern:

> By him I was brought vpp
>   in godlie pietie
> In modest chearefullnes,
>   & sad sobrietie.

Moulsworth wants these womanly characteristics to be remembered when anyone begins to condemn her for daring to write. In addition, the claim that her father taught her these particular traits undercuts the response to her bold assertion that women should have their own school:

> ... the muses ffemalls are
> and therfore of Vs ffemales take some care
> Two Vniuersities we haue of men
> o thatt we had but one of women then (ll. 31–34)

By presenting herself as a pious, modestly cheerful, sober (and by implication dutiful) daughter, she suggests that university learning will not detract from her virtues or make her any less feminine.

With wit, confidence, and directness like that later seen in Bradstreet's description of her critics, Moulsworth follows her call for a women's university with a playful boast of what educated women could do: "O then thatt would in witt, and tongs surpasse / All art of men thatt is, or euer was" (ll. 35–36). The self she reveals here ironically contrasts with the persona she had earlier established. The father Moulsworth created might have taught her "godlie pietie," "modest chearefullness, & sad sobrietie," but the daughter learned more lively lessons as well.

Martha Moulsworth's "Memorandum": Crossing the Climacteric

Susie Paul

Undeniably we are taken with voices and stories that speak to us in particularly knowing ways about where and who we are in our lives at the very moment we read. True, Martha Moulsworth has the audacity to complain about the lack of educational opportunities for women of her day and the worthlessness of learning in women in the cold commerce of the marriage market, and that is fine. But for this middle-aged reader approaching the borderland of the climacteric and the long country beyond, Martha's "Memorandum" is a map, and, as it turns out, a treasure map. For here on this side of the change we do fear the passage; we have been taught either to dread the drab invisibility of the aging woman or to tremble at the consequences of embracing the powerful role of crone. Across 350 years Martha shows us that if we do the hard work of confronting the lives we have lived, despising and cherishing what is rightly despised and cherished, then letting go, we can claim for ourselves a blessing.

Martha's voice rises out of the past on a surge of recent voices discussing growing older: Barbara Walker's *The Crone*, Carolyn Heilbrun's *Writing a Woman's Life*, Gloria Steinem's *Revolution from Within* and "Doing Sixty," Betty Friedan's *The Fountain of Age*, Erica Jong's *Fear of Fifty*, Lois Banner's *In Full Flower*, and Germaine Greer's *The Change*, to name only some. Early in her book, Germaine Greer recounts a conversation with a friend in distress about growing older and losing her beauty. Greer responds with longing: "I needed," she writes, "role models for a woman learning to shift the focus of her attention away from her body ego towards her soul, but for the life of me then and there I could not summon to

113

mind a single one."[1] I would offer Martha as just such a role model. Ultimately, her "Memorandum" is not about the past; rather it is about the place she has come to—serenity, power, and, above all, freedom.

Early in her poem, Moulsworth writes, "My Name was Martha, Martha tooke much payne / our Sauiour christ hir guesse [guest] to entertayne / God gyue me grace my Inward house to dight" (ll. 17–19). Name this balance, name it a recognition that we must all answer the call of the spirit as well as the call of the world, but consider too that Martha, on her fifty-fifth birthday, shifting from past to present tense, knows to gird herself for trials to come. The movement that Martha calls "Inward" is the woman's "journey ... towards wisdom" that Greer claims "is as long as the headlong rush of our social and sexual career."[2] Martha begins by confronting her anger. In the vocabulary of seasons and the climate of colors, this poem's landscape is wintry, except for one hot point, a single flash of color: "My ffather ... arayd in scarlett" (ll. 21; 26), symbol of knowledge and the sanction of a great university from which women were excluded. Ironically scarlet is the very color of carnality of which she has been washed clean so that she may be daughter of a heavenly as well as earthly father. Is her phrasing a barb, intricately crafted and concealed? Certainly her bold assertion that "in witt" the educated woman's achievement would surpass "All art of men" (ll. 35–36) is softened by her claim to have lost what she learned—all of which she credits to her father—and her acknowledgement that it was not as "marketable" anyway as the gold of virginity.

Despite such tactics, her expression of resentment and anger is brave not just because she is a woman, but because she is an aging, even, for the time, aged woman. Such complaining could bring down upon her the charge of being a hag or crone, that third and much feared manifestation of the Goddess's three aspects, the symbol of "death, winter ... the waning moon," the wise crone.[3] Of course Martha is much too pious and privileged to suffer an even more perilous charge, though her position on women's education is a kind of heresy. Martha speaks forthrightly in a world that sel-

---

[1]Greer, *The Change: Women, Aging, and the Menopause* (New York: Knopf, 1992), 12.

[2]*The Change*, 12.

[3]See Barbara Walker, *The Woman's Encyclopedia of Myths and Secrets* (San Francisco: Harper, 1983), 187.

dom tolerated such outspokenness in its women and especially its aging women. So she ceases to be what Carolyn Heilbrun (and also Gloria Steinem) terms a "female impersonator" and answers the call (centuries before Heilbrun conceived of it) that "we should make use of our security, our seniority, to take risks, to make noise, to be courageous, to become unpopular."[4]

Loyalty to father and priest and husband after husband structures Martha's life and poem. Such an illustrious domestic career was for a woman of her time something to celebrate. Yet the way she presents it allows her also to escape what she honors. She kills the husbands off, evokes them twice, first living, then contains each in a story, until he rises up out of his strong flesh and marches away as a spirit, hand in glove with a saint to the world beyond this one. She is left alone and utterly free of them. It is a kind of brilliant tactic: "My husbands all on holly dayes did die / Such day, such waie, they to the S^{ts} did hye" (ll. 73–74). She both buries and releases them.

The hope she describes for her favorite husband's resurrection is an important transition in the poem and its process. The feast day on which he died "comes in that season wch doth bringe / vppon dead Winters cold, a lyvlie Springe" (ll. 91–92). There is such an urge to life in the lines that follow that it is sexual. Aside from the evocation of his "Bodie" "budd[ing]" with "life" (ll. 93–94), these lines come in a rush of regular music after the line "His Bodie winteringe in the lodge of death" (l. 93)—broken as it is by four consecutive unstressed syllables. The small explosions of "budd" and "Breath," "incorruption" and "power" (ll. 94–95) also contribute to the energy of the passage.

At some level the "Memorandum" is a poem in which a woman who is still a sexual creature considers the option of remarrying. The scripture to which she alludes here, 1 Corinithians 15:42–43, reads: "So also is the resurrection of the dead. It is sown in corruption; it is raised in incorruption: It is sown in dishonor: it is raised in glory. It is sown in weakness; it is raised in power." Given the turn away from marriage the poem finally takes, perhaps the final vision of her third husband—in his spiritual "power"—represents her passage from a sexual to a spiritual urgency or imperative. She must feel the crescendo of her own complex yearnings and voice, for she comes back quietly to Christ, not quite rhyming "power" and "Sauiour" (l. 96), unwilling or unable

---

[4]Heilbrun, *Writing a Woman's Life* (New York: Norton, 1988): 126; 131.

fully to echo it. After such fullness, wondering which shall be her heavenly husband seems merely a diversionary tactic, or perhaps not. She reasserts their distance, all three safe in heaven, she left with her "Widowehood" (l. 108). Earlier in the poem, after describing her "easie darlings life" with her last husband (l. 66), she asks, "whatt would a women old or yong haue more?" (l. 68). Could it be the power to choose not to give herself away, not to define herself in terms of another's needs again, the power to hold herself apart and enjoy the treasure of who and where she is? Greer writes of the "consequences" of aging for a woman, saying that "At first she may cling to her old life, trying to claw back something of what she poured into it so unstintingly, but eventually, her grieving done, her outrage stilled, she must let go. Only if she lets go can she recover her lost potency" (373–74).

If this is a winter poem, it is not bleak and frigid; rather it is cool and serene. Yet if we survey the poem as a landscape, we still spy one splash of fire, the scarlet cape the father wears upon his back. At fifty-five, Martha probably no longer sheds month by month the scarlet cape inside her, but holds the wiseblood within. She is full of wisdom, enough to appreciate, as 1 Corinthians 15 also says, that "There is one glory of the sun, and another glory of the moon." "The Virgins life is gold," Martha writes; "the Widowes siluar" (ll. 109–10), the silver the waning moon sheds and drops as cool coins into our open hands, the silver of our hair. These are treasures she teaches us how to claim as she finally does: "I loue siluar well" (l. 110).

Biblical Resonance in Moulsworth's "Memorandum"

Robert C. Evans and Neil P. Probst

From Thomas Hassall's funeral sermon, we know that Martha Moulsworth was a careful reader of scripture, but the same fact is also clearly evident from her "Memorandum" itself. The margins of her poem are sprinkled with precise Biblical citations, yet Moulsworth hardly ever simply cites or echoes scripture; instead, she more typically transmutes and digests it, making it an integral part of her own poetic design. In fact, several essays in this volume discuss her artful use of allusions. Professor Curtis Perry, for example, notes how the repetition "Martha, Martha" in l. 17 of the "Memorandum" directly echoes the words of Jesus in Luke 10:41, while Professor Susie Paul nicely notes how Moulsworth's allusion to 1 Corinthians 15:42 (at l. 95) sends us back to St. Paul's immediately preceding words: "*There is* one glory of the sun, and another glory of the moon ..." (1 Corinthians 15:41). As Professor Paul points out, this phrasing anticipates the striking conclusion of Moulsworth's poem, with its emphasis on the respective values of gold (associated with virgins) and silver (associated with widows). Both these examples show that Moulsworth does not merely parrot scripture. Instead, she invites us to ponder it by first pondering it herself.

Typical of her poem's capacity for such allusive nuance is the first of its many biblical citations. Moulsworth decorates the margins of her work with numerous references to scripture, but only the first is so emphatically open-ended. Thus, when Moulsworth refers to God as the being "in whome we are, & liue" (l. 10), a marginal note reminds us that she is alluding to Acts 17:28, which describes God as the one in whom "we live, and move, and have our being." However, Moulsworth appends to this note a significant addendum: by following the numbers with the abbreviation "&c" (i.e., *et cetera*), she deliberately invites us to consider the relevance of the immediately ensuing biblical verses. And, as it turns out, these are quite relevant indeed to the complicated themes, tone, and meanings of her work. Here as elsewhere, Moulsworth demonstrates a subtle and complex artistry.[1]

If we read, for example, not only the specific verse Moulsworth cites but also the ones that run from that point to the conclusion of Acts 17, we notice how this whole passage helps justify the poem's existence and foreshadow its complicated texture. For instance, immediately after describing God as the Being in whom we each individually "have our being," St. Paul tells the Athenians that this conclusion is supported by various classical or pagan writers themselves. Thus he notes that "certain also of your own poets have said, For we are also his offspring" (Acts 17:28).[2] This comment is relevant to Moulsworth's own project in various ways. In the first place, it shows Paul's own familiarity with classical learning and his willingness to cite it in support of Christian teachings. These facts help justify Moulsworth's own later expression of interest in classical languages and classical learning; anyone who might question a Christian's interest in such matters would be reminded here that Paul himself found such knowledge useful. Furthermore, the idea that we are offspring of God is echoed a few lines later by Moulsworth herself, who explains how, through christening, she became the daughter both "of earthly parents, & of heauenlie ffather" (l. 15). In other words, Paul's reference to "offspring" both prepares for and ratifies Moulsworth's subsequent expression of the same idea. Finally, Paul's citation of poets in

---

[1]Quotations from Moulsworth's "Memorandum" are taken from the text printed in *"My Name Was Martha": A Renaissance Woman's Autobiographical Poem*, ed. Robert C. Evans and Barbara Wiedemann (West Cornwall, CT: Locust Hill Press, 1993), 4–8.

[2]We quote from the King James version, although we have also consulted the other Renaissance translations reprinted in *The New Testament Octapla: Eight English Versions of the New Testament in the Tyndale-King James Tradition*, ed. Luther A. Weigle (New York: Thomas Nelson, n.d.). The only Renaissance rendering reprinted there that departs significantly from the phrasing of the Authorized version is, as one might expect, the Catholic translation, which says that in God "we live and move and be" (766).

support of his Christian message helps legitimize Moulsworth's own decision to write a poem herself. Paul apparently valued poems enough to read them, cite them, and use them to support Christian teachings. All in all, then, Moulsworth's subtle allusion to this one verse from Paul helps variously authorize her own poem and pronouncements.

The immediately following verse in Paul's address to the Athenians is also relevant to Moulsworth's poem. Paul proclaims that since we *are* the "offspring of God, we ought not to think that the Godhead is like unto gold or silver, or stone, graven by art and man's device" (verse 29). This passage resonates with Moulsworth's several later references to valuable metals, as when she puns that "Lattin" (a kind of brass) "is not the most marketable mariadge mettal" (marginal note next to line 38), or when she concludes her poem by saying, "the Virgins life is gold, as Clarks us tell / the Widowes siluar, I loue siluar well" (ll. 109–10).[3] The Biblical passage, in other words, emphasizes imagery that Moulsworth (herself the wife of a goldsmith) also chose to highlight in her work.[4] Similarly, Paul's immediately following words, which warn of the need for repentance (verse 30), are relevant to Moulsworth's preoccupation with spiritual readiness (ll. 19–20) and also to her emphasis on the afterlife (ll. 93–102). By the same token, Paul's emphasis in Acts 17:31 on Christ as both a judge and redeemer (sent to punish sinners and raise the dead) anticipates the concluding section of Moulsworth's poem (especially ll. 83–102), while the apostle's stress on the "resurrection of the dead" (verse 31) foreshadows several phrases from Moulsworth's conclusion (see especially ll. 81, 88, 93–96, and 99).

However, perhaps the most intriguing possible link between Paul's words and Moulsworth's poem involves the very last verse of Acts 17. That passage, verse 34, mentions how, in response to Paul's message, "certain men clave unto him, and believed: among the which *was* Dionysius the Areopagite, and a woman named Damaris, and others with them." This passage has obvious implications for Moulsworth's "Memorandum." First, it shows, in the

---

[3]For more on the pun on "Lattin," see Professor Anne Lake Prescott's essay in this volume. Indeed, it was Professor Prescott who first noted this pun.

[4]On Moulsworth as the wife of a goldsmith, see the long biographical essay by Robert Evans in this volume.

person of Dionysius, an ideal reconciliation of classical learning
and Christian belief—precisely the kind of reconciliation
Moulsworth both advocates and achieves in her poem.[5] Dionysius
embodies the same kind of union between intellect and faith that
Moulsworth calls for and demonstrates in her "Memorandum."
Even more intriguing is the reference to the "woman named
Damaris," since this figure symbolizes the kind of thoughtful
feminine intelligence that Moulsworth herself both speaks for and
displays. Damaris was one of the few Athenians who listened
thoughtfully to Paul's words and responded properly to them. She
thereby behaved as many men did not. She thus symbolizes the
potential of all women to hear, consider, and acknowledge God's
call. She is a perfect representative of female intelligence and potential, and any reader of Moulsworth's "Memorandum" who re-
called that Damaris was one of Paul's few Athenian converts
would find it hard to question Moulsworth's later stress on the
value of feminine thoughtfulness.[6] Damaris, like Moulsworth herself, demonstrated a kind of intellectual independence uncommon
for women of her day; she symbolized the proposition that feminine learning need not conflict with Christian faith. Finally, the
possibility that Damaris may have been the *wife* of Dionysius only
underscores another important theme of Moulsworth's
"Memorandum": its celebration of wedded love, of marriage as a
partnership of souls.[7] If Damaris *was* the wife of Dionysius, then

---

[5]Anthony Low discusses Moulsworth's use of classical rhetorical devices in an essay elsewhere in this volume. Dionysius, of course, was for
centuries mistakenly identified as the author of a very influential body of
neo-Platonic theological texts; for a lengthy discussion, see the article by
Jos[eph] Stiglmayr in the *Catholic Encyclopedia*, ed. Charles G. Herbermann,
et al., 15 vols. (New York: Encyclopedia Press, 1913), 5: 13–18.

[6]Jean Calvin, obviously an important Renaissance interpreter, stresses
the significance of Damaris's conversion: "Since Luke names only one man
and one woman, it appears that at the beginning the number of believers
was small. For the *others*, whom he mentions, remain as it were on the
fence (*medii*), because they were not rejecting Paul's teaching out of hand,
but they had not been so seriously affected that they attached themselves
to him as disciples.... it is very likely that Damaris was a woman of the
first rank." See *Calvin's Commentaries: The Acts of the Apostles 14–28*, trans.
John W. Fraser, ed. David W. Torrance and Thomas F. Torrance (Grand
Rapids, MI: Eerdmans, 1991), 127.

her example only shows that a thoughtful, intelligent woman could also be not only a good Christian but a faithful spouse. And Moulsworth's decision to allude to this entire Biblical passage only shows the artful complexity that characterizes her poem as a whole.

Numerous other examples of Moulsworth's artful allusiveness could easily be discussed at length, but here we wish only to mention them and comment briefly. One might note, for instance, Moulsworth's marginal citation of Luke 24:29 at l. 20. That verse describes how the resurrected Christ, visiting his disciples "toward evening, … went in to tarry with them." Clearly this passage is relevant to Moulsworth's desire that Christ should with her "supp, & stay all night." However, the passage also anticipates the strong emphasis on resurrection that characterizes the final section of her poem. Yet if one reads the verses that precede the one Moulsworth cites (that is, the verses that provide the immediate context for her citation), one notices many other points of contact with the "Memorandum." In fact, Luke's entire Chapter 24 forcefully stresses the different reactions of men and women to the evidence of the resurrection, and in Luke's presentation of those reactions, the women come off quite well. It is the women, for instance, who first visit the sepulchre and discover that the body of Jesus is missing and that the tomb is being guarded by angels (Luke 24:1–8). Yet when the women (including "Mary Magdalene, and Joanna, and Mary *the mother* of James, and other *women that were* with them") return and describe their experiences to the apostles, they are met with a kind of skepticism and condescension that might unfortunately seem all too typical of male responses to women: "And their words seemed to them [i.e., the disciples] as idle tales, and they believed them

---

[7]For a good discussion of Damaris, see the entry on her in the *Anchor Bible Dictionary*, ed. David Noel Freedman, 6 vols. (New York: Doubleday, 1992), 2:5. Significantly, the author of that entry, Ben Witherington, III, argues that this passage shows "the typical Lukan male-female parallelism, where Luke attempts to show that the gospel affects and benefits men and women equally" (5). On the tradition of Damaris as the wife of Dionysius see, for example, Jacobus de Voragine, *The Golden Legend*, trans. Granger Ryan and Helmut Ripperger (New York: Longmans, Green, 1941), 619. The view of Damaris as wife of Dionysius goes back at least to John Chrysostom; see the entry on Damaris in Ronald Brownrigg, *Who's Who in the New Testament* (New York: Holt, Rinehart and Winston, 1971).

not" (Luke 24:11). Only when Peter runs to the sepulchre to confirm the women's report does the truth sink in, yet even at this
point the men seem unconvinced that the resurrection has occurred. They know only that the body has vanished. The women
have seen and reported a vision, but the men disbelieve them.

In fact, when Christ soon visits the disciples, they fail to recognize him, for "their eyes were holden that they should not know
him" (Luke 24:16). This verse is only one of several in the chapter
that strongly stresses (like Moulsworth's opening lines) the failure
or the ability to *see*. Moulsworth describes how her birth "did open
first theis eis, and shewed this light" (l. 3), and Luke 24 similarly
emphasizes the attainment of vision. In fact, the widely known
Geneva translation, in its marginal glosses, underscores this emphasis. Commenting on Luke 24:16, for instance, the Geneva gloss
notes that "This [verse] declareth that we can neither se, nor vnder-
stand til God open our eyes." Similarly, commenting on Luke
24:28, the Geneva gloss notes that "Christ did bothe shut their eyes
and open the*m*, [because] he wolde kepe them in suspens til his
time came to manifest himself vnto them."[8] It seems intriguing that
the women, who are strongly emphasized throughout Luke 24 (see
also, for instance, verses 22–23), are granted immediate perception
of the angels and of the evidence of the resurrection, while the men
at first fail to perceive Christ when he appears and also doubt the
women's report. As the Geneva gloss notes concerning the men's
perplexity, "Hereby appeareth y[t] they had faith, although it was
weake." The women, in contrast, seem in this respect to "surpasse"
the men (to use the verb Moulsworth herself uses when she con-

---

[8]See *The Geneva Bible: A Facsimile of the 1560 Edition*, introd. Lloyd E.
Berry (Madison: University of Wisconsin Press, 1969).

A similar emphasis on vision occurs in the verses surrounding another Biblical citation Moulsworth lists in connection with l. 20 of her
poem—Revelation 3:20: "Behold, I stand at the door, and knock: if any
man hear my voice, and open the door, I will come in to him, and will sup
with him, and he with me." This verse is echoed when Moulsworth hopes,
concerning Christ, that "he wth me may supp," but it seems worth noting
that the immediately preceding verse reads as follows: "I counsel thee to
buy of me gold tried in the fire, that thou mayest be rich; and white raiment, that thou mayest be clothed, and *that* the shame of thy nakedness do
not appear; and anoint thine eyes with eyesalve, that thou mayest see."
The final clause seems relevant to Moulsworth's opening emphasis on vision, while gold imagery is also strongly emphasized in her poem.

templates the true potential of women; l. 35). Luke's 24th chapter, then, seems relevant to Moulsworth's "Memorandum" in more ways than one, not the least of which is its emphasis on the actual and potential worth of women's experience. One might also note the chapter's strong emphasis, as in Moulsworth's poem, on the number three (see verses 7, 13, 21). Or one might note how the chapter, like the poem, emphasizes mutual supping (verse 30; l. 20).

The account of the same events in Matthew (28:1–20) does not emphasize the women's experiences nearly as strongly as the account in Luke, nor does it emphasize as strongly the flawed perceptions and faith of the men. The account in Mark (16:1–20) does prominently emphasize the women, but it also suggests that they fail as a group to report their vision to the men; this task is left to Mary Magdalene, who is granted a separate vision. The male disciples disbelieve her, but they also disbelieve two of their own, so that the division between the reactions of the sexes is not emphasized as prominently in Mark as it is in Luke. Finally, the account in John (20:1–31) emphasizes the experiences of the women as a group much less strongly than the account in Luke. Moreover, the first two male disciples to arrive at the scene are given much more emphasis and seem much more trusting, while Mary Magdalene at first fails to perceive the risen Christ when he presents himself to her. When Mary reports her vision to the male disciples, she is met with no reported skepticism, and in fact the disciples themselves immediately acknowledge Christ when he presents himself. Only Thomas doubts.

In other words, Moulsworth (deliberately?) alludes to the one scriptural account (Luke's) that most strongly emphasizes the faith and perceptiveness of women in general and the incredulity and smugness of men as a group.

However, the subtlety of Moulsworth's allusiveness here is by no means unique. In fact, nearly all her scriptural citations resonate in unexpected ways when examined closely. At l. 85, for instance, she cites the third verse of Jude to support her claim that Christians should fight for their faith. Yet the cited verse also emphasizes that that faith was first transmitted to the "saints"—also a key word in the final third of Moulsworth's poem. Similarly, Moulsworth's allusion (at l. 95) to 1 Corinthians 15:42 not only provides a source for her reference to "Ris[ing] in incorruption," but also links her poem to a passage of scripture that exhibits the same kind of rhetorical balance as the "Memorandum." Thus, Paul writes that the human body "is sown in corruption; it is raised in incorruption." The larger passage also emphasizes the word "sown" in a way that strongly supports Moulsworth's adjacent imagery of the "budd of life" (l. 94), just as the passage strongly distinguishes between the spiritual and the natural in ways that anticipate Moulsworth's later distinction between earthly marriage and heavenly union. By the same token, her allusion at l. 96 to Philippians 3:21 reminds us of the distinction between the "vile body" of unredeemed mortals and the "glorious body" of Christ. The allusion thereby supports her emphasis, in the whole final portion of her poem, on the themes of physical death and spiritual resurrection.

These themes are also relevant to her next scriptural citations—to verses 18 and 30 of Matthew 22. The first of these verses introduces the passage containing the famous distinction between things belonging to God and things belonging to Caesar (a distinction that parallels Moulsworth's own emphasis on the contrasts between body and soul, earth and heaven, earthly marriage and spiritual union). Most obviously her citation allows her to confront the problem she raises explicitly in her poem: which of her three earthly husbands will be her mate in heaven? She echoes Christ's reply to the Sadducees, who had posed a similar question concerning a woman who had been married in succession to seven brothers. Yet her allusion is relevant to her poem in ways that transcend the obvious, since the Sadducees are identified as those who "say that there is no resurrection" (Matthew 22:23). They thus deny a central emphasis of the final portion of Moulsworth's poem. Moreover, in recounting the story of the much-married woman, Matthew reports that after the death of her seventh husband, "last of all the woman died also" (22:27). Clearly this fact is relevant to Moulsworth's strong sense of her own mortality, implying that the purpose of her "Memorandum" is not only to commemorate the passings of her three husbands but to prepare for her own.

Finally, Moulsworth's last biblical citation (to Ecclesiastes 4:12) is completely typical of her intelligent allusiveness. The cited passage is echoed almost verbatim in Moulsworth's claim that "A threefold cord ... hardlie yett is broken" (l. 105). Moulsworth uses this echo to argue that the bonds formed by three marriages are so strong that there is no point in marrying again (or "knittinge here a fourth knott," as she puts it in l. 104). Yet the passage from Ecclesiastes 4 is actually part of an argument on *behalf* of establishing human links:

> [9] Two are better than one; because they have a good reward for their labour. [10] For if they fall, the one will lift up his fellow; but woe to him *that is* alone when he falleth; for *he hath* not another to help him up. [11] Again, if two lie together, then they have heat: but how can one be warm *alone*? [12] And if one prevail against him, two shall withstand him; and a threefold cord is not quickly broken.

Given this context, Moulsworth's allusion seems remarkably complex and even poignant. She is, after all, now alone; she no longer has a husband's hand to help her up; she no longer has a husband's body to warm her on cold November nights. She might easily have used this passage from Ecclesiastes to justify another earthly marriage: if a three-fold cord is strong (she might have reasoned) would not a four-fold cord be even stronger? Would not marrying a fourth husband help her overcome the loneliness that this scripture so memorably describes and that she so clearly felt? In the end, however, she uses the cited scripture to justify an independent life supported by a spiritual link with God. Instead of choosing marriage once again, she opts for widowhood. Two may indeed be better than one, and if two lie together they may indeed have heat. In the final analysis, however, Moulsworth chooses to remain one—with herself and with God.

To read Moulsworth's poem with the scriptures near at hand is to read as Moulsworth obviously wrote. By echoing God's word, she praises both Him and it, thus demonstrating her humility and dependence. Yet she also thereby claims Biblical sanction and authority for her poem, even as she sends us back to the source of all truth. By continuously alluding to her culture's most well-known text, she continuously illuminates and illustrates her own skill and creativity. By prompting us to return to scripture, she encourages all her readers—women *and* men—to seek and contemplate true knowledge.

Autobiographical Approaches

"My Inward House":
Women's Autobiographical Poetry
in the Early Seventeenth Century

Josephine A. Roberts

One of the most startling features of Martha Moulsworth's autobiographical poem is the narration of her life in the past tense, as if she were already dead. Yet Moulsworth was not alone in adopting this unusual visionary role: Elizabeth Grymeston confesses she composed her *Miscellanea. Prayers. Meditations. Memoratives* (1604) from the perspective of "a dead woman among the living."[1] Indeed, one of the dominant forms of autobiographical poetry before Moulsworth's time was the dream-vision, with a long heritage stretching back to Macrobius in the fifth century.[2] According to the genre of the dream-vision, the troubled sleeper often undertakes a journey in quest of knowledge, guided by a host of allegorical figures. The dream-vision was an autobiographical genre particularly appealing to women, beginning with Christine de Pizan's *Le Livre de la Cité des Dames* (1405), in which the dreamer narrates her frustrations in trying to construct a tradition of women authors, historians, and philosophers.[3]

---

[1]All quotations from Grymeston's work refer to the third expanded edition of *Miscellanea. Prayers. Meditations. Memoratives* (undated, but before 1609), STC 12409, sig. A2v.

[2]For background on the genre of the dream vision, see James Winny, *Chaucer's Dream-Poems* (New York: Barnes and Noble, 1973) and B.A. Windeatt, *Chaucer's Dream Poetry: Sources and Analogues* (Cambridge: Cambridge University Press, 1982).

[3]*The Book of the City of Ladies*, trans. Earl Jeffrey Richards (New York: Persea Books, 1982). See Maureen Quilligan's recent study, *The Allegory of Female Authority: Christine de Pizan's Cité des Dames* (Ithaca: Cornell University Press, 1991).

For early English women writers, the dream-vision offered a number of rich possibilities. On the one hand, the narrator could allegorize her spiritual struggle, as does Elizabeth Melville, Lady Culross in *Ane Godlie Dreame* (1606). Although Melville provides few individualizing details of her life, she does describe the dreamer's terror of slipping into the mouth of hell, only to be rescued at the last instant by Christ. The dreamer suddenly awakens, to the shocked recognition that she is still alive. The moment of awakening is reversed in Rachel Speght's "The Dreame," published as the first poem in her collection, *Mortalities Memorandum* (1621). In Speght's dream-vision her allegorical guides are all female, and they specifically introduce her to a catalogue of great women writers of antiquity, including poets, historians, astronomers, and rhetoricians, in the manner of the *Cité des Dames*. The dreamer, led onwards by Desire to learn more, is suddenly turned aside by an unexplained event: "some occurrence called me away."[4] Dismayed by her "quenched hope" of gaining more knowledge, the dreamer proceeds to describe her own earlier writings against the misogynist adversary Joseph Swetnam, and then confronts a far more formidable foe, the figure of Death attacking her mother. When the dreamer awakens, she is shocked to discover that her mother is in fact dead. Like Melville, Speght invokes the comfort of Christ's presence, but the poem culminates in a tribute to her love for her mother. The very title of Speght's collection, *Mortalities Memorandum*, suggests some precedent for "The Memorandum of Martha Moulsworth."

Several early seventeenth-century women authors also modified the genre of the dream-vision to provide for a more secular setting. In *Salve Deus Rex Judaeorum* (1611), Aemilia Lanyer includes a dream-vision in her dedicatory poem, "The Authors Dreame" to Mary Sidney, Countess of Pembroke. Instead of an apocalyptic landscape, she sets the dream in the Idalian grove, where the classical goddesses Minerva, Bellona, Diana, Aurora, and Flora gather to pay homage to a mortal woman seated in Honor's chair. In keeping with the genre, the dreamer undertakes a journey led by Morpheus, who describes the writings of the distinguished woman, at last revealed as the Countess of Pembroke. Lanyer's poem is autobiographical in that she relates gaining access to the manuscript verse translations of the Psalms prepared by

---

[4]*Mortalities Memorandum, with a Dreame Prefixed, imaginarie in manner; reall in matter* (1621), STC 23057, 8.

Sir Philip Sidney and the Countess (who, Lanyer claims, "farre before him is to be esteemd"; l. 151). Awakening before she has a chance to speak directly to the Countess, the dreamer resolves that she will dedicate her poems to her literary predecessor. Through the medium of the dream-vision, Lanyer boldly disregards the barriers of class and rank that would ordinarily separate her from direct association with the Countess and situates herself in close relation to the most distinguished female patron of sixteenth-century England. Lanyer's poem also demonstrates the imaginative potential of the dream-vision as a way of surmounting the obstacles that would restrict and constrain women. The dream motif runs throughout *Salve Deus Rex Judaeorum*: in an end note "To the doubtfull reader," the author explains the title came to her "in sleepe many yeares before I had any intent to write in this maner."[5] The dream-vision is also central to her major religious poem, where she draws upon a single biblical verse to recreate the figure of Pontius Pilate's wife, who experiences a prophetic dream of Christ.[6] Pilate disregards her warning vision, but for Lanyer it is proof of the ability of women to acquire knowledge and wisdom.

Yet even Lanyer seems to have sought a more direct means of describing personal experience than was afforded by the older genre of dream-vision. As we have seen, the allegorical framework of the poem often involved the veiling of personalizing details, as in Speght's poem where the reader never learns precisely what caused the sudden end of her education, or what part her mother may have played in relation to her writing career. It is all the more significant that Lanyer discovers an alternative mode to relate a key event from her life. In "A Description of Cooke-ham," appended to her religious verse, Lanyer chooses the setting of a country estate in Berkshire, where she shared a carefree existence with her patron, Margaret Clifford, Countess of Cumberland, and her daughter, Anne Clifford. Unlike "The Authors Dreame," here Lanyer sees herself in intimate contact with her social superiors, who enjoy with her a love of learning and a life of religious meditation. As Ann Baynes Coiro has noted, Lanyer is painfully aware of the difference in class (the "parters in honour"; l. 108) that separate her from her patrons, but she also recalls nostalgically the brief

---

[5]*The Poems of Aemilia Lanyer: Salve Deus Rex Judaeorum*, ed. Susanne Woods (New York: Oxford University Press, 1993), 139.

[6]The story of Pilate's wife appears only in Matthew 27:19, not in the other gospels.

time in which she lived secure in an all-female paradise, free from the demands of husbands and creditors.[7] Lanyer's "Cooke-ham," the most directly autobiographical of all her surviving works, is a beautifully balanced poem, with the first half describing the estate in spring time, followed by her account of the coming of winter brought on by the departure of the ladies. Like Moulsworth's "Memorandum," the seasons in "Cooke-ham" serve as an emotional framework for the poem reflecting the speaker's own changing states of mind.

Lanyer's contemporary, Lady Mary Wroth, also sought new forms for autobiographical poetry. Her sonnet sequence, *Pamphilia to Amphilanthus*, begins with the motif of the dream-vision, with Pamphilia asleep, witnessing Venus in the act of commanding Cupid to place a flaming heart within her chest: "I, waking hop'd as dreames itt would depart / Yet since: O mee: a lover I have binn."[8] The sonnet sequence describes Pamphilia's troubled relationship with the inconstant Amphilanthus ("lover of two"), and while it may be read autobiographically, Wroth avoids including any physical details that might specifically identify the male lover. Only within her vast prose romance, *The Countess of Montgomery's Urania* (1621), does Wroth turn to provide defining characteristics that link Amphilanthus to her first cousin, William Herbert, third Earl of Pembroke. Throughout the fiction, Amphilanthus' fatal attraction to beautiful women becomes apparent to Pamphilia, but she refuses to criticize him, choosing instead to blame herself for his philandering. Yet at the end of Book III, Pamphilia narrates the thinly disguised tale of Lindamira ("Wonderful beauty" or "Lady Mary") to her servant and confidante, who quickly recognizes that the story "was something more exactly related then a fixion."[9] Lindamira describes a double betrayal—by the Queen she has served and by the man she has secretly loved. Lindamira's tale outrages its narrator Pamphilia, who finds "her estate so neere agree with mine" (425) that she writes a series of seven sonnets "to conclude my rage against him" (at once Lindamira's lover, Pamphilia's Amphilanthus, and Wroth's Herbert). Pamphilia's anger, suppressed in the courtly form of the Petrarchan sonnet sequence, finds more

---

[7]"Writing in Service: Sexual Politics and Class Position in the Poetry of Aemilia Lanyer and Ben Jonson," *Criticism* 35 (1993): 357–76.

[8]*The Poems of Lady Mary Wroth*, ed. Josephine A. Roberts (Baton Rouge: Louisiana State Univ. Press, 1992), Poem 1, ll. 13–14.

[9]*The Countesse of Mountgomeries Urania* (1621), STC 24051, 429.

direct expression in "Lindamira's Complaint." Here the speaker contrasts her "twise seaven yeares" of devotion, with her lover's callous abandonment. Beginning with a farewell, in which she characterizes her beloved as the life-giving sun, the speaker progresses through a series of seven stages of separation. The numerology is not accidental, for as in Moulsworth's poem, the numbers form a carefully chosen pattern. St. Augustine regarded seven as a number representing "perfect completeness," a concept derived from Neo-Pythagorean number theory.[10] Whereas seven is often associated in the Bible as a number of servitude and expiation, it also became identified with the common medieval notion of the seven steps to perfection.[11] Here in constructing the sequence of seven sonnets, Wroth seems to draw upon these concepts to suggest how Pamphilia achieves a perfection of love that is not contingent on reciprocation. The final sonnet bluntly acknowledges the disapproval of outsiders (who accuse her of "mistrust and Jelousie" [1. 2]), but affirms the purity of a love that surmounts even betrayal.

In the autobiographical poems of Lanyer and Wroth, there is clearly a strong element of defensive justification. When we turn to Martha Moulsworth's poem, the natural tendency is to question what aspects of her life Moulsworth felt needed explanation. Perhaps the manuscript provides a hint, for centered beneath her name is a single word: "Widdowe." From plays, pamphlets, and jest books we know that in the seventeenth century the widow was a perennial target of satire. A volume of *Characters*, first published in 1615 and attributed to John Webster, pointedly contrasts "A vertuous Widdow," who mourns for the loss of her husband and resists all temptation to remarry, with "An ordinarie Widdow," who cunningly amasses great wealth through successive remarriages.[12] Webster's graphic description of the lascivious widow with her piles of plate and jewels reflects the negative stereotype, exploited in materialistic seventeenth-century London society. Proverbs about widows also perpetuated the stereotype, particularly one

---

[10]Vincent Foster Hopper, *Medieval Number Symbolism: Its Sources, Meaning, and Influence on Thought and Expression* (New York: Oxford University Press, 1938), 79.

[11]Hopper cites the seven years Jacob served Leah and then Rachel (Genesis 29), 24. He also refers to the seven steps to perfection, 18.

[12]*The Complete Works of John Webster*, ed. F.L. Lucas, 4 vols. (London: Chatto and Windus, 1927), 4:38–39.

which circulated in Moulsworth's time: "Take heed of a person marked and a widow thrice married."[13] One indication of the conflicting pressures placed on widows may be found in the prose romance *Urania*, where Wroth describes how, following the deaths of their husbands, wealthy women became the targets of persistent suitors. Wroth (who herself remained a widow for over forty years) highlights a small group of women, particularly the widow Queen of Naples and Lady Pastora, who resisted the immense pressures to remarry. Interestingly, as Moulsworth looks back over her life, she affirms her decision to wed three times, as well as her present choice to remain alone. Above all, she defies societal stereotyping that would assign her to one oppressive and overwhelmingly negative category.[14]

After Moulsworth enumerates the deaths of all three husbands, she poignantly turns to address the subject of her departed children: "butt roote, & ffruite is dead, wch makes me sad" (l. 72). In a single line, she confronts a devastating loss, but her reticence underlines her grief. For many Renaissance women, the writing of a book of advice for one's children was a socially acceptable form of autobiography.[15] Perhaps one of the best examples relevant to Moulsworth's poem is Elizabeth Grymeston's collection of prose meditations, interspersed with poetry, written for her son Berny, the sole survivor of nine children. Grymeston in the dedication to her son refers to her own declining physical condition, her husband's suffering, and even her own mother's "virulent" wrath against her. But despite these trials, Grymeston sought to leave her

---

[13]See Morris P. Tilley, *A Dictionary of Proverbs in England in the Sixteenth and Seventeenth Centuries* (Ann Arbor: University of Michigan Press, 1950), H 372. Tilley also records such gems as, "He who marries a widow will often have a dead man's head thrown in his dish" (W 336), and "The rich widow weeps with one eye and casts glances with the other" (W 340).

[14]Yet she is clearly sensitive about three husbands, as revealed by her biblical allusion to how the Sadduces confronted Christ with the test question concerning a widow and her seven husbands. Moulsworth cites Matthew 2:30, but the episode is also reported in Mark 12:18–27 and Luke 20:27–38.

[15]On mothers' books of advice, see Elaine V. Beilin, *Redeeming Eve: Women Writers of the English Renaissance* (Princeton: Princeton University Press, 1987), 266–85, and Betty S. Travitsky, "The New Mother of the English Renaissance: Her Writings on Motherhood," in *The Lost Tradition: Mothers and Daughters in Literature*, ed. E.M. Broner and Cathy Davidson (New York: Unger, 1980), 33–43.

son a book in which he might see "the true portraiture of thy
mothers minde."[16] In its final version, organized into twenty meditations, Grymeston reveals an impressive range of reading in the
classics (Seneca, Virgil, Terence, Pindar), the church fathers
(Augustine, Ambrose, Gregory, Jerome, Chrysostom), and the English poets (Southwell, Spenser, Harington, Daniel).[17] This portrait
of her mind is organized numerologically, so that the thirteenth
chapter is a Good Friday's "Meditation of the Crosse," and the volume culminates in the Penitential Psalms and a final section of
"Memoratives." Some of the latter sound remarkably like Polonius'
advice to Laertes, but one of the most dramatic has special relevance to Moulsworth's poem:

> There is no moment of time spent, which thou art not count-
> able for, and therefore when thou hearest the clocke strike,
> thinke there is now another houre come whereof thou art to
> yeeld a reckening; and by endeavouring to spende one houre
> better than another, thou shalt come to some better perfec-
> tion in Christianity.[18]

Although Moulsworth has no surviving children to serve as
her primary audience, she desires to give an accounting (literally, a
counting) of the hours, as Grymeston describes. Her poem does
indeed offer a portrait of her mind, revealing a range of learning
that may not be as extensive as Grymeston's, but shows a strong
knowledge of the Bible and of church history (such as evidenced
by her marginal reference to the Byzantine historian Nicephorus
Callistus). To some extent the verses Moulsworth creates become
her "offspring," although she herself never makes the overt comparison. Significantly, two autobiographical women poets writing
twenty years later, "Eliza" and An Collins, who were both without
children, explicitly treated their verse as their heirs. Although we
do not know the author's complete name, *Eliza's Babes: Or the Virgins Offering* (1652) contains a number of autobiographical elements, including addresses to her brother, sister, and husband.
"Eliza" proudly contrasts her divine "babes" with mortal chil-

---

[16]*Miscellanea*, sig. A2v.

[17]Ruth Hughey and Philip Hereford, "Elizabeth Grymeston and Her
Miscellanea," *The Library* 15 (1934–35), 61–91. Hughey and Hereford's in-
valuable study traces Grymeston's sources and shows how she frequently
modified them for artistic effect. They argue that the poetry in the volume
was not her own, but copied from other authors.

[18]*Miscellanea*, sig. H4.

dren.[19] Similarly, An Collins, who describes herself as suffering from physical affliction and forced to live in confinement, nevertheless celebrates her creative powers in "Another Song" from her *Divine Songs and Meditacions* (1653):

> Yet as a garden is my mind enclosed fast
> Being to safety so confind from storm and blast
> Apt to produce a fruit most rare,
> That is not common with every woman
> That fruitfull are.[20]

Whereas Collins refers to the garden of her mind, Moulsworth chooses the corresponding image of the "Inward house" (l. 19). In keeping with the biblical persona of Martha, the diligent housekeeper, she surveys her house, to put all in order. Her autobiographical poem contains some elements of the epitaph, a classical genre that was also a socially acceptable form of autobiographical writing for women.[21] Yet the dates in the margins of Moulsworth's manuscript are not those of her husbands' deaths, but of her own marriages. As Moulsworth measures the length of each union, she self-consciously invests the raw figures with meaning and significance, providing a link between the "numbers" of time and the "numbers" of poetry. Her attempt to make sense of the span of life is in many ways typical of the epitaphs written by women in honor of their deceased children. For example, Elizabeth Egerton describes the death of her son Henry, who "lived dayes as many as

---

[19]In a witty poem, "Eliza" argues for the superiority of her "babes" over mortal offspring:

> "To a Lady that bragg'd of her children"
> Thine did proceed from sinful race,
> Mine did from the heavenly dew of grace
> Thine at their birth did pain thee bring,
> When mine are born, I set and sing.

Eliza's Babes: Or the Virgins Offering. Being Divine Poems and Meditations (1652), 54.

[20]An Collins, *Divine Songs and Meditacions*, ed. Stanley Stewart. Augustan Reprint Society Pub. 94 (Los Angeles: William Andrew Clark Memorial Library, 1961), 57.

[21]Mary Ellen Lamb discusses the prominence of the epitaph as a classical form employed by Elizabeth, Mildred, and Katherine Cooke in the sixteenth century: "The Cooke Sisters: Attitudes toward Learned Women in the Renaissance," in *Silent But for the Word*, ed. Margaret P. Hannay (Kent: Kent State University Press, 1985), 107–25.

my years," the sum of twenty-nine.[22] Similarly, Katherine Philips wrote a moving epitaph in honor of her first child Hector, who died (she says) "in forty days," a figure which Philips possibly exaggerates, to create symmetry with her "twice forty months" of wedlock.[23] By attributing meaning and significance to the bare numbers, these authors find purpose even in the most fleeting of lives.

Moulsworth's "Memorandum" thus draws upon three of the dominant modes of autobiographical writing by women of the early seventeenth century. Rejecting the medieval form of the dream-vision, Moulsworth writes instead as one "broad waking," fully aware of the cold November day as she sits before her fire. Like her contemporaries Lanyer and Wroth, she seeks an alternative form to describe her personal experience in more direct and immediate detail. Yet she still retains the visionary stance of the narrator of the dream-vision and the circular framework of the journey. In keeping with the genre of the mother's legacy, Moulsworth creates a portrait of her mind for future generations, even as she implicitly acknowledges that her work must be a "memorandum" for children other than her own. Finally, her poem incorporates several elements from the classical form of the epitaph, a fitting genre for a woman learned in Latin. Yet as she commemorates her husbands and children, ascribing meaning to the numerical span of their lives, she ultimately provides for us a vivid portrait of her own "Inward house."

---

[22]See the text of Egerton's poem, "On my Boy Henry," in *Kissing the Rod: An Anthology of Seventeenth-Century Women's Verse*, ed. Germaine Greer, et al. (New York: Farrar Straus Giroux, 1988), 117.

[23]Elizabeth H. Hageman points out that Hector Philips actually lived less than two weeks, but the number forty is associated in Christian numerology with "periods of privation and trial": "The Matchless Orinda" in *Women Writers of the Renaissance and Reformation*, ed. Katharina M. Wilson (Athens: Univ. of Georgia Press, 1987), 568. Hageman provides the text of "Orinda upon Little Hector Philips," 599.

"My muse is a tell clocke":
The Paradox of Ritual Autobiography in
Martha Moulsworth's"Memorandum"

Curtis Perry

The first four lines of Martha Moulsworth's "Memorandum" locate her autobiographical writing in a precise ritual context:

> The tenth day of the winter month Nouember
> A day which I must duely still remember
> did open first theis eis, and shewed this light
> Now on thatt day uppon thatt daie I write[1]

"Remember" here means something like "memorialize," since presumably Moulsworth does not actually recall her own birth. Consequently, insofar as Moulsworth's poem is itself the performance of this dutiful memorialization, her writing is described as the observance of a ritual. This formulation is elaborated by the description—in the marginalia—of the poet's muse as a "tell clocke," a description which suggests that the poem is merely a passive recording of the inevitable and regular passage of time's "yearly stroke" (l. 7).

This model of writing, of course, differs considerably from a more conventional notion of autobiography as a work "(1) *primarily* written to give a coherent account of the author's life ... , and (2) composed after a period of reflection and forming a unified narra-

---

[1]The "Memorandum" is reproduced in *"My Name Was Martha": A Renaissance Woman's Autobiographical Poem,* ed. Robert C. Evans and Barbara Wiedemann, (West Cornwall, CT: Locust Hill Press, 1993). All citations will be given parenthetically, either by line number or, in the case of marginalia, by page number.

tive."[2] If this definition stresses the shaping agency of the author, Moulsworth's account of writing-as-ritual seems here to deny any authorial intervention. At stake in these different versions of autobiography are different versions of memory, for if traditional autobiography involves the constitution of a unified life through a process of re-collection, Moulsworth's introductory lines promise merely a reiterative memorialization of the past events. Here we might notice too that the more familiar notion of autobiography dovetails nicely with the modern conception of memory and personal identity formulated most powerfully for us by Locke:

> to find wherein personal identity consists, we must consider what *person* stands for;—which, I think, is a thinking intelligent being, that has reason and reflection, and can consider itself as itself, the same thinking thing, in different times and places.[3]

For Locke, reason and recollection are coterminous with personal identity. Consequently, if Locke inaugurates a modern tradition of thinking about memory and identity, then what we tend to think of as autobiography is precisely the literary expression of this modern conception of self.[4]

Moulsworth's "Memorandum" implicitly engages questions about the relationship between personal identity and autobiography when, for example, it describes the day of writing as "the birth day of my selfe, & and of theis lynes" (l. 6); however, by describing writing as "tell clocke" memorialization—by denying that the autobiographical project is structured by a process of reasoned, reflective consideration—Moulsworth's poem raises questions for its readers about the kind of personal identity it describes. Since Moulsworth's poem seems—at least in its initial formulation—to hinge on a kind of memory less closely bound to our modern notions of identity, we are invited to wonder not only if the "lynes"

---

[2]Paul Delany, *British Autobiography in the Seventeenth Century* (London: Routledge & Kegan Paul, 1969), 1.

[3]Locke, *An Essay Concerning Human Understanding*, 2 vols., ed. Alexander Campbell Fraser (New York: Dover, 1959), 1: 448.

[4]The Lockean tradition is nicely encapsulated in the anthology *Personal Identity*, ed. John Perry (Berkeley: University of California Press, 1975). See also the useful discussion of Lockean identity, autobiography, and the keeping of diaries in Felicity A. Nussbaum's "Toward Conceptualizing Diary," in *Studies in Autobiography*, ed. James Olney (New York and Oxford: Oxford University Press, 1988), 128–40.

are autobiographical in anything like a modern sense of the word, but also if the "selfe" they sketch is in any way recognizable to us.

In order to get at the peculiarities of Moulsworth's formulation, it is useful to distinguish between what Roland Greene has called "fictional" and "ritual" aspects of poetry.[5] By "fictional," Greene refers not to the truth or falsehood of a narrative, but rather to its presentation of an "implicit plot that unfolds within a hypothetical world," or to the sense a text gives that it tells a distinct story from a distinct perspective.[6] A reader responds to the "fictional" aspects of a text by using them to piece together a unified and unique narrative. "Ritual," by contrast, names those aspects of a poem (including elements like non-referential sounds, numerologies, rhyme schemes, and so on) which "organize" the text "in the reader-vocalizer's immediate experience."[7] A poem in which "ritual" elements predominate will encourage the reader to apprehend it as a score for repeatable performance—we might think of an incantation, for example—and it will de-emphasize those aspects of authorial voice that make the text seem specific to one person's experience.

With its necessary emphasis both on details of an individual's experience and on that individual's voice, one would think of autobiography as a mode in which what Greene calls "fictional" would necessarily dominate. To be sure, since the "Memorandum" traces an individual life in some detail, it is primarily a "fictional" or narrative text. What seems remarkable to me about the "Memorandum," however, is the way it allows "ritual" aspects to intrude on the telling of a life story. We can point out, for example, the formal "ritual" aspects of the poem. In keeping with her description of her muse as a "tell clocke," Moulsworth's poem consists of 110 lines—a couplet for each of her 55 years of age.[8] This structuring device deflects attention from the details of the life toward the material presence of the poem as a disciplined act of ritual remembrance. The same could be said for the simple repetitive couplets, which continually refocus our attention on the formal demands of

---

[5]Greene, "Sir Philip Sidney's *Psalms*, The Sixteenth-Century Psalter, and the Nature of Lyric," *Studies in English Literature, 1500–1900* 30 (1990): 16–40. See also Greene's *Post Petrarchism: Origins and Innovations of the Western Lyric Sequence* (Princeton: Princeton University Press, 1991), 5–21.

[6]Greene, "Sir Philip Sidney's *Psalms*," 21.

[7]Greene, "Sir Philip Sidney's *Psalms*," 20.

[8]Isobel Grundy's essay in this collection provides an exhaustive review of the numerological structures that organize the "Memorandum."

the poem. This deflection is implicit in the poem's marginalia, where Moulsworth writes "my muse is a tell clocke, & echoeth everie stroke wth a coupled rhyme so many times viz 55." If the act of writing is described as mere echo—the transparent accounting of the passage of time—then perhaps the details of the life are not what is important in the poem so much as the act of recording them.

A second and closely related point is that this formulation denies any special relationship between having lived the life and being able to memorialize it. The act of writing is not, for example, given here as an exploration of personal experiences, nor would the description of the writing process as echoic seem to imply the development of any carefully individuated subject-position. Furthermore, it need hardly be pointed out that most of the "Memorandum" commemorates the life of Martha Moulsworth by noting her participation in public rituals: the life is organized by a litany of rituals including Moulsworth's birthdays, her christening, her weddings, her periods of mourning, and the "holly dayes" (l. 73) upon which each of her husbands dies. These ritual occasions— rather than adumbrating a unique subjectivity—mark precisely the moments where Moulsworth's life intersects most obviously with publicly constituted values, behaviors and meanings. By the same token, the poem dwells predominantly on Moulsworth's socially inscribed roles in relation to men.

The poem goes out of its way on one occasion to insist precisely that Martha was always part of a public, ceremonial system of loyalties:

> In carnall state of sin originall
> I did nott stay one whole day naturall
> The seale of grace in Sacramentall water
> So soone had I, so soone become the daughter
> of earthly parents, & of heavenlie ffather (ll. 11–15)

That the details of the narration consist largely of public events and social bonds is cognate with the formulation of the muse as a "tell clocke"—each foregrounds what Greene would call the "ritual" aspects of the text by attempting to evacuate the narrative of specific, idiosyncratic authorial perspective. What is left seems to present a model of the self defined not by a history of personal experiences, but rather as both the performer of a ritual action and as a series of publicly inscribed events and relations.

I will return to this paradoxical notion of a "ritual" autobiography, but first I want to step back for a moment to consider in general terms how we might relate the oxymoronic quality of this formulation to larger structural paradoxes built into commonplace ideas about women—and hence about women's writing—in Renaissance England. It should be obvious, first of all, that the authorial passivity implied by the notion of "tell clocke" memorialization in Moulsworth's poem reflects a reticence about authorship perfectly understandable in a culture which took it as proverbial that "an eloquent woman is never chaste."[9] Given the common currency of this association between chastity and silence, it is not surprising that much of the writing of educated Renaissance Englishwomen was cast as ritual observance or translation. Thus, for example, Germaine Greer has referred to the tradition of death-bed poems by women to their husbands as a series of "mnemonics for female magnanimity," and has described the bulk of seventeenth-century womens' religious versification as "a discipline intended to focus concentration on well-worn pious truisms."[10] This kind of ritual literary production was admissible both because it asserted pieties, and also because it presented itself as meditative discipline rather than as eloquence. With some notable exceptions, those women writers who nevertheless sought eloquence generally had to do so by taking advantage of the few modes and stances—meditational devotion, translation, and so on—permissable to them.[11]

Gary Waller describes precisely this problem when he writes that, for Renaissance women writers, "a very condition of their ability to write is the acceptance of constraints which deny them authentic speech."[12] For Waller, this poses a central problem for critics:

> the voices of opposition or counter dominance are heard
> only as murmers against the discourse of power which at-

---

[9]This proverb is quoted by Margaret Hannay in her "Introduction" to *Silent But for the Word: Tudor Women as Patrons, Translators, and Writers of Religious Works*, ed. Margaret Patterson Hannay (Kent, OH: Kent State University Press, 1985), 4.

[10]Greer, "Introduction," in *Kissing the Rod: An Anthology of Seventeenth-Century Women's Verse*, ed. Germaine Greer, Susan Hastings, Jeslyn Medoff, and Melinda Sansone (New York: Farrar, Straus, Giroux, 1989), 11, 12.

[11]On this point generally see the essays collected in *Silent But for the Word*.

[12]Waller, "Struggling into Discourse: The Emergence of Renaissance Women's Writing" in *Silent But for the Word*, 246.

tempts, by the subjection of language, to suppress its loud silences. How does one speak more eloquently of such silences? How might *we*?[13]

We might begin to respond to this question by wondering what
exactly "authentic speech" means, and who has it? Presumably
even the most privileged of speakers—a Ben Jonson, say, or even a
King James—is given voice only through the conventions and assumptions of his culture. Foucault, in a passage Waller quotes, argues that

> The fundamental codes of a culture—those governing its
> language, its schemas of perception, its exchanges, its tech-
> niques, its values, the hierarchy of its practices—establish for
> every man, from the very first, the empirical orders with
> which he will be dealing and within which he will be at
> home.[14]

That these "fundamental codes" often acted to stifle for women the
kinds of expression which they enabled for men does not make a
male courtier's writing, in the last analysis, any more "authentic"
than a woman's meditation.

If everyone writes from within these codes, then all writing
can be seen as a kind of negotiation, a process of finding a position
within the field determined by these codes. For some the process is
a great deal easier than for others, but it is important to remember,
with Raymond Williams, that within these fundamental codes "no
mode of production and therefore no dominant social order and
therefore no dominant culture ever in reality includes or exhausts
all human practice, human energy, and human intention."[15] What
this suggests to me is that while it may be valid, having taken an
olympian perspective on the English Renaissance as a whole, to
describe women's writing cumulatively as "loud silences" and
"murmers," the task for the critic lies in tracing the ways that individual texts by women manage to negotiate space for themselves
within restrictive social codes.

I am thinking here of Ann Rosalind Jones's observation that
"to think in terms of negotiation rather than coerced repetition or
romantic rejection of literary models opens up a whole spectrum of

---

[13]Waller, "Struggling into Discourse," 246.

[14]Foucault, *The Order of Things: An Archaeology of the Human Sciences*
(New York: Vintage Books, 1973), xx.

[15]Williams, *Marxism and Literature* (Oxford: Oxford University Press,
1977), 125.

women's responses to the logics of power."[16] In reading Moulsworth's "Memorandum," what this means is that while we may not be able to reconstruct an authentic "selfe" from the silences of the poem, it is nevertheless possible to reconstruct the conditions in which the ambiguities involved in this model of "tell clocke" memorialization make sense as the strategic narrative obfuscations of a writer who "accepts the dominant ideology ... but particularizes it and transforms it" in order to find a voice.[17]

As a simple example, consider the poem's final lines: "the Virgins life is gold, as Clarks vs tell / the Widowes siluar, I loue siluar well." These lines pick up the language of the dowry from earlier in the poem, where a marginal note opines that "Lattin is nott the most marketable mariadge mettall" (5). Implicit here is the system that Gayle Rubin has called "the traffic in women"—the system of exchange in which women are transferred between men in order to solidify reciprocal kinship bonds that help constitute social order.[18] As Rubin points out, such a system cannot accept women as independent agents within this social system: since they are exchanged, they cannot be the exchangers. Moulsworth's final two lines reiterate and accept this commonplace association between women and money while simultaneously asserting her own independent agency within a system of traffic by hinting at a kind of self-possession.

More generally, Moulsworth's "Memorandum" manages to articulate some radical ideas within a poem that in many ways conforms to and accepts the dominant ideologies of a patriarchal society. Her call for a university to educate women, to give one example, is strikingly explicit both in its assertion of women's potential and in its articulation of injustice:

> Two Vniuersities we haue of men
> o thatt we had but one of women then
> O then thatt would in witt, and tongs surpasse
> All art of men thatt is, or euer was (ll. 33–36)

---

[16]Jones, *The Currency of Eros: Women's Love Lyric in Europe, 1540–1620* (Bloomington: Indiana University Press, 1990), 4.

[17]Jones, *The Currency of Eros*, 4. On the concept of "negotiation," and what it means to read women's texts with this concept in mind, see 2–4 and 201 n.6.

[18]Rubin, "The Traffic in Women: Notes on the 'Political Economy' of Sex," in *Toward an Anthropology of Women*, ed. Rayna R. Reiter (New York and London: Monthly Review Press, 1975), 157–210.

More broadly, though we cannot be sure what role Moulsworth played in the preservation or transmission of her poem, the decision to memorialize her own story in a poem which evidently was then allowed at least a very limited circulation suggests that the author saw her story as in some sense worthy of record.

If Moulsworth's poem makes progressive claims—implicitly and explicitly—these claims are enabled by the poem's strategic responses to cultural codes. Mary Beth Rose has described how, during the seventeenth century, women "began not simply to record the deeds of their male relatives, but to explore their own identities and experience in autobiographical form."[19] As a participant in the developments Rose describes, Moulsworth's "Memorandum" shows us that these early autobiographical explorations required complicated negotiations: if the poem explores Moulsworth's identity, it does so precisely by describing herself as a passive recorder, and by memorializing her male relatives. What this means in the case of Moulsworth's ritual autobiography is that by emphasizing both the publicly inscribed ritual quality of the "selfe," and the passive, disciplined ritual quality of the "lynes," Moulsworth is able within the bounds of propriety to write an autobiography that articulates (and embodies) some radical notions about women.

In fact, I want to argue that the "Memorandum" is at its most sophisticated precisely where it most concretely engages this negotiation, poising the naming of a "selfe" against the ritual quality of its "lynes." Moulsworth writes

> My name was Martha, Martha tooke much payne
> our Sauiour christ hir guesse to entertayne
> God gyue me grace my Inward house to dight
> that he wth me may supp, & stay all night (ll. 17–20)

As a marginal note makes clear, Moulsworth here refers to the Biblical Martha who, with her sister Mary, hosted Jesus. The Biblical story (Luke 10:38–42) tells of sibling rivalry: Mary sits at Jesus's feet; Martha, who is "cumbered about much serving," complains to Jesus that her sister is not helping and is in turn rebuked for caring

---

[19]Rose, "Gender, Genre, and History: Seventeenth-Century English Women and the Art of Autobiography," in *Women in the Middle Ages and the Renaissance: Literary and Historical Perspectives*, ed. Mary Beth Rose (Syracuse: Syracuse University Press, 1986), 245.

too much about the petty tasks of this world and for neglecting the work of salvation.[20]

We might read the line "My name was Martha, Martha tooke much payne" as an important moment of self-naming within the poem. Robert Evans, for example, has described Moulsworth's description of her namesake as a canny self-positioning in which she associates herself with the biblical Martha's pains but carefully distances herself from her namesake's petty worldliness: Moulsworth's "pains" are taken in the care of the "Inward house."[21] What interests me here, though, is Moulsworth's use of actual language of scripture, for the verse she quotes is this: "And Jesus answered and said unto her, Martha, Martha, thou art careful and troubled about many things" (10:41). It is not surprising that Moulsworth's narrative should weave in a literal quotation of Jesus's "Martha, Martha." After all, we can expect that Moulsworth was deeply familiar with the exact words of the brief scriptural story of her namesake. What is odd here, however, is the way that the scriptural echo subtending the line erupts within this moment of careful self-positioning as a kind of ritual incantation. It points away from the "fictional" axis of the narrative ("I am Martha, and I define myself in a certain relation to another Martha"), and calls attention to an alternative, "ritual" axis in which the quotation of scripture ("Martha, Martha") is perhaps more important than the positioning or description of self.

That these two axes should be so tightly—carefully?—interwoven at the moment in the poem where Martha names herself and in effect positions herself in relation to scripture suggests to me that in some sense the poem is *about* the paradoxes implicit in the idea of ritual autobiography. For one way to read the conflicting pulls in this compacted line would be to say that they remind us that in this poem the act of self-naming is simultaneously an active process of reasoned reflection and a passive process of ritual inscription of a public text.

---

[20]Luke, 10:40. I quote the story from the King James Version. It would be possible, I think, to relate this story to Moulsworth's autobiography in a number of ways. Perhaps, having had three husbands, Moulsworth too felt "cumbered about much serving" and subtly expresses her regret at not having been able to dedicate her life to sitting at the feet of Christ?

[21]This is how Robert Evans read the moment in *"My Name Was Martha,"* 17.

That the goal of the poem is somehow to negotiate a voice and identity from within the system of restrictions limiting women's eloquence is corroborated by Moulsworth's citation of Acts 17:28: "In him we live, and move, and have our being; as certain of your own poets have said." The reminder that Christians become fully agents only by surrendering to Christ is simultaneously a reminder of the analogous paradox in the situation of Moulsworth: she can only have a "being" in some negotiated relation to restrictive discourses, and can only construct an authorial voice for herself by imagining it as passive. This scriptural citation, in other words, encapsulates the paradoxes involved in Martha's self-naming, since in that instance we also saw that Moulsworth could describe and position herself only from within a ritual invocation of scripture.

It is interesting to speculate that Moulsworth found, in the relationship between Christ and the believer, a model for the paradoxical negotiation involved in writing a woman's ritual autobiography.[22] If the Christian finds an authentic self only by ceding all agency to Christ, Moulsworth is able to write her life only by ceding the kind of shaping agency involved in what we think of as autobiography and writing instead a "tell clocke" memorandum of a publicly inscribed series of relationships and events. The parallel in effect glosses the strategic functioning of Moulsworth's acceptance of various social strictures governing the conduct of women, an acceptance which authorizes her to record and circulate her own story as well as to express some truly progressive notions.

---

[22]Other women writers responded similarly to the Christian believer's enabling passivity. Wendy Wall, for example, presents a comparable description of Amelia Lanyer's authorizing use of Christ in her essay "Our Bodies / Our Texts?: Renaissance Women and the Trials of Authorship," *Anxious Power: Reading, Writing, and Ambivalence in Narrative by Women,* ed. Carol J. Singley and Susan Elizabeth Sweeney (Albany: State University of New York Press, 1993), 64: "in couching the presentation of her book in language that suggests that she is delivering the savior to female readers, Lanyer inverts the textual dynamic in which the writer asserts control over his book by figuring it as in need of governance."

Research Sources on Seventeenth-Century Women's Autobiography

Karen Worley Pirnie

Early modern women's autobiographical writing is a field that offers wide opportunity for the scholar. A few women have received written notice, but much of this is "background" critical work, leaving ample room for new studies of the self-constitutive aspects of these women's writings. Excerpts from the work of numerous Renaissance women are available in anthologies (see Access to Primary Sources below), making them accessible to scholars interested in exploring this field.

Any research should begin with the exhaustive bibliographical articles in *English Literary Renaissance (ELR)*. These provide comprehensive lists organized by categories: Background Studies, Editions, Various Genres, and Studies of Individual Authors. *ELR* 24 (1994) includes "Recent Studies in Women Writers of Tudor England, 1485–1603 (1990 to mid-1993)" by Georgianna M. Ziegler (229–42) and "Recent Studies in Women Writers of the Seventeenth Century, 1604–1674 (1990–mid-1993)" by Sara Jayne Steen (273–74). For earlier sources, see Elizabeth Hageman's "Recent Studies in Women Writers of Tudor England," *ELR* 14 (1984): 409–25, and "Recent Studies in Women Writers of the English Seventeenth Century," *ELR* 18 (1988): 138–67.

Autobiography

General works about autobiography

James Olney, editor of *Autobiography: Essays Theoretical and Critical* (Princeton: Princeton University Press, 1980), and Paul De-

lany, author of *British Autobiography in the Seventeenth Century*
(New York: Columbia University Press, 1969), are acknowledged
experts in the genre. Both authors consider the definition and theory of autobiography as expressive of both the individual writer
and her historical period. In addition to offering essays on the
genre, Olney's book includes Mary G. Mason's essay on the first
female autobiographers in English (discussed in Critical Work,
below). Delany devotes a chapter to "Female Autobiographers,"
six women who wrote in the late seventeenth century; his "Check-
List of Seventeenth-Century Autobiographers" includes only nine
more women, all later than Martha Moulsworth.

Women's autobiography

   A trio of books published in the late 1980s looks specifically at
the ways women write their lives. *The Private Self: Theory and Practice of Women's Autobiographical Writings*, edited by Shari Benstock
(Chapel Hill: University of North Carolina Press, 1988), includes
two excellent essays on women's assumption of authority and female ego formation. *A Poetics of Women's Autobiography: Marginality
and the Fictions of Self-Representation*, by Sidonie Smith (Bloomington and Indianapolis: Indiana University Press, 1987), considers
both gender and historical placement in the first section
("Theoretical Considerations") and includes full chapters on
Margery Kempe and Margaret Cavendish (see sections on them below). Estelle C. Jelinek, in *The Tradition of Women's Autobiography:
From Antiquity to the Present* (Boston: Twayne, 1986), examines the
unique content and form that differentiate women's autobiographical writing from that of men: personal subject matter and "a mul-
tidimensional, fragmented self-image" (xiii). Jelinek discusses Julian of Norwich and Margery Kempe among the earliest autobiographers, comparing their books with male spiritual autobiographies; not surprisingly, she finds a greater need for self-justification in the women's work. Jelinek's chapter on the seventeenth
century provides an overview of spiritual and secular autobiographies, virtually all written in the latter half of the century, after
Moulsworth's poem. Interestingly, Jelinek notes two of Moulsworth's themes in several of these later works: ancestral history
and marital love.

Forms of autobiographical writing: autobiography, diaries, letters

Bella Brodzki and Celeste Schenck (in the introduction to their anthology, *Life/Lines: Theorizing Women's Autobiography* [Ithaca: Cornell University Press, 1988]) propose "a feminist reading of autobiography" as "nonrepresentative, dispersed, displaced subjectivity" (6). Schenck's essay in the collection, "All of a Piece: Women's Poetry and Autobiography," further suggests that all women's writing expresses the fragmented conditions of female life, whether or not a specific work is intentionally self-representational. Most critics, however, specifically exclude diaries, journals, or letters in their considerations of autobiographical writing. This controversy over what constitutes autobiography suggests possibilities for future critical work, since more early modern women's letters and diaries survive than explicitly autobiographical memoirs.

Seventeenth-Century Women (and Precursors)

English Women's Voices 1540–1700, ed. Charlotte F. Otten (Miami: Florida International University Press, 1992), reprints 46 documents written by women, arranged by subjects of interest to women: abuse, prison life, political petitions, marriage, health, childbirth, and religion. The volume includes autobiographies, as of Mrs. Alice Thornton and Lady Anne Halkett, as well as diaries, letters, instructions, and testimonies in legal proceedings. In the nineteen-page bibliography of women writers between 1540 and 1700, only 25 entries predate Moulsworth.

Her Own Life: Autobiographical Writings by Seventeenth-Century Englishwomen, ed. Elspeth Graham, Hilary Hinds, Elaine Hobby, and Helen Wilcox (London and New York: Routledge, 1989), reprints substantial excerpts from the autobiographical writings of thirteen seventeenth-century women. The earliest, from Anne Clifford's private diary, is dated 1616–17. The remaining twelve postdate Moulsworth, ranging from 1653 to 1691, and, unlike Moulsworth's poem, were written for publication. The introduction discusses political and religious conditions as well as the notion of self inherent in autobiographical writing. The volume's extensive bibliography includes seventeenth-century publications, modern publications of seventeenth-century texts, and secondary sources. The women included, and the dates of their excerpted works, are as follows: Anne Clifford (1616–17), An Collins (1653), Anna Trapnel (1654), Margaret Cavendish (1656), Susanna Parr (1659), Katharine Evans and Sarah Cheevers (1662), Mary Carleton (1663), Alice Thornton (1668), Sarah Davy (1670), Anne Wentworth (1677), Hannah Allen (1683), and Joan Vokins (1691).

Mentioned in both of Hageman's bibliographical articles, Betty Travitsky's *The Paradise of Women: Writings by Englishwomen of the Renaissance* (Westport, CT: Greenwood Press, 1981) is still a fine starting point for students of Renaissance women's writing. Travitsky's collection prints excerpts from personal writings, letters, and diaries of 17 writers from the sixteenth and early seventeenth centuries, including many contemporaries of Moulsworth.

Critical work

To date, critical work on early modern women's autobiographical writing has been limited to a few women, noted individually below. Mary G. Mason's essay "The Other Voice: Autobiographies of Women Writers" (in Olney, above in General Works; reprinted in Brodzki and Schenck, above in Forms) makes a strong case for viewing the three writers listed individually below (Julian of Norwich, Margery Kempe, and Margaret Cavendish) as the first female autobiographers in English, because they establish patterns that women today still follow in writing about their own lives. These patterns distinguish women's life-writing from men's by defining an identity that evolves in relation to an "other." Julian of Norwich creates herself in relation to the Christian God; Margery Kempe also relates to Christ, but remains a wife and mother; Margaret Cavendish constitutes herself as part of a double portrait with her husband. (Anne Bradstreet is also included in Mason's discussion, but because she is considered an American writer, she has been omitted here.) Moulsworth clearly fits this pattern in her repeated self-definition through her relationships with God, her father, and her husbands. Kate Greenspan (in "The Autohagiographical Tradition in Medieval Women's Devotional Writing," *a/b: Auto/Biographical Studies* 6:2 [1991]: 157–68) suggests that spiritual autobiographies, although "seldom autobiographical in the modern sense" (158), can be interpreted within the genre of hagiography—the writing of saints' lives. The authority of such writings derives from the writers' experience, and both Julian of Norwich and Margery Kempe do refer to real events in their lives.

Mary Beth Rose's essay "Gender, Genre, and History: Seventeenth-Century Women and the Art of Autobiography" (in *Women in the Middle Ages and the Renaissance: Literary and Historical Perspectives*, ed. Mary Beth Rose [Syracuse: Syracuse University Press, 1986], 245–78) discusses four late seventeenth-century women: Margaret Cavendish, Anne Halkett, Ann Fanshawe, and Alice Thornton. In the work of these four women, all postdating Moulsworth, Rose sees the emergence of "modern conventions of autobiography as a distinctly personal, secular, and introspective literary form" (245). In contrast with the earlier mystical autobiographers, Rose's four subjects write about themselves in the real world of contemporary relationships and events, resolving in their work the conflict between their private and public selves.

Sandra Findley and Elaine Hobby, in their essay "Seventeenth Century Women's Autobiography" (in *1642: Literature and Power in the Seventeenth Century* [University of Essex, 1981], 11–36), discuss as autobiographers five women born between 1620 and 1625: Anne Halkett, Mary Rich (Countess of Warwick), Ann Fanshawe, Margaret Cavendish, and Lucy Hutchinson. They include diaries and journals as autobiographical writing, and their major thematic concerns are the meaning of marriage and women's efforts to enter the domain of public life. More recently, Helen Wilcox, in her essay "Private Writing and Public Function: Autobiographical Texts by Renaissance Englishwomen" (in *Gloriana's Face: Women, Public and Private, in the English Renaissance*, ed. S.P. Cerasano and Marion Wynne-Davies [Detroit: Wayne State University Press, 1992], 47–62), also considers letters, diaries, and journals as autobiographical writings, and her subjects were all unpublished during their lifetimes. She discusses diaries and journals of Moulsworth's contemporaries Lady Margaret Hoby (1571–1633) and Grace Mildmay (1552–1620) and the later Lady Anne Clifford (1590–1676) and Dorothy Osborne (1627–95), as well as memoirs of Lady Anne Halkett (1622–99), Lady Elizabeth Delaval (1649–1717) and Lady Ann Fanshawe (1625–80).

Individual Women Writers

Julian of Norwich (1342–1416)

Lynn Staley Johnson, "The Trope of the Scribe and the Question of Literary Authorship in the Works of Julian of Norwich and

Margery Kempe," *Speculum* 66 (1991): 820–38, finds that Julian and Margery Kempe (see below) used their scribes as "means of maintaining control over the texts they profess neither to control nor to aspire to control" (820). Johnson analyzes Julian's narrative persona and representation of experience, comparing these elements in earlier short and later longer texts of her *Showings*. Elona K. Lucas, "Psychological and Spiritual Growth in Hadewijch and Julian of Norwich," *Studia Mystica* 9:3 (Fall 1986): 3–20, traces Julian's personal spiritual development through her mystical journey, with extensive quotes. For a theological (rather than autobiographical) notion of self, see Ritamary Bradley, "Perception of Self in Julian of Norwich's *Showings*," *Downside Review: A Quarterly of Catholic Thought* 104 (1986): 227–39.

Margery Kempe (1373–1439)

A current collection of essays on Margery Kempe and her *Book* (*Margery Kempe: A Book of Essays*, ed. Sandra J. McEntire [New York: Garland, 1992]) illustrates the continuing opportunity for scholars interested in the work as autobiography. Of twelve recently written essays, only two begin specifically to approach the way in which Kempe inscribes herself: Sandra McEntire, in "The Journey into Selfhood: Margery Kempe and Feminine Spirituality" (51–69), uses modern psychology for insight into the uniquely female experience of spirituality, making connections between Kempe's spiritual awakening and her discovery of herself and suggesting (implicitly) further analysis of how Kempe presents this self in writing. Eluned Bremner, in "Margery Kempe and the Critics" (117–35), applies principles of French feminism and deconstruction to analyze how Kempe achieves autonomy within a patriarchal discourse that strives to deny her sexual being.

Peter Dorsey, "Women's Autobiography and the Hermeneutics of Conversion," *a/b: Auto/Biographical Studies* 8 (1993): 72–90, also considers the problematical "relationship between the traditions of the spiritual autobiography and women's life-writing" (72), finally defending the conversion trope as a valid form of self-expression for the female subject. He sees in Kempe's *Book* a challenge to the patriarchy and grounds his own interpretation in the work of other critics. (Dorsey also discusses Anne Bradstreet's autobiographical poems, although she has been omitted from this chapter.)

M.K. Johnson's article, "'No Bananas, Giraffes, or Elephants': Margery Kempe's Text of Bliss," *Women's Studies* 21 (1992): 185–96, considers *The Booke of Margery Kempe* "the first autobiography in English" (185) and sets out to "dismantle the reading strategies that have marginalized Kempe's *Book*" while proposing new terms for reading Kempe (188). Essentially offering a feminist rereading of Kempe aimed at understanding how she interprets her world and "inscribes the female body into her text" (190), Johnson applies concepts from Roland Barthes and Hélène Cixous. In the same issue of *Women's Studies*, W. Harding analyzes allusions and representations of motherhood in Kempe's *Book* and the letters of Margaret Paston in an article entitled "Medieval Women's Unwritten Discourse of Motherhood: A Reading of Two Fifteenth-Century Texts." Noting that Kempe presents her maternal and wifely roles as subordinate to her spiritual concerns, Harding finds Kempe's "bodily communication ... disruptive and challenging" (207–8). Janel M. Mueller, in an essay entitled "Autobiography of a New 'Creatur': Female Spirituality, Selfhood, and Authorship in *The Book of Margery Kempe*" (in *Women in the Middle Ages and the Renaissance: Literary and Historical Perspectives*, ed. Mary Beth Rose [Syracuse: Syracuse University Press, 1986], 155–71), also characterizes Kempe's as "the first autobiography in English" (155) and as displaying a more specifically personal autobiographical design than Julian of Norwich's *Showings*. Mueller documents the self-justification in Kempe's *Book* that, she feels, differentiates it from other spiritual "autobiographies."

Karma Lochrie, in her article "*The Book of Margery Kempe*: The Marginal Woman's Quest for Literary Authority," *Journal of Medieval and Renaissance Studies* 16 (1986): 33–55, summarizes Kempe's narrative as a journey in search of justification as a mystic and literary authority as a writer. Lochrie specifically explores the meaning and effects of writing an autobiography, concluding with the sad irony that for the illiterate Kempe, the act of inscribing her life alienated her from her own life: "Kempe as an author becomes a cypher to herself" (55). However, Lynn Staley Johnson (see Julian of Norwich above) provides evidences that Kempe was "a self-conscious author" (833) in her uses of the scribe to situate herself in a literary community as well as to validate her own authority. Nancy Lenz Harvey, "Margery Kempe: Writer as Creature," *Philological Quarterly* 71 (1992): 173–84, shares this respect for Kempe as a writer, describing Kempe's self-conscious view of her written work as a manifestation of her ideas. Harvey analyzes Kempe's choice of vocabulary and incident, and speculates on possible influences.

Sidonie Smith (see Women's Autobiography above) devotes a chapter to the ways in which Kempe's autobiography simultaneously accepts the ideology of female subordination and challenges it by appropriating authority. In a more theoretical approach, Sarah Beckwith, in "Problems of Authority in Late Medieval English Mysticism: Language, Agency, and Authority in the *Book of Margery Kempe*" (*Exemplaria* 4:1 [March 1992]: 171–99), reads Kempe through the discourses of Mikhail Bakhtin and Marxist critics, attempting to resolve the inherent conflict between Kempe's spirituality, with its "essentialist version of selfhood" (178), and her dramatic self-production. Beckwith places this conflict within the larger late medieval anxiety over clerical authority and especially clerical control of language, giving this essay broad interest to adherents of many literary theories.

Finally, Dorothea Siegmund-Schultze, "Some Remarks on the *Book of Margery Kempe*," *Fifteenth Century Studies* 7 (1983): 329–44, places Kempe at the emergence of autobiography as a new genre. Siegmund-Schultze sees Kempe as a "mirror of her time" (331), and identifies many characteristics of Kempe's writing coincidentally shared by Moulsworth. Both seek social esteem through their husbands and fathers; both exhibit a bourgeois concern with money; and both show a strong sense of family ties.

Margaret Cavendish (1625–1674)

A Glorious Fame: The Life of Margaret Cavendish, Duchess of Newcastle, 1623–1673, by Kathleen Jones (London: Bloomsbury, 1988), is an excellent starting point for any reading of Cavendish's autobiographical writings. Inspired by and largely using Cavendish's own words, Jones chronicles Cavendish's life, looking for feminist impulses in her experiences and writings. She notes in Cavendish several themes also explored by Moulsworth, particularly education for women and concern for family heritage. For a thematic, rather than autobiographical parallel with Moulsworth, see Annette Kramer, "'Thus by the Musick of a Ladyes Tongue'": Margaret Cavendish's Dramatic Innovations in Women's Education," *Women's History Review* 2:1 [1993]: 57–80.

Catherine Gallagher, "Embracing the Absolute: the Politics of the Female Subject in Seventeenth Century England," *Genders* 1 (1988): 24–39, explores the contradiction between Cavendish's "proto-feminism" and her political conservatism in a socio-political analysis of Cavendish's self-constitutive writings, in particular *The Blazing World* and *Sociable Letters*, which Gallagher reads as self-constitutive works. Gallagher concludes that Cavendish's political absolutism ironically excluded her as a woman from any but the most subservient subject positions, making a fantasy of monarchy the only possible expression of her self-assertion. In contrast, Rachel Trubowitz, "The Reenchantment of Utopia and the Female Monarchical Self: Margaret Cavendish's *Blazing World*," *Tulsa Studies in Women's Literature* 11 (1992): 229–46, suggests that Cavendish's Utopia "is at once culturally subversive and politically nostalgic and, as such, uniquely accommodates her construction of female subject in imperial terms" (230). For a theoretical response to Gallagher's analysis of women writing from within the aristocracy, see Mary Ellen Lamb's essay on Lady Anne Clifford in "Others" below.

Sidonie Smith (see Female Autobiography above) includes a chapter on Cavendish's self-disclosure and desire for public recognition. James Fitzmaurice, "Fancy and Family: Self-Characterizations of Margaret Cavendish," *The Huntington Library Quarterly* 53 (1990): 198–209, defends Cavendish from adverse critics, contending that she consciously created three distinct personae to defend herself against social opposition to women's publishing. Fitzmaurice refers to Cavendish's letters and poems and quotes from contemporaries Bathsua Makin and Dorothy Osborne. In a more recent article, "Margaret Cavendish on Her Own Writing: Evidence from Revision and Handmade Correction," *Papers of the Bibliographical Society of America* 85:53 (1991): 297–398, Fitzmaurice finds self-constitutive elements in corrections Cavendish made to printed versions of her work. Using comparative textual criticism, Fitzmaurice concludes that these careful corrections belie Cavendish's pose as a harmless eccentric; indeed, her revised preface to *The Life of William Cavendish*, according to Fitzmaurice, characterizes her as a serious historian.

Moira Ferguson, in "A 'Wise, Wittie and Learned Lady': Margaret Lucas Cavendish," her introduction to the Cavendish section of *Women Writers of the Seventeenth Century* (ed. Katharina M. Wilson and Frank J. Warnke [Athens: University of Georgia Press, 1989]), calls Cavendish's preface "a late autobiographical sketch" (312). Ferguson gives both this preface and Cavendish's explicit autobiography, "A True Relation of My Birth, Breeding and Life," a feminist psychological reading, concluding that Cavendish was both "shy and eager to be noticed" (309) and thus explaining the contradictions in Cavendish's work. Excerpts from "A True Relation" in Ferguson's essay (not included in the selections that follow) deal with several dominant themes also found in Moulsworth's poem: family ties, paternal status, finances, education, and her husband.

Others

These women did not write autobiographies *per se*, but critics identify self-constitutive elements in their work. Their themes may be of interest to scholars seeking precursors or parallels for Moulsworth.

Katherine Parr, last wife of Henry VIII (1512–1548) wrote a conversion narrative, *Lamentation of a Sinner*, in 1545–46, which is discussed by Janel Mueller in "A Tudor Queen Finds Voice: Katherine Parr's *Lamentation of a Sinner*," *The Historical Renaissance: New Essays on Tudor and Stuart Literature and Culture*, ed. Heather Dubrow and Richard Strier (Chicago: University of Chicago Press, 1988): 15–47. Examining Parr's possible literary models for the source of her subjectivity and authority, Mueller finds that Parr intentionally feminized her voice to demonstrate that gender can be accommodated within Protestantism (35). In the opening section of Parr's *Lamentation*, dealing with her conversion experience, she successfully presents herself as a universalized subject (25).

Dorothy Leigh, "The Mother's Blessing" (1616) and **Elizabeth Joceline, "The Mother's Legacie to her Vnborn Child" (1624)** are discussed by Christine Sizemore in "Attitudes Toward the Education and Roles of Women: Sixteenth-Century Humanists and Seventeenth-Century Advice Books," *University of Dayton Review* 15:1 (Spring 1981): 57–67. Both women wrote conventional advice books, Leigh's addressed to her three nearly-grown sons and Joceline's to her husband as she anticipates her possible death in childbirth. Sizemore provides biographical and historical background information for both authors and genre, with generous excerpts to support her claim that "the two women also indicate their individual personality and experience" (65). Her emphasis is on women's education and social roles.

Lady Anne Clifford (1590–1676). Discussing self-representation in Lady Anne Clifford's diaries, Mary Ellen Lamb, in "The Agency of the Split Subject" (*ELR* 22 [1992]: 347–68), contends that Clifford managed to reconcile contradictions between her socio-political position and her sex, "interpellating herself into a dominant, rather than a subordinate, subject position in her culture" (349). Clifford is also discussed by Helen Wilcox (see Critical Work above). Like Lamb, Wilcox observes that Clifford conflated her public and private functions in her efforts to gain control of her father's lands and ancestral home.

Elizabeth Egerton (1626–63), the step-daughter of Margaret Cavendish, left a collection of journalistic writings probably written between 1648 and 1663. In "'His wife's prayers and meditations': MS Egerton 607," *The Renaissance Englishwoman in Print: Counterbalancing the Canon* (ed. Anne M. Haselkorn and Betty S. Travitsky [Amherst: University of Massachusetts Press, 1990], 241–60), Betty Travitsky calls Egerton's writings, "akin to autobiography" (246). She finds in Egerton's writing the same pattern of defining self through relationships that we see in Moulsworth and other female autobiographers.

Gender Issues:
Education, the Muses, and Widowhood

"The Muses Females Are":
Renaissance Women and Education

John T. Shawcross

An exciting outcome of the woman's movement of the last two decades has been the discovery of women authors of the past. Aside from a few women writers before the Romantic period in literature began, women were not represented in anthologies or college courses or encyclopedias of literature. Names were not even known, let alone writing available. Male domination of literary history not only ignored women, looking backward, but had even contemporaneously in earlier periods, like the English Renaissance, suppressed publication and records of their existence. I do not imply on purpose, but because women just didn't matter. Of course, contributory to such a state of affairs have been the continuing social stratifications which still cannot believe that a noncollege-educated person could have written the plays ascribed to William Shakespeare. The author had to have been one of the aristocracy, an Oxford or Cambridge man, according to the socially prejudiced. Such a caste system placed even women of higher social rank in inferior positions as far as things like seriousness in writing or competency in nonephemeral art were concerned. However, more than simply rediscovering women writers, attention should be paid their writing and its content within the full range of all literature.

The discovery and publication of Martha Moulsworth's "Memorandum," dating in 1632, is another significant piece of evidence of the preceding. Salient points which I pursue here, already remarked on by Robert C. Evans and Barbara Wiedemann in their commentaries on the poem, are the education afforded this woman and attitudes toward it, and gendered relationships of writing persisting in many people's minds, even today in arguments about cross-gender writing.[1] What writing, if any, women were expected (allowed?) to engage in fell under general rubrics of domestic matters, letters, diaries or other personal statements, translations, and pleasant poetry, and the education which some might experience, therefore, produced literacy, a knowledge of foreign languages, and domestically useful knowledge (like needlework). In a catalogue of Basic Books for Women, 1475–1640, Suzanne W. Hull[2] lists (in addition to a few items like Aemilia Lanyer's *Salve deus rex Judaeorum*) prayerbooks for women, cookbooks, medical advice and cures, gardening advice (often by men, of course), and such as Barnabe Rich's *The excellency of good women. The honour and estimation that belongeth unto them. The infallible markes whereby to know them* (1613), a treatise on women's good and bad qualities. But it is clear that it as well as other works in praise of women like William Heale's *An Apologie for Women* (1609)—later called *The Great Advocate and Orator for Women*—are built on stereotypes aided by the influence of the Theophrastan character such as "Sir Thomas Overbury's" *The Good Wife*, as Rosemary Masek has pointed out.[3] The gender categorizations seem ubiquitous and even today unending. A work like Daniel Tuvill's *Asylum Veneris, or A Sanctuary for Ladies* (London: Printed by Edward Griffin, 1616), which argues that women should have the same access to learning as men, is indeed rare.

Aside from the unfounded masculine/feminine dichotomy that this supports, such categorizing has delimited the reading of women's writing in various ways, by both men and women. Mary Sidney Herbert, the Countess of Pembroke, has almost always been relegated to mere translator of the psalms or of Phillipe de Mornay or Robert Garnier. Women—allegedly having an aptitude for language—could be taught foreign languages and could thus be the conduit to bring the ideas and writing achievements of men from other countries to the English-speaking world. In the case of the psalms, as I have noted elsewhere,[4] the Countess is not merely

---

[1]Compare the series of essays in *Cross-Gender Writing*, ed. John T. Shawcross, a special issue of *The CEA Critic* 56 (1993).

[2]In *Chaste, Silent & Obedient* (San Marino: Huntington Library, 1982).

[3]"Women in an Age of Transition: 1485–1719," *The Women of England From Anglo-Saxon Times to the Present*, ed. Barbara Kanner (Hamden: Archon Books, 1979).

[4]See "The Authority of the Writer" forthcoming in *LIT Literature Interpretation Theory*. The Psalm is quoted from J.C.A. Rathmell's edition (New

making the psalms available to an English-speaking public in yet another version; she is interpreting them in literary forms to be judged not only on the divine and moral precepts made more meaningful and pertinent to a God-fearing people, but on their literary achievements. Psalm C, *Jubilate Deo*, for instance, is cast as a sonnet, with a rhyme scheme of abab bcbc cdcd ee. The Petrarchan octave sets forth God's creation of and benevolence toward humankind, which should be acknowledged by song (praise). The sestet admonishes that he should be hymned for his eternal mercy and truth. Implication is that such praise is just. Repetition emphasizes: "We are his flock," "We are his folk"; chiasmus implies the Christ: "All good, all grace ... He of all grace and goodnesse is the spring." Its comparison with the King James version makes clear how the psalm has been developed into a satisfying poem, not simply a translation. Compare "Enter into his gates with thanksgiving, and into his courts with praise" and "With thankfullnesse O enter then his gate: / Make through each porch of his your praises ring." The Countess's "each porch" plays upon the image George Herbert was to employ in *The Temple* prior to entry into the Church, but even more literarily significant, it plays upon the porch of the ear through which these sung praises will ring. Her final couplet, "Tyme in noe termes his mercy comprehends, / From age to age his truth it self extends" is poetic worlds beyond "His mercy is everlasting, and his truth endureth to all generations." We can appreciate John Donne's allusion to her as Moses's sister Miriam in his poem on the Sidneys' psalm translations, for he refers to Exodus 15:21 where the Song of Miriam is quoted: "Sing ye to the Lord, for he hath triumphed gloriously: the horse and his rider hath he thrown into the sea." The Countess's psalm translations (and her adjustments of what probably were her brother Philip's early attempts[5]) deserve to be read and evaluated as poetry, which reading not even women critics searching for Renaissance women's achievements have generally discerned. Too

York: New York University Press, 1963). *The Tragedie of Antonie* is the 1595 London edition.

    [5]Compare the textual study by Noel Kinnamon and his conclusions as to the Countess's return to the Hebrew text for correction and clarification and her relationship with texts of the earlier psalms assigned to Philip— "The Sidney Psalms: The Penshurst and Tixell Manuscripts," *English Manuscript Studies* 2 (1990): 139–61. See also Sallye Sheppeard's discussion of the Countess's poetic achievement in "On the Art of Renaissance Translation: Mary Herbert's Psalm 130," *Texas College English* 18 (1985): 1–3.

frequently women's "translations" are viewed as *not* providing "a voice more her own."

For another instance, we should remark that the Countess's "translation" of Garnier's *The Tragedy of Antonie* likewise presents lyrics separable from the full drama, like that on death in five stanzas:

> Alas, with what tormenting fire
> Us martyreth this blind desire
> To stay our life from flying!
> How ceaselessly our minds doth rack,
> How heavy lies upon our back,
> This dastard fear of dying!

Or the conclusion to the third act where the chorus of Egyptian soldiers comments on Antony's suicide:

> How abject him, how base! think I,
> Who, wanting courage, cannot die
> When need him thereto calleth;
> From whom the dagger, drawn to kill
> The cureless griefs that vex him still,
> For fear and faintness falleth.

Must we point out the attention to English prosody and rhyming, the effective alliteration and the weak catalectic syllables limping off when death prevails?

For the most part women of the period avoided publication[6] and a woman who did publish was seen as "rediculous" or as a "hermaphrodite in show, in deed a monster."[7] One who allowed her work to appear—and to early and current acclaim—was Anne Bradstreet, the American poet, whose dates are ca. 1612 through 1672. Born in England as Anne Dudley, she migrated to the Colonies with her recently married husband, Simon Bradstreet, in

---

[6] See Margaret J.M. Ezell, *The Patriarch's Wife: Literary Evidence and the History of the Family* (Chapel Hill: University of North Carolina Press, 1987), 64–83.

[7] See James Fitzmaurice, "Fancy and the Family: Self-Characterizations of Margaret Cavendish," *Huntington Library Quarterly* 53 (1990): 198–209. He is quoting Dorothy Osborne on Margaret Cavendish, Duchess of Newcastle—*Letters from Dorothy Osborne to Sir William Temple*, ed. G.C. Moore Smith (Oxford: Oxford University Press, 1928), 37. For Edward Denny, Baron of Waltham's remark on Lady Mary Wroth, see Josephine A. Roberts' edition of *The Poems of Lady Mary Wroth* (Baton Rouge: Louisiana State University Press, 1983), 33–34.

1630, joining others of the early religiously disaffected. Hers was the first volume of American poetry published, being *The Tenth Muse Lately Sprung Up in America*, printed in London in 1650.[8] A new and expanded edition, called *Several Poems Compiled with Great Variety of Wit and Learning*, was published in 1678 in London by her nephew John Rogers. The male creation of literary canon and the effect of the caste system can be seen in the dismissal of her that Moses Coit Tyler penned in *A History of American Literature During the Colonial Period 1607–1765* (New York: G.P. Putnam's, 1898), I, 292. Alongside his cogent remarks on male Colonial writers, Tyler tells us that Bradstreet was "sadly misguided by the poetic standards of her religious sect and of her literary period." He thus plainly ignores the verse that has been particularly admired by women critics today, the personal poems, and joins them in reading the poems which reflect a study of English and French male authors of the later Renaissance period as mere imitations and unhappy apprentice work. But Bradstreet has not been accorded her due, just as the Countess of Pembroke has not, by some critics who stress only a feminine ideological agenda, not the literary achievement. A case in point is Adrienne Rich's preface to Jeannine Hensley's edition.[9] Rich's concentration on certain poems only and her apparent ignorance of a full panoply of female and male authors lies behind her remark, "Until Edward Taylor, in the second half of the century, these were the only poems of more than historical interest to be written in the New World. Anne Bradstreet was the first non-didactic American poet, the first to give an embodiment to American nature, the first in whom personal intention appears to precede Puritan dogma as an impulse to verse." All those "firsts" are questionable; but more noticeable is the diametric view of her evaluation to that of Tyler, who saw only the dogma as impulse. Bradstreet should be considered as "poet" (not just "woman poet") with evaluation alongside her male colleagues—an evaluation which will place her very high among them. A contemporary view of the work of Margaret Cavendish, Duchess of Newcastle, by a feminist significantly remarked that she "by her own Genius, rather than any timely Instruction over-tops many grave 'Gown-

---

[8]The first *American* publication by an American poet was Philip Pain's *Daily Meditations: Or, Quotidian Preparations for, and Considerations of Death and Eternity* (Cambridge, MA: 1668).

[9]*The Works of Anne Bradstreet*, ed. Jeannine Hensley (Cambridge, MA: Belknap Press of Harvard University Press, 1967).

Men.'"[10] All Bradstreet's poems should be given the meaningful scrutiny that some of them have been given, not dismissed because they do not fit the circumspect attitudes of either female or male critics.[11]

At times polemics dominate Renaissance women's writing, as in Lanyer's important preamble to her poetic collection or in direct attack like 'Esther Sowernam's' *Ester hath hang'd Haman* (1617) or the also pseudonymous *Jane Anger her protection for women. To defend them against the scandalous reportes of a late surfeiting lover, and all other like venerians that complaine so to bee overcloyed with womens kindnesse* (1589). In a talk in September 1990, "Looking for the Female Debater," Ann R. Jones discussed the debate-training accessible to women, rhetorical handbooks, and rhetorical virtuosity. One of the best examples of successful polemical writing by a woman, and employing the (unfortunately necessary) strategy of masquerade, is Bathsua Makin's *An Essay to Revive the Antient Education of Gentlewomen* (London, 1673), although written somewhat earlier.[12] Makin uses the ploy of masquerade to enable the controlling male populace to read the book's arguments and thereby accept their cogency. Were the author to be recognized as a woman, men would undoubtedly simply have dismissed it. Makin lies directly and says, "I would not suggest a thing prejudicial to our Sex"—except that in reality she isn't lying because she means the female sex though the male reader be duped. Her 'essay' stresses acquisition of mathematics and foreign languages and more by women:

---

[10]Bathsua Makin in *An Essay* discussed below.

[11]See my *Intentionality and the New Traditionalism: Some Liminal Means to Literary Revisionism* (University Park: Pennsylvania State University Press, 1991), 198–200, for a brief literary discussion of three poems by Bradstreet. Robert D. Arner has remarked, "She is a far richer writer than has yet been acknowledged even in the best studies about her"—*American Writers Before 1800: A Biographical and Critical Dictionary*, ed. James A. Levernier and Douglas R. Wilmes (Westport: Greenwood Press, 1983), I, 192.

[12]Confusions in the identity of Bathsua Reginald (rather than Pell) Makin are clarified by Jean R. Brink in "Bathsua Reginald Makin: 'Most Learned Matron,'" *Huntington Library Quarterly* 54 (1991): 313–26. See also the important statements by Frances Teague, "New Light on Bathsua Makin," *Seventeenth-Century News* 49 (1986): 16, and "Bathsua Makin: Woman of Learning," *Women Writers of the Seventeenth Century*, ed. Katharina M. Wilson and Frank J. Warnke (Athens: University of Georgia Press, 1989), 285–88.

I would not deny them the knowledge of grammar and rhetoric, because they dispose to speak handsomely. Logic must be allowed, because it is the key to all sciences. Physic, especially visibles, as herbs, plants, shrubs, drugs, etc., must be studied because this will exceedingly please themselves, and fit them to be helpful to others. The tongues ought to be studied, especially the Greek and Hebrew: these will enable to the better understanding of the Scriptures.

The mathematics, more especially geography will be useful: this puts life into history. Music, painting, poetry, etc., are a great ornament and pleasure. Some things that are more practical are not so material, because public employments in the field and courts are usually denied to women. Yet some have not been inferior to many men even in these things also.

Makin, as a man, confutes the naysayers before they speak: "We cannot be so stupid as to imagine that God gives ladies great estates merely that they may eat, drink, sleep, and rise up to play" (which as any reader of the Bible should know means to have sexual intercourse lustfully). The objection that no persons will marry educated daughters is answered by three refutations; that "Women do not desire learning" is rejoined by "neither do many boys" and "Women are of low parts" by "So are many men." Makin had been governess to Charles I's children in the 1630s and 40s, and began a school for women in the 50s, and out of these experiences come her principles for education.

Makin's remarks reflect the gender ideology related to social class that Tina Krontiris has discussed,[13] and women's "office" in public and private matters, based generally on custom and ideology, that is examined in a collection of recent essays.[14] Makin's course of study for women greatly broadens what women of the aristocracy and certainly the middle class engaged: it goes well beyond woman's "sweet attractive grace" in such things as poetry and makes inroads on man's "contemplation" (words employed by Milton to epitomize a contrast between the genders). Yet perhaps because the anticipated audience is male, there is a gendered drawing back in "allowed," in "physic" being of "visibles," in

---

[13]Tina Krontiris, *Oppositional Voices: Women as Writers and Translators of Literature in the English Renaissance* (London: Routledge, 1992).

[14]S.P. Cerasano and Marion Wynne-Davies, eds., *Gloriana's Face: Women, Public and Private, in the English Renaissance* (Detroit: Wayne State University Press, 1992).

artistic "ornament and pleasure," and in the general denial of "public employments."

The information in Martha Moulsworth's poem "Memorandum" places her within the world implied above that a seventeenth-century middle class woman might experience. Her father was apparently a clergyman, a doctor of divinity, one of good but middle social status. Her education seems to have been that which might be expected for a female child of an educated man of "godlie pietie" (l. 27), private instruction since the "Two Vniuersities we haue" are only "of men" (l. 32), and pervasive knowledge of the Bible. This education was "Beyond my sex & kind," that is, beyond what was usual for a woman then. She learned Latin,[15] though her lack of its use in intervening years lost its facility; yet that matters little for "Lattin is nott the most marketable mariadge mettall" (marginal note to l. 38). As she says, "Had I no other portion to my dowre / I might have stood a virgin to this houre," a situation that women today still encounter or believe they encounter. With Moulsworth's third husband, who apparently had some public influence and connections, she held strong domestic "office" both in exercising her "will in house" and the "purse in Store."

We today who espouse equality of the sexes are gratified to read in this poem the lament over the lack of a university "of women," but we might question the continued genderfication Moulsworth expresses in "then / O then thatt would in witt, and tongs surpasse / All art of men thatt is, or euer was" (ll. 34–36). We also might question the satisfaction she finds in her private "office" *only*: "I had my will in house, in purse in Store / whatt would a women old or yong haue more?" (ll. 67–68). Perhaps an epitome of this continued genderfication and satisfaction with what purports to be woman's lot is seen in Moulsworth's "the muses ffemalls are

---

[15]I might note, despite the antagonism of some twentieth-century commentators on John Milton because of prejudice against his inferred religious ideas and his political positions, that he made sure that two of his daughters were literate in reading and writing and that he taught them foreign languages (at least Latin) and that all three daughters were instructed in sewing (the trade of making gold and silver lace, particularly), enabling them to earn their own livings, if need be, as it seems to have been for all three, who left his home before 1670. Rather than condemning him as some kind of tyrannic father figure forcing them to learn, such commentators should have commended him for his actions. (The oldest daughter, Anne, was mentally slow and lame, the possible physical cause being uncertain although speculations have been advanced.)

/ and therfore of Vs ffemales take some care" (ll. 31–32). The nine
Muses, we remember, were the daughters of Mnemosyne (memory) and Zeus, but though they performed at festivals usually under the leadership of Apollo (the god of music and poetry), they
did not produce myths themselves or any with themselves as foci.
Rather they brought humanizing qualities to males, inspiration for
poetry, and divine wisdom. A female university might create a superior group of women who might surpass the art of men in wit
(knowledge) and tongues (language), as Moulsworth notes, for
they are "muses," that is, poets, in the most obvious meaning of
the statement. But the statement also thus maintains a gender-divi-
sioning we too often hear even today. The statement, less obviously and probably not intended by the author, places women as
"muses" who, in their inspiration of men or lack thereof, must be
courted or flattered ("of Vs ffemales take some care"; l. 32). Is there
a threat in that last phrase? Is it pointing out that women are necessary to men for their seemingly own achievements? The lines insufficiently advance a collaboration of female and male than
would be more modernly desired.

　　We cannot expect a seventeenth-century person, female or
male, to have the concepts of sexual equality that some of us today
believe in (but only a relatively few "some"), yet it should be remarked that Moulsworth maintains the division of "offices" and
the Pauline injunction of husband and wife.[16] The education which
she tells us she experienced or demonstrates has some similarities
to the suggestions for Makin's "Education of Gentlewomen": literacy, language acquisition, poetic achievement, certain kinds of
knowledge. It is a big step in the right direction, but it is channeled
through a sexually divided marital world, a class-stratified world,
and a world in which gendering of activities of the mind prevails.
The transitional state of change in gender-thinking is very important, here in the seventeenth century, and it is led primarily,
though not exclusively, by women; yet maintained are certain ideological positions, often the result of religious indoctrination (with
its biblical underpinnings) and of marital status and sexual attitudes. These are matters we literary students should remember in

---

[16]Ephesians 5:22–24: "Wives, submit yourselves unto your own husbands, as unto the Lord. / For the husband is the head of the wife, even as
Christ is the head of the church: and he is the savior of the body. / Therefore as the church is subject unto Christ, so let the wives be to their own
husbands in every thing."

reviewing the work of such people as Edmund Spenser, the Duchess of Newcastle, John Milton, and Katherine Philips.

Makin, in an elegy for Lady Elizabeth Langham in 1664, reflects this same world that Moulsworth reveals for the woman of seventeenth-century England:

> ... So good in all relations, so sweet
> A daughter, such a loving wife, discreet
> A mother; though not hers, not partial
> She loved, as if they had been natural.
> To th'Earl and Ladies she a sister rare,
> A friend, where she professed, beyond compare.
> ... and her studies meant
> To share some for her languages, which she
> In Latin, French, Italian happily
> Advanced in with pleasure; what do I
> Recount her parts? her memory speaks more
> Than what can be, or hath been said before:
> It asks a volume, rather than a verse ...[17]

(The second and third lines above refer to her step-children.) The elegy is an apostrophe to a woman—really any woman—of accomplishment whose "new Transcendent Name, to th'world unknowne" is "Not writ in marble, but the saint's white stone." Reference is to Revelation 2:17: "To him that overcometh will I give to eat of the hidden manna, and will give him a white stone, and in the stone a new name written, which no man knoweth saving he that receiveth it." It is the same text that Bradstreet alludes to in the last lines of "Contemplations": "But he whose name is grav'd in the white stone / Shall last and shine when all of these are gone." Though woman—Langham, Bradstreet, Moulsworth—may not be known to the world at large, she is known to God and is rewarded by God. Her name may not be written in much-prized marble, seemingly unaffected by time, with its impurities seen in its mottling, but it is recorded in the pure white stone of ordinary life, transcending saint-like to the only audience of significance, God.

---

[17]"Upon the much lamented death of the Right Honourable, the Lady Elizabeth Langham," Huntington Library, Hastings Collection, MS HA 8799.

Early Modern Women
and "the muses ffemall"
Frances Teague

The silence of early modern women has been broken by the recovery of such non-aristocratic writers as Martha Dorsett Moulsworth, Bathsua Reginolles Makin, or Aemelia Bassano Lanyer.[1] That list includes only three Englishwomen who studied languages, wrote their ideas down, and saw them turned into print; others exist as well. Yet despite the recovery of such writers, a puzzle remains. While women *could* learn, write, even publish, most who were capable of such pursuits did not even consider doing so, while those few who did felt sufficiently uncomfortable that they sought out other learned women to form networks of support.

One obvious reason both for women's general reluctance to be identified as female authors and for their perception that they needed support is the culture's dismissal, even disapproval of such activity. I want to examine one manifestation of such disapproval, namely, an expressed fear of female intercourse with the muses. In classical mythology, the nine muses who inspired and aided artists were female: Calliope, muse of epic poetry; Clio, of history; Erato,

---

[1]For accounts of these writers, see Martha Moulsworth, *"My Name Was Martha": A Renaissance Woman's Autobiographical Poem,* eds. Robert C. Evans and Barbara Wiedemann (West Cornwall, CT: Locust Hill Press, 1993); Jean Brink, "Bathsua Reginald Makin: 'Most Learned Matron,'" *Huntington Library Quarterly* 54 (1991): 215–28; Frances Teague, "The Identity of Bathsua Makin," *Biography* 16 (1993): 1–17; Barbara K. Lewalski, "Of God and Good Women: The Poems of Aemilia Lanyer," in *Silent But for the Word,* ed. Margaret Hannay (Kent: Kent State University Press, 1985). Scholars have neglected such writers more than they have aristocratic women writers. The latter's social rank has meant their inclusion in literary history, although they have too often been regarded as patrons and poetesses, rather than as writers who deserve serious consideration.

of love poetry; Euterpe, of lyric poetry; Melpomene, of tragedy; Thalia, of comedy; Polyhymnia, of sacred poetry; Terpsichore, of choral song and dance; Urania, of astronomy. An extension of this myth often identified poetry as female as well. But at least two different accounts existed about what happened when a woman writer sought out the muses.

Martha Moulsworth makes the statement that "the muses ffemalls are" (l. 31) in defending her own ability to write and her exercise of that skill in crafting her autobiographical poem. Speaking of the way that her father allegedly educated her, she says:

> ... Beyond my sex & kind
> he did wth learninge Lattin decke [my] mind
> And whie nott so? the muses ffemalls are
> and therfore of Vs ffemales take some care
>   (ll. 29–31)

Clearly she sees the female nature of these muses as providing her with a justification: if poetry has traditionally been associated with women, she seems to ask, why may she not share in that association by writing herself? To extend the metaphoric identification, she implicitly regards herself in a sustaining relationship with the muses. She and they share common interests and pursuits, and this commonality is, in turn, her authorization for writing. As a consequence, she argues, the muses "take some care" of women who seek learning because of that shared sexual identification. Later in the poem she speaks of how she gave up her Latin, which "is nott the most marketable mariadge mettall" (margin, l. 38), when she gave up her virgin state to marry. Although "the virgin Muses I loue well," she tells the reader, she "Bid virgin life ffarewell" (ll. 41–42) and with her marriage gave up any claim to the muses' support for her learning. Moulsworth, then, imagines the muses as chaste and learned women who provide support to virgins who emulate them.

One might make a very different analysis of a woman writer's relation to the muses. In an influential feminist anthology published in 1974, Louise Bernikow provided such an analysis, grounding it in an implicit critique of the psychologist Erich Neumann:

> A woman ... learn[s] that poetry is a woman, either historically or metaphorically. What is she to make of this information? If poetry is a woman, why is every woman not a natural poet? Or is she? If a woman becomes more sophisticated

in her study of such matters, she will turn to Eric [*sic*] Neumann and learn that the combination of male poet and female muse symbolizes the erotic aspect of the creative act.
She will find that interesting, and then she will begin to wish
to apply that information to herself. She will find it difficult.

Do women poets see themselves in homosexual relationship to the muse? Can women poets see themselves in any
relationship to the muse? Does the figure become maternal
and the relationship of poet to muse fit any analysis yet
made by anyone? It is not hard to speculate that if a woman
sticks with Neumann's analysis and applies it to herself, the
psychic conflict caused by that vision might lead her to elim-
inate the erotic completely. Alternatively, she might identify
with the male poet and end up perceiving the muse-poet relationship, like everything else, through the grid of male
sensibility.[2]

Bernikow's analysis makes it clear that centuries after Moulsworth
and her contemporaries tried to justify their writing, questions
about the appropriateness of women's writing remain. Her speculation that one might interpret the relation between a woman
writer and the muse as potentially lesbian is, in fact, precisely what
some of Martha Moulsworth's contemporaries did see. The relationship that Moulsworth suggests—one of sustaining companion-
ship among and nurturing models for women—becomes one that
other early modern writers regard as sexually ambiguous and con-
temptible. Thus Ben Jonson rebukes Cecily Bulstrode, whom he
names as the Court Pucell, for her writing by making the sexual
nature of the writer's relationship to the muse explicit:

> What though with tribade lust she force a muse,
> And in an epicoene fury can write news
> Equal with that, which for the best news goes,
> As airy light, and as like wit as those?[3]

"Tribade" means "lesbian."[4] Jonson condemns this woman poet
who writes, he thinks, inappropriately and impertinently about

---

[2]Louise Bernikow, "Introduction," *The World Split Open: Four Centuries
of Women Poets in England and America, 1552–1950* (New York: Vintage,
1974), 18.

[3]Quotations of Jonson's work are taken from *Ben Jonson: The Complete
Poems*, ed. George Parfitt (New Haven: Yale University Press, 1982).

[4]The word "tribade" is rare. Jonson uses it on one other occasion, in
poem 10 of *Forrest*. In the poem he also associates the epithet with classical
deities upon whose sexuality he casts doubt: after rejecting as his "active

him. That condemnation is explicitly of her sexuality: she is a "pu-cell" or whore, she is "epicoene," she is a lesbian rapist who forces the muse of poetry in "tribade lust." The imagery is singularly ugly. It is not, alas, unique.

Thus when Edward Denny, Baron of Waltham, objected to Lady Mary Wroth's *Urania*, he wrote a poem assailing her as "Hermaphrodite in show, in deed a monster, / As by thy words and works all men may conster ...."[5] Wroth's publication of her words, the work that she has made from language, allows all men to "conster" or understand her true nature: she is monstrous, a hermaphrodite. And in the anthology *Kissing the Rod*, Germaine Greer comments on how frequently seventeenth-century women who write are assailed as sexually immoral; indeed, she calls those booksellers who encouraged women writers "pimps."[6] Those who are hostile toward women of learning associate the muse of poetry with ambiguous gender identity. A woman who invokes the muse is, at best, a slut, and at worst, a lesbian rapist.

One final example shows a woman writer acknowledging this negative formulation of the myth. In "Upon the Saying that My Verses Were Made by Another," Anne Killigrew implicitly recognizes the potentially lesbian relationship that she has with the muse even as she insists upon her heterosexuality. The poem begins with a prayer:

> Next Heaven, my Vows to thee, (O Sacred *Muse!*)
> I offer'd up, nor didst thou them refuse.
>   O Queen of Verse, said I, if thou'lt inspire
> And warm my Soul with thy Poetique Fire,
> No Love of Gold shall share with thee my Heart,
> Or yet Ambition in my Brest have Part,
> More Rich, more Noble I will ever hold
> The *Muses* Laurel, than a Crown of Gold.

---

muse" the goddess Pallas Athena, whom he calls a "mankind maid," he rejects "light Venus" and her "tribade trine," i.e., the three Graces. Jonson clearly associates the female muse with women of uncertain gender orientation.

[5]The poem is quoted in *The Poems of Lady Mary Wroth*, ed. Josephine A. Roberts (Baton Rouge: Louisiana State University Press, 1983), 32–33.

[6]Germaine Greer, "Introduction," *Kissing the Rod: An Anthology of Seventeenth-Century Women's Verse*, eds. Germaine Greer, Susan Hastings, Jeslyn Medoff, and Melinda Sansone (New York: Farrar Straus Giroux, 1989) offers a discussion of the sort of attacks on their sexuality that women writers faced (see esp. 20–30).

An Undivided Sacrifice I'le lay
Upon thine Altar, Soul and Body pay;
Thou shalt my Pleasure, my Employment be,
My All I'le make a Holocaust to thee.[7]

The language is sensual. To receive "Poetique Fire," the speaker will offer up not simply her heart, but even her body and soul, laying these on the muses' altar. Burning her all in a Holocaust, she will have as her pleasure only the muses. Such language hints at precisely the sort of homoerotic construction that Jonson had made explicit in his poem. In the next stanza, the speaker comments on what happens when the muse granted her prayer: "pleasing Raptures fill'd my Ravisht Sense," she sought out the beauty of Apollo's Daphne, and she was as filled with "Rapture and Delight" as those struck by Cupid's arrows. Clearly the speaker is in love with the Muse, and her language is erotically charged as a consequence of her passion.

Yet subsequent stanzas suggest that she regards the eroticism of her language as a mistake. The speaker is shocked when publication leads her not to "Honour, [but] brought me shame!" Readers claim her verse is written by others and rip away her plumes and laurels. Humiliated, she turns for support to the memory of Orinda, "her Sexes Grace," arguing that Orinda was not sexually attractive to anyone, save through her transforming poetry. The last stanza identifies the speaker as "a Maide" (i.e., virgin) who still seeks to be "Divinely Inspired and possest"; now she seeks such union not with a female muse (as in ll. 1 or 3), but rather with Phebus, i.e., with Apollo who had ravished Daphne, that nymph whom the persona had previously found attractive (l. 61). The myth of union with the muse must be radically altered if Killigrew is to make use of it; her muse must be masculine, not the "Queen of Verse."

Yet Moulsworth's formulation of the myth—that the muses aid and can be identified with learned women—is not unique. When Anne Bradstreet's poetry was published she was identified as "The Tenth Muse Newly Sprung Up in America," hardly a title to be used if it implied anything negative. And in a remarkable work, *An Essay to Revive the Ancient Education of Gentlewomen in Religion, Manners, Arts & Tongues, with an Answer to the Objections against This Way of Education* (London, 1673), Bathsua Reginolles Makin

---

[7]See Greer, et al., eds., *Kissing the Rod*, 303–5.

uses a version of the myth similar to Moulsworth's. Makin argues that

> We may infer from the stories of the muses that this way of education [i.e., educating women] was very ancient. All conclude the heroes were men, famous in their generation, therefore canonized after their deaths. We may, with like reason, conclude Minerva and the nine muses were women famous for learning whilst they lived and therefore thus adored when dead.
>
> ...
>
> It may now be demanded, by those studious of antiquity, why the virtues, the disciplines, the nine muses (the devisers and patrons of all good arts), the three graces should rather be represented under the feminine sex, and their pictures be drawn to the portraitures of damsels and not have masculine denominations and the effigies of men?[8]

As do Moulsworth and Bradstreet, Makin identifies the muses as female figures sympathetic to learned women and models for such women to follow. Such references to the muses as we find in work by Moulsworth, Makin, or Bradstreet suggest that a second version of the myth was available for women who chose to write in the early modern period. The muse might be seen as the poet's lovers and the relationship between a woman and the muse as homoerotic, threatening, and shameful. But an alternate version existed in which women, divine and mortal, came together in mutuality to enjoy models for accomplishment and support for education.

Such networks of friendship and support are, of course, quite common among women in western culture. The traces of such networks survive in the correspondence learned women left and in their frequent allusions to one another in their own work. We know, for example, that all the women mentioned in this essay were participants to some extent in supportive relationships with other women.

In her essay, Makin catalogues virtually every learned woman of her day (including several she taught), she maintained a correspondence with Anna Maria von Schurman in Utrecht, and she established a school for girls when she was in her seventies. Lanyer consistently dedicates her work to aristocratic women and speaks of the Duchess of Kent as the woman who trained and guided her. Elegies on Bulstrode (including one in her praise by Jonson, who

---

[8]Makin, Wing, M309, n.p.

had not intended his vicious attack to be published) make it clear that she was regarded as an important figure among the gentle-women at court, one who led others in intellectual games. Lady Mary Wroth's model was, of course, her aunt, Mary Sidney, the Countess of Pembroke; and at court Wroth was associated with a number of women who themselves wrote and who patronized male authors. Killigrew, who alludes to Orinda (Katherine Phillips) as a model in literary pursuits, served as a Maid of Honour to Mary of Modena together with her friend and fellow poet, Anne Kingsmill, the Countess of Winchelsea. Cut off from other women writers, Anne Bradstreet nevertheless read and wrote of great women like Semiramis and Queen Elizabeth I. The editors of *Kissing the Rod* note possible allusions in Bradstreet's work to the Countess of Pembroke and Dorothy Leigh and comment on a personal connection to the writer Elizabeth Knyvet. For each of these women writers, then, a network of women who provide guidance and support is important. The only one who mentions no such network is Martha Moulsworth, the woman who left the muses behind when she wed, and only returned to poetry when she was alone after her third husband's death. For her, marriage displaced poetry and the female muses; others in her culture clearly feared that the process would work in reverse and that a relationship with the muse would displace marriage and men. To write was sexually suspect, for to write was to find support from women, not men.

Educating Women and the Lower Orders

Jean R. Brink

In 1543 an act passed the English parliament prohibiting bible-reading to all women except gentlewomen and to the lower orders of both genders—groups (as Sir Geoffrey Elton has since observed) "too ill-instructed and volatile to be allowed to read such heady stuff."[1] The men who wrote this act appear to have linked class and gender; biology and social status were perceived as establishing intellectual and educational boundaries. Attitudes such as these became complicated during the long reign of Elizabeth Tudor (1558–1603), a queen whose reputation for learning was celebrated in tribute after tribute. Roger Ascham, her tutor and author of *The Schoolmaster*, for example, uses her fluency in Greek and Latin to illustrate the efficacy of his double translation method of teaching languages:

> ... our most noble Queen Elizabeth, ... ever took yet Greek nor Latin grammar in her hand after the first declining of a noun and verb, but only by this double translating of Demosthenes and Isocrates daily without missing every forenoon, and likewise part of Tully every afternoon, for the space of a year or two, hath attained to such a ready utterance of the Latin, and that with such a judgment as they be few in number in both the universities, or elsewhere in England, that be in both tongues comparable with her Majesty.[2]

One of the unfortunate legacies of Joan Kelly-Gadol's essay "Did Women Have a Renaissance?" has been an inclination to disparage the possibility that a learned queen had any impact on attitudes

---

[1]Geoffrey Elton, *England Under the Tudors*, 3rd ed. (London and New York: Routledge, 1991), 199.

[2]Roger Ascham, *The Schoolmaster* (1570), Folger Library Series (Charlottesville: University Press of Virginia, 1974), 87.

toward education for women. In one influential study, for example, we are told that "Elizabeth I failed to make other than the impact of a 'token' woman on the patriarchal attitudes of the early modern period."[3]

It has become a commonplace to insist that sixteenth- and seventeenth-century women who were celebrated for their learning were regarded even in their own day as privileged exceptions. The discovery of the manuscript of Martha Moulsworth's "Memorandum" in Beinecke, Osborn MS fb 150 testifies to the literacy and intellectual curiosity of a previously unknown woman.[4] Martha Moulsworth belonged to the gentry, but her social status and lineage raised her to the status enjoyed by women whose families had been elevated to the peerage.

In her autobiographical poem, she claims that her father "Beyond my sex & kind / ... did wth learninge Lattin decke [my] mind" (ll. 29–30). Since Moulsworth's father died when she was quite young, he cannot personally have instructed her, but she credits him with having done so. She poignantly insists that women are not intellectually inferior to men:

> Two Vniuersities we haue of men
> o thatt we had but one of women then
> O then thatt would in witt, and tongs surpasse
> All art of men thatt is, or euer was
> Butt I of Lattin haue no cause to boast
> ffor want of vse, I longe agoe itt lost (ll. 33–38)

Not only was Martha Moulsworth literate, but she also conceived of a society in which educational opportunities might be extended

---

[3]Joan Kelly-Gadol, "Did Women Have a Renaissance?," in Renate Bridenthal and Claudia Koonz, eds., *Becoming Visible: Women in European History* (Boston: Houghton Mifflin, 1977), 137–64; Lisa Jardine, *Still Harping on Daughters: Women and Drama in the Age of Shakespeare* (Totowa, NJ: Barnes and Noble, 1983), 194; A. Heisch, "Queen Elizabeth and the Persistence of Patriarchy," *Feminist Review* 4 (1980), 45–78; "The Influence of Humanism on the Education of Girls and Boys in Tudor England," *History of Education Quarterly* 25 (1985), 57–70. For a more balanced assessment, see Betty S. Travitsky, "Placing Women in the English Renaissance," in *The Renaissance Englishwoman in Print: Counterbalancing the Canon*, ed. Anne M. Haselkorn and Betty S. Travitsky (Amherst: University of Massachusetts Press, 1990), 3–41.

[4]For details, see Martha Moulsworth, *"My Name Was Martha": A Renaissance Woman's Autobiographical Poem*, ed. Robert C. Evans and Barbara Wiedemann (West Cornwall, CT: Locust Hill Press, 1993).

to women, allowing them the opportunity to contribute to culture. Her case cannot be generalized to the extent of claiming that most seventeenth-century women were literate and educated, but her comments show that it was possible for women who belonged to the gentry to value learning for its own sake. Moulsworth's views on education challenge the revisionist studies that persistently debunk the view that humanism opened up educational opportunities for women. To the Martha Moulsworths of the seventeenth century it may not have mattered that Elizabeth I belonged to the ruling class and occupied a privileged position. The idealized achievements of those who were celebrated for their learning in their own time and in the next generation—the daughters of Sir Thomas More, the daughters of Sir Anthony Cooke, Lady Jane Grey, and Elizabeth I—served as models of female potential. Families who educated their daughters in emulation of these exceptional women established traditions that were passed on to the next generation.[5]

The Educational Theories of
Richard Mulcaster and Bathsua Makin

If, however, Martha Moulsworth had decided to set up a school and had been writing a tract for the general public in the hope of attracting prospective students, then she probably would have exercised very different rhetorical strategies. The published work of Richard Mulcaster, the headmaster of Merchant Taylors' School in London, shows that he is concerned about the reactions of his audience to his educational theories. And the same concern is likely, if somewhat less certain, to have been the case when Bathsua Makin published her *Essay to Revive the Antient Education of Gentlewomen, in Religion, Manners, Arts & Tongues* (1673). Nearly a century divides these two educators, and we know much too little about the circumstances of the publication of these treatises to be able to deduce chronological shifts in attitudes between the sixteenth and seventeenth centuries. Nevertheless, we have sufficient

---

[5]Margaret J.M. Ezell, *The Patriarch's Wife: Literary Evidence and the History of the Family* (Chapel Hill: The University of North Carolina Press, 1987), 13.

information concerning their lives and works to be able to interrogate their attitudes toward class and gender.

Compared with Bathsua Makin, Richard Mulcaster was professionally and educationally very privileged. He was a younger son born into a prominent Carlisle family and attended Eton College, where William Barker was his schoolmaster. He matriculated at King's College, Cambridge, but received his B.A. in 1554 from Peterhouse. It is also possible that he attended Oxford. In 1558 he was the representative of Carlisle in the House of Commons. As headmaster of the Merchant Taylors' School in London, he had an impressive influence on his students. His pupils included Edmund Spenser, Thomas Kyd, Thomas Lodge, six of forty-seven translators of the King James version of the Bible, and five bishops. He taught Ralph Huchenson, President of St. John's, Oxford; John Peryn, Regius Professor of Greek at Oxford; and John Spenser, President of Corpus Christi College, Oxford, and chaplain to the learned King James I. Lancelot Andrewes, Bishop of Chichester, Ely, and Winchester, had a portrait of Mulcaster above the door of his study and left an inheritance to Mulcaster's son Peter.[6]

Bathsua Reginald Makin was the daughter of Henry Reginald, a schoolmaster who belonged to the circle of Samuel Hartlib. Reginald received mixed reviews from at least one of his students. His pupil Sir Simonds D'Ewes describes Henry as a kindly but not especially competent man who rewarded his students' accomplishments with raisins.[7] D'Ewes, however, thought that Reginald was far less gifted than his daughter:

> He had a daughter named Bathshua, being his eldest, that had an exact knowledge in the Greek, Latin, and French tongues, with some insight also into the Hebrew and Syriac; much more learning she had doubtless than her father, who was a mere pretender to it; and by the fame of her abilities, which she had acquired from others, he got many scholars which else would never have repaired to him nor have long staid with him. (63)

When Bathsua was married, Simonds D'Ewes commented that he was invited to the wedding; he also describes her in his diary as

---

[6]John Buckeridge, "A Sermon Preached at the Funeral of ... Lancelot, Late Lord Bishop of Winchester ...." *XCVI Sermons by ... Lancelot Andrewes*, ed. William Laud and John Buckeridge. 5th ed. (London, 1661), 791.

[7]*The Autobiography and Correspondence of Sir Simonds D'Ewes*, ed. James Orchard Halliwell, Esq., 2 vols. (London: Richard Bentley, 1845), 1:65.

the "greatest scholler, I thinke, of a woman in England" (68). Bathsua married, bore at least one child who survived, and, after she
was widowed, supported herself by tutoring. Among her pupils
were the Princess Elizabeth (daughter of Charles I) and the daughters of Lucy Hastings, Countess of Huntingdon.[8]

Makin's choices were strictly limited by the prevailing mores
that restricted professional opportunities for women. She was employed in the school that her father ran. Once that school closed,
her principal means of supporting herself would have been to act
as a tutor to noble women or gentlewomen. Since she was born in
approximately 1600, she must have been nearly seventy-three
when the *Essay* was printed. If, as is suggested in the "Postscript"
to the *Essay*, she was starting a school in Tottenham-High-Cross for
young girls at her age, then she was truly a remarkable woman.[9]

There is no particular reason to assume that the headmaster of
Merchant Taylors' School in London would have more rigid views
on class than gender or that he would be distinctly less egalitarian
than a female educator, but that is in fact the case. In 1581 Richard
Mulcaster published *Positions Wherein Those Primitive Circumstances
Be Examined, Necessarie for the Training Up of Children*, and in the following year he brought out *The First Part of the Elementarie which
Entreateth of Right Writing of our English Tung*. In 1586 he opened a
private school of his own, but it was not a financial success. In 1594
he tried his second private school, but two years later he yielded to
his creditors and closed his school on Milk Street and became
headmaster of St. Paul's School. In *Positions* Mulcaster devotes
Chapter 38 to the following proposition:

> [t]hat young maidens are to be set to learning, which is
> proved by the custome of our countrey, by our duetie to-
> wardes them, by their naturall abilities, and by the worthy
> effectes of such as haue bene well trained. The ende
> wherunto their educations serueth, which is the cause why &
> how much they learne. Which of them are to learne, when

---

[8]For further biographical information, see my "Bathsua Reginald
Makin: 'Most Learned Matron,'" *Huntington Library Quarterly* 54 (1991):
313–26.

[9]*An Essay to Revive the Antient Education of Gentlewomen, in Religion,
Manners, Arts & Tongues With An Answer to the Objections against this Way
of Education* (London: J.D., 1673), 42–43. All references will be to this edition; page numbers will be cited parenthetically in the text.

they are to begin to learne. What and how much they may
learne. Of who and where they ought to be taught.[10]

Even though he acknowledges that his audience may think that he
should have concentrated on boys and remained silent about girls,
Mulcaster cannot resist stating that his own commitment to education for young women engages him "toothe and naile" (167).

He marshals support for female education from Plato and concludes that:

> Which being thus, as both the truth tells the ignorant, and
> reading shewes the learned, we do wel then perceaue by
> *naturall men* and *Philosophicall reasons*, that young *maidens* de-
> serve the traine: by cause they have that treasure, which be-
> longeth vnto it, bestowed on them by *nature*, to be bettered
> in them by *nurture.* (171)

Gender is not viewed as determining intellectual potential, but
Mulcaster regards class as decisive: Parents should treat their
daughters just as they treat their sons, having the same restraint in
"cases of necessitie" and the same freedom in "cases of libertie"
(175).

We know that education affected social status. The graduate of
a university was entitled to designate himself a gentleman. Mulcaster, however, seems unwilling to pursue these implications and
to entertain the possibility that class was an arbitrary accident of
birth.

Even though he was the headmaster of the Merchant Taylors'
School, he seems to have despised the developing commercial class
whose economic success enabled them to claim a higher status for
their children:

> As for *riche* men which being no *gentlemen*, but growing to
> wealth by what meanes soeuer, will counterfeat *gentlemen* in
> the education of their children, as if money made equalitie,
> and the purse were the preferrer, and no further regard:
> which contemne the common from whence they came,
> which cloister vp their youth, as boding further state: they be
> in the same case for *abilitie*, though farre behinde for *gentili-
> tie*. (194)

---

[10]*Positions Wherein Those Primitive Circumstances Be Examined, Necessarie for the Training Up of Children* (London: T. Vautrollier for T. Chare,
1982), X4 [166]. All further references will be to this edition; page numbers
will be cited parenthetically in the text.

Mulcaster recognizes that intelligence can be found in all classes, but he remains strongly committed to a hierarchical society with definite class boundaries:

> But as they came from the common, so they might with more commendacion, continue their children in that kinde, which brought vp the parentes and made them so wealthy, and to impatronise themselues vnto a degree to farre beyond the dounghill. (194)

Poor men's sons, who have sufficient ability, can be sent to school, but then there will need to be some kind of civil patronage.[11] More seems to be at stake here, however, than a pragmatic attitude toward financing education. It seems clear that the headmaster of the Merchant Taylors' School held socially liberal views on the education of women, but that he retained deep prejudices about extending educational opportunities to those "new men" who could not claim to be members of the gentry.

In contrast, Makin adopts rational and enlightened educational views in regard to both gender and class. Makin's use of a masculine persona has been criticized as giving a "conservative tone to much of her essay."[12] Surely, however, her use of this persona is merely a rhetorical ploy designed to disarm critics of the school that she is advertising. In a note immediately following the dedication, she tells the reader: "I am a man myself, that would not suggest a thing prejudicial to our Sex" (5) and prints a letter from another gentleman who raises objections to educating his daughters. The *Essay* is a response to such objections as women do not need to be educated because "the end of Learning is to fit one for publick Employment, which Women are not capable of" (7).

Like Mulcaster, Makin assures her audience that she is advocating education for gentlewomen, whose class entitles them to leisure: "those that are mean in the World, have not an opportunity for this Education" (22). She then continues:

> My Meaning is, Persons that God hath blessed with the things of this World, that have competent natural Parts, ought to be educated in Knowledge; That is, it is much better they should spend the time of their Youth, to be competently instructed in those things usually taught to Gentlewomen at

---

[11]David Cressy, "Educational Opportunity in Tudor and Stuart England," *History of Education Quarterly* 163 (1976): 305–6.

[12]Hilda Smith, *Reason's Disciples: Seventeenth-Century English Feminists* (Urbana: University of Illinois Press, 1982), 102–3.

> Schools, and the overplus of their time to be spent in gaining
> Arts, and Tongues, and useful Knowledge. (22)

Nevertheless, it is clear from her examples of the advantages enjoyed by educated women that she believes in broadly based educational opportunities.

For Bathsua Makin, social class does not define educational
potential: "Maids," she tells, "that cannot subsist without depending, as Servants may chuse their places, to attend upon honourable
Persons, or to be imployed in Nurseries; by their Conversation, to
teach Tongues to Children" (26). Far from despising those in trade
or business, she insists that educated women could help their husbands in their "Trades, as the Women [do] in Holland" (27). Merchants are to be admired. Rather than disdaining those who gain
status by their own industry, Makin comments that "the Duke of
Florence is a great Marchant; Noblemen in *England*, and Gentlemen
in *France*, think it disparagement to them to be so" (35).

Richard Mulcaster and Bathsua Makin, like Martha Moulsworth, consider it important to educate women. Moulsworth, because she was writing a meditational poem, makes the most out-
spoken claim for women. However, her declaration that if given
the opportunity to attend universities, women would surpass men
has to be understood as a consequence of private discourse. Although Mulcaster and Makin strongly agreed on equal educational
opportunities for women, their attitudes toward class fundamen-
tally differed. It may be that the idea of educating the lower orders
was more potentially threatening than that of educating women.

Mulcaster ≠ Educating ↓class women
Makin = educating ↓class women

"The Widdowes Silvar":
Widowhood in Early Modern England[1]

Esther S. Cope

Saying, "I love silvar well," Martha Moulsworth declared her contentment with widowhood.[2] Her statement seems to challenge the conceptual frameworks of the patriarchal society of early modern England that emphasized a woman's marital status and reflected contemporary assumptions about female vulnerability and dependence. The church viewed a woman as virgin, wife, or widow, and the law regarded her as either a *feme sole* (alone) or a *feme covert* (under the cover or protection of her husband or father). The seemingly disparate characteristics of widowhood fit uneasily into these categories. A widow, though she was a *feme sole*, had been married; in her widowhood, she might have some property and thus some economic independence; through her experiences, she might also have gained self-assurance. In response to the anomaly of widowhood contemporaries offered a plethora of advice purporting to guide the widow through the potential dangers of her situation. The abundance of myths and frequently rude jokes about wealthy widows who ultimately became victims of

[1]This paper is based in part upon research done at the Huntington Library (abbreviated "HEH" herein). I am grateful to the Huntington for its fellowship support and to the University of Nebraska-Lincoln for a leave. I owe special thanks to scholars at the Huntington for their questions and suggestions as I was working on this. Lois Schwoerer read a draft and also offered valuable comments. Robert Evans sent me an early version of his biographical essay about Martha and thus enabled me to draw upon some of the new material that he and others have found about her.

[2]See line 110 of "The Memorandum of Martha Moulsworth" in "*My Name Was Martha*": *A Renaissance Woman's Autobiographical Poem*, ed. Robert C. Evans and Barbara Wiedemann (West Cornwall, CT: Locust Hill Press, 1993), 4–8. In quotations, *i/j* and *u/v* have been modernized.

their own schemes to remarry were another illustration of the society's anxieties about widowhood.[3] In plays of the period the sheer numbers of women described as widows are a striking contrast to the relatively few men identified as widowers, even though many of those men had lost their wives.[4]

The facts about widows and widowhood belie the popular fictions, whose conflicting images of widows' capability and utter helplessness provide hints of the reality beneath their portrayals. Although a comprehensive survey of the topic remains to be done and available data about the numbers of widows are too limited to be useful, evidence shows that, despite the society's tendency to let widowhood itself define a woman's condition, the experiences and circumstances of widows in early modern England could be very diverse.[5] Widows were wealthy and impoverished, old and young; some managed their affairs capably while others proved hopelessly inept.[6] Many, like Martha, were widowed more than once.

---

[3]For examples of advice, see I.L., *The Lawes resolutions of womens rights: or The Lawes Provision for Woemen* (London, 1632) or Richard Brathwaite, *The English Gentlewoman* (London, 1631); sermons were another important vehicle for advice to widows, e.g., Robert Harris, "Samuels Funeral: or a sermon preached at the funerall of Sir Anthonie Cope. [1630]: to Lady Anne Cope, [widow]," in *Six Sermons, preached on severall texts and occasions* (1627); or John Ley's sermon for Mrs. Jane Ratcliffe. The full title states his purpose (*A Patterne of Pietie. or The Religious life and death of that Grave and gracious Matron, Mrs. Jane Ratcliffe Widow and Citizen of Chester, Of whom the discourse is framed and applied so as the commemoration of the dead may best serve to the edification of the living, whether men or women, whereof part was preached and this whole written* [London, 1640]). Concerning myths and jokes, see Charles Carlton, "The Widow's Tale: Male Myths and Female Reality in 16th and 17th Century England," *Albion* 10:2 (1978): 118–29; also "A merry new Song of a rich Widdowes wooing that married a young man to her owne undoing," *The Pepys Ballads*, ed. Hyder Edward Rollins (Cambridge, MA: Harvard University Press, 1929), 1: 257–61.

[4]Thomas L. Berger and William C. Bradford, Jr., *An Index of Characters in English Printed Drama to the Restoration* (Englewood, CO: Microcard Editions Books, 1975) give eighty-eight entries for widows compared to three for widowers. I am grateful to Michael Warren and James Riddell for this reference.

[5]For data, see Peter Laslett, *Family Life and Illicit Love in Earlier Generations* (Cambridge: Cambridge University Press, 1977), 199–208. I am grateful to Roger Schofield for this reference.

[6]See Joel T. Rosenthal, "Aristocratic Widows in Fifteenth-Century England," in *Women and the Structure of Society: Selected Research from the*

The following brief survey of widowhood in Martha Moulsworth's era will examine some stereotypes in the light of evidence about some individual widows.

The "forlorn" or "poor" widow appears frequently in both literary and historical sources from early modern England. She served to represent any suffering or beleaguered figure—plague-ravaged London, England during the civil wars, or the church.[7] The biblical injunctions to care for the widowed and the fatherless encouraged charitable donations and offered a moral basis for claims of relief. In many communities bequests provided a small amount of money each week for a poor widow. Elsewhere there were almshouses, such as Mary Price's in Hereford which supported six poor widows or single women.[8] Among the papers of judges and other officials are numerous petitions in which widows, calling themselves "poor," sought assistance in recovering land or monies, fending off creditors, handling other legal business, or obtaining outright relief.[9] Poverty was certainly a real possibility for widows, but it is not always easy to separate anxieties about income and desire for greater financial security from actual want.

When widows were poor, contemporaries expected that they would seek to remarry in order to allay financial hardship.[10] Some widows acted accordingly. The Earl of Huntingdon's widowed mother acknowledged that both she and her friends thought remarriage might save her from becoming a "beggar." She told her son that she hoped to find someone who would "chearfuly bayer"

Fifth Berkshire Conference on the History of Women, ed. Barbara J. Harris and JoAnn K. McNamara (Durham, NC: Duke Press Policy Studies, Duke University Press, 1984), 36–47.

[7]John Vicars, *Englands Hallelu-jah* (1631), stanza 76; Eleanor Douglas, *Prayer* (1644), 4–5; also Daniel Featly, *The Practice of Extraordinarie Devotion* 1630, 661 (church as a widow).

[8]E.M. Leonard, *The Early History of English Poor Relief* (Cambridge: Cambridge University Press, 1900), 211n–212.

[9]See, for example, the case of Jane Mitforth who was left with a debt and then had additional difficulties because, through her attorney's negligence, a court had ruled against her (HEH, EL 6050–52), the case of Lady Anne Allott who was trying to get money owed her (HEH, EL 5987), or that of Margery Biwaters who was trying to get property (HEH, EL 6006).

[10]See Barbara J. Todd, "The Remarrying Widow: A Stereotype Reconsidered," in *Women in English Society 1500–1800*, ed. Mary Prior (London: Methuen, 1985), 54–92.

her debts and be her "servant as well as a husband."[11] In many cases sources tell us only that women remarried, not why they did so. Although Hannah Allen's taking an apprentice for her second husband ostensibly allowed her to remain in the book trade as well as giving him entry into it, records suggest that she became less active thereafter. During the five years between the death of Benjamin Allen and her remarriage she had sold books and used her imprint in a way that was distinct from his previous practice.[12]

Neither considerations of income nor guild or company regulations governing practice of a trade or business can explain whether widows remarried. In contrast to Hannah Allen, other printers' widows did not remarry but continued working as printers.[13] Barbara Todd's study of Abingdon, Oxfordshire, suggests that occupational circumstances, that is how involved a woman was in the business and how easy it may have been for her to manage it on her own, have some correlation with remarriages. The widows of merchants or maltsters were, accordingly, less likely to marry again than were widows of artisans.[14]

By common law, a widow was entitled to a third of her late husband's estate, but few women actually received that much by the early seventeenth century. The Statute of Uses of 1536 (27 Hen. VIII, c. 10) meant that an agreement made prior to marriage, rather than the common law, often determined widows' inheritance. These arrangements tended to deprive them of benefits from increases in their husbands' estates over the years of marriage.[15]

---

[11]HEH, Hastings correspondence, HA 2433, [Edmonds, Lady] Sarah [(Harington)] Hastings [Kingsmill Zouche] to [her son] the earl of Huntingdon, 9 July [1626]. The need to find a protector to assist her in her battle for her estates may explain Lady Anne Clifford's second marriage (Barbara Lewalski, *Writing Women in Jacobean England* [Cambridge, MA: Harvard University Press, 1993]), 129.

[12]Maureen Bell, "Hannah Allen and the Development of a Puritan Publishing Business, 1646–51," *Publishing History* 26 (1989): 5–66.

[13]Maureen Bell, "Hannah Allen and the Development of a Puritan Publishing Business, 1646–51," 46.

[14]Barbara J. Todd, "The Remarrying Widow: A Stereotype Reconsidered," 69–71.

[15]Eileen Spring, *Law, Land, & Family: Aristocratic Inheritance in England, 1300 to 1800* (Chapel Hill: University of North Carolina Press, 1993). Spring challenges some of the conclusions of both Amy Louise Erickson, "Common Law Versus Common Practice: The Use of Marriage Settlements in Early Modern England," *Economic History Review*, 2nd ser. 43:1

Countering what might have been a financial incentive to remarry were the increasing numbers of husbands who were also stipulating that their widows were to have their portions only so long as they remained widows.[16] The prophet Eleanor Davies, who remarried in defiance of such a provision made by her lawyer husband, engaged in a series of law-suits to overthrow it. She complained bitterly about the fate of widows and came to discover that her second husband was more of a hindrance than a help as she tried to recover estates that she believed were hers.[17]

Stories of widows who contributed to their own undoing by unwise remarriages illustrated the commonplace that the loss of a husband meant that a woman's "head is cut off, her intellectuall part is gone."[18] An oft-repeated cautionary tale, which some sources credit to Stow, told of a wealthy London widow whose marriage to a much younger and less wealthy man devastated her estate and drove her to suicide.[19] The exception that proved the rule for contemporaries was the occasional wealthy widow who secured very favorable provisions in a second marriage. Catherine, duchess of Buckingham, whose affairs attracted attention because her husband, before his assassination, had been the king's favorite, did this. In the marriage agreement she negotiated with the earl of

---

(1990): 21–39, and Maria Cioni, *Women and the Law in Elizabethan England* (New York: Garland Publishing, 1985).

[16]Barbara J. Todd, "The Remarrying Widow: A Stereotype Reconsidered," 54–92. Robert Evans's transcripts of the wills of Martha's husbands show that none of them imposed this condition in their bequests to her.

[17]See Esther S. Cope, *Handmaid of the Holy Spirit* (Ann Arbor, MI: University of Michigan Press, 1992), 46–49, 102–7, 135. In her tract, *Prayer* (1644), Davies made references to the widow's position as "forlorn" and "woful" (4–5); see also her *Restitution of Prophecy* (1651), 37, 40. Lady Anne Clifford's second husband gave her as little assistance as her first in her lengthy struggles to obtain the estate that her father had left her (see V. Sackville-West, ed. *The Diary of the Lady Anne Clifford* [London: William Heinemann, Ltd., 1923]).

[18]I.L., *The Lawes resolutions of womens rights: or The Lawes Provision for Woemen* (London, 1632), 232. Brathwaite says much the same thing (Richard Brathwaite, *The English Gentlewoman* [London, 1631], 111); see also Daniel Rogers, *Matrimoniall Honor* (London, 1642), 78–79.

[19]Alex Niccholes, *A Discourse of Marriage and Wiving* (1615), 18; see also "A merry new Song of a rich Widdowes wooing, That married a young man to her owne undoing," *The Pepys Ballads*, ed. by Hyder Edward Rollins (Cambridge, MA: Harvard University Press, 1929), 1: 257–61.

this. In the marriage agreement she negotiated with the earl of
Antrim, she protected her children's interests in her own considerable fortune.[20]

Less notorious widows, including Martha Moulsworth, who
competently managed their families, fortunes, and affairs were not
the stuff for gossip or drama. The funeral sermon that Thomas
Hassall preached for Martha suggests that she was one of those
widows who gained notice as examples of another popular stereotype, the "reverend widow."[21] Like her "forlorn" counterpart, the
reverend widow had a biblical basis that influenced contemporary
rhetoric. Her primary virtues were modesty and devoutness, but
the exemplary practice of those qualities often also meant making a
mark in the secular world. Among the many virtues that the Rev.
John Collings found in Frances Hobart was how well she had han-
dled the debt and estate her husband left so that "in a few years,
she had shortned his debt, *Six thousand pounds.*"[22] Chester widow
Jane Ratcliffe had made religion a central part of her daily life and
performed much charitable service in her community while successfully managing the brewery which Mr. Ratcliffe had oper-
ated.[23]

An important part of the image of "reverend" widows was
their remaining as widows rather than remarrying. Neither
Frances Hobart nor Jane Ratcliffe had married again after the death
of her husband. Rev. John Ley, who memorialized Jane Ratcliffe as
a "patterne of pietie," described her "firme resolution to forebeare

---

[20]Jane H. Ohlmeyer, *Civil War and Restoration in the Three Stuart King-
doms: The Career of Randal Macdonnell, Marquis of Antrim, 1609–1683* (Cambridge: Cambridge University Press, 1993), 31. Laud described her as
having "dealt very nobly with her children" (*Works*, 7: 124).

[21]Richard Brathwaite, *The English Gentlewoman* (London, 1632), p. 68,
refers to the "reverend" widow. I am grateful to Robert Evans for sending
me information about Hassall's sermon for Martha.

[22]John Collings, *Par Nobile. Two Treatises* (London, 1669), 10.

[23]Peter Lake, "Feminine Piety and Personal Potency: The 'Emancipation' of Mrs Jane Ratcliffe," *The Seventeenth Century*, 2:2 (1987): 146. John
Ley, *A Patterne of Pietie. or The Religious life and death of that Grave and gracious Matron, Mrs. Jane Ratcliffe Widow and Citizen of Chester, Of whom the
discourse is framed and applied so as the commemoration of the dead may best
serve to the edification of the living, whether men or women, whereof part was
preached and this whole written* (London, 1640), 43, 133–34. John Collings
presents a similar picture of Lady Frances Hobart in *Par Nobile. Two Treatises* (London, 1669), 24, 32–34.

marriage and to rest in the state of widowhood since the death of her husband."[24] According to Collings, Frances Hobart "grew to be something *superstitious* in this thing not only resolving (through Gods assistance) to go to her Grave having *been only the Wife of one Husband*; but almost looking upon it as a piece of her duty, and often reckoning it a piece of the honour of her *fathers house*, that none of her Noble sisters (left Widow) had married a second time."[25]

Contemporaries expected that widows would manifest their grief for their husbands by wearing mourning clothes. The sober garb of Lady Anne Clifford in the third panel of the triptych that she commissioned in 1646 when her second husband was still living was typical of what was expected of widows. Jane Ratcliffe, in contrast, had not "relapsed to meaner raiment" in her widowhood.[26] Ley explained her defiance of custom on two grounds. Because Mr. Ratcliffe had twice been Lord Mayor of the City of Chester, his widow felt she must not "come too much below the condition wherein she was placed," and she did not want, by changing her dress, to seem to give too much attention to clothing which she deemed an outward and worldly thing.[27]

Martha Moulsworth's lines about being content with "the Widowes silver" suggest that, after the death of her third husband, she had accepted the advice so often repeated in contemporary sermons.[28] Even though she had twice abandoned widowhood for remarriage, she also acknowledged some loyalty for each of the three men she married. When she was first widowed, she fell into the group of widows who, according to Todd's evidence, were most likely to remarry—those widows who were youngest, whose

---

[24]John Ley, *A Patterne of Pietie* (London, 1640), 77.

[25]John Collings, *Par Nobile. Two Treatises* (London, 1669), 10.

[26]The triptych is reproduced in Elspeth Graham, Hilary Hinds, Elaine Hobby, and Helen Wilcox, eds., *Her Own Life: Autobiographical Writings by Seventeenth-Century Englishwomen* (London: Routledge, 1989), 6. On Clifford see also V. Sackville-West, ed., *The Diary of the Lady Anne Clifford* (London: William Heinemann, Ltd., 1923). Momford, uncle to Eugenia, the widow in *Sir Gyles Goosecap*, told her, "Alas Neece, y'are so smeard with this willfull-widdows-three-yeeres blacke weede, that I never come to you, but I dreame of Coarses, and Sepulchres, and Epitaphs, all the night after" (*Sir Gyles Goose-cappe Knight. A comedy lately acted with great applause at the private House in Salisbury Court* [London, 1636], a reference I owe to Leah Scragg).

[27]John Ley, *A Patterne of Pietie* (London, 1640), 133–34.

[28]"The Memorandum of Martha Moulsworth," l. 110.

marriages had been shortest, and whose children were young.[29] Martha had one small child and was carrying her second when Mr. Prynne died, and only a year passed between his death and her marriage to Mr. Througood [Thorowgood].[30] That cannot explain her final marriage, which occurred after a longer interval and a longer marriage, although she suggested that in Mr. Molesworth she found a companion who allowed her the freedom that some women obtained only in widowhood.[31]

Martha attributed the notion of the "Widowes silvar" to "Clarks" (ministers) rather than to St. Jerome, whose description of widowhood as the second degree of chastity (virginity was the first) was probably the source of her image. Jerome's portrayals of the widows he knew were cited again and again in sermons of the day and appeared in Ley's writing about Jane Ratcliffe.[32] Also prominent in contemporary sermons were the widows of the Bible, particularly the widow of Sarepta (1 Kings 9:17–24), the importunate widow (Luke 18:3–5) and the widow whose two mites, Jesus said, were more than the money given by others (Mark 12:42).[33] Although none of Martha's biblical references dealt specifically with widows, their stories offered models with which she and her contemporaries were surely familiar.

---

[29]Barbara J. Todd, "The Remarrying Widow: A Stereotype Reconsidered," 54–92.

[30]I owe this information to Robert Evans.

[31]"The Memorandum of Martha Moulsworth," ll. 66–68.

[32]Hieronymous [Jerome], *Select Letters of St. Jerome*, ed. by F.A. Wright (London: William Heinemann Ltd., 1933), Letter 22: to Eustochium. The English edition of Jerome's letters which appeared in 1630 did not include either the Letter to Eustochium or Letter 54 to Paula on Marcella and the sack of Rome (Hieronymous [Jerome], Saint. *Certaine selected epistles of Hierome. As also the lives of Saint Paul the first hermite, Of Saint Ilarion the first Monke of Syria, and of S. Malchus.* Translated into English. M.DC.XXX: [1630]). For contemporary citations of Jerome, see, for example, John Ley, *A Patterne of Pietie* (London, 1640), 5, 6, 10–11, 16, 26, 40, 41, 79, 81, 124, 179–80; also Richard Brathwaite, *The English Gentlewoman* (London, 1631). I have not found any sermons or books of advice that actually used gold and silver to describe virginity and widowhood.

[33]Robert Harris, *Six Sermons, preached on severall texts and occasions* (1627), "Samuel's Funerall," 16; "Peters Enlargement upon the Prayers of the Church" [seventh ed.], 19. John Ley, *A Patterne of Pietie* (London, 1640), 11. Sampson Price, *The Clearing of the Saints Sight* (London, 1617), 32.

Freed from obligations to her husband, the ideal widow was supposed to serve God. As *The Lawes Resolutions of Womens Rights: or The Lawes Provision for Woemen* (which, although written earlier, was printed in 1632, the year when Martha wrote) put it, the widow should "learne to cast her whole love and devotion on him, that is better able to love and defend her than all the men in the world."[34] Jane Ratcliffe left extensive devotional writings which Ley incorporated in his text, and Frances Hobart, according to Collings, was rarely without her Bible.[35]

Both Jane Ratcliffe and Frances Hobart were among the widows whose religious lives included close friendships with clergy. As the work of Diane Willen has shown, in many instances these relationships were reciprocal rather than those of the stereotypical widow, who, in the absence of her husband, was helpless without the guidance and rule of a male.[36] John Ley told of Jane Ratcliffe's "sacred services" from which she "scrupulously shunned the presence of men, especially of Ministers."[37] To determine her position on the much contested point of kneeling to receive the sacrament, she read books and consulted various divines. Once she had reached her own conclusion, she talked to other women about it.[38] Nevertheless she was not the "she-precise hypocrite" whom the caricaturists described as wanting to preach.[39] She did not challenge the social order. Ley contrasted her eloquence in prayer (he had apparently overheard one of those private services) with her "silence" in "common conversation."[40] If she violated any of the strictures upon conduct that the books imposed upon widows, and if, by loving society "albeit her intentions relish[ed] nothing but sobriety," she gave "speedy wings to spreading infamy," he did

---

[34]I.L., *The Lawes Resolutions of Womens Rights: or The Lawes Provision for Woemen* (London, 1632), 232.

[35]John Ley, *A Patterne of Pietie* (London, 1640), 26–27, 45ff; John Collings, *Par Nobile. Two Treatises* (London, 1669), 26.

[36]Diane Willen, "Godly Women in Early Modern England: Puritanism and Gender," *Journal of Ecclesiastical History*, 43:4 (1992): 561–80.

[37]John Ley, *A Patterne of Pietie* (London, 1640), 63.

[38]John Ley, *A Patterne of Pietie* (London, 1640), 45–51, 63, 85–89, 143–48. Also see Peter Lake, "Feminine Piety and Personal Potency: The 'Emancipation' of Mrs Jane Ratcliffe," *The Seventeenth Century*, 2:2 (1987): 143–65.

[39]See John Earle, *Micro-Cosmographie. Or A Peece of the World Discovered; In Essayes and Characters* (London, 1628), no. 43.

[40]John Ley, *A Patterne of Pietie* (London, 1640), 60.

not say so.[41] The strong faith and sense of identity in Martha's poem present a similar image although the poem does not tell us very much about the details of her life in that third widowhood.

Martha's experiences as a widow and the *lacunae* in our knowledge about her serve as a useful reminder of both the diversity among early modern English widows and how little we know about them. Their society looked at them as widows, and modern research about them is only in its initial stages. Many questions remain unanswered: How far were the experiences of widows shaped by their society's preoccupation with widowhood and its notions about the conduct appropriate for widows? To what extent did a woman's widowhood rather than her age, status, wealth or other factors determine the condition and quality of her life? How does widowhood differ from the marital separations that women, like Katharine Courteen, Anne Clifford, or Eleanor Davies/Douglas, experienced?[42]

Dated 1633, just a year after Martha composed her poem, is a volume entitled "Certaine Collections of the Right honorable Elizabeth late Countess of Huntingdon for her owne private use."[43] Although the Countess may not have used the book, she presumably had gathered the biblical verses and other devotional material recorded in it.[44] She was not a widow. Her husband of many years survived her when she died in 1633, but she, like Martha, was thinking about death.[45] In contrast to the faith that allowed Martha to look to the resurrection, sin and the need to repent preoccupied the Countess. Neither woman's views were original. Both echoed beliefs found among the religious authorities of the time. Their

---

[41]See Richard Brathwaite, *The English Gentlewoman* (London, 1631), 110. A case in King's Bench, 4 Jac. revolved in part around the withdrawal of an offer of marriage as a consequence of reports of a woman's incontinency (John March, *Actions for Slaunder* [London, 1648], 91–92).

[42]John Collings, *Par Nobile. Two Treatises* (London, 1669); V. Sackville-West, ed., *The Diary of the Lady Anne Clifford* (London: William Heinemann, Ltd., 1923); E. Cope, *Handmaid of the Holy Spirit.*

[43]HEH, EL 6871.

[44]In addition to the multitude of biblical citations, she tells us that she has drawn from: "the booke of ye practise of pietie"; "Mr. A:H: Booke" concerning the "Lords Supper"; "Dr. Andrewe's booke of sermons"; and "Dr Halls Meditations." For both Andrewes' sermons and A.H.'s book, she provides some page numbers.

[45]The countess died 26 January 1633/34.

presentations nevertheless help to delineate the women as individuals rather than simply women or widows.

To her contemporaries Martha may have been primarily a widow at the time when, at age fifty-five and widowed for the third time, she wrote her poem. That poem is one of few available descriptions of early modern widowhood written by a widow. Its spiritual perspective is that offered by the clergy and based on the Bible and Christian tradition, but its expression is Martha's. She tells us about herself, not just about widowhood.

Appendices

Appendix 1

Old- and Modern-Spelling Versions of the Yale Text of Moulsworth's "Memorandum," with Photographic Reproductions

The manuscript of Martha Moulsworth's "Memorandum" occurs in a commonplace book (Osborn MS fb 150) currently housed in the Beinecke Library at Yale University. Although the pages on which the poem appears are unnumbered, the work occurs near the end of the manuscript volume. The poem is preceded by many blank pages, although most of the other texts included in this commonplace book are political in nature. A bookseller's account that accompanied the manuscript to Yale suggests that all of these prose works date from before 1632 (that is, before the composition of Moulsworth's poem). Apparently the volume was once owned by Marmaduke Rawdon of London, the son-in-law by marriage of Martha Moulsworth. The bookseller's account describes and dates the finished prose pieces the volume contains:

> The complete texts are "A Discourse of the High Court in Parliament" (30 pp., before 1629), "A general collection of all the offices of England, with the fees belonging to them, being in the Kings gift" (48 pp., ... before 1629), "A copies [sic] of the information exhibited in the Starr chamber ... against Francis Cotton ... John Selden, *et al.* ... (20 pp., 1629 ...), "The true Coppies of all the gentlemen bearing Armes in the Artillarie Garden taken out of the Roule deliuered to my Mr. Captayne Marmaduke Rawdon" (6 pp., 1631).

The bookseller also mentions several incomplete pieces: "'The Battle of Newport by Sr. Francis Vere' (7 pp., unfinished, undated), a list of towns taken by the states of Holland from Spain in 1629, and the draft of a power of attorney by Captain Rawdon, 21 December 1631."

Moulsworth's "Memorandum," then, seems to have been inscribed in the rear of a manuscript once owned by her step-daughter's husband; whether the handwriting of this text belongs to Moulsworth herself is uncertain, although the style of writing is noticeably different from that of the political prose in the front of the volume, which seems to have been written by a secretary or servant of Marmaduke Rawdon ("my Mr."). It would seem that the volume was a private text not intended for very wide circulation.

Moulsworth's poem is written in a neat, relatively clear hand from the early seventeenth century. In the following transcription, line numbers have been added in square brackets. Brackets have also been used to set off the various marginal notes that run alongside the manuscript version of the poem itself; these notes were apparently composed by Moulsworth. In the transcript, punctuation and spelling have been left unchanged, and in the few places where a word is missing, crossed out, or corrected, these facts have been appropriately indicated. Explanatory notes, indicated by marginal symbols, follow the transcription.

The present transcription differs in a few insignificant details from the transcript printed in the first edition. For a list of these corrections, see the beginning of the accompanying notes.

Nouember the 10ᵗʰ 1632
† The Memorandum of Martha Moulsworth
Widdowe

The tenth day of the winter month Nouember
A day which I must duely still remember
did open first theis eis, and shewed this light
†   Now on thatt day* vppon thatt daie I write
                       Nouember 10ᵗʰ 1632
This season fitly willinglie combines   [5
the birth day of my selfe, & of theis lynes
†   The tyme the clocke, the yearly stroke is one
thatt clocke by ffiftie fiue retourns hath gonn
How ffew, how many warnings itt will giue
he only knowes in whome we are, & liue   [10

[*beginning next to line 7:* my muse is a tell
clocke, & echoeth
euerie stroke wth
a coupled ryme
so many tymes
viz 55
Acts 17.28.&[?]]

In carnall state of sin originall
I did nott stay one whole day naturall
The seale of grace in Sacramentall water
so soone had I, so soone become the daughter
of earthly parents, & of heauenlie ffather   [15
† some christen late for state, the wiser rather.

† My Name was Martha, Martha tooke much payne
                                        [Luke 10: 14
† our Sauiour christ hir guesse [sic] to entertayne
God gyue me grace my Inward house to dight
† thatt he wth me may supp, & stay all night   [20
                                        [Reuela: 3.20:

My ffather was a Man of spottles ffame
                                        [Luke 24.29
of gentle Birth, & Dorsett was his name
He had, & left lands of his owne possession
† he was of Leuies tribe by his proffession
his Mother oxford knowenge well his worth   [25
† arayd in scarlett Robe did send him fforth.
By him I was brought vpp in godlie pietie
† In modest chearefullnes, & sad sobrietie
Nor onlie so, Beyond my sex & kind
† he did wth learninge Lattin decke mind [sic]   [30
And whie nott so? the muses ffemalls are
and therfore of Vs ffemales take some care
Two Vniuersities we haue of men

o thatt we had but one of women then

——[NEW PAGE]——

O then thatt would in witt, and tongs surpasse   [35
All art of men thatt is, or euer was
Butt I of Lattin haue no cause to boast
† ffor want of vse, I longe agoe itt lost
                              [Lattin is nott the most
                                marketable mariadge
                                          mettall
Had I no other portion to my dowre
I might haue stood a virgin to this houre   [40
Butt though the virgin Muses I loue well
I haue longe since Bid virgin life ffarewell
Thrice this Right hand did holly wedlocke plight
† And thrice this Left with pledged ringe was dight
three husbands me, & I haue them enioyde   [45
Nor I by them, nor they by me annoyde
all louely, lovinge all, some more, some lesse
though gonn their loue, & memorie I blesse.

Vntill my one & twentieth yeare of Age
                              [1 Husband, Mr Nicolas
                              Prynne, Aprill 18
                              1598
I did nott bind my selfe in Mariadge   [50
My springe was late, some thinke thatt sooner loue
† butt backward springs doe oft the kindest proue
My first knott held fiue yeares, & eight months more
† then was a yeare sett on my mourninge score
My second bond tenn years nine months did last   [55
                              [2^d Mr Tho: Througood
                                   ffebruary 3 1604
† three years eight Months I kept a widowes ffast

The third I tooke a louely man, & kind
† such comlines in age we seldome ffind

[3ᵈ Mʳ Beuill
Moulsworth
June 15, 1619

† ffrom Mortimers he drewe his pedigre
† their Arms he ~~bought~~ bore, nott bought wᵗʰ Heraulds fee   [60
third wife I was to him, as he to me
third husband was, in nomber we agree
eleuen years, & eight months his autume lasted
a second spring to soone awaie itt hasted
† was neuer man so Buxome to his wife   [65
wᵗʰ him I led an easie darlings life.
† I had my will in house, in purse in Store
whatt would a women old or yong haue more?

Two years Almost outwearinge since he died
And yett, & yett my tears ffor him nott dried   [70
I by the ffirst, & last some Issue had
butt roote, & ffruite is dead, wᶜʰ makes me sad

——[NEW PAGE]——

† My husbands all on holly dayes did die
Such day, such waie, they to the Sᵗˢ did hye
† This life is worke-day euen att the Best   [75
butt christian death, an holly day of Rest
† the ffirst, the ffirst of Martirs did befall
† Sᵗ Stevens ffeast to him was ffunerall
the morrowe after christ our fflesh did take
this husband did his mortall fflesh fforsake   [80
† the second on a double sainted day
† to Jude, & Symon tooke his happy way
† This Symon as an auncient Story Sayth
† did ffirst in England plant the Christian ffayth

[Niceph: Histo:

Most sure itt is thatt Jude in holy writt   [85

[Jude ver: 3

† doth warne vs to Mayntayne, & ffight ffor itt

In wch all those thatt liue, & die, may well

hope wth the S^{ts} eternally to dwell

† The last on St Mathias day did wend

vnto his home, & pilgrimages ende   [90

this feast comes in that season wch doth bringe

vppon dead Winters cold, a lyvelie Springe

His Bodie winteringe in the lodge of death

Shall ffeele A springe, wth budd of life, & Breath

† And Rise in incorruption, glorie, power   [95

[corrin: 15.42

† Like to the Bodie of our Sauiour

[phillip: 3.21

In vayne itt were, prophane itt were ffor me

† Wth Sadnes to aske wch of theis three

[Matt: 22.18

I shall call husband in ye Resurrection

ffor then shall all in glorious perfection   [100

Like to th'immortall heauenlie Angells liue

who wedlocks bonds doe neither take nor giue

[verse 30

Butt in the Meane tyme this must be my care

of knittinge here a fourth knott to beware

† A threefold cord though hardlie yett is broken   [105

Another Auncient storie doth betoken

[Ecclesiast 4.12

† thatt seldome comes A Better; whie should I

then putt my Widowehood in Jeopardy?

the Virgins life is gold, as Clarks vs tell

the Widowes siluar, I loue siluar well.   [110

Textual Notes

The present transcription differs from the transcript published in the first edition in a few insignificant respects. In the following list of changes, the appropriate line number is followed by the original reading, then by a bracket, then by the corrected reading. (All essays in the present volume incorporate these changes.)

18 her] hir; **21** that] thatt; **23** profession] proffession; **30** learning] learninge; **37** But] Butt; **38 margin** not] nott; **40** have] haue; **58 margin** Moulswoorth] Moulsworth; **60** not] nott; **64** it] itt; **68** what] whatt; **85** that] thatt; **87** that] thatt; **103** But] Butt; **108** jeopardy] Jeopardy

Title: "Memorandum": literally, "[It is] to be remembered"; with perhaps the additional sense of a memento or souvenir of Moulsworth's life.

4: "on thatt day* vppon that day": probably wordplay meaning "on that same day and also about or concerning that day"

7: In Moulsworth's marginal note, the spelling and meaning of the word followed by a question mark are uncertain. This is one of the few cases in the MS where the handwriting has proven indecipherable. Clearly the word is a verb; however, rather than suggesting a possibility, we have chosen to transcribe the word as it appears. "Tell clocke": according to the *OED*, one who "tells the clock," meaning "to count the hours as shown by a clock; hence, to pass one's time idly." The final part of the Biblical citation is also unclear and thus concludes with an added question mark. Probably the phrasing intended was "&c" (i.e., "etc."). That is, Moulsworth clearly alludes to Acts 17:28, but she may also find the following few verses relevant to her meaning: "For in him we live, and move, and have our being; as certain also of your own poets have said, For we are also his offspring.... he hath appointed a day, in which he will judge the world in righteousness by *that* man whom he hath ordained" (Acts 17:28–31). Interestingly, one of those who responded to Paul's call in this instance was "a woman named Damaris" (Acts 17:34).

16: "for state": with a view toward public dignity, pomp, and ceremony; "rather": earlier

17: Moulsworth seems to have misremembered or miscopied the location of the reference to Martha, which should be Luke 10:41. In context the passage reads as follows: "Now it came to pass, as they went, that he entered into a certain village; and a certain woman, named Martha, received him into her house. And she had a sister, called Mary, who also sat at Jesus' feet, and heard his word. But Martha was cumbered about much serving, and came to him, and said, Lord, dost thou not care that my sister hath left me to serve alone? Bid her, therefore, that she help me. And Jesus answered, and said unto her, Martha, Martha, thou art careful and troubled about many things. But one thing is needful, and Mary hath chosen that good part, which shall not be taken away from her" (Luke 10:38–42). St. Martha was traditionally considered the "prototype of the busy housewife"; see J.C.J. Metford, *Dictionary of Christian Lore and Legend* (London: Thames and Hudson, 1983), 168.

18: "guesse": guest

20: "Behold, I stand at the door, and knock; if any man hear my voice, and open the door, I will come in to him, and will sup with him, and he with me" (Revelation 3:20). The next scriptural citation also seems relevant to this line: "But they constrained him, saying, Abide with us; for it is toward evening, and the day is far spent. And he went in to tarry with them" (Luke 24:29).

24: "Leuies tribe": among the ancient Hebrews, the Levites were a religious caste descended from Levi, son of Jacob. They held no portion of land in Canaan (Deuteronomy 18). Perhaps this fact is relevant to Moulsworth's claim in l. 23 about her father's lands. Robert Dorsett held various ecclesiastical offices.

26: Scarlet colored robes were traditionally presented to doctors of divinity or the law.

28: "sad": settled, firmly established; strong; orderly, grave, serious; dignified; mature (*OED*).

30: Surely this was meant to read "decke my mind."

38: "want of vse": lack of practice or exercise

44: "dight": adorned, prepared

52: "backward": late, delayed

54: "score": record or account; the sum recorded to a customer's debit (*OED*).

56: "widowes fast": abstinence as an expression of grief

58: Bevill Molesworth is mentioned in a letter dated 1603, written by Sir Robert Cecil (chief minister of James I) and addressed to the Lord Chief Baron and the other Barons of the Exchequer: "I am certified by my deputies in my farm of silk that Henry Southworth and Bevill Mowlsworth, two of his Majesty's waiters of the port of London, have been much envied by some of the officers of the port, and often unjustly molested by others both for their endeavours to serve his Majesty and their diligence to assist my deputies .... I understand also that an English bill is depending before you in the Court of Exchequer preferred by one William Gerrard against Mowlsworth and Southworth, which I am informed is but matter of molestation, because the suit is not brought against them by due form of law .... As I am not willing to entreat for any favour if they have evil demeaned themselves, so am I unwilling they should enure unjust molestation for their employment in my farm, or be hindered from his Majesty's service .... I knowing well what is fit to be recommended to persons in your place, who are to proceed upon proofs and not allegations, do only in general show you my desire to have them favoured as far as is reasonable." Well before he married Martha, then, Molesworth seems to have been a man who enjoyed some influence and connections. See Great Britain, Historical Manuscripts Commission, *Calendar of the Manuscripts of the ... Marquess of Salisbury*, part XV (London: HMSO, 1930), 362–63.

59: "Mortimers": an ancient noble family, especially prominent in the fourteenth century

60: "Heraulds fee": this alludes to the notorious abuses by which bogus coats of arms could be purchased from corrupt heralds

65: "Buxome": Gracious, indulgent, favorable; obliging, amiable, courteous, affable, kindly; blithe, jolly; obedient, compliant, humble (*OED*).

67: "Store": provision and maintenance of household necessities

73: "roote, & ffruite": i.e., the fathers and the children. This pairing of words has Biblical precedents; see, for instance, Proverbs 12:12.

75: "worke-day": probably a variant of "work-a-day"—i.e., routine, laborious; distinguished from a holiday or day of rest

77–78: For details of St. Stephen, see Acts 6–7, esp. 7:54–60. His holiday falls on 26 December.

81–82: 28 October. "Apart from appearing in lists of the Apostles and being present at Pentecost, Simon receives scant attention in the [New Testament], but legend links his later exploits with those of St. Jude. According to Craton's *Ten Books* (probably dating from the 4th century) and Abdias's *Apostolic History* (617–21), the two apostles conducted their evangelical missions in Syria, Mesopotamia and Persia" (Metford 228).

83: Thomas Fuller, in his *Church History of Great Britain* (ed. J.S. Brewer, 6 vols. [Oxford: Oxford University Press, 1845]) cites as the source of this legend Dorotheus, whom he identifies as the "bishop of Tyre under Diocletian and Constantine the Great" (1:11–12).

84: The marginal note probably refers to Nicephorus Callistus (ca. 1256–ca. 1335), a Byzantine historian, whose "principal work, a 'Church History,' narrates in 18 books the events from the birth of Christ to the death of the Phocas (610).... In 1555 it was translated into Latin and played an important part in the controversial literature of the time ...." See *The Oxford Dictionary of the Christian Church*, ed. F.L. Cross (London: Oxford University Press, 1966), 953.

86: "... ye should earnestly contend for the faith which was once delivered unto the saints" (Jude, verse 3).

89: Saint Matthias's day is 24 February.

95: 1 Corinthians 15:42 says of "the resurrection of the dead" that "It is sown in corruption; it is raised in incorruption."

96: Philippians 3:21 promises that Christ "shall change our vile body, that it may be fashioned like his glorious body, according to the working by which he is able even to subdue all things unto himself."

98: The Sadducees, "who say that there is no resurrection," confronted Jesus with the story of a woman who had been married successively to seven brothers, all of whom died. They continued: "Therefore, in the resurrection whose wife shall she be of the seven? For they all had her. Jesus answered and said unto them, Ye do err, not knowing the scriptures, nor the power of God. For in the resurrection they neither marry, nor are given in marriage, but are like the angels of God in heaven" (Matthew 21:23, 28–30).

105: "a threefold cord is not quickly broken" (Ecclesiastes 4:12).

107: For the proverb "seldom comes the better," which was widely current in the sixteenth century, see Morris Palmer Tilley, *A Dictionary of the Proverbs in England in the Sixteenth and Seventeenth Centuries* (Ann Arbor: University of Michigan Press, 1950), 46.

November the 10th 1632

The Memorandum of Martha Moulsworth
Widdowe

The tenth day of the winter monte, November
A day which I must duely still remember
did open first theis eies, and shewed this light
Noe on that day vppon that daie I write
The season fitly, willingly combined
the birth day of my selfe & of theis lyns
The tyme the clocke the yearly stroke is one
that clocke by Httie tíme restored gate gone
How theis, how many warnings it will gine
He only knowet in whome we are & líve

In carnall state of sin originall
I did nott stay one whole day naturall
The seale of grace in Sarramentall water
So soone had I, so soone became the daughter
of earthly parents, & of heavenlie father
some christian late for grace, the soyson rather

My Name was Martha Martha tooke much payne
our Saviour Christ her guest to entertaine
God gyve me grace my Inward house to digt
that he woth me may suppe & stay all night

My Father was a Man of spotted flame
of gentle Birth & Dossett was his name
He had, Left Lands of his owne possession
he was os Levied twise by his profession
His Mother oxford knowenge was his worth
arayd in scarlett Robe did send him forth
By him I was brought vpp in goodie pietie
In modest chearefulnes, & sad sobrietie
Nor onlie so, Beyond my sex & kind
he did with learninge Lattin deck the mind
And whie nott so? the muses femalle are
and therfore of vs femalle take some care
Two vniuersities we haue of men
o that we had but one of women then

November 10th 1632

my muse is a tel
clocke in crossltie
eueric stroke tells
a couplet & mine
so many, tymes
Vee 55
Acts 17.28.3

Luke 10. 14

Reutla: 3. 20.
Luke 24. 29

Lattin is nott the most
marketable matriadge
potrall

them thatt would in witt and songs surpasse
All art off men thatt is, or ever was
Butt J for Lattin have no cause to boast
ffor want of vse J longe agoe itt loste
Had J no other portion to my dowre
J might have stood a virgin to this howre
Butt though the diving Muses J love well
J have longe since this virgin like ffarewell
Thrice this Right hand did holy wedlock pligtt
And thrice this Left with pledged ringe was digtt
three husbands me J have them enioyde
nor J by them, now they by me annoyde
all lovely, lovinge all, some more, some lesse
though gonn their love & memorie J blesse,

1 Husband Mr Nicolas
Prgane, Aprill 18
1598

Untill my one & twentieth yeare of Age
J did nott bind my selfe in mariadge
My springe was late, some thinke that sooner love
butt bakkward springes doe oft the findest prove
My first knott held fine yeares & eigtt montes more
then was a yeare lett on my mourninge score

2m Tho: Throwgood
February 3 1604

My second bond tenn yeares nine montes did last
three yeard eigtt Montes J kept a widowes ffast

3d Mr Bewill
Moulsworth
June 15 1619

The third J tooke a lovely man & kind
Such goodnes in age no ffloome ffind
ffrom Mortimers he drewe his pedigre
their Arms he bore their longst with stewardes ffe
third wife J was to him, as he to me
third husband was, in nomber we agree
Eleven yeard & eigtt montes his autumn lasted
a second Spring to soone away itt hasted
was never man so Buxome to his wife
with him J had an easie darlingt life
J had my will in house in purse in Store
so hatt would a womb old or yong have more?
Two yeard almost outwearinge since he diedd
And yett, & yett my teard ffor him nott driedd
J by the ffirst & last some Jssue had
butt roott, & fruits is dead, wich makes me sad

My husbands all on jolly dayes did die
Fryeday, hurt wait, they to the st did hye
This life is work-day even att the best
but christian ~~death~~ an holly day off rest
the first, the first off Martirs did befall
st stevens ffast to him was ffinenbrace
the morrow after christmos ffast did take
this husband did his mortall ~~ffeast~~ fforsake
the second on a double sainted day
te ffinde, & Symon tooke his gayry way
This Symon as an auncient storye sayth
Niceph: Histo: did first in England plant this christian ffayth
Jude ver. 3 Most sure it is leat ffirst in holy writ
doth warne us to Maentayne, & fight ffor it
An seck all these that live & die may will
have holy the sts eternally to dwell
The last on st Mathias day did solenly
unto his tombe & pilgrimages true

this feast comes in that season wch doth bringe
upon dead winters cold a lyvelie springe
His bodie winteringe in the lodge of death
shall ffeele A springe, wch buds off life & breath
1corin: 15.42 And rise in incorruption, glorie, power
1phillip: 3.21 Like to the bodie of our Saviour

An vayne it were, prophane it were ffor me
Matt: 22.18 doth Sadures to aske wch of these three
Shall call husband in the Resurrection
ffor then shall all in glorious perfection
Like to th'immortall heavenlie Angells live
Verse 30 who wedlocks bond doe neither take nor give
Butt in the meane tyme this must be my care
of knittinge here a ffourth knot to beware
A threefold cord though hardlie yett is broken
Ecclesiast Another clearion storie doth betoken
4.12 that seldome comes A better woe should I
then putt my widoowhood in Jeopardy?
the virgins life is gold, as Clarke doe tell
the widoowes Silvar, I love Silvar well.

November the 10th 1632
† The Memorandum of Martha Moulsworth
 Widow

The tenth day of the winter month November
A day which I must duly still remember
Did open first these eyes, and showed this light
† Now on that day upon that day I write
                                        November the 10th 1632
This season fitly willingly combines   [5
The birthday of my self, and of these lines
† The time the clock, the yearly stroke is one
 That clock by fifty five returns hath gone
 How few, how many warnings it will give
 He only knows in whom we are, and live   [10
              [*beginning next to line 7:* my muse is a tell
                                   clock, and echoeth
                                   every stroke with
                                   a coupled rhyme
                                   so many times
                                   viz[.] 55
                                   Acts 17[:]28 [etc]

In carnal state of sin original
I did not stay one whole day natural
The seal of grace in sacramental water
So soon had I, so soon become the daughter
Of earthly parents, and of heavenly father   [15
† Some christen late for state, the wiser rather.

† My name was Martha, Martha took much pain
                                        Luke 10:14
† Our savior Christ her guest to entertain
 God give me grace my inward house to dight
† That he with me may sup, and stay all night   [20
                                        Revela[tion] 3[:]20

My father was a man of spotless fame

Luke 24:29

Of gentle birth, and Dorset was his name
He had, and left lands of his own possession
† He was of Levi's tribe by his profession
His mother Oxford knowing well his worth   [25
† Arrayed in scarlet robe did send him forth.
By him I was brought up in godly piety
† In modest cheerfulness, and sad sobriety
Nor only so, beyond my sex and kind
† He did with learning Latin deck [my] mind   [30
And why not so? The muses females are
And therefore of us females take some care
Two universities we have of men
Oh that we had but one of women then

————[NEW PAGE]————

Oh then that would in wit, and tongues surpass   [35
All art of men that is, or ever was
But I of Latin have no cause to boast
† For want of use, I long ago it lost

Latin is not the most
marketable marriage
metal

Had I no other portion to my dower
I might have stood a virgin to this hour   [40
But though the virgin muses I love well
I have long since bid virgin life farewell
Thrice this right hand did holy wedlock plight
† And thrice this left with pledged ring was dight
Three husbands me, and I have them enjoyed   [45
Nor I by them, nor they by me annoyed
All lovely, loving all, some more, some less
Though gone their love, and memory I bless.

Until my one and twentieth year of age
                          1 husband, Mr[.] Nicolas
                          Prynne, April 18
                          1598

I did not bind myself in marriage   [50
My spring was late, some think that sooner love
† But backward springs do oft the kindest prove
My first knot held five years, and eight months more
† Then was a year set on my mourning score
My second bond ten years nine months did last   [55
                     2^d Mr[.] Tho[mas] Througood
                     February 3 1604
† Three years eight months I kept a widow's fast

The third I took a lovely man, and kind
† Such comeliness in age we seldom find
                        3^d Mr[.] Bevill
                        Moulsworth
                        June 15, 1619

† From Mortimers he drew his pedigree
† Their arms he ~~bought~~ bore, not bought with herald's fee   [60
Third wife I was to him, as he to me
Third husband was, in number we agree
Eleven years, and eight months his autumn lasted
A second spring too soon away it hasted
† Was never man so buxom to his wife   [65
With him I led an easy darling's life.
† I had my will in house, in purse[,] in store
What would a woman old or young have more?
Two years almost outwearing since he died
And yet, and yet my tears for him not dried   [70
I by the first, and last some issue had
† But root, and fruit is dead, which makes me sad

————[NEW PAGE]————

My husbands all on holy days did die
Such day, such way, they to the saints did hie
† This life is work-day even at the best   [75
But Christian death, an holy day of rest
† The first, the first of martyrs did befall
† Saint Steven's feast to him was funeral
The morrow after Christ our flesh did take
This husband did his mortal flesh forsake   [80
† The second on a double sainted day
† To Jude, and Simon took his happy way
† This Simon as an ancient story sayeth
† Did first in England plant the Christian faith

                                    Niceph[orus]: Histo[ria]

Most sure it is that Jude in holy writ   [85

                                            Jude ver[se] 3

† Doth warn us to maintain, and fight for it
In which all those that live, and die, may well
Hope with the saints eternally to dwell
† The last on Saint Mathias' day did wend
Unto his home, and pilgrimage's end   [90
This feast comes in that season which doth bring
Upon dead winter's cold, a lively spring
His body wintering in the lodge of death
Shall feel a spring, with bud of life, and breath
† And rise in incorruption, glory, power   [95

                                    1 Corinthians 15:42

† Like to the body of our savior

                                            Phillip[ians] 3:21

In vain it were, profane it were for me
† With sadness to ask which of these three

                                            Matthew 22:18

I shall call husband in the resurrection
For then shall all in glorious perfection   [100
Like to the immortal heavenly angels live

Who wedlock's bonds do neither take nor give

verse 30

But in the meantime this must be my care
Of knitting here a fourth knot to beware
† A threefold cord though hardly yet is broken   [105
Another ancient story doth betoken

Ecclesiastes 4:12

† That seldom comes a better; why should I
Then put my widowhood in jeopardy?
The virgin's life is gold, as clerks us tell
The widow's silver, I love silver well.   [110

Appendix 2

Transcripts of the Wills
of Martha Moulsworth
and Her Three Husbands

The following transcriptions are based on documents currently held at the Public Record Office in Chancery Lane, London. The PRO reference numbers for the wills are as follows: Martha Moulsworth (PROB 11/197); Bevill Molesworth (PROB 11/159); Thomas Thorowgood (PROB 11/126); Nicholas Prynne (PROB 11/103). Line breaks are indicated by "/" marks.

The Will of Martha Moulsworth

IN THE NAME OF GOD AMEN I Martha Molesworth of Hoddesdon in the countie of Hartford widowe / weake in bodie, yet by gods goodnes of good understanding / and of sound memorie doe for the better quieting of my minde, and declaration / thereof to [blank space in will] Survive ordaine and make this my last will and testam*ent* / in forme followeing ffirst I bequeath my Soule both in life and death into the / mercifull handes of Allmightie God my creator who gave it mee my bodie I com*m*itt / to the'arth from whence it came to be decentlie buried at the discretion of my executrix / herevnder named Item I giue and bequeath vnto the children and grandchildren that are / vnmarried nowe of my loveing kinsman Symon Edmondes of London Alderman / the severall legacies followeing, to be paid and [word unclear; raised?] to them onelie out of the / money oweing to mee vpon a Surrender by William Parnell Tenant of the Mannor / of [blank space in will] in the countie of M[iddlesex] to the said children, and grandchildren I

say I doe / giue one hundred and fiftie poundes of lawfull Englishe money, that is to say, To / Symon Edmonds the eldest
Sonne twentie poundes, To Thomas the second sonne other /
twentie poundes / To Elizabeth Edmonds other twentie poundes
To Sarah Edmonds / other twentie poundes To Hugh Wood the
sonne of my cozen Hugh Wood and Martha / his wife tenn
poundes To Christopher Parke the sonne of my Cozen Christopher
/ Parke, and Anne his wife [blank space in will] tenn poundes And
the rest of the said som*m*e of One / hundred and fiftie poundes I
leave to be disposed of by my said kinsman Alderman / Edmonds
amongst his other children (which to my remembrance I haue not
seene) / as hee shall thinke fitting And it is my will and minde that
those legacies being paid / out of the Surrender aforesaid, the rest
of the money due by the said Surrender shall accrew / to my executrix, my meaneing being that this Surrender shalbe to the vses
aforesaid / and to noe other vse or vses Item I giue and bequeath
to william Pryn of Lincolnes / Inn in the countie of Middl*esexe* esquire the som*m*e of five poundes Sterling hee being my / husband
Pryns godson and mine Item I giue vnto Marmaduke Rowdon /

[New Page]

Son of my executrix one hundred poundes sterling to be paid vnto
him at the end of two yeares / next after my decease if hee shalbe
then liveing Item I giue to Beuill Rowdon her sonne / two hundred poundes sterling to be paid vnto him at the end of two yeares
next after my / decease if hee shalbe then liveing Item I give to
Robert Rowdon her sonne two / hundred poundes Sterling to be
paid vnto him at the end of two yeares next after my decease / if
hee shalbe then liveing Item I giue to Marmaduke Rowdon sonne
of Thomas Rowdon / two hundred poundes sterling to be paid
when hee shall come to the age of seaven yeares / And in case the
said Marmaduke shall departe this life before hee attaine the said
age / of seaven yeares, then I giue those two hundred poundes to
the said Thomas Rowdon / his ffather Item I give to my cozen
Thomas Willys of London Chaundler five poundes / sterling Item
I give to my cozen Anne fforster widowe three poundes sterling /
Item I give to Martha Henne [?] the parcell of table lynnen; on
which I lent her / ffather tenn poundes Item I give and bequeath to
Martha Rowdon daughter of my / executrix, one thousand
poundes of lawfull money of England Item I give & bequeath /
vnto the two daughters of my loveing freind and Grandson Edward fforster of London / Marchant the som*m*e of three hundred

poundes sterling (that is to say) To Elizabeth the / eldest, one hundred and fiftie poundes to be paid vnto her at the end of two yeares next / after my decease if shee shalbe then liveing, and if dead, then that one hundred and fiftie / poundes to be paid vnto Martha her sister, And vnto the said Martha the second daughter of / the said Edmond the somme of one hundred and fiftie poundes to be paid vnto her at the end / of two yeares next after my decease, if shee shalbe then liveinge, and if dead, then that / one hundred and fiftie poundes to be paid vnto the said Elizabeth her sister, The said somme / of three hundred poundes to be in full discharge of all promised bills, bonds, covenants / whatsoever by mee made vnto the said Edmond fforster Item I give to Edmond fforster / Sonne of the said Edmond two hundred poundes sterling Item I give to Edward Roberts / my auncient Servant fowre shillinges everie moneth dureing his naturall life, the first / paiement thereof to beginne on the first daie of the first moneth that shall happen / after my decease, and soe to continue dureing his life Item I give to my daughter in law / Elizabeth Lucey my gold ring with five Diamonds in itt, and to Martha her daughter / my greate chaine of gold Item I give to my said Grandson, Edmond fforster / and to William Bowger [?] and Henrie Crewe tenn poundes a peece The rest and / residue of all my goodes, chattells, debts, Iewells, plate, money, lands of inheritance, / ffee simple, and Coppiehold I give and bequeath vnto my daughter in lawe Dame / Elizabeth Rawdon alias Elizabeth Rowdon alias Thorowgood, whome I doe hereby make / and ordaine full and sole executrix of this my testament and last will And I doe / hereby intimate declare and publishe that the reasons which doe enduce and cause / mee to be so liberall and beneficiall vnto my said daughter in lawe Rowdon, and to / her children, and grandchildren before named in bestoweing the most parte of my estate / on them, and giveing my inheritance as aforesaid are as followeth That Thomas Thorowgood / my late deceased husband, and ffather of the said Dame Elizabeth Rawdon left mee / a plentifull estate of chattles and landes and other hereditaments, which I have enioyed / thees manie yeares, And for that the said Dame Elizabeth and her said children, and / grandchildren have ever bene loveing and kinde vnto mee and allwaise diligent & / carefull of mee both in sicknes and in health, in soe much that shee and they have / gayned and deserve my love, and I doe love her the said Dame Elizabeth as / if shee were my owne child, and I love the said children, and grandchildren / as if they were my owne And I doe hereby revoake and

Comptermande all / former and other wills legacies, and bequests by mee heretofore made giuen and / bequeathed In wittnes whereof to this my present testament conteyning therein / my last will I the said Martha Molesworth have sett my hand and seale Dated / the nyneteenth daie of July Anno one thousand six hundred ffortie six And in the / two and twentieth Yeare of the raigne of our Soveraigne Lord Charles by the grace of

[New Page]
God King of England Scotland ffrance, and Ireland defender of the ffaithe /
Martha Molesworth Signed sealed and by the within named Martha Molesworth pub= / lished, and declared to be her last will and testament the nyneteenth daie of Iuly one thousand / six hundred fortie six within written in the presence of Tho Hassell Tho [illegible] / Basill fforster Tho Hen

——[END]——

The Will of Bevill Molesworth

IN THE NAME OF GOD AMEN This seaventeenth daie of ffebruary One thousand sixe hundred thirtie beinge the sixt yeare / of the Raigne of our Soveraigne Lord Charles by the grace of God of England Scotland

[New Page]
ffraunce and Ireland kinge defender of the faith &c Bevill Molesworth of Hodsden in the / Countie of Hertford Esquier weake in bodie with age and sicknes accordinge to the Common condicion / of nature, yet enioyinge the freedome of spiritt in vnderstandinge and memory by gods gratious good- / =nes, doe this in his feare for the better quietinge of my minde and declaracion thereof to such as shall / survive, ordaine and make this my last will and Testament disavouchinge and revokeinge all former wills / whatsoever. My first care is to make my peace with God through the mediacion of Jesus Christ whom as / I acknowledg mine onely redeemer, soe I seeke none other Mediator or Saviour, by his only merritt and / mediacion desireing and expectinge free pardon of all my sinnes, soe that my soule being quitted from the guilt / of originall and accuall sinnes maie enioye that happines in his heav-

enly kingdome by him purchased and / promised to all the elect.
My bodie I committ to the ~~earth~~ Comon Purgatory of the earth to
bee buried in / Broxburne Church vnder that stone where my
deare sonne Bevill Molesworth lyeth, there to rest vnder / hope
vntill the generall resurreccion of the iust, wch I most assuredly
beleeve Item I give to the poore of / the Towne of Hodsdon in the
parishes of Broxburne and Amwell tenne pounds to bee distributed / amongst them at the tyme of my buriall with indifferent
respect to the necessitie of the persons in either / parish by the
ioynt care and discreccion of the Ministers Churchwardens and
Overseers for the poore then / beinge, of both the said parishes
indifferently Item whereas I have certayne poore houses or Tenements lyinge in / the parish of Broxburne aforesaid purchased of
one Lowen, now in the tenure and occupacion of Bonny / and
Lawuye beinge lett for the yearely rent of fiftie shillings a yeare,
my will is that the rent of the said / houses or tenements after my
decease bee thus disposed (namely that the Vicar of Broxburne for
the tyme / beinge and his Successors forever shall preach one sermon yearely by waye of a Commemoracion at the / parish Church
of Broxburne the next Sabaoth daie after my buriall In considera-
cion of wch his paines my / will is, he soe preachinge shall have
out of the rent of the said Tenements twenty shillings yearely And
at / the same tyme amongst such poore persons of the parish of
Broxburne as shalbe present at the said sermon / and present
themselves to the Minister and Churchwardens after the Sermon to
bee distributed by the / discrecion of the said Minister and
Churchwardens other twenty shillings The tenne shillings remayning / my will and meaninge is shall by the care of the said Minister
and Churchwardens bee imployed towards / the reparacions of
the said Tenements as need shall require, and the faire and decent
maintayninge of / the pavements in the Church about the said
stone, vnder which my body shall lye buried Item whereas / I have
certayne houses or tenements leased out for tearme of yeares to
come scituate or beinge in the / Old change in London My will
and meaninge is that the whole rent and profitt of all the said tenements / shall come vnto Martha my wife duringe her naturall life
And after her decease vnto my daughter / Grace the wife of
Thomas Hill of London Gentleman duringe her naturall life alsoe
And after / the decease of my said daughter Grace, to discend to
Bevill Hill sonne of the said Thomas & Grace / Hill and his heires
for ever Provided allwaies and my will and meaninge is in the dis-
posinge of the / said Tenements to her my said daughter Grace

and Bevill Hill in manner and forme above= / =written, that it bee with this condicion, That whereas amongst certaine lands lyinge in Hammersmith / in the parish of ffullham lately by mee disposed, and by waie of contract assured as a dower with / Elizabeth my daughter married to ffrauncis Lucy Esquire There is some parte of the said land Coppie / =hold to the lord Bishopp of London, and accordinge to the Custome to bee passed by surrender which / for want of Tennants ready to take the said surrender was not ~~sett downe~~ soe donne at the tyme of the said contract / Therefore my will and meaninge is for the makeing good of my true intencion in the said contract with / the said ffrancis Lucy my sonne in lawe, for that parte of the dower to him intended and promised, That / if my said daughter Grace Hill and Bevill Hill her sonne shall after my decease (being therevnto / required by the said ffrancis Lucy, the said parcell of Coppiehold soe defectively left over) take vp in Court / and imediately surrender freely and fully to the said ffrancis Lucy accordinge to the said contract That / then my said bequest of the forenamed Tenements lyinge in the parish of St Mary Magdalens in the / old change London shall accordingly stand good to my said daughter Grace Hill duringe her naturall / life, and after her decease to her sonne Bevill Hill and his heires for ever But if the said Grace and / Bevill shall refuse to passe the said Surrender accordinge to this mine appointment in manner afore= / said, then I give and bequeath All those my houses or tenements in Saint Mary Magdalens in the Old /

[New Page]

Change above named after the decease of Martha my wife to him my said sonne in lawe ffrancis Lucy / and his heires for ever Item whereas I have two acres of arrable land more or lesse lyinge in Ryefeild in / the parish of Broxburne now in the tenure or occupacion of one William Ayres lett together wth some / other lands which I hold in the right of Martha my wife duringe her naturall life As alsoe a certaine / parcell of meadowe in the Comon meade by mee lately purchased of one Boreham ioyninge to the lands / of Marmaduke Rowden of London My will and meaninge is, that all the said parcells of meadowe and / arrable ground shall remayne to her my said wife Martha duringe her naturall life And after her decease / I doe give and bequeath all the said parcells vnto Marmaduke Rowden of London and his heires forever Item I give and bequeath a certayne Cottage or Tenement lyinge in the parish of Lewsham in the County / of Kent lately in the tenure or occupacion of Widdow Harrison, and now in the tenure of one Belton / at five nobles rent per Annum imediately after my decease, to the releife of the poore people of / Lewsham aforesaid for ever, deductinge out of the said rent tenne shillings yearely for the Minister being / for ever for one sermon preachinge as at Broxburne Lastlie I give and bequeath to Martha my wife / all my goods and Chattells, lands, and leases whatsoever not formerly disposed beinge in the parish of / Lewsham in Kent above named duringe her naturall life ~~after~~ And after her decease vnto my daughter Grace / the wife of Thomas Hill above named duringe her naturall life alsoe And after the decease of the said / Martha and Grace To Bevill Hill abovenamed and his heires for ever The residue of all my goods / and Chattells whatsoever and wheresoever not otherwise disposed (my debts being paid funerall rights decently / performed &c), I fully and whollie give and bequeath vnto Martha my wife whom I alsoe do constitute & / ordaine of this my last will and testament full and sole Executrix In witnes whereof I have herevnto sett / myne hand and seale the ~~daie and~~ yeare and daie above written Bevell Molesworth Signed, sealed, & delivered / by the said Bevill Molesworth as his last will and Testament the yeare and daie prefixed in presence / of Tho. Hassall William Kinge Sara Lewin ./

———[END]———

The Will of Thomas Thorowgood

IN THE NAME OF GOD AMEN I Thomas Thorowgood / of Hodsdon in the parishe of Broxborne in the Countie of Hertford gent beyng / visited by the hand of god and vnder the Arrest of bodilie sicknes yet in respect of / my mynde and vnderstanding well setled and resolued by gods greate mercy do / thus ordayne and make my last will and testament vizt: ffirst I bequeathe my / Soule and better parte to hym my Creator and Redemer whose I whollie am / holding fast by that guifte of faithe which he hathe bestowed vppon me the assurance / of his grace and mercey in the free and full pardon of all my synnes thoroughe the / alone and all sufficient meritt and mediacion of Jesus Christ thoroughe whome I / allso beleue to obteyne etearnall life and an Inheritaunce amongest the Saintes / in the Caelestiall kingdome which assurance I haue

euer held by gods grace and / therein desire hym I maye con-
tinewe even to the end. My bodie I committ to the / Earthe from
whence yt came to be buryed in Broxborne aforesayed when god
shall / call me to rest in the common bed of corruption to the generall resurrection of the iust / which I allso steadfastlie beleue and
hopefullie expect. Touching my worldlie goodes / and the Re-
maynder of that portion which god of his free goodnes allotted
vnto me for / the Comforte of my life I thus dispose thereof by the
permission of my good god & / the free assent of Martha my wife
by waye of Dower of Ioynture estated in the Mayne / of my estate
that is to saye: Imprimis whereas I haue certaine Tenements without / Algate in London late william Thorowgoods my father deceased, my will and desire / ys that the whole righte and possession of the saied Tenements or howses shall presently / after my
deathe descend and come vnto Elizabeth my daughter wife of
Marmaduke / Rawdon of London and the heires of her bodie
lawfullie begotten for euer. Item I giue / and bequeathe vnto the
saied Elizabeth the present state and possession of a certaine /
Mesuage or Tenement in Hodsdon aforesayed commonlie called or
knowne by the name of / the white Hynde nowe in the tenure or
occupacion of one Smithe as allso one other / Tenement adioyning
therunto nowe in the tenure or occupacion of one Page: Bothe /
which saied Tenements with there appurtinances my will is
shoulde come plenallie and presently / to my saied Daughter and
her heires for euer as before All that my meadowe grounde / bey-
ing fyve acres more or lesse lying in the Common meades of
Hodsdon aforesayed / latelie purchased of John Thorowgood my
neiphue to descend presentlie to her my / saied daughter without
deduction of thyres to my wife or any other incombrance / whatsoeuer. Item I giue vnto my saied daughter three guilt potts of silver plate / and one silver salt suteable which were my fathers As
allso of all the houshold stuffe / remayning in the house which
was her graundfather Highams of all kyndes I

[New Page]
giue vnto my saied daughter by my Wifes willing assent her free
and full choise presently / Item to Marmaduke Rawdon my sonne
in lawe I giue one hundred poundes of currant / Englishe money
parte of a portion promised to be paied vnto hym his heires or as-
signes / by myne executrix presentlie after my decease. Item to
Thomas Rawdon my graundchilde / I giue three parcell guilte
broade Bowles of silver plate which were my ffathers to / be

presentlie deliuered as a remembraunce of my loue to hym. Item I giue and bequeathe / vnto my sister Anne Lewin widowe fyve poundes a yere of currant englishe money to be / payed her yerelie by myne executrix at twoe seuerall and vsuall tymes in the yere by equall / portions so longe as she my saied executrix and my saied Sister shall liue togeather / Item to Humfrey Downes my brother Sara Goughe Elizabeth Rowley and Mary / Downes my sisters: To william Lewin my Cosin and Sarah his wife I giue fortie / shillinges a peece to make eache of them a ryng in remembraunce of my loue to be by / myne executrix presentlie performed. Item to the poore of the towne of Hoddsdon / I giue fower nobles a yere of currant englishe money to be payed for euer by myne / heires & executors out of the Rent of that Tenement where Gilderson nowe dwelleth / Item to Thomas Hassell vicar of Amwell I giue twentie shillinges a yere of / currant englishe money to be yerelie payed vnto hym by myne heires and executors / out of the tenement adioyning to my nowe dwelling howse so longe as he contineweth / his vsuall exercise of preaching at Hoddesdon Chappell as allso to hym fortie / shillinges of present money as a remembraunce desyring that he may preache at / my buriall And that the vicar of Broxborne giving waye therunto shall haue suche fees / as are due to hym. Moreouer my Will and meaning ys that concerning all my Landes / howsoeuer disposed of in my life ~~tyme~~ (whereso my wife hath a Ioynture) or ordered in / this my will in manner and forme aforesayed which fullie and whollie my meaning / ys should after the decease of Martha my wife descend to Elizabeth my daughter / and the heires of her bodye lawfullie begotten for euer. yf so be yt shoulde please god that / she my saied daughter should dye without suche lawfull yssue Then my will ys that / all my saied Landes should be equallie deuided & not by waye of Sale but in free / estate and tenure betwixt Marmaduke Rawdon my sonne in lawe William Lewyn and / William Downes my neiphues soe equallie deuided betwixt them to remayne to them / and theire heires for euer. Lastlie my will ys that all my goods and Chattells / whatsoeuer vnbequeathed (my debts beyng payed Legaceys performed and funeralls / discharged shall fullie and whollie come vnto Martha my wife whome I ordayne and / make of this my last will and Testament full and sole executrix. And this I / avouche for my last will revoking all other former willes according to the playne / Letter and meaning thereof beyng noe where either enterlyned or defaced. / Witnesse myne hand and seale this twentie and fowrthe daye of October in the /

yeare of grace one thowsand sixe hundred and fifteene. Thomas Thorowgood. Signed sealed and avouched for his last will and Testament the yere and daye / aboue written in the presence of vs Thomas Luther Edward Roberts

———[END]———

The Will of Nicholas Prynne

IN THE NAME OF GOD AMEN The sixe and twentieth daye of december / Anno d*omini* One thowsande sixe hundred and three and in the yere of the Reigne of oure / Sovereigne Lord James by the grace of god kinge of Englande Scotlande ffraunce and / Irelande [*marginal insertion*: defender of ye faith &c y^t / is to saie of England / fraunce & Ireland ye first] the firste and of Scotlande the seaven and thirtithe I Nicholas Pryne Citizen / and Goldsmithe of London beinge at this present sicke in bodye but of good and perfect / mynde remembraunce and vnderstandinge thancks be to almighty god doe declare and / make this my pr*es*ente Testament and last will in manner and fourme followeinge (that is / to saie) ffirste and principallie I give and com*m*ende my soule vnto god almightie assuredlie / trustinge and believinge by the only merritts deathe and passion of Ihesus Christe my Savior / and Redeemer to have salvation and free pardon and Remyssyon of all my synnes and eternall lief / in the kingdome of heaven wth the faithefull and elect Children of god and my bodye I comytte / to the earthe to be buried in the parrishe Churche of St Mathewe (of wch parrishe I am nowe a / parrishoner) in suche *Christ*ian sorte and manner as to my Executrix and lovinge wief hereafter / named shall seeme expedient And for suche temporarie and earthelie goodes as it hathe / pleased almightie god of his goodnes to endowe and blesse me wth My Will thereof is in mann*er* / and fourme as hereafter followeth (That is to saie) That accordinge to the custome of the Citie / of London there shalbe an equall division thereof in three p*a*rtes One equall thirde p*a*rte whereof / I give and bequeathe vnto my lovinge wief Martha Pryne to hir owne proper vse One oth*er* / thirde p*a*rte thereof vnto and amongest my Sonne Richarde Pryne and the Childe or Children / wherw^th my saide wief nowe goeth to be payde as is vsuall by the custome of the saide Cittie of / London And th'other thirde parte I reserve to my self to dispose as hereafter is expressyd (that / is to saie) Item I give and bequeathe vnto the Companye of Goldsmithes of London to th'intent / and for that they shall bringe my Body to buryall the Somme of Tenn poundes of lawfull mony / of Englande to make a parcell or peece of plate in remembraunce of me whiche Tenn poundes I / will shalbe payde w^{th}in three yeeres next after my deceasse Item I give and bequeathe to fower / of the poore Almes menn of the saide Companie whome I will shall beare my Corps to the / buriall (that is to saie) James Collins Simon Herringe Robert ffleminge and George / Durrant To euerie of them Tenn shillings for their paines And I give moreover to the said / James Collins to th'ende he shall see that a good Coffin be provided for mee ffourtie shillinges / Item I give and bequeathe to Mr John Presse Clerck Person of the saide parrishe churche / of St Mathewe ffive poundes And to everie of his three children nowe lyvynge twentie shill*ings* / a peece wch legacies to be payed to him and them w^{th}in one yeare and a half next after my decesse / Item I give and bequeathe to my Aunte Anne Pryne wyddowe Sixe poundes thirtene shillinges / and fower pence And to my Brother Thomas Pryne ffyve poundes and ffourtie shillinges more / to make him a Ringe And to everie of his Children nowe lyvynge ffourtie shillings My sayde / Aunts Legacie and the legacie given to my saide Brother Thomas and his children to be paide / w^{th}in twoe yeeres next after my decesse Item I give and bequeathe to my Brother in lawe Henrie / Loftus Twentie poundes and to my Sister in lawe nowe his wief Sixe poundes thirtene shillings / and fower pence to be payde as is last aforesaide Item I give and bequeathe to my Sister / Batten fourtie shillings and to Erasmus hir Sonne Twentie shillings and to Thomas hir / Sonne and Elizabeth hir daughter fourtie shillings a peece to be payde w^{th}in two yeres / next after my deceasse Item I give and bequeathe to Mr William Sherston nowe Maior of / the Cittie of Bathe Three poundes to make him a Seale ringe of goulde And to his Sonne Peter / Sherston ffourtie shillings to make him a Ringe to be paide and delivered to them w^{th}in twoe yeres / next after my decesse Item I give and bequeathe vnto my Brother James Pryne ffyve pounds / to be payde vnto him as is last aforesaide And I give and bequeathe vnto Priscilla Roberts / that nurssed my Sonne Richarde ffourtie shillings to be paide w^{th}in twoe yeares after my decesse / The Remainder and residue of my said Thirde p*ar*te remayninge vnbequeathed I give and / bequeathe vnto the saide Martha my Wief and to and amongest the saide Richard Pryne my / sonne and the Childe or Children wherew^{th} my saide wief nowe goeth p*a*rte and p*a*rte like to be / payde vnto my saide Children at suche tyme as their p*a*rtes and por*ci*ons of and in the thirde

[New Page]

p*a*rte due to them of my saide goodes and chattells oughte to be payde as by the custome of the saide / Cittie of London is vsuall But yf anie of them or all of them shall happen to decease before / That then my will is that my said wief shall have to hir owne proper vse the p*a*rte and por*ci*on / of suche of them as for soe shall happen to deceasse devised and bequeathed to them of and in the / Remainder and residue of my saide thirde p*a*rte And I ordaine and make the saide Martha / my wief my full and sole Executrix of this my pre*sen*t Testament and Last will And Oue*r*seers / of the same the above named Henrie Loftus and John Presse In wittnes whereof I the said / Nicholas Pryne have hereunto left my hande and sealle the daie and yeares firste aboue written / Nicholas Pryne Signed sealled and published by the saide Nicholas Pryne for his last will & / Testament in the pre*sen*ce of George Shother Ocr[?] of Alexander Ashnest

——[END]——

Persons Mentioned in the Wills
of Martha Moulsworth and Her Husbands

The following persons are mentioned in the wills of Martha Moulsworth and her three husbands. This list is provided for the convenience of readers and as an aid to future research. When Moulsworth's first, second, and third husbands are mentioned by name, the abbreviations "(M1)," "(M2)," and "(M3)" are cited to help clarify relationships.

ASHNEST, Alexander: a witness to the will of Nicholas Prynne (M1).

AYRES, William: occupant, at the time of preparation of the will of Bevill Molesworth (M3), of arable land belonging to Molesworth in Ryefield in the parish of Broxbourne. Molesworth held this land in the right of Martha during her natural life.

BATTEN, Elizabeth: daughter of "my Sister Batten" mentioned in the will of Nicholas Prynne (M1); Prynne left Elizabeth forty shillings.

BATTEN, Erasmus: son of "my Sister Batten" mentioned in the will of Nicholas Prynne (M1); Prynne left Erasmus twenty shillings.

BATTEN, My Sister: unspecified relative, perhaps a sister-in-law, to whom Nicholas Prynne (M1) left forty shillings.

BATTEN, Thomas: son of "my Sister Batten" mentioned in the will of Nicholas Prynne (M1); Prynne left Thomas forty shillings.

BELTON, unspecified: current occupant of a tenement or cottage in Lewisham in the county of Kent; this tenement, previously occupied by the widow Harrison, was the property of Bevill Molesworth (M3); he left most of the annual rent from this property to the poor of the parish.

BOREHAM, unspecified: previous owner of land purchased by Bevill Molesworth (M3) in Hoddesdon; this land lay next to land owned by Marmaduke Rawdon of London, Molesworth's son-in-law. This land was to remain in Martha's possession during her natural life but then descend to Marmaduke Rawdon of London and his heirs forever.

BOWGER, William: Martha leaves him ten pounds; his relation to her is unspecified.

COLLINS, James: one of the four poor almsmen of the Goldsmiths' Company to whom Nicholas Prynne (M1) left ten shillings each to carry his corpse for burial. Collins was given an additional forty shillings to see that a good coffin was provided.

CREWE, Henrie: Martha leaves him ten pounds; his relation to her is unspecified.

DOWNES, Humfrey: Thomas Thorowgood (M2) calls Downes his "brother," although this presumably means brother-in-law. Downes was apparently the husband of Mary Downes. Given forty shillings to make a ring of remembrance. Presumably Martha's brother-in-law by marriage.

DOWNES, Mary: Thomas Thorowgood (M2) calls her his sister; she was presumably married to Humfrey Downes. Thomas Thorowgood left her forty shillings to make a ring of remembrance. Presumably Martha's sister-in-law.

DOWNES, William: Thomas Thorowgood (M2) calls him his nephew. If Thorowgood's daughter Elizabeth were to die without lawful issue, William Downes was to inherit one-third of Thorowgood's property after the death of Martha. The other inheritors would be Marmaduke Rawdon of London and William Lewin, another of Thomas Thorowgood's nephews. Presumably William Downes was the son of Humfrey Downes and Mary Downes.

DURRANT, George: one of the four poor almsmen of the Goldsmiths' Company to whom Nicholas Prynne (M1) left ten shillings each to carry his corpse for burial.

EDMONDES, Elizabeth: daughter or granddaughter of Symon Edmondes the Alderman of London (Martha's "loving kinsman"). Martha leaves Elizabeth twenty pounds.

EDMONDES, Sarah: daughter or granddaughter of Symon Edmondes the Alderman of London (Martha's "loving kinsman"). Martha leaves Sarah twenty pounds.

EDMONDES, Symon: eldest son of Symon Edmondes the Alderman of London (Martha's "loving kinsman"). To the younger Symon Martha leaves twenty pounds.

EDMONDES, Symon: Alderman of London; called by Martha her "loving kinsman"; she leaves legacies to his unmarried children and grandchildren. Apparently living at the time she wrote her will; she allows him to distribute some money among his remaining children, whom (to her remembrance) she has not seen.

EDMONDES, Thomas: second son of Symon Edmondes the Alderman of London (Martha's "loving kinsman"). Martha leaves Thomas twenty pounds.

EDMONDES, unspecified children: children of Symon Edmondes the Alderman of London (Martha's "loving kinsman"). Martha allows him to divide fifty pounds among them, although she notes that she does not remember seeing them.

FLEMINGE, Robert: one of the four poor almsmen of the Goldsmiths' Company to whom Nicholas Prynne (M1) left ten shillings each to carry his corpse for burial.

FORSTER, Bassil: a witness to the will of Martha Moulsworth.

FORSTER, Edmond [Edward?], the elder: merchant of London whom Martha describes as her loving friend and grandson. She leaves his two daughters a total of three hundred pounds. This bequest to his daughters serves to discharge any debts that Martha Moulsworth owes him. Martha leaves him an additional ten pounds.

FORSTER, Edmond, the younger: son of Edmond Forster the elder (a merchant of London whom Martha describes as her loving friend and grandson). The younger Edmond Forster thus seems to have been her great-grandson. She leaves him two hundred pounds sterling.

FORSTER, Elizabeth: daughter of Edmond Forster the elder (a merchant of London whom Martha describes as her loving friend and grandson). Martha leaves Elizabeth one hundred and fifty pounds. If Elizabeth dies within two years of Martha's death, this sum should be paid to her sister, Martha Forster.

FORSTER, Martha: second daughter of Edmond Forster (a merchant of London whom Martha describes as her loving friend and grandson). Martha Moulsworth leaves Martha Forster one hundred and fifty pounds. If Martha Forster dies within two years after Martha Moulsworth's death, her inheritance should be paid to her sister, Elizabeth Forster.

GILDERSON, unspecified: occupant of a tenement in Hoddesdon owned by Thomas Thorowgood (M2); four nobles a year from the rent of this tenement were left to the poor of Hoddesdon.

GOUGHE, Sara: Thomas Thorowgood (M2) calls her his sister and leaves her forty shillings to make a remembrance ring. Presumably, then, Martha's sister-in-law.

HARRISON, Widow: recent occupant of a cottage or tenement belonging to Bevill Molesworth (M3) lying in the parish of Lewisham in the county of Kent; the annual five nobles of rent from this property were left to the poor of Lewisham, except for ten shillings to be paid to the parish minister for preaching an annual sermon.

HASSALL, Thomas: Vicar of Amwell; friend of Martha. Her second husband, Thomas Thorowgood, left Hassall twenty shillings a year out of the tenement adjoining Thorowgood's dwelling house so long as Hassall continued his usual exercise of preaching at Hoddesdon chapel. Thorowgood also left Hassall forty shillings as a remembrance for preaching at Thorowgood's funeral. A witness to the will of Bevill Molesworth (M3). A witness to the will of Martha Molesworth.

HENNE [?], unspecified father: father of Martha Henne; he apparently borrowed ten pounds from Martha Moulsworth in exchange for a parcel of linen. Martha Moulsworth leaves this linen to Martha Henne.

HENNE [?], Martha: Martha leaves her a parcel of table linen on which Martha had lent Martha Henne's father ten pounds.

HEN, Thomas: a witness to the will of Martha Moulsworth. Could he be the unspecified Henne who was the father of Martha Henne?

HERRINGE, Simon: one of the four poor almsmen of the Goldsmiths' Company to whom Nicholas Prynne (M1) left ten shillings each to carry his corpse for burial.

HIGHAM, grandfather: Grandfather of Elizabeth Thorowgood Rawdon, the daughter of Thomas Thorowgood (M2). Silver products and other household stuff once belonging to Higham were left by Thomas Thorowgood to Elizabeth.

HILL, Bevill: son of Grace and Thomas Hill; grandson of Bevill Molesworth (M3). Grace was Bevill Molesworth's daughter and thus Martha's step-daughter. Bevill Hill would thus have been the step-grandson of Martha. After the death of Martha Moulsworth (his step-grandmother) and Grace Hill (his mother), Bevill Hill was to inherit property in Lewisham parish, Kent, once owned by his grandfather Bevill Molesworth (M3).

HILL, Grace Molesworth: daughter of Bevill Molesworth (M3); thus apparently step-daughter of Martha. Grace was the wife of Thomas Hill, a gentleman from London. After the death of Martha, Grace was to inherit the rent and profits of tenements in the Old Change at London belonging to Bevill Molesworth (M3). After the death of Grace, this income was to be inherited by Bevill Hill, the son of Grace and her husband Thomas and the grandson of Bevill Molesworth (M3). After the death of Martha, Grace was to inherit property once owned by Bevill Molesworth (M3) in the parish of Lewisham, Kent.

HILL, Thomas: husband of Grace Hill, daughter of Bevill Molesworth (M3). Thomas Hill would thus have been the step-son-in-law by marriage of Martha.

KINGE, William: a witness to the will of Bevill Molesworth (M3).

LEWIN, Anne: a widow; sister of Thomas Thorowgood (M2). Apparently living in the same house as Martha at the time Thomas prepared his will. He left his sister five pounds a year, to be paid by Martha as long as Anne Lewin lived in the same house with Martha.

LEWIN, Sarah: wife of William Lewin, whom Thomas Thorowgood (M2) calls his cousin; Thorowgood left Sarah forty shillings to make a remembrance ring. A witness to the will of Bevill Molesworth (M3).

LEWIN, William: Thomas Thorowgood (M2) calls Lewin his cousin and leaves him forty shillings to make a remembrance ring.

LEWIN, William: Thomas Thorowgood (M2) calls this William Lewin his nephew. If Thorowgood's daugher Elizabeth were to die without lawful issue, this William Lewin was to inherit one third of Thorowgood's property after the death of Martha, to be divided with William Downes and Marmaduke Rawdon of London. Presumably this William Lewin was the son of William Lewin (whom Thorowgood calls his cousin) and his wife Sarah.

LOFTUS, Henrie: brother-in-law of Nicholas Prynne (M1), who left him twenty pounds. Presumably this was *not* Martha's brother but rather the brother of a previous wife of Nicholas Prynne, or (less likely) perhaps the husband of Nicholas Prynne's sister. Appointed as an overseer of Nicholas Prynne's will.

LOFTUS, Unnamed Sister-in-law: Wife of Henrie Loftus; Nicholas Prynne (M1) left her six pounds, thirteen shillings, and four pence.

LOWIN, unspecified: Bevil Molesworth (M3) purchased tenement property in Hoddesdon from this person; out of the yearly rent money from this tenement (fifty shillings), twenty shillings were to be used to pay the Vicar of Broxbourne and his successors for a yearly commemorative sermon. Twenty shillings were to be distributed to the poor of Broxbourne who attended the sermon. The remaining ten shillings were to be used for necessary repairs to the tenement and also to maintain the pavement surrounding the stone under which Bevill Molesworth was buried. Possibly this person was the William LEWIN whom Thomas Thorowgood (M2) called his cousin, or the William LEWIN whom Thomas Thorowgood (M2) called his nephew.

LUCY, Elizabeth Molesworth: daughter of Bevill Molesworth (M3); married to Francis Lucy, Esquire. Presumably Elizabeth was the sister of Grace Molesworth Hill. In her will, Martha leaves Elizabeth Lucy, her daughter-in-law, a gold ring with five diamonds in it.

LUCY, Francis: husband of Elizabeth Molesworth Lucy, who was the daughter of Bevill Molesworth (M3). Thus Francis was the son-in-law of Bevill Molesworth (M3) and the son-in-law by marriage of Martha. He was to receive properties belonging to Bevill Molesworth in the parish of St. Mary Magdalens in the Old Change, London.

LUCY, Martha: daughter of Elizabeth Molesworth Lucy and Francis Lucy; Martha Moulsworth's step-graddaughter. The elder Martha leaves the younger Martha a great chain of gold.

LUTHER, Thomas: witness to the will of Thomas Thorowgood (M2).

MOLESWORTH, Bevill: third husband of Martha; with her, presumably, the parent of Bevill Molesworth, a son who died young. Father of Grace Hill, apparently Martha's step-daughter.

MOLESWORTH, Bevill: son of Bevill Molesworth (M3). Presumably Martha's son. His father desired to be buried under the same stone with his son in Broxbourne church.

PAGE, unspecified: occupant of a tenement next to the White Hind in Hoddesdon at the time Thomas Thorowgood (M2) prepared his will. Thorowgood left this tenement to his daughter Elizabeth.

PARK, Anne: wife of Christopher Park the elder, Martha's cousin; presumably mother to Christopher Park the younger.

PARK, Christopher, the elder: Martha's cousin; husband of Anne Park; father of Christopher Park the younger.

PARK, Christopher, the younger: son of Christopher Park the elder, Martha's cousin. She leaves the younger Christopher Park ten pounds.

PARNELL, William: tenant of an unnamed manor in the county of Middlesex who owed Martha money.

PRESSE CHILDREN: three children of John Presse, parson of the parish church of St. Matthew. Nicholas Prynne (M1) left each child twenty shillings apiece.

PRESSE, John: Clerk parson of the parish church of St. Matthew; bequeathed five pounds by Nicholas Prynne (M1), a member of his parish. Appointed as an overseer of Nicholas Prynne's will.

PRYNE, Anne: widow, aunt of Nicholas Prynne (M1), who left her six pounds, thirteen shillings, and four pence in his will.

PRYNE, James: brother of Nicholas Prynne (M1), who left James five pounds.

PRYNE'S CHILDREN, THOMAS: unspecified number of children of Thomas Pryne, brother of Nicholas Prynne (M1), who left them forty shillings.

PRYNE, Thomas: brother of Nicholas Prynne (M1), who left him five pounds and forty shillings more to make a ring.

PRYNNE, Nicholas: Martha's first husband; citizen of London; goldsmith; parishoner at Church of St. Matthew (in London's Friday Street) at the time of his death. Godfather of William Prynne, the famous puritan pamphleteer.

PRYNNE, Richard: son of Martha's first husband, Nicholas Prynne (M1). Along with Martha, Richard was Nicholas Prynne's major heir.

PRYNNE, CHILD OR CHILDREN: offspring with whom Martha was pregnant at the time Nicholas Prynne (M1) composed his will.

PRYNNE [PRYN], William: of Lincoln's Inn, London, the godson of Martha and her first husband, Nicholas. William Prynne wrote famous and controversial puritan pamphlets before and during the Civil War. Martha leaves William five pounds sterling.

RAWDON, Bevill: son of Marmaduke Rawdon of London and his wife Elizabeth (the step-daughter of Martha). Bevill Rawdon was thus Martha's step-grandson. She leaves him two hundred pounds sterling.

RAWDON, Elizabeth: Daughter of Thomas Thorowgood (M2); married to Marmaduke Rawdon of London; inherited properties in London and Hoddesdon from her father, including the White Hind in Hoddesdon. She and her lawfully begotten heirs were to inherit all of Thomas Thorowgood's lands after the decease of Martha. Executrix of Martha's will. Martha leaves the bulk of her estate to Elizabeth because Elizabeth's father, Thomas Thorowgood, left Martha a plentiful estate, and because Elizabeth and her children and grandchildren were always loving and kind to Martha and always diligent and careful of her in sickness and in health; she and they have gained and deserve Martha's love;

Martha loves Elizabeth as if she were Martha's own child, and she loves Elizabeth's children and grandchildren as if they were her own.

RAWDON, Marmaduke, son of Thomas Rawdon: Thomas Rawdon was the son of Elizabeth Thorowgood Rawdon and Marmaduke Rawdon of London; Thomas's son Marmaduke was therefore the grandson of Elizabeth and the great-step-grandson of Martha. Martha leaves him two hundred pounds sterling, to be inherited when he reaches the age of seven years. If he should not survive, the money is to go to his father, Thomas Rawdon, Martha's step-grandson.

RAWDON, Marmaduke the younger: son of Marmaduke Rawdon of London and his wife Elizabeth. Elizabeth was Martha's step-daughter and executrix. The younger Marmaduke Rawdon was thus Martha's step-grandson. She leaves him one hundred pounds sterling.

RAWDON, Marmaduke of London: son-in-law of Thomas Thorowgood (M2); married to Thorowgood's daughter Elizabeth; thus son-in-law by marriage of Martha. Rawdon was bequeathed one hundred pounds in Thorowgood's will. If Rawdon's wife Elizabeth were to die without lawful issue, Rawdon was to inherit Thorowgood's property and divide it equally with Thorowgood's nephews William Lewin and William Downes.

RAWDON, Martha: daughter of Elizabeth Thorowgood Rawdon, Martha's step-daughter and executrix; Martha Rawdon was thus Martha's step-granddaughter. Martha leaves her one thousand pounds [!].

RAWDON, Robert: the son of Marmaduke Rawdon of London and his wife Elizabeth, Martha's step-daughter from her second marriage. Robert Rawdon was thus Martha's step-grandson. She leaves him two hundred pounds sterling.

RAWDON, Thomas: grandchild of Thomas Thorowgood (M2); son of Thorowgood's daughter Elizabeth and her husband Marmaduke Rawdon of London. Inherited silver plate from Thomas Thorowgood as a remembrance of love; the plate once belonged to Thomas Thorowgood's own father, William.

ROBERTS, Edward: witness to the will of Thomas Thorowgood (M2). In her own will, Martha Moulsworth mentions an Edward

Roberts as her "ancient servant"; she leaves him four shillings every month during his natural life.

ROBERTS, Priscilla: woman mentioned in the will of Nicholas Prynne (M1); Roberts nursed Prynne's son Richard; Prynne left her forty shillings.

ROWLEY, Elizabeth: Thomas Thorowgood (M2) calls her his sister and leaves her forty shillings to make a remembrance ring. Presumably Martha's sister-in-law.

SHERSTON, Peter: son of William Sherston, mentioned in the will of Nicholas Prynne (M1). Prynne left Peter Sherston forty shillings to have a ring made.

SHERSTON, William: mayor of the city of Bath at the time Nicholas Prynne (M1) composed his will. Prynne left Sherston three pounds to make himself a seal ring of gold.

SHOTHER, George: a witness to the will of Nicholas Prynne (M1).

SMITH, unspecified: occupant of the White Hind in Hoddesdon at the time Thomas Thorowgood (M2) prepared his will; Thorowgood left the White Hind to his daughter Elizabeth.

THOROWGOOD, John: nephew of Thomas Thorowgood (M2). Thomas purchased five acres of meadow ground in Hoddesdon from John not long before preparing his will. He left the property to his daughter Elizabeth.

THOROWGOOD, William: father of Thomas Thorowgood (M2); mentioned in the latter's will. William once owned tenements "without Algate in London."

WILLYS, Thomas: a chandler (i.e., maker or seller of candles) of London; Martha's cousin; she leaves him five pounds sterling.

WOOD, Hugh, the elder: Martha's cousin.

WOOD, Hugh, the younger: son of Hugh Wood the elder; presumably Martha's nephew; she leaves him ten pounds.

WOOD, Martha: wife of Hugh Wood the elder, Martha's cousin. Presumably the mother of Hugh Wood the younger.

Appendix 3

Thomas Hassall's Funeral Sermon
on Martha Moulsworth

(with explanatory notes by Ann Depas-Orange)

Hassall's sermon appears in MS Don.g.9., a manuscript currently held at the Bodleian Library, Oxford. The first half of this small volume is given over to a funeral sermon by John Joanes commemorating Marmaduke Rawdon, Martha Moulsworth's stepson-in-law. In the following transcription of Hassall's sermon, each boldfaced virgule or slash-mark ("/") indicates a line break. Two such marks are used to indicate gaps of space between lines. Explanatory notes, cited by folio number and prepared by Ann Depas-Orange, follow the text of the sermon itself.

[Folio 31r]
To / The right Vertuous Lady / Dame Elizabeth Rawdon // Madame // How deeply I stand / indebted to the happy / memory of our deare freind / decease'd (who in her lyfe= / tyme made her house as / myne) your selfe, w'h many / others, can wittnesse myne / acknowlidgment in publick / And how much I still owe / to your manyfold fauours / (who haue made mee as / one of your owne family,) / lett your owne vertue / tell you in priuate /

[31v]
The two principall / pillours of these two / Houses are fallen both / together; and wee yet / seruiue, to mourne their / losse, to blesse their me= / morye: Their bodyes / are reposed in a smale / parcell of ground; / And their memorye / recorded in this little / Mannell. [sic] A smale Vrne / will hold the ashes of / a great Prince; So little /

243

remaynes to vs heere / when wee are dead. // It was not a mistake / on the Messenger, Death, / but the decree of the / Commander, God; /

[32r]

which called them away / before my selfe; who had / the aduantage of them both / in yeares, but not so ripe / for that blessing. // Somewhat remaynes for mee / yet to doe, wᶜʰ I desyre / may bee the will of my / Master; And this little / that I haue done, vppon / this sadd occasion, I *present* / to the eye of your priuate / censure. Let it lye by yᵘ /as a Monument of yᵉ dead / to bee looked vppon, not / looked into; least it should / eyther reuiue yʳ owne sor= / rowes; or discouer the / faylings of // Your obliged seruant // Thomas Hassall //

[33r]

A / Commemoration Sermon / preached at Hodsdon Chappel / on Weddensday being / October the 28ᵗʰ / 1646 / Being the feast of / Simon and Jude / Apostles // And the daye of our / Monethly Fast / by an Ordinance / of Parliament / In memoriall of Mr.ˢˢ / Martha Molesworth / late of Hodsdon Widdowe / deceased //

[34r]

Introductio. / This daye is Ordayned / for a daye of Fasting / And our Sceane (as yee / may see) fitted for mour= / ning (fasting and mour= / ning sute well together) / The twise-martyred Saints / Simon, and Jude, are / content to waue their / iust right in the daye, / and as Cloase mourners / in this sadd meetinge / to beare a part in our / Common sorrowes. // Somewhat is to bee sayd / to expresse our losse / somewhat to reuiue our Comfort //

[34v]

The Text // Luke 10. Verse 42. // One thing is necessary. / When facility, and necessity / meete together in com= / manding to vs a duty / (that it is easy to bee / learned, and necessary / to be practized) hee is / iustly to be blamed, / and worthily ponished / that neglects it. // And such is this lesson / in my text; Facile quia / vnum; Importans quia / necessarium. One thing / is necessarye. //

[35r]

One thing is necessarye. // A thing may bee sayd to / bee necessary in 3 respects / First in respect of the / Ineuitablenesse of yᵉ Conditio*n* / wᶜʰ being such as cannot / bee auoyded, a man must / learne to make a vertue / of necessity, by willingly / submitting himself vnto it // Secondly in the respect of / that necessary Concernment /

wch it carryes along wth it / when Illud vnum est in [illegible] / omnium, so that all other / things seeme to bee inclu= / ded In illo vno // Thirdly in respect of that / vnchangable Consequence //

[35v]

which depends vppon it / wherein a man can neyther / Act, nor Erre but once, / admitting neyther a re= / peale, if good; nor a re= / paire, if euell. // This Vnum necessarium / is our Disce mori (the / subiect of our present / discourse, the occasion / of our present meeting) / then which I knowe / not any one thing more / neces- sary, considered by / those three respects fore= / mentioned. // For first it is of absolute / necessity, and by no state / to bee auoyded //

[36r]

Statutum est Omnibus / mori semel, It is appoyn= / ted to all men to dye once. // Secondly It is of spetiall / Concernement to euery man / who pretends interest in Christ / For if in this lyfe only / wee had hope in Christ / wee were of all men most / miserable: But our lyfe / lyes hid wth Christ, in God / and Death only makes / a pas- sage for the Soule / to lyfe, and glorye. // Thirdly It is this One, / this last Act of Death / which once playd, deter= / mins of all for- merly / done by vs, and resolues / that great Question //

[36v]

What shall become of vs; / For as the tree falles, / so it lyes. Ex- pundlo [sic] / aeternitas: Tyme past, / present, and to come, / all included In vno / mortis articulo, so to / make vs eternally happy, / or eternally miserable. / One thing is necessary. // I haue therefore made / choice of theise words, / a part of Christs sermon / to Martha then liuing, / to make them ye ground /of my Sermon of Martha / now deceased; to showe / how our Disce mori / is that vnum necessarium //

[37r]

W^ch all men pretend to heare / but no man is willing to / learne: wee would bee / allwayes in the theorick / (content to discourse of / death, and reade lectures / of mortification) but for / the practick; wee had / rather see it well noted / by others; then expe= / ri- mented in our selues / Hoc vnum non nobis / adhuc necessarium; / wee are not yet prepared / to dye; And if it were / but conuenient only, / and not necessary to dye / wee could bee content / to dis- pence with it for / euer //

[37v]

Two words make two / parts of my Text / vnum necessarium / the
first is the soule / the second yᵉ body of yᵉ text / In Vno enim inest
aliquod / Diuinum, The Name / of Vnitye imports a / Diuinity: In
Necessario / inest aliquid Humanum / It sauours of Man to / bee
subiect to Necessity // First God him selfe, / and the most re= /
markable works of / God, are represented / to vs in Vnityes. / Deus
enim est Vnus / There is but one God //

[38r]

There is but one God, and / one Mediatour betwixt / God, and
man, wᶜh is yᵉ man / Jesus Christ. 1 Tim: 2.5 / And this is eternall
lyfe / to knowe thee, the only / true God, and whome / thow hast
sent Jesus Christ / John: 17.3. // So agayne for yᵉ works of God /
God made but one Sunne / to giue light, and lyfe to / the whole
worlde; yet / neyther doe yᵉ innumera= / ble company of Starrs /
enuye, or oppose yᵗ singu= / ler glory of the Sunne / from whose
beames they / all receiue their luster: //

[38v]

Nor maligne yᵉ distinction / of their owne condition, / though one
Starre doe / differ from another in / glorye. 1 Cor: 15.41. // So God
made of one blood / all Nacions to dwell on / the face of the Earth, /
and appoynted them / both their tymes of being / and place of
habitation / Acts: 17.26. // So God made at first / but one Man
(neq*ue* hoc / sine mysterio) to shewe / a visible representation / of
the Inuisible God, / And to giue a necessary //

[39r]

Instruction to reasonable / Man of that Diuinity / which consists in
Vnitye. // For to that purpose speaks / the Prophet Mallachy: 2.15 /
asking and resoluing yᵉ question / Quare vnum, who but one? /
when hee had abundance / of Spirit. Bycaus hee / would preserue a
holy seede / Pluralityes cause polutions. // Church, and Common
wealth / were wont to count their / happynesse to consist in / lin-
eall succession of plants / deriued from their first / rootes, seildom
mended / by transmutation. // So God him self calles to / his people
//

[39v]

Heare me all yee that / followe after rightuousnesse, [sic] / and yee
yᵗ seeke the Lord; / Looke vnto the Rock from / whence yee were
hewen, / and to the pitt, whence / yee were digged. // Considder
Abraham yʳ / father; and Sara that / bare you; I called him / alone,

and blessed him / and increased him etc / Isay. 51.1 etc // Yea still, the higher wee / come to perfection, the / neerer to vnity. // When the Apostle would / sett forth the Church / of Christ, in her best / puritye //

[40r]

Then Vnus est Dominus / vna Fides, vnus Baptismus / Ephe: 4.5. And it is / too manifest that y^e mul= / tiplicity of theise, hath / made a nullity in all these. // And lastly, when y^t great / Restauration shall come, / wch the faythfull expect, / then Concludenda sunt / omnia in Vno; Then God / shall bee all in all. 1 Cor: 15:28 // Neyther in the Interim / can wee expect y^e Comfort / of our promised Reformation / Donec omnes in vno con= / uenimus; Till agreing / all in one, wee hold the / Vnity of the Spirit in the / bond of peace. //

[40v]

I stand not heere to dispute / the Question eyther of / Monarchy, or Monopoly / though some are of opinion / that there is a Vnum / necessarium in both these, / In the one, for security / of State policy: In the / other, for restraynt of / Popular Libertye // Sed Quae supra nos, nihil / ad nos. My vnum / necessarium stands be= / fore mee; The Obiect / of Death; and y^e Medi= / tation of mans mortality / The second part of my text / to which I now come // Vnum necessarium //

[41r]

The Necessity of Deaths / remembrance stands in a / threefold Consideration // First It is Necessary for / thee to remember, thow / must dye. That thought / will take thee of [sic] from many / idle, vnlawfull, and impious / actions. // Secondly It is necessary for / thee to prepare thy selfe / for death; That will / quiet thy Conscience, and / in the hower of death, ease / thee of many feares, and / clostuastions [sic; illegible] // Thirdly It is necessary for / thee to Considder, what / shall become of thee after / death. //

[41v]

This will moderate / both presumption, and / Desperation; yea and by / Judging thy selfe, preuent / the following Judgement / both of God, and Man. // The serious meditation / of Mans mortality, / is the strongest motiue / to Mortification; For / if the remembrance of / Death, That Kinge of / terrours (as Job calles it) / calle not to repentance, / nothing can: for the / wages of sinne is death, / and he that is loath / to dye, will be affrayd / to sinne. //

[42r]

There is no Epithete so / propper to Sinne, as to calle / it Deadly
Sinne; for it rely [sic] / giues a deadly blowe indeede / if wee
rightly Considder it. // It is Sinne that destroys / the Image of God
in the / Soule of man; a deadly / blowe, and feawe sensible / of it;
For Consuetudo pec= / candi, tollit sensum peccati / Custom in
sinning, takes / away the sence of sinne // It is sinne that destroyes /
the peace of God in the / Conscience of man, a deadly / blowe
againe, from whence / arise our continuell feares / and distractions
//

[42v]

It is Sinne that destroyes / the Trueth of God in a / mans Profession.
Omnis / homo mendax; Hense / euery man learnes to / playe the
Hypocrite, / Dissimulando cum Deo, / vt dissimulet peccatum /
apud homines; Dissem= / bling with God, that / hee may hyde his /
sinnes from men. // It is Sinne that destroys / the Light of God in
the / lyfe of man: so many / cloudes of sinne arise / dayly, that thy
light / cannot shine before men / to glorifye thy Father / wch is in
heauen //

[43r]

Lastly It is Sinne y^t destroyes / the Comfort of God in the / Death of
man; by then / mustering together all thy / Sinns; by laying wide
open / the booke of thy Conscience, / by presenting to thee that /
wch before, thow would not / reguard, nor remember, / The Daye
of Judgement. // Many sadd spectacles are / then presented to dying men / wch y^e bystanders see not, / or conceiue them to bee but /
fancyes, and spectors of the / distempered brayne. / And those
many strong / pangues, cold swetts, sore / tremblings, and gastly /
shreekings //

[43v]

proceede not only from the / strength of Nature, in / that hard
conflict be= / twixt Life, and Death, / As from the passion of / the
Soule; the terrour / of the Conscience, y^e feare / of Hell; that Worme
/ beginning then to gnawe, / which neuer dyeth, / that Fire to kin-
dle, w^ch / is neuer to bee quenched. // O then, Thow Man of / many
thoughts, remem= / ber this one; and make / this vnum necessarium / thy dayly meditation / It is a Lesson worth thy / learning,
Disce mori. //

[44r]

Take the Preacher his / Counsaile: Remember thy / Creatour, now in y^e dayes / of thy youth: of thy health / of thy strength, of wealth / of thy greatnesse; yea in the / middest of all thy pleasures, / and successive proiects, / yea remember, That for / all these, God will bringe / thee to Judgment | Eccle: 11.9 | If thow forgettest / this One thinge, thow / canst make good vse of / nothing. // Secondly remember, Hoc / vnum est necessarium / and matters of necessity / are not to bee slightly / handled. //

[44v]

Three things therefore / are necessary, In this / One Act of Death, to bee / desyred of euery dying / Man, and Woman. // 1° To send a good Testimony / before thee. // 2° To carry a good Consci= / ence with thee // 3° To leave a good Report / behind thee // For the first. Non potest / esse mors mala, quem / praecesita vita bona / It cannot be an euell / death, wch followes a / good lyfe: For God is / not vnrighteous, that / hee should forget y^r / worke, and labour //

[45r]

Of loue, which yee showe / to his Name &c Heb: 6:10 / If Cornelius his prayers, / and almes, could call downe / an Angell from heauen / to Comfort him in well-doing / Fide nondum rectificata / His fayth not being yet / well informed; How much / more shall that Sacrifize / of our pious actions, bee a / sweete sauour to God / Fide iam Iustificata, / our fayth being approued / and wee by fayth Iustified / For with such sacrifizes / is God pleased. Heb: 13.16 // And bee not deceaued, for / God is not mocked, what a man sowes, the same hee / shall reape. //

[45v]

It is not the abortiue / Mort-maine of a dijnge / Testator; nor ye Inforced / performance of a formal / Executor, wch commends / thy piety, or adds to thy / Merit: (wch bee matters / rather of Course, then / Conscience) Nam quae / non fecimus epsi, vix ea / nostra voco; Wee can / hardly call that our owne / wch is drawne through / the hand of an other man // Besydes that common / experience tells vs / such pious Donations / runne many hazzards, / Are seildome true handed / or longe liued. //

[46r]

For the Second / Conscientia mille testes / If all the Records in the / World were burn't; and / not a man to stand vpp / with thee, at the daye of / Judgment; yet thyne owne / Conscience would cast /

downe thy countenance / with Caine, not daring to / looke vppon the face of that / All-seing God; and stand / alone as Accuser, Witnesse / and Judge; To giue Judge= / ment against all men / And to rebuke all y^e vngodly / amongst men, of all their / wicked deedes w^{c}h they / haue impiously committed, / And of all their cruell spea= / kings, so audatiously vttered / Jude vers: 15 //

[46v]

Thow therefore y^t pleadest / so much for libertye of / Conscience, and holdest it / for so great a tyranie / for any man to insult / ouer thee, or giue lawes / to thy tender Conscience; / play not the Tyrant with / thyne owne Conscience, / Doe not inforce thyne owne / Conscience, against thyne / owne knowledge and / profession. Take heede / of playing the Hypocrite / whilst thow liuest; or y^e / Dissembler, when thow / lyest a dyinge: Such a / Conscience will proue thy / Judas, Qui prodidit Do= / minum, qui perdidit / scipsum [sic] //

[47r]

For the Third. / Memoria Justi benedicta / A good Name well purchased / is a blessing in it self / It is not the verball Orator / who stands vp to plead for thee / Nor the marble Monument / which seemes to commend thee / which can tye mens tongues / from speaking trueth of thee / But thy hated Name / shall be bandyed vpp, and / downe the World with / obloquye; And thy parti= / culer sinns remembred / as a part of thy iust ponish= / ment in this worlds Purgatory / Greatness cannot outdaze it [sic] / nor policy preuent it. //

[47v]

Coniah his sentence shall / bee made good against thee / Thow shalt dye vnlamented / No man shall mourne for / thee saying; Alas my / brother, Alas my sister / Alasse that noble Lord, / alasse his glory. And / thy Buriall shall bee / sutable (without sollem= / nity, without decency) / Thow shalt bee buryed / as an Asse is buryed, / euen drawne, and cast / forth, without the gates / of Jerusalem / see Jerimye 22. / Verse: 18: 19 /

[48r]

And all this, and more then / all this (if this bee not yet / sufficient) speakes but the / mynd of my Text, And / commends to Vs all this / Memoriall, and preparation / for Death, This Vnum / necessarium // One thing is necessarye. // But I forgett my selfe / and that one thing necessary / whome all this principally / concernes; And but

for / which, all that hath bin / sayde, needed not to haue / bin spoken; I meane the / Memoriall of our deceased / Sister Mi^{ss}. Martha /
Molesworth, whose Obsequies / calle vs together. //

[48v]

And my vnum necessarium / begins heere, being by her / dying
vote desyned to / this duty: And to whose / liuing desert, I owe so /
much, and can paye so / little; that you must / take mee but as a
Com= / pounder; willing ra= / ther to staule the dept, / then to discharge it. // I knowe it will be expected I should speake much of /
her, being of so longe / acquaintance wth her / (for I see not that
face in / all this Assembly, w^{ch} / hath knowne her longer / then my
selfe); //

[49r]

And during all that tyme / so much obliged to her, / (that the reality and Con= / stancy of her fauours to / mee, may neuer bee forgotten) / And, which is more, That / In all this tyme of our so /
longe acquaintance (I / speake it to Gods glorys) / As there neuer
was any / break of vnkindnesse betwixt / vs: so neuer any occasion
/ for which I might haue / wished, I had not knowne her // She was
no stranger in / this place, hauing liued / heere the better half of /
her tyme; and that part / which might best speake / her. //

[49v]

Whose manner of lyfe and / conuersation is so well / knowne to all,
that it / were but a wast of / tyme to repeat it to you. / And I chal-
lendge euen / Justice it selfe to doe / her right in what shee / de-
serued well; and dare / euen Detraction to speak / it's worst in re-
peating / what she did euell. // Yet these are those same / Licentiate
tymes, in w^{ch} / Ius datum sceleri, / hath brought that woe / vppon
vs, denounced / by the Prophet Isaye / Chap: 5. Vers / 21 / 22 //

[50r]

To Call Euell good, and / Good euell, Darkenesse light, / and Light
darknesse; Bitter / sweete, and Sweet bitter / wherein men are wise
in / their owne eyes, and prudent / in their owne opinions /
Quando noua virtuq*ue*, noua / pietas, est maledicere, / et male-
facere, eminen= / tissimis, et excellentisi= / mis rebus, simul
[illegible] / tam in sacris, quam [illegible] // The new Vertue, and
new / Piety, is to speake euell, / and doe euell, to y^e most / eminent,
and excellent / things, and persons, both / in the Church, and in /
the Commonwealth. //

[50v]

Yet lett not Trueth bee / affrayd to remember her / Integrity, Iustice, Pietye, / and well formed Charitye / And, to saye muche in /
one worde; Shee liued / many yeares without / Scandall; and dyed /
without a Curse. // To adde to these gene= / ralls, some particulers
// Her Byrth was generous / descended from honest / parents, well
knowne / and respected in their / tymes, and places. / The worshipfull / House, and Name / of Dorsett //

[51r]

Her Education in such / thewes, and manners, as / were most
propper, and / commendable to her sexe / yea euen to Arts and
Letters // Wherein, though left as an / Orphane, to the care of others
/ (her parents dijing, whilst / shee was yongue) yet when / my father, and mother for= / sooke mee, God tooke mee vp / sayth
Dauid; And as shee / receiued the benefitt of / her Education from
others / so shee thankfully com= / municated the same bles= / sing
to those, who beinge / not her owne, were by / mariage of their fathers / committed to her tuition //

[51v]

Her Mariage beginning / in the Pryme of her yeares / was noteworthy, hauing / had three Husbands, / all louing to her, and be= /
loued of her; so that shee / would many tymes saye / They were all
so good, / that she knew not / which was the better. // Her Lyfe, a
patterne of / Modesty, Discression, / Hospitality, Frugality / to others of her Sexe / who neyther in Youth, / nor Age neede to scorne /
her Example // But after all comes Death / to make ye Catastrophe //

[52r]

Which though ministring / occasion of sorrowe to her / suruiuing
freinds, yett sett / a Crowne vppon all these / precedent passages //
The hand of God pleased / by a tedious, and paynefull / sicknesse
(which in all / her former dayes shee / had not bin acquainted w^th)
/ to make her weary of lyfe, / and better prepared for death / And,
in trueth, it moued / many tymes a mixt pas= / sion of sorrowe,
and ioye / in her visiting freinds, to / heare, and see how patient= /
ly shee indured, how ear= / nestly she desyred her dissolution //

[52v]

And that wch is worthy / our remembrance, and not / vnworthy y^e
obseruation / This vnum necessarium / the Arte of dying well / was
skillfully practized / by her; when during the / tyme of her restraynt / being vnder y^e Blackrodd / of this her Visitation / shee

sought to deceiue / the tediousnesse of soli= / tude, and sicknesse, / with reading good Bookes, / her constant Companions, / and faythfull Cownsellers; // And withall, so discreetely / she ordered her studyes, / that they might not seeme / tedious. //

[53r]

Mixing Ciuell, wth Eccle= / siasticall Historyes, and in / both finding concurrences / with the present tymes // That Booke of Bookes, the / Holy Bible was neuer / longe from her; attended / with some other Handmayds / tractats of piety, healpes / to Deuotion // And, both to healpe her / owne memorye; and to / communicate the frute / of her studyes to others / she had lyinge by her / pen, Inke, and paper / wherewith she noted such / matters as were of spetiall / consequence, quoting the / places, to commend them / to others. //

[53v]

But she hath now taken / her leaue of vs, and of all / these; leauing vs, and all / these behynd her; to the / increase of our sorrowes, / who are parted from her / But to the comfort of her / owne soule, wch doutlesse / hath caryed ye quintesence / of those Collections wth her. // And this is the / breefe History of our / deceased freind Mi^ss / Martha Molesworth, / And thus you haue the / modell of our Martha / her vnum necessarium // One thing is necessarye //

[54r]

And what now remayneth for mee // Vnum quidem hoc mihi / necessarium, vt semper mori= / ens lugeam huius mortis / memoriam, non sine morte / mihi redimendam; Mors / autem mea dabit dolori / finem, Mors Christi / vitae initium // This one thing remaynes as / necessary for mee, Euer to / bemoane the memory of / her death, to mee by death / only to be redeamed: / For my death shall giue / an end to my sorrowe, / And the death of Christ / the beginning of Comfort. //

[54v]

This place espetially / obliged mee to her memoriall / This place therefore fitts best her Monument / And in the ruines of / this place, wee may all / considder our owne / mortality // Our vnum necessarium / is still to remember, and / prepare for the daye / of our dissolution / That so wee allso, with / this our Sister, and all / others departed in the / fayth of Christ Jesus / may haue our perfect / consummation, and bliss //

[55r]

both in body, and soule / in that eternall, and euer= / lasting Glory. // To which hee bring vs / who hath so clearely brought vs / euen Christ Jesus that / Righteous // To whome wth the Father / and the Holy ghost / Three persons / and one God / bee ascribed / all / Honor, Glory, and Prayes / now, and for euer more // Amen.

Notes
Prepared by Ann Depas-Orange

31v. *The two principall pillours*: Referring to the deaths of both Marmaduke Rawdon (of London and Hoddesdon) and Martha Moulsworth in 1646.

31v. *Mannell*: Probably "manual," i.e., "A small book for handy use.... In the mediaeval Church, a book containing the forms to be observed by priests in the administration of the sacraments, etc." (*OED*).

33r. *Hodsdon Chappel*: the chapel in the center of Hoddesdon had been a point of rivalry between the competing vicars of Broxbourne and Amwell parishes. Moulsworth and the Rawdon family had supported the claims of Hassall (vicar of Amwell).

33r. *Simon and Jude*: Moulsworth refers to these saints in her "Memorandum" (ll. 81–86). Her second husband, Thomas Thorowgood, died on their feast day.

34v. *Luke 10 Verse 42*: Moulsworth herself alludes to this Biblical incident in her poem (ll. 17–18), although in her marginal note the number of the verse is misremembered or miscopied. The whole relevant passage reads as follows: "[38] Now it came to pass, as they went, that he [Jesus] entered into a certain village: and a certain woman named Martha received him into her house. [39] And she had a sister called Mary, which also sat at Jesus' feet, and heard his word. [40] But Martha was cumbered about much serving, and came to him, and said, Lord, dost thou not care that my sister hath left me to serve alone? bid her therefore that she help me. [41] And Jesus answered and said unto her, Martha, Martha, thou are careful and troubled about many things: [42] But one thing is needful: and Mary hath chosen that good part, which shall not be taken away from her."

35r. *Illud vnum est* ... : This is rendered in the immediately following English words.

35r. *In illo vno*: "In that one [thing]."

35v. *Vnum necessarium*: "One necessary thing."

35v. *Disce mori*: The meaning of this term is explained in the immediately following parenthetical phrase.

36r. *Statum est Omnibus* ...: This is rendered in the immediately following English words. Hassall seems to be echoing Hebrews 9:27.

36v. *Martha then living*: I.e., the Biblical Martha mentioned in Luke 10:38–42.

37r. *mortification*: Subjecting the body, appetite, or passions to control by practicing abstinence or self-denial; rendering oneself "dead" to the world or the flesh (*OED*).

37v. *Vno enim inest*: Paraphrased in the following English phrase. For a Biblical parallel, see 1 Corinthinians 8:4.

37v. *In necessario inest* ...: Paraphrased in the following English words.

37v. *Deus enim est Vnus*: Rendered in the following English words. For Biblical parallels, see 1 Corinthians 8:6 and 1 Timothy 2:5. Hassall soon cites the latter verse (see 38r).

38r. *1 Tim: 2.5*: I.e., 1 Timothy 2:5: "[5] For *there is* one God, and one mediator between God and men, the man Christ Jesus ...."

38r. *John: 17.3*: I.e., John 17:3: "[3] And this is life eternal, that they might know thee the only true God, and Jesus Christ, whom thou hast sent."

38v. *1 Cor: 15.41*: I.e., 1 Corinthians 15:41: "[41] *There is* one glory of the sun, and another glory of the moon, and another glory of the stars: for *one* star differeth from *another* star in glory."

38v. *Acts 17:26*: "[26] And [God] hath made of one blood all nations of men to dwell on all the face of the earth, and hath determined the times before appointed, and the bounds of their habitation ...." In her "Memorandum," Moulsworth herself alludes to a subsequent verse: "[28] For in him [God] we live, and move, and have our being; as certain also of your own poets have said, For we are also his offspring." See the marginal note next to line 7 of her poem.

38v. *neque hoc sine mysterio*: "and this not without mystery."

39r. *Prophet Mallachy: 2.15*: I.e., Mallachi 2:15: "[15] And did he not make one? Yet had he the residue of the spirit. And wherefore one? That he might seek a goodly seed. Therefore take heed to your spirit, and let none deal treacherously against the wife of his youth."

39r. *Quare vnum, who but one?*: Perhaps a slip of the pen occurred here, since this Latin phrase would more accurately be translated "Why [or wherefore] one?"

39r. *Pluralities*: In ecclesiastical terminology, this could mean the holding of two or more benefices simultaneously by one person, or, alternatively, such a benefice held concurrently by more than one person (*OED*). Such pluralities had long been a subject of criticism.

39r. *Transmutation*: This whole passage almost certainly alludes to contemporary political matters; Hassall (as would be expected) seems to have favored the Royalist cause. "Transmutation" means a change or shift (*OED*).

39v. *Heare me all yee*: Isaiah 51:1–2 reads as follows: "[1] Hearken to me, ye that follow after righteousness, ye that seek the Lord: look unto the rock *whence* ye are hewn, and to the hole of the pit *whence* ye are digged. [2] Look unto Abraham your father, and unto Sarah *that* bare you: for I called him alone, and blessed him, and increased him." Once again Hassall seems to be offering implied political commentary favoring the Royalist position.

39v. *the Apostle*: I.e., Paul.

40r. *Vnus est Dominus*: Ephesians 4:5 stresses that there is "[5] One Lord, one faith, one baptism ...." Hassall uses this verse to argue that the multiplicity of contemporary religious positions threatens to nullify the ideal harmony of the Church.

40r. *Restauration*: "Restoration," i.e., "The reinstatement of man in the divine favour or in a state of innocence" (*OED*).

40r. *Concludendo sunt omnia in Vno*: 1 Corinthians 15:28 reads as follows: "[28] And when all things shall be subdued unto him, then shall the Son also himself be subject unto him that put all things under him, that God may be all in all."

40r. *Donec omnes in vno conuenimus*: This is paraphrased in Hassall's ensuing English sentence. For a biblical parallel, see (for example) Ephesians 4:13: "[13] Till we all come in the unity of the faith, and of the knowledge of the Son of God, unto a perfect man, unto the measure of the stature of the fulness of Christ."

40v. *Monarchy, or Monopoly*: Hassall again alludes to contemporary political issues.

40v. *Sed Quae supra nos, nihil ad nos*: "Things which are above us are nothing to us." Hassall now backs away from commenting any further on contemporary political controversies.

41r. *of*: I.e., "off."

41r. *clostuastions*: no such word appears in the *OED*, although the context seems to suggest that Hassall understood it to mean something like "anxieties."

41v. *Mortification*: "The action of mortifying the flesh or its lusts; the subjection of one's appetites and passions by the practice of austere living, esp. by the self-infliction of bodily pain or discomfort" (*OED*).

41v. *That Kinge of terrours (as Job calles it)*: See Job 18:14: "[14] His confidence shall be rooted out of his tabernacle, and it shall bring him to the king of terrors."

41v. *the wages of sin is death*: See Romans 6:23: "[23] For the wages of sin *is* death; but the gift of God *is* eternal life through Jesus Christ our Lord."

42r. *rely*: I.e., "really."

42r. *Consuetudo peccandi, tollit sensum peccati*: Paraphrased in the following English words.

42v. *Profession*: A public vow or declaration, especially of a religious nature; the declaration of belief in or obedience to religion; hence, the faith or religion which one professes (*OED*).

42v. *Omnis homo mendax*: I.e., every man is mendacious, deceptive, given to lying. For a biblical parallel see (for instance) Isaiah 9:17: "[17] ... every one *is* an hypocrite and an evildoer ...."

42v. *Dissimulando eum Deo ...*: Paraphrased in the immediately following English words.

42v. *thy Father wch is in heauen*: Perhaps an allusion to the Lord's Prayer; see Matthew 6:9.

43r. *fancyes*: I.e., figments of the imagination.

43r. *pangues*: I.e., "pangs," pains.

43v. For biblical parallels see, for example, Mark 9:44–48. Verse 44 speaks of hell as a place "Where their worm dieth not, and the fire is not quenched." See also, for example, Isaiah 66:24 for similar sentiments.

43v. *Thow Man of many thoughts*: Perhaps this alludes to Psalm 94:19: "[19] In the multitude of my thoughts within me thy comforts delight my soul."

43v. *Disce mori*: see 35v and note.

44r. *Preacher his Counsaile*: I.e., the Preacher's counsel or advice; the word "Ecclesiastes" was often translated as "the Preacher."

44r. *Remember thy Creatour ...*: An allusion to Ecclesiastes 12:1: "[1] Remember now thy Creator in the days of thy youth, while the evil days come not, nor the years draw nigh, when thou shalt say, I have no pleasure in them ...."

44r. *Eccle: 11.9*: Ecclesiastes 11:9 reads as follows: "[9] Rejoice, O young man, in thy youth; and let thy heart cheer thee in the days of thy youth, and walk in the ways of thine heart, and in the sight of thine eyes: but know thou, that for all these *things* God will bring thee into judgment."

44r. *Hoc vnum est necessarium*: "This one thing is necessary."

44v. *Non potest esse mors mala ...*: This is paraphrased in the immediately following English sentence.

44v. *For God is not vnrighteous ...*: See Hebrews 6:10: "[10] For God *is* not unrighteous to forget your work and labour of love, which ye have shewed toward his name, in that ye have ministered to the saints, and do minister."

45r. *Cornelius his prayers*: I.e., "Cornelius's prayers." Cornelieus was a Roman centurion who practiced Jewish law without having become circumcised. He is a traditional example of a gentile convert to Christianity. See Acts 10:2–4, where he is described as "[2] A devout *man*, and one that feared God with all his house, which gave much alms to the people, and prayed to God alway. [3] He saw in a vision evidently about the ninth hour of the day an angel of God coming in to him, and saying unto him, Cornelius. [4] And when he looked on him, he was afraid, and said, What is it, Lord? And he said unto him, Thy prayers and thine alms are come up for a memorial before God."

45r. *Fide nondum rectificata*: Paraphrased in the immediately following English words.

45r. *Fide iam Iustificata*: Paraphrased in the following English phrase. See, for example, Galatians 3:24: "[24] Wherefore the law was our schoolmaster to *bring us* unto Christ, that we might be justified by faith." See also, for instance, Romans 3:28, Romans 5:1, and Galatians 2:16.

45r. *Heb: 13.16*: i.e., Hebrews 13:16: "[16] But to do good and to communicate forget not: for with such sacrifices God is well pleased."

45r. *God is not mocked …*: See Galatians 6:7: "[7] Be not deceived, God is not mocked: for whatsoever a man soweth, that shall he also reap."

45v. *Mort-maine*: "A metaphorical expression in English legal use—'dead hand'—for impersonal ownership; posthumous control exercised by the testator over the uses to which property is to be applied" (*OED*).

45v. *Testator*: "One who makes a will, *esp.* one who has died leaving a will" (*OED*).

45v. *Executor*: "A person appointed by the testator to execute or carry into effect his will after his decease" (*OED*).

45v. *matters rather of Course*: Probably referring to the way in which one handles his/her affairs before dying; the customary process or procedure one carries out, such as making a will, before death.

45v. *Nam quae non fecimus epsi …*: Paraphrased in the lines that immediately follow.

45v. *Donations*: Probably referring to legacies, endowments, or other charitable benevolences.

45v. *true handed*: Probably suggesting that legacies are not always properly administered by the testator's executor(s).

46r. *Conscientia mille testes*: "The conscience is a thousand witnesses."

46r. *Caine*: After his sacrifice was not accepted by God, Cain attacked and killed his brother, Abel. When first asked about his brother by God, Cain lied and was then banished from holy ground. See especially Genesis 4:5–

6, which refers to Cain's fallen countenance after his sacrifice was rejected; see also 4:9.

46r. *Jude vers: 15*: I.e., Jude 1:14–15: "[14] And Enoch also, the seventh from Adam, prophesied of these, saying, Behold, the Lord cometh with ten thousands of his saints, [15] To execute judgment upon all, and to convince all that are ungodly among them of all their ungodly deeds which they have ungodly committed, and of all their hard *speeches* which ungodly sinners have spoken against him."

46v. *Thow therefore y* pleadest ...: Apparently an allusion to contemporary politics, probably aimed at religious dissenters.

46v. *profession*: Probably referring to public utterances or assertions.

46v. *Take heede of playing the Hypocrite*: Perhaps there is an echo here of Matthew 6:1–2: "[1] Take heed that ye do not your alms before men, to be seen of them: otherwise ye have no reward of your Father which is in heaven. [2] Therefore when thou doest *thine* alms, do not sound a trumpet before thee, as the hypocrites do in the synagogues and in the streets, that they may have glory of men. Verily I say unto you, They have their reward."

46v. *Qui prodidit Dominum, qui perdidit scipsum*: "Scipsum" should probably read "seipsum." Judas betrayed the Lord and thus ruined himself.

47r. *Memoria Justi benedicta*: This is paraphrased in the following English sentence. For a similar Biblical sentiment, see Proverbs 10:7: "[7] The memory of the just *is* blessed: but the name of the wicked shall rot."

47r. *outdaze*: I.e., outshine or outdazzle it in brightness.

47r. *policy*: I.e., cleverness, calculation, shrewdness, strategy.

47v. *Coniah his sentence*: Coniah (Jeconiah/Jehoiachin) is driven from the land he desires most; no one, including his own family, will weep for him or even care when he dies. See next note.

47v. *Jerimye 22. Verse: 18:19*: I.e., Jeremiah 22:18–19: "[18] Therefore thus saith the Lord concerning Jehoiakim the son of Josiah king of Judah; They shall not lament for him, *saying*, Ah my brother! or Ah sister! they shall not lament for him, *saying*, Ah lord! or, Ah his glory! [19] He shall be buried with the burial of an ass, drawn and cast forth beyond the gates of Jerusalem."

48v. *her dying vote*: This might possibly read "her dying note." If "vote" is the word intended, then it could mean Moulsworth's dying prayer or intercession; or petition or request; or ardent wish or desire (*OED*). If "note" is the word intended, then perhaps Hassall refers to a final written request.

48v. *I owe so much*: Moulsworth had long been a firm supporter of Hassall; for details, see the essay entitled "The Life and Times of Martha Moulsworth" (by Robert Evans) included in this volume.

48v. *Compounder*: "One who compounds for a liability, debt, or charge: one who compounds a felony or offence; one who pays a lump sum in discharge of recurrent payments to which he is liable" (*OED*). "To compound" in the sense Hassall uses here meant to "settle (a debt) by agreement for partial payment" (*OED*).

48v. *staule*: I.e., stall or postpone payment.

48r. *discharge*: I.e., pay in full.

49v. *Ius datum sceleri*: The mantle of law is given to wickedness—i.e., wickedness is made legal.

49v. *the Prophet Isaye Chap: 5. Vers 21 22*: I.e., Isaiah 5:20–21 in the King James Version: "[20] Woe unto them that call evil good, and good evil; that put darkness for light, and light for darkness; that put bitter for sweet, and sweet for bitter! [21] Woe unto *them that are* wise in their own eyes, and prudent in their own sight!"

50r. *Quando noua virtuq*ue …: This is paraphrased in the ensuing English passage.

51r. *thewes*: The *OED* defines a "thew" as a custom, usage, or general practice; a custom or habit of an individual; a good quality or habit; a virtue. Hassall's phrasing in this passage is reminiscent of lines 27–30 of Moulsworth's "Memorandum."

51r. *dijing*: I.e., "dying."

51r. *when my father, and mother forsooke mee* …: See Psalm 27:10: "[10] When my father and my mother forsake me, then the Lord will take me up."

51v. *Pryme*: I.e., her youth or first age.

51v. *all louing to her, and beloued of her*: This is reminiscent of line 47 of Moulsworth's "Memorandum."

52r. *precedent*: preceding in time; antecedent; just-mentioned (*OED*).

52v. *Arte of dying well*: On this convention of medieval and Renaissance thought see, for instance, Mary Catherine O'Connor, *The Art of Dying: The Development of the Ars Moriendi* (New York: Columbia University Press, 1942). For some representative texts see, for example, Nancy Lee Beaty, *The Craft of Dying: A Study of the Literary Tradition of the "Ars Moriendi" in England* (New Haven: Yale University Press, 1970).

52v. *Blackrodd*: I.e., "black rod," referring to the Gentleman Usher of the Black Rod, who carried "an ebony rod crowned with a golden lion" and who acted as "the sovereign's personal attendant in the House of Lords.... it is Black Rod who summons the members of the Commons to the Upper House to hear a speech from the throne or to witness the royal assent being given to a Bill.... In 1642 Charles I attempted to impeach five members of the Commons by personally entering the chamber, only to find that those he sought had fled. Thereafter the doors of the Commons' chamber have by tradition always been closed in the face of Black Rod and he is obliged to knock three times with his staff before being admitted." See the *Illustrated Dictionary of British Heritage*, ed. Alan Isaacs and Jennifer Monk (London: Market House Books, 1986), 38–39.

52v. *Visitation*: "The action, on the part of God or some supernatural power, of coming to, or exercising power over, a person or people for some end" (*OED*).

53r. *concurrences*: I.e., parallels with or similarities to current issues, events, or persons.

53r. *places*: I.e., "A particular part, page, or other point in a book or writing.... A (short) passage in a book or writing, separately considered, or bearing upon some particular subject .... A subject, a topic" (*OED*).

53v. *all these*: I.e., her notes and papers.

53v. *quintesence*: I.e., quintessence, the most essential part; a highly refined essence or extract; the purest or most perfect form of some quality; the most perfect embodiment of the typical qualities of a thing (*OED*).

54r. *Vnum quidem hoc mihi ...*: This is rendered in the immediately following English passage that consumes the rest of this page.

54v. *This place*: I.e., Hoddesdon Chapel. On Moulsworth's active support of Hassall and the chapel, see Evans, "The Life and Times of Martha Moulsworth" (in this volume).

Appendix 4

More Poems by Martha Moulsworth?

Robert C. Evans

It hardly seems likely that the "Memorandum" is the only poem Martha Moulsworth wrote. In his funeral sermon, Thomas Hassall (one of her oldest friends) makes it clear that Moulsworth was a literate, educated woman who loved "reading good Bookes," which he called "her constant Companions and faythfull Cownsellers" (52v).[1] Even as death approached, she spent her time reading not only the Bible but also "Ciuell" and "Ecclesiasticall Historyes" (53r), along with other "tractats of piety" and "healpes to Deuotion" (53r). In addition, Hassall makes clear that Moulsworth transcribed the fruits of her reading, not only for her own benefit but also to share with others (53r). She was, then, an avid reader and note-taker, and it is not hard to imagine her writing other works besides the "Memorandum." That poem, indeed, displays a skill and conscious artistry that suggest it was probably not unique. As yet, however, no other poems by Moulsworth are definitely known to survive.

Poems by members of Moulsworth's circle of friends, family, and acquaintances do exist, mainly in a manuscript held at the British Library (MS Add 18,044). This volume contains writings by such figures from Moulsworth's life as Edmond Forster, Edmund Parlett, and Thomas Hassall himself. In addition, the manuscript transcribes numerous poems copied (sometimes with attribution, sometimes not) from the works of famous Renaissance writers, including Herbert, Vaughan, Crashaw, Daniel, Drayton, Donne, and many others. Most intriguingly, however, the manuscript also contains scores of poems whose first lines are not listed in the stan-

---

[1]For the full text of the sermon, see Appendix 3 of this volume.

dard index.[2] Most of these poems, obviously, are probably *not* by Moulsworth. A few, however, just might be. Unfortunately, since the vast majority are unascribed, determining who wrote most of them is likely to prove a difficult if not impossible task. Yet their existence remains a tantalizing fact—one that awaits further investigation.[3]

One other poem *possibly* by Moulsworth presents itself. This is the brief lyric inscribed in the stone that rests above the grave containing her third husband and final child, both named Bevill Molesworth. That poem, now worn down and just barely legible, reads as follows:

> Now seaunty seaun yeares past (myne only Sonne)
> I'me come vnto thee my lifes glasse is runne
> Thou hadst the shorter I the longer howre
> Both equall now I hope th'eternall power
> For Christs blood shed will rayse out of this dust
> Our flesh to resurrection of y[e] Just.

Did Martha write this work? Certainly she might have. The composition of this poem would have preceded the writing of the "Memorandum" by only about two years, and the themes and techniques of the works do bear some comparison. Both emphasize such motifs as death, time, and resurrection, and the balance of this poem's third line is highly reminiscent of a characteristic technique of the "Memorandum."

In the end, however, the poem cannot be confidently ascribed. It could have been written by Moulsworth, but it could just as easily have been written by various other authors. These include Thomas Hassall, Edmund Parlett (the vicar in whose church the father and son were buried), other members of the extended Molesworth family, and even Bevill Molesworth himself. Certainly the voice adopted is his, and we know from his will that he left explicit

---

[2]See Margaret Crum, *First-Line Index of Manuscript Poetry 1500–1800 in Manuscripts of the Bodleian Library Oxford*, 2 vols. (New York: Modern Language Association, 1969).

[3]Four other notebooks owned and transcribed by a close relative of Martha Moulsworth contain poems and other works; these manuscripts are presently in private hands. I have examined them closely and have found nothing in them that is ascribed to Moulsworth. Like the British Library MS, however, they contain numerous unascribed works. I thank the owner for allowing me to inspect them.

instructions that he should be buried with his son.[4] Possibly, then, he left this poem as his own final testament. Yet whether the poem was written by a friend, a relative, her husband, or even by Moulsworth herself, the work provides one more small piece of the context from which her own "Memorandum" emerged.

---

[4]For the full text of Molesworth's will, see Appendix 2 of this volume.

"A Suter for My Sealfe":
A Letter, 1610, from Ane Lawraunce
to Thomas Sutton

Transcribed and Edited by Joseph P. Crowley
Introduced by Patricia N. Hill

In May 1610 a young unmarried woman, Ane Lawraunce, addressed a lengthy letter to "The ridght worshipfull Mr [Thomas] Sutton" in an attempt to persuade him to include her among those to be named in his will as beneficiaries.[1] This request came only after he had refused her a loan of two hundred pounds, for want of adequate security. Ane Lawraunce's appeal may strike one as brazen, even bizarre; but it becomes less so when put in the context of Thomas Sutton's career and reputation.

By 1610, Thomas Sutton (1532–1611) was an elderly man of enormous wealth with neither a will nor direct heirs.[2] His situation and, apparently, his behavior led many London theatre-goers to speculate that Sutton had been the title character in Ben Jonson's *Volpone*, first staged in 1606.[3] Sutton's early life is obscure. In the 1570's he was a coal dealer in Northern England, and by 1582, he had settled in London as a prosperous money lender: hence Ane Lawraunce's initial contact with him. By the 1590's the presence of a great fortune and the absence of a will led to widespread discussion of that fortune's likely disposition, as well as a circle of would-be heirs, including an illegitimate son. Sutton seems to have attracted the loyalty and service of a number of people with promises (or hopes) that he would provide for them in the future.

From one of these, the courtier Sir John Harington, Sutton gained support in Parliament for the passage of an act giving him the authority to establish a charitable foundation. It was to this foundation, a residence and school for indigent men and boys, that Sutton bequeathed the largest part of his estate, literally on his deathbed. His identification with Volpone as a crafty manipulator of others' greed gradually faded, and he has been remembered primarily as the philanthropist responsible for one of England's most famous charitable institutions, the Charterhouse.

Perhaps it was his reputation as a man interested, potentially at least, in assisting the needy that prompted Ane Lawraunce's letter. She was certainly unable to afford his lending services, and refers to her father as a "poore gentelman"; further, she claims to be too infirm to earn her own living. But it is not to Sutton's compassion that she makes her strongest appeal; rather it is to his self-interest. Her letter reads like a sermon, taking as its text Matthew 6:19–21, Jesus' comparison of Earthly with Heavenly Treasure. Though the terms of her argument are essentially religious, they are thus expressed in a vocabulary the worldly Sutton could well understand.

The contrast between the two treasures runs through the letter like a refrain. Earthly wealth is merely lent to the Christian to enable him to do good deeds, a point she reinforces with several other allusions to Matthew's gospel, and with reminders of death's nearness and consequences: death strips a man of his earthly wealth and subjects him to a divine judgment based on how he has used that wealth. She even offers two exempla to that effect, one vaguely similar to the plot of *Everyman*, the second evocative of Luke's parable of the crafty servant (16:1–4). Lawraunce is extraordinarily blunt in her self-assumed role as Sutton's spiritual director. She reminds him that he is indeed elderly, that death is a daily threat, and that he therefore needs to concern himself with this disposition of his soul (and, as the reader discovers, his will as well).

With a last admonition that he attend to his salvation, Lawraunce returns to the point at hand: her need of money. Here too she appeals to scripture to justify her petition: God tells her to seek and ask what she needs (Matthew 7:7–9). Did Lawraunce recognize the irony? Jesus told his followers to address their pleas to the Heavenly Father; she addresses hers to an earthly banker.

No one can read this letter without wondering about the fate of its author: a highly literate, clever, bold young woman seemingly without resources other than her own wit. In an earlier age, she might have been a nun; in a later age, a governess. One can only hope, for her and with her, "that if my life in this wourlde be lounge, and sharpe, yet in the worlde to com it will be Joyfull and everlasting."

Notes

1. Lawraunce's letter is presently housed (along with other Sutton documents) at the Corporation of London, Greater London Record Office. Its reference number is ACC 1876 F3 351. We thank Charterhouse and the GLRO for permission to print our transcript of Lawraunce's letter.

2. On Sutton's life see, for instance, two articles by Neal R. Shipley: "Thomas Sutton: Tudor-Stuart Money-Lender," *Business History Review* 50 (1976): 456–76, and also "A Possible Source for Volpone," *Notes and Queries*, n.s. 39 (1992): 363–69. In addition, see Hugh Trevor-Roper, "Thomas Sutton," *Carthusiana* 20.1 (October 1948): 2–8.

3. On this issue see, for instance, Margaret Hotine, "Ben Jonson, Volpone, and Charterhouse," *Notes and Queries*, n.s. 38 (1991): 79–81.

Transcript
Ane Lawraunce to Thomas Sutton

Too the ridght worshipfull / Mr Sutton; at his loginge in / fleatestreate; at a wolendrapers / nere Sainte Dounstounes / Churche; thes delyuer; or at / his house in Hauckney[1]

---

[1]This address is written in the same hand as the letter itself; presumably both were penned by Lawraunce. The letter is long and broad in size, with very small margins; Lawraunce manages to cram a great many words onto two pages, yet her handwriting is generally very clear. The following transcription retains the original spelling. Most of Lawraunce's intended meanings are clear (although "one," for instance, can sometimes mean either "one" or "on" or "own"). When confusion seems likely to result from her spelling, the modern equivalent is inserted in brackets, preceded by an equal sign: e.g., "one [= own]." Glosses on Lawraunce's usages are also inserted within brackets. Virgules or slashes ("/" marks) are inserted, in boldface, to indicate the line-breaks in Lawraunce's letter. On occasion Lawraunce herself uses such slash marks, preceded by a colon

Sir before I knew yow. Reporte gaue me mutch asuraunce of yowr cristian disposition wich Imbouldened me / to be a suter unto yow for the lendinge me too houndred poundes, aquaintinge yow with my occationes to yowes [= use]² / the saime;³ whearein at my firest,

---

and double space, to indicate new stages in her developing argument. In the transcription, a new paragraph has been inserted wherever she makes these marks. Pointed brackets ("< >") have been used to insert missing words or letters.

Fleet Street is still an important thoroughfare in London. St. Dunstan's church is mentioned in connection with the street by John Stow in his famous *Survey of London* (London: Dent, n.d.). Hackney was a fashionable suburb about three miles north of St. Paul's Cathedral; see Fran C. Chalfant, *Ben Jonson's London* (Athens: University of Georgia Press, 1978), 90. Woolendrapers were dealers in cloth.

²Most of Ane Lawraunce's spellings that are strange or non-standard to us of the twentieth century are among the various early forms of the particular words as listed in the *Oxford English Dictionary* entries for the words. Examples include *ar* (for *are*), *bed* (*bid*), *doo* (*do*), *goo* (*go*), *home* (*whom*), *lounge* (*long*), *mutch* (*much*), *one* (*on*), *one* (*own*), *then* (*than*), *to* (*too*), *too* (*two*), and *yowse* (*use*). However, some of her spellings are not to be found among the early forms listed in the *OED* and probably were of limited provenance, if not idiosyncratic to Lawraunce. Examples include *furdar* (*further*), *searu-* (*serv-*), *yewse* (*use*), *youndge* (*young*), and the two extensively attested patterns (1) of spelling *-dgh(-)* where modern spelling has *-gh(-)* (e.g. *althoudgh*, *broudght*, *moudght* (*might*), *ridght*, *thoudgh*, *thoudghtes*) and (2) of spelling word final *-ufe* after a vowel (or voiced consonant) where modern spelling has *-ve* (e.g. *aboufe*, *conceaufe*, *craufe*, *graufe*, *leaufe*, *receaufe*, *searufe*, and also *desearufes* and *liufes*. This last pattern does not hold when a *-d*, *-inge*, or *-th* ending follows or with the verb *liue*). Lawraunce's form *deathe* where *deafe* is called for is probably a mistake; *ouft(e)* for *ought* may be a mistake, but it occurs both times *ought* is called for.

Ane Lawraunce is remarkably consistent in her spelling of specific words, whether her spellings are common ones or not.

³Ane Lawraunce uses semicolons rather liberally in her letter. In all but two of the 132 occurrences, the semicolon is followed by single spacing rather than double spacing (excluding occurrences at the end of a line). Moreover, the two instances of double spacing after a semicolon could have been accidental rather than intentional. Of the 132 semicolons, 62 (47%) occur between independent clauses; 22 (17%) occur between an independent clause and a dependent clause (or *vice versa*); and 48 (36%) occur in places other than between clauses (for example, in a series). In certain instances, Lawraunce seems to use a present participial phrase as a

and seconde conferences[4] I founde yow so fauorable, as I trusted greately / one yowr frindeship thearein; yet afterwardes when I hoped most theareof yow weare fardest from / doinge me that good I desired; wich if yow had don thoudgh I coulde not giue yow sitch [= such] security wich / worldly wise men to [= too] mutche staundes upon; yet by godes healpe I woulde with all possible speade as / Justly haue paide that mony againe and interest for it as if the Excheacor of Einglaunde had bin my / Seaurety [= surety] for doinge it; Also I shoulde euer haue bin uery thaunkefull, and most bounde unto yow for / that good deade; wich god, that louethe the goode worke and the wourkeman woulde haue rewarded whoo / is an euerlastinge frinde to thous that dothe his will and indeauores to liue acordinge to his commaundementes / withoute wich, he respecktes no persones; so in him the fountaine of goodnes that knouse [= knows] all the wisdom, / honores, pleasures, and Treasures of this worlde to be folishnes I only troust:

And because I now / conseaufe yow ar to [= too] worldly affeckted; or else to mutch draune, or carried by the perswationes of som from / doinge that good whilest yow ar liuinge wich in the eande will be best for yowr sealfe; I haue chiefely / for yowr good, and partely for my one [= own] wrote this wich I pray yow reade and consider well of; for it is / truthe withowte desimulation, and sitch, as if the eyes of yowr soulle be not starke blinde, the eares of / yowr harte quite deathe [read: deafe], and yowr conscience sealed by to[5] sinne,[6] yow shall finde to be better Treasure, by / me a poore

---

full clause (for example: "praieinge yow not to delaye yowr amendment from day to day"; and also: "Concludinge thes matteres wich desearufes to be eandeles with thes wordes"). In doing the above syntactical analysis, where there was reason for considering the participial structure a sort of elliptical clause (as with the two examples above: for instance, "[As I am] praieinge yow not to delaye ..."), I counted it as a clause. Where there was less reason for considering the structure a clause (for example, "addinge thes wordes thereto"; or "prayeing yow to excepte ... ;") I did not.

[4]This phrasing seems to imply that Lawraunce had actually met with Sutton.

[5]The manuscript has "to" instead of an expected "its" or the like.

[6]This three-part clause may take many of its details and ideas from Matthew 13:13–17: "[13] Therefore speak I to them in parables: because they seeing see not; and hearing hear not, neither do they understand. [14] And in them is fulfilled the prophecy of Esaias, which saith, By hearing ye shall hear, and shall not understand; and seeing ye shall see, and shall not

gentelwoman, and a maide willingly gathered to bestowe one yow, then sitch as I desired to / borrowe of yow or all the like this worlde afourdes, wheareof for one man god has leante yow a large / portione; but nether wife nor childe of yowr one to posses the saime when he shall sende his messinger / Deathe for yow[7] at what time yow must leaufe it all behinde yow pearaduenture to sitch wich more / desires to haue the saime then yowr lounger life heare, and neuer prayes for yowr healthe, and / happines in the life to com; for sitch faullse frindes this worlde afourdes to many:

And now I / beseitch yow sir; wisely consider, and beare in mynde; That when Deathe comes yowr body / must to the earthe from wheance it cam; and yowr soulle goo before god to giue acounte how yow / haue liued, yewsed, and bestowed that Tallente[8] he has here lente yow of pourpose to doo good with / unto his nedy memberes wich ar yowr poore Brotheres, and Sisteres in Crist Jesous that wauntes them, / to home [= whom] Crist commaundes yow both to giue and leande Quickely; willingly, chirfully, and frely withoute / groginge [= grudging]; addinge thes wordes theareto; That whosoeuer lendeth to one of thous [= those] doth it unto the lorde;[9] / and whosoeuer giueth but a cope [= cup] of coulde water in his naime; shall thearefore, receaufe a Thousaunde / foulde;[10] againe our Sauioure saiethe that

---

perceive: [15] For this people's heart is waxed gross, and *their* ears are dull of hearing, and their eyes they have closed; lest at any time they should see with *their* eyes and hear with *their* ears, and should understand with *their* heart, and should be converted, and I should heal them. [16] But blessed *are* your eyes, for they see: and your ears, for they hear. [17] For verily I say unto yow, That many prophets and righteous *men* have desired to see *those things* which ye hear, and have not heard *them*."

[7]Like later phrasing, this passage is reminiscent of the morality play *Everyman*, in which Death is indeed sent as God's messenger.

[8]Perhaps Lawraunce is alluding to the famous parable of the talents (Matthew 25:14–29), which stresses the need to use one's gifts as God intends. See also Luke 19:12–27.

[9]See Proverbs 19:17: "He that hath pity upon the poor lendenth unto the Lord; and that which he hath given he will pay him again."

[10]See Matthew 10:42: "And whosoever shall give to drink unto one of these little ones a cup of cold *water* only in the name of a disciple, verily I say unto you, he shall in no wise lose his reward." See also Mark 9:41: "For whosoever shall give you a cup of water to drink in my name, because ye belong to Christ, verily I say unto you, he shall not lose his reward."

a good Tree brindgethe fourth good frute;[11] also that faithe /
withoute charity is a ded faithe[12] and profites not to saluation, and
whosoeuer has not bothe of them / can not haue benifitt of the
Deathe, and merites of Iesus Crist and be saiued, and yet to [= too]
many doo / ouer bouldely presume one godes mercey upon faithe
onely and so rides post to hell wheance they / can not retourne; till
then; neuer remembringe godes Iustis wich is no less then his
merceye, bothe / infinyte, and cannot be seperated; whearefore in
the naime of god whilest yow haue leasure lett / yowr greatest care
be to preuent that eandeles misery; and in Crist pourchase yowr
saluation by / repentaunce, faithe, hope, charitye, good workes,
and euery way amendement of life; so shall yow be / most happey
when Deathe Comes; for a good life causes a godly eande,[13] and as
the Tree faulles it / lies:[14]

And now I pray yow for yowr good giue me leaufe to tell yow
a Talle, or Too [= Two]; not impertinent to / the matter; and
wheareof yow may maike comfortable yewse [= use]; and eare it
be lounge yow will finde / the like proued upon yowr sealfe ether
for yowr good or otherwise as it shall please god to giue yow grace
/ or suffer yow to doo whilest yow ar liuinge; they ar not of Diues,
and Lazarous home yow haue often / hard of,[15] but my first taille
is:

---

[11]See Matthew 7:17: "Even so every good tree bringeth forth good
fruit; but a corrupt tree bringeth forth evil fruit."

[12]Based on James 2:17: "Even so faith, if it hath not works, is dead,
being alone." See also James 2:20: "But wilt thou know, O vain man, that
faith without works is dead?"

[13]It was proverbial that a "good life makes a good death." See the
Oxford Dictionary of English Proverbs, 3rd. ed. rev. by F. Wilson (Oxford:
Oxford University Press, 1970), 321, which cites sixteenth- and seventeeth-
century attestations.

[14]See Ecclesiastes 11:3: "If the clouds be full of rain, they empty *themselves* upon the earth: and if the tree fall toward the south, or toward the
north, in the place where the tree falleth, there it shall be." For the proverbial versions of this idea, see M. Tilley, *A Dictionary of Proverbs in England
in the Sixteenth and Seventeenth Centuries* (Ann Arbor: University of Michigan Press, 1950), M64 and T503.

[15]On Dives (the rich man who winds up in hell) and Lazarus (the poor
man who ascends into heaven), see Luke 16:19–31.

Theare was a man had three frindes;[16] Too of them he loued intirely, the other / he maide littele acounte of; this man was sent for before his kinge and desired his first frinde to goo with / him but he woulde not; yet he broudght him parte of his way; then he desired his seconde frinde to goo / with him and he coulde not yet gaue him somthinge for a remembraunce; last of all he went to his Thurde / frinde of home [= whom] he maide least reconinge and he went with him to the kinge and aunswared for him in all / matteres whatsoeuer; so man in this worlde beinge sent for by Deathe comes to his wife, children, or frindes / to goo with him, but they will not yet they will bringe him to his graufe; then he desires his goodes, and / substaunce to goo with him, and they cannot yet they will giue him a sheate; but his conscience will goo / with him, and before the Throune of god aunsweare for him, Thearefore haue greate caire to be of a good / conscience; and whilest yow ar here prouide as a kinge did of home I shall tell yow my seconde talle;;[17] / Theare was a country, wheare the commones did chouse theare kinge, and at ther pleasures woulde banishe him / into a far country almost naiked; but one kinge more wise then the rest so soune as he was chosen / sent continuall prouision into that country wheare he shoulde goo, that when his one [= own] peopell did / banishe him he moudght [= might] be royally receaued; and liue most princely theare; Euen so yow may now / prouide in this worlde that when Deathe comes for yow god, his Aungelles, and saintes may Joyfully receaufe / yow into heauen;[18] whearefore withoute furdar delay Tender yowr one soulles good; liue godly, and / remember that Deathe will steall upon yow as a Theife;[19] Also that the laite lorde Treasorer whoo no doute / hoped to liue as lounge as yow was sodenly sent for;[20] I neide not tell yow that Sir

---

[16]The ensuing tale has much in common with the early sixteenth-century morality play *Everyman*.

[17]Miss Lawraunce may have added the second semicolon here because the first is obscured by bleed-through from the other side.

[18]See Luke 16:9: "And I say unto you, Make to yourselves friends of the mammon of unrighteousness; that, when ye fail, they may receive you into everlasting habitations."

[19]This clause is probably loosely based on one or more of the following: 1 Thessalonians 5:2, 2 Peter 3:10, and Revelation 3:3 and 16:15.

[20]This apparently refers to Thomas Sackville, first Earl of Dorset and Baron Buckhurst (1536–1608), who served as Lord Treasurer from 1603–08. The account of his life in the *Dictionary of National Biography* notes that he "died suddenly at the council-table at Whitehall on 19 April 1608."

John Spenser is ded;[21] / whoo if before he diede had giuen but the Twentye parte of his worldly wealthe to the poore and nedy members / of crist had don a heauenly deade upon earthe, for wich, his soulle now undowtedly shoulde haue had / a heauen [sic] rewarde; praieinge yow not to delaye yowr amendment from day to day; nether to be / ouer secure in yowr one conseate;[22] but whilst yow ar liuinge withowte furdar detraction this day / begin to be as cairefull to prouide heauenly Treasure for yowr soulle; as yow haue bin in gettinge earthly / for yowr body;[23] and expeckt Deathe daly; be feairefull of hell, and more desirous of heauen then all this / worldes wealthe; and althoudgh yow se this new yeares springe, knowe yowr sommer is past; and / that yow ar nere the faulle of the leaffe; and yowr gray hares ar messingeres sent to bed [= bid] yow prepaire yowr / body for the graufe, and yowr soull for god whoo has aldredy giuen yow a lounge time only to repent and doo / good, not leasure to sinne; whearefore from heancefourthe acounte no better of goulde and siluer then of red / and white earthe wich can searufe [= serve] maunes [= man's] tourne but for a shorte time; also know that yowr body, wich / is mutch more precious

---

[21]This probably refers to the Sir John Spencer (d. 1610) who served as Lord Mayor of London. According to the *Dictionary of National Biography*, after he came to London "he was so successful that he became known as 'Rich Spencer.'" He was accused of using shady business practices, lived in a sumptuous house, and in his final years was famous for refusing to contribute to voluntary collections. The *DNB* reports that he "died, at an advanced age, on 3 March 1609–10 .... His funeral was on a most sumptuous scale.... True to the last to his parsimonious principles, Spencer left none of his immense wealth to objects of public benevolence or utility." In many respects, then (including background, wealth, and recentness of death), Spencer seems to have been an ideal example for Lawraunce to cite.

[22]This phrase may be loosely derived from one or more of the following scriptural texts: Proverbs 26 and 28; Romans 11:25 and 12:16; and Job 37:24.

[23]See Luke 12:20–21: "[20] But God said unto him, *Thou* fool, this night thy soul shall be required of me: then whose shall those things be, which thou hast provided? [21] So *is* he that layeth up treasure for himself, and is not rich toward God." See also Matthew 6:19–21: "[19] Lay not up for yourselves treasures upon earth, where moth and rust doth corrupt, and where thieves break through and steal. [20] But lay up for yourselves treasures in heaven, where neither moth nor rust doth corrupt, and where thieves do not break through nor steal: [21] For where your treasure is, there will your heart be also."

then mony withoute yowr soull is a corropte carcase, and yowr soulle withoute / god a sepulker of sinne, and that man was maide only to searufe god in this life, and then to inioye / euerlastinge life in heauen; for wich cause; all cristianes shoulde haue greate caire how they liue; and the / youngest men ouft [= ought] to thinke continually one the graufe; for ther liufes ar unsertaine, and oftentimes / shortened by casewalties; but the Thoudghtes of oulde men shoulde alwaies dwell thearein for phisike / cannot lounge presearufe them; and yet commonly the nearear thous ar to theare eandes; the more; covityous; / and desirous they ar of goulde, and siluer earthes uadinge [= fading] treasure:

I haue red that the ritch / philosopher Socrates cast his goulde into the sea knowinge he shoulde be more happye withowte mutch / then with it; and the wise Profitt Daued prayed as well against ritches as pouerty; also Peter, and John; the /

——[END OF FIRST PAGE OF MANUSCRIPT]——

eldest, and derest Aposteles of crist saide goulde and siluer haue I noune;[24] but the Diuell saide all this is myne;[25] god graunte / yow may so liue here, that afterwardes yow may be in the state of thous saintes not that Diuell; and so yow / may if whilste yow haue leasure yow repent that time past whearein yow have not searued god and liued / as yow oufte [read: ought] and begin to be charitable, mercifull, and liberaull, not wrestelinge lounger against the cries of / yowr one conscience in gatheringe, and heapinge together that before naimed earthly Treasure wich / worldely men ouer mutch esteames and drawes to many of them from god to the diuill; whearefore in / the naime of god, and his Son Criste reast yow now from thouse laibores for of sitch ritches yow haue / enufe alredy, and beande yowr holle forces for the searuis of god doinge his will, and obaienge his / commaundementes; so asuredly shall yowr life, and deathe be good, yow happey, and blessed that euer / yow weare borne, for then yow shall one day heare Crist pronounce this sentence both upon yowr soulle and / body; goo into euerlastinge life; wheare yow shall for euer inheret that

---

[24]See Acts 3:6: "Then Peter said, Silver and gold have I none; but such as I have give I thee ...."

[25]See Luke 4:6: "And the devil said unto him [Jesus], All this power will I give thee, and the glory of them: for that is delivered unto me; and to whomsoever I will give it."

euerlastinge life; wheare yow shall for euer inheret that heauenly Treasure wich no / mortall eye has seine, eare harde of; or harte can conseaufe; nether Can the wisdom of men or Aungeles / expres it;[26] wich Treasure aboufe all otheres I beseitch yow be most cairfull to gett, then will yowr / conscience goo chirefully with yow, and before the Throune of god aunsware Joyfully for yow;[27] Also / consider what incompirable gladnes will be at the generaull resurrection in yowr soulle and body / at ther meatinge, and Joynyinge together againe to inioye euerlastinge life;[28] Concludinge thes matteres / wich desearufes to be eandeles with theise wordes; That all healpes to saluation can be no more / then ar neidefull; nor any perswationes more uehement then necessary to clouse up the latter / daies of a worldely manes life with a cleare sonsett wich god graunte yow may haue to yowr / eandeles comforte:

:And now to eande my lounge letter, sithince god has giuen yow a lounge / life; and a large portion only to searufe him, and doo good as aforesaide; wheareby at the eande / of this unsertaine, and shorte life, yow may be asured of a seartaine one for euer in his / heauenly kingdom; I heareby most humblye desire yow for the loue yow beare to that place, yowr / Sauioure Criste, godes eternaulle presence, and yowr one soulle; from hencefourthe to haue ~~sitch~~ / a cairefull, and good regarde of yowr one saluatyon; and Also sitch a frindely respeackte of / me wich in Cristian duty unfainedly wishese yow well; and desires to speande my pilgramaige of / this life in the feare, fauor, and loue of god wheareby I may afterwardes be asured of a better; that / if yow will not for my present prefermente wich I aquainted yow with lende me upon my one [=own] / security the mony I desired to borrowe; yet that yow will in a godly, fatherly, Cristian and frindly / disposition towardes me be pleased; from this time fourthe; to repute, excepte [read: accept], taike, and number / me amoungest thous wich yow haue, and shall maike choyse of to be yowr

---

[26]Based on 1 Corinthians 2:9: "But as it is written, Eye hath not seen, nor ear heard, neither have entered into the heart of man, the things which God hath prepared for them that love him."

[27]The situation here may be partly, remotely, derived from Hebrews 4:16: "Let us therefore come boldly unto the throne of grace, that we may obtain mercy, and find grace to help in time of need."

[28]This refers to the common Christian belief that the soul and body would meet and reunite on the day of general resurrection; see, for instance, John Donne's poem "The Relic."

and shall maike choyse of to be yowr adopted children; or / chosen frindes one home yow porpose, and will bestowe sitch worldly wealthe when god shall / caull yow oute of this life as heare he has lente yow,[29] The rewarde wheareof yow shall asuredly / finde in heauen before yow prepaired by him wich for that good worke, and Charitable deade will be / a father, and frinde to yow foreuer; and to him I will not faill ouften, and earnestly to pray for / yowr healthe, and happines in this life, and yowr euerlastinge Joyes in the life to com; wich / howsoeuer yow ar, or may be dissposed towardes me, with all my harte I humbly desire him to / graunte yow, whoo has promised to here, and graunte the praieares of his faithfull and obediente / searuauntes:

And now to shew yow the cause why I am a suter for my sealfe; it is because; / yow haue mutch of this worldes goodes wich I waunte [i.e., lack]; and wishe no more of but for my / necessary maintaynaunce;: yow <are> oulde; and I youndge, Thearefore am like to outeliue yow wich / I desire not, Also my one [= own] father beinge but a poore gentelman is not able to prefer me, or / doo for me as he is willinge; and my sealfe thorowe infirmyties in my heade and eyes cannot / taike sitch paines for my one good as I am also willinge; and thearefore feares wauntes to com / upon me; wich to preuente I am commaunded by godes worde both to seike and axe [= ask];[30] and by / him yowr heauenly father; am sent unto yow whoo knowes yow can healpe me; and thearefore / willes me in his naime and his sonn Cristes to axe of yow this I sewe for; for whous saikes / I trust yow will graunte me the saime; saieinge this far for my sealfe; that if yow knew / me; my harte, dispositions; desires, and willingnes to liue as all thous ar knoune to god; yow / beinge one of his woulde not for any worldly wealthe denye me what here I humbly desire; but / howsoeuer yow shall doo thearein; I hope to be comforted hearewith, that if my life in this / wourlde be lounge, and sharpe, yet in the worlde to com it will be Joyfull and euerlastinge; so / seasinge, and leauinge my sute unto yowr godly wisdom; and yow unto him whoo neuer / leaueth his; I craufe pardon; prayeinge yow to excepte [= accept] this my lenton labor as a Token of good / will towardes yow; as well as for my one

---

[29]The punctuation mark here could be a semicolon instead of a comma. There is a dot above, but it is exactly at the crossing point of the two strokes of an *x* on the other side and thus may be bleed-through.

[30]See Matthew 7:7: "Ask, and it shall be given you; seek, and ye shall find; knock, and it shall be opened unto you." See also Luke 11:9.

good; wich at Easter last I had sent but that then I / harde yow weare far of [= off] in the countrey, and aboute Whitsontide next god permittinge me; I will / sende to know yowr worshipes pleasure to this parte of my letter wich consearnethe my sealfe; / humbly beseachinge yow that it may be in a line or too under yowr haunde; and howsoweuer it shall / be I will rest thaunkefull; and satisfied thearewithe; from my fatheres house now at Battersea[31] / in Surry Too milles from london, this xuth day of may 1610

yowr worshipes welwisher:
and humble peticioner /

Ane Lawraunce

---

[31]Battersea was an ancient borough near London, bordered on the north-east by Lambeth.

Appendix 6

Women Writers of the English Renaissance: A Chronology of Texts and Contexts

Prepared by Eric Sterling

1558: b. Joan Thynne (letter writer); b. Anthony Bacon; b. Robert Greene; d. Mary Tudor. Elizabeth ascends the throne upon Mary's death and restores the Anglican religion in England.

1559: b. George Chapman. Act of Supremacy (Elizabeth becomes head of Anglican Church); Act of Uniformity (mandatory church attendance). *Mirror for Magistrates* (first edition).

1560: b. Margaret Clifford, Countess of Cumberland; b. Frances Walsingham, Lady Essex (letter writer—to her husbands Sir Philip Sidney and Robert Devereux [Earl of Essex] and to Robert Cecil); b. Thomas Hariot. Publication of Geneva Bible (strongly Protestant, Calvinist). First Bible to divide chapters into verses and to use Roman type rather than Gothic. Anne Locke, a friend of John Knox, translates *Sermons of John Calvin, upon the songe that Ezechias made after he had bene sicke, and afflicted by the hand of God*. She dedicates the translation to the Duchess of Suffolk. Elaine Beilin believes that Locke's "conviction that she was a part of God's Providence overcame any doubts she may have had as a female author."

1561: b. Mary Sidney (Countess of Pembroke; editor, devotional writer; sister of Sir Philip Sidney); b. Francis Bacon; b. Robert Southwell. Hoby's translation of Castiglione's *Il Cortegiano*; Norton's and Sackville's *Gorboduc, or Ferrex and Porrex* (first English play in blank verse).

1562: b. Penelope Rich (1563?), letter writer and object of Sir Philip Sidney's *Astrophil and Stella*; b. Samuel Daniel. Religious Wars begin in France. In England, Homily on Marriage ordered to be read regularly at church. Lady Anne Bacon's translation of Bishop John Jewel's *Apologia pro Ecclesia Anglicana* (*Apologie or Aunswer in defence of the Church of England*), the first complete statement in English defending Anglicanism against Roman Catholicism.

1563: b. Michael Drayton; b. Elizabeth Grymeston (writer of mother's advice books); d. John Bale. Thirty-nine Articles of Anglican Church. Foxe's *Acts and Monuments (Book of Martyrs)*; on Protestant heroes. Sackville's induction included in second edition of *The Mirror for Magistrates*.

1564: b. William Shakespeare; b. Christopher Marlowe; b. Galileo; d. John Calvin; d. Michelangelo. Second, enlarged edition of Lady Anne Bacon's translation of the *Sermons of Bernadine Ochine (to the number of 25) concerning the predestination and election of God* (first ed. 1551). Bacon's publisher, to assure readers that a modest woman can publish and engage in intellectual pursuits, asserts in his preface that Bacon is a "wel occupied Jentelwoman, and verteouse mayden ... whose shamfastnes would rather have supprest theym, had not I to whose handes they were commytted halfe agaynst her wyll put them fourth... If oughte be erred in the translacion, remember it is a womans yea, a Gentylwomans, who commenly are wonted to lyve Idelly, a maidens that never gaddid farder than hir fathers house to learne the language." Lady Bacon also translates *An Apologie or answere in defence of the Church of Englande with a briefe and plaine declaration of the true Religion professed and used in the same*.

1565: Mary (Queen of Scots) marries Lord Darnley (Henry Stuart) and joins the Catholic Alliance.

1566: b. James Stuart; d. Thomas Hoby. Mary Stuart gives birth to James, the future King of England and Scotland.

1567: b. Thomas Nashe. Darnley murdered (probably with Mary Stuart's complicity); Mary Stuart marries one of the murderers (Earl of Bothwell). Mary forced to abdicate. James becomes King of Scotland at the age of one. Elizabeth Whitney's *Copy of a letter, lately written in meeter, by a younge Gentilwoman: to her vnconstant Louer*. Whitney, a poet, is the sister of poet Geoffrey Whitney, author of *Choice of Emblems* (1568).

1568: b. Aemilia Lanyer (poet); d. Roger Ascham. Mary Stuart flees to England, where she is arrested. Publication of the Bishop's Bible (more moderate than the Geneva Bible), advocated by Elizabeth.

1569: b. John Davies. Northern rebellion (led by Duke of Norfolk), to install Mary Stuart as Queen of England, fails.

1570: Pope Pius V excommunicates Elizabeth and says that he deposes her. Grace Mildmay begins her *Journals and Papers* (1570–1617). She writes, for the benefit of her daughter Mary, *For the Workhouse: a Book of Prescriptions and Recommendations Collected and Copied by her Daughter* (still unpublished). The work contains advice, Protestant meditations, cures, and recipes; it also provides a clear sense of what life was like for a sixteenth-century Englishwoman. Ascham's *Schoolmaster*.

1571: b. Lady Margaret Hoby (author of earliest known diary by a British woman, covering years 1599–1605); b. Esther (Hester?) Kello (writer and calligrapher); b. Johannes Kepler. Parliament passes bill limiting clergy's forced subscription only to doctrinal Article of Faith. Ridolfi Plot (to depose Elizabeth for Mary) fails.

1572: b. John Donne; b. Ben Jonson; b. Thomas Dekker; d. John Knox. St. Bartholomew Massacre of French Huguenots. Duke of Alencon courts Elizabeth.

1573: b. Earl of Southampton. Isabella Whitney's *Sweet Nosgay, Or pleasant posye: contayning a hundred and ten Phylosophicall flowers.* George Gascoigne's *Hundred Sundrie Flowers.*

1574: b. Elizabeth Clinton (Countess of Lincoln, advice book writer); b. Anne of Denmark (wrote *Letters to King James,* married to King James and participant in Ben Jonson's masques); b. Lady Anne Southwell (poet and letter writer); b. Joseph Hall.

1575: b. John Webster; b. Cyril Tourneur; b. Thomas Heywood. Beginning of a correspondence, later published as *Two Elizabethan Women: Correspondence of Joan and Maria Thynne 1575–1611,* edited by Alison Wall.

1576: b. John Marston; d. Lady Joanna Lumley (translator); d. Lady Frances Abergavenny (poet). Treaty of Ghent; Sack of Antwerp. The Theatre (first permanent theatre building in England) built by James Burbage. Mary Sidney, age 15, marries middle-aged Earl of Pembroke—his third marriage. Her uncle, Robert Dudley, becomes a favorite of Queen Elizabeth and is reputed the most influential and powerful man in England. Lady Joanna Lumley, the first translator of a Greek tragedy into English, dies. The play, *The Tragedie of Euripides Called Iphigeneia, Translated out of the Greake into Englisshe,* had appeared in the mid 1550s. She also had translated *Epistola ad Dominum Patrem.*

1577: B: MARTHA MOULSWORTH; b: Anne, Countess of Arundel, who wrote treatises on childbirth and child rearing; b. Robert Burton; b. Peter Paul Rubens. Sir Francis Drake initiates voyage around the world.

1578: b. Lady Katherine Paston (correspondent for her husband in financial affairs); b. Maria Thynne (letter writer); b. William Harvey; d. George Gascoigne. Nine of Isabella Whitney's poems appear in Richard Jones's *Gorgeous Gallery of Gallant Inventions.* Margaret Tyler's translation of the chivalric romance *The First Part of the Mirrour of Princely Deedes and Knyghthood: Wherein Is Shewed the Worthinesse of the Knight of the Sunne, and His Brother Rosicleer, Sonnes to the Great Emperour Trebatio, with the Straunge Love of the Beautiful Princesse Briana, the Valiant Acts of Other Noble Princes and Knights,* originally written by Diego Ortunez de Cala horra. In her epistle to the reader, Tyler defends a female's desire to write (on any topic) and to pursue intellectual activities. She writes about war (a topic usually reserved for men), yet she anticipates the criticism she will receive. She claims that since men dedicate works to women (and thus have female patrons), women may read, think, and study. Barbara McGovern refers to Tyler as "the first true English feminist." Holinshed's *Chronicles* (first edition). Lyly's *Euphues, the Anatomy of Wit*.

1579: b. John Fletcher; b. John Webster. Union of Utrecht. John Stubbs loses right hand for writing *The Discovery of a Gaping Gulf*, in which he disapproves of Elizabeth's proposed wedding to the Duke of Alencon. Spenser's *Shepheardes Calender*.

1580: d. John Heywood; d. Raphael Holinshed. Drake returns from voyage. The Pope fails in his attempt to return Ireland to Roman Catholicism. Montaigne's *Essays* (I–II).

1581: b. Lady Jane Cornwallis (author of private correspondence, 1613–44); b. Prudentia Deacons (Catholic nun who translated *The mantle of the spouse* [n.d.]); b. Lucy Harington, Countess of Bedford (patroness and poet); b. Thomas Overbury. Recusancy laws tightened against Catholics (forcing them to attend Anglican services and to receive the sacrament). Elizabethan regime executes three priests.

1582: b. Elizabeth Weston. Gregorian Calendar adopted by Catholic countries in Europe. Roman Catholic English translation of New Testament published at Rheims. Old Testament translation published in 1609. Thomas Bentley publishes *The Monument of Matrones: conteining seven severall Lamps of Virginitie, or distinct treatises*, an anthology of religious literature by women. Bentley claims that his book is "more proper and peculiar for the private use of women than heretofore hath beene set out by anie," thus implying a distinction between male and female piety. The collection includes Queen Elizabeth's translation of Marguerite de Navarre's *Le Miroir de L'Ame pecheresse*, a work by Grace Mildmay, Frances Aburgavennie's *Praiers made by the right Honourable Ladie Frances Aburgavennie* and *The Precious Perles of Perfect Godliness*, Jane Grey's *Certaine Effectuall praier* and *Exhortation*, Katherine Parr's *Lamentacion of a Sinner* (originally published in 1547) and *Prayers stirryng the mynd unto heavenlye medytacions* (originally published in 1545), and Elizabeth Tyrwhitt's *Morning and evening praiers, with diverse Psalmes, Hymnes, and Meditations*. In Tyrwhitt's work, the persona is a sinner, a "miserable, wretched woman."

1583: b. Philip Massinger. Throckmorton Plot (to rescue Mary Stuart) fails; thousands of Catholics arrested.

1584: b. Lucy (Elizabeth) Knatchbull (autobiographer); d. Duke of Alencon. Puritans fail in attempt to reform Church. Several poems in Richard Jones's *Handful of Pleasant Delights* may be by Isabella Whitney. Anne Wheathill publishes *A handfull of holesome (though homelie) hearbs, gathered out of the goodlie garden of Gods most holie word*. Wheathill dedicates her work to women and discusses her dilemma in writing what she wishes while not breaching feminine decorum.

1585: b. Mary Ward (wrote letters to the Pope in which she advocated education for women and wrote travel narrative for her voyages from 1606–1618); b. William Drummond; b. Elizabeth Cary (Lady Falkland, poet, dramatist, translator). James agrees to rule as a Protestant.

1586: b. Lady Elizabeth Lindsey (letter writer); b. John Ford; d. Sir Philip Sidney. Babington Plot (to murder Elizabeth and replace her with Mary) discovered, with Mary clearly an accomplice. Pope Sixtus V offers King Philip of Spain one million crowns to invade England. Church permission required for any publication in England. Sir Philip Sidney, who had been tutored by MARTHA MOULSWORTH'S FATHER, dies of a wound inflicted in battle.

1587: b. Lady Mary Wroth (poet, fiction writer); Mary Stuart executed. The Pope decrees crusade against England. Marlowe's *Tamburlaine*. Kyd's *Spanish Tragedy*. Holinshed's *Chronicles* (second edition), used by Shakespeare and Marlowe. Dorothy Arundell writes (c. 1587–1597) the *Life of Fr. Cornelius, the Martyr*. Elizabeth Saunders writes letter of a visit to her family. Saunders was arrested for trying to restore Catholicism to England and once escaped from prison in order to attend Mass.

1588: b. Thomas Hobbes; d. Duke of Guise. England defeats the Spanish Armada. "Martin Marprelate" attacks on Anglicanism by Puritans begin. Marlowe's *Tamburlaine, Part II*. Montaigne's *Essays* (III).

1589: Civil war in France between Protestant and Catholic factions ensues after murder of Henry III. Henry of Navarre becomes king. Shakespeare begins writing plays (*1 Henry VI*). Jane Anger's *Jane Anger, her Protection for Women* published, the first work by an Englishwoman that discusses the Renaissance gender controversies. Anne Dowriche publishes a poem, *The French Historie: A Lamentable Discourse of three of the chiefe, and most famous bloodie broiles that have happened in France for the Gospell of Jesus Christ*. Marlowe's *Jew of Malta*. Puttenham's *Art of English Poesie*.

1590: b. Lady Anne Clifford (diarist, biographer, letter writer educated by Samuel Daniel); d. George Puttenham; d. Francis Walsingham. King James marries Anne of Denmark. Bishops Whitgift and Bancroft attack Puritan ministers. Spenser's *Faerie Queene* (I–III). Sir Philip Sidney's *Arcadia* published. Anne Locke Prowse translates *Of the markes of the children of God, and of their afflictions. To the faithfull of the Low Countrie. By John Taffin*.

1591: b. Agnes More (translator); b. Robert Herrick. Hacket's Conspiracy (Puritan who called himself King of Europe). *Arden of Feversham*. Sir Philip Sidney's *Astrophil and Stella* published.

1592: b. Alice Osborne (wrote petition to Parliament in the later 1650s, *The Case of the Lady Wandesford*); b. Henry King; d. Robert Greene; d. Michel de Montaigne. Plague besets London. Shakespeare at work on poems and sonnets. Elizabeth recalls Essex from France. Ralegh angers Queen Elizabeth by marrying Elizabeth Throckmorton (one of the queen's ladies-in-waiting) without the queen's permission. Recusancy rolls indicate that

Elizabeth Grymeston, a Roman Catholic writer of advice books, is fined for not attending the Anglican church. Publication of the Countess of Pembroke's translation of Robert Garnier's *Marc Antonie* and Philippe de Mornay's *Discours de la Vie et de la Mort*. In the 1590s, she also translates Petrarch's *Trionfo della Morte* and finishes the translation of the Psalms begun by her brother Philip. Although she does not publish her translation of the Psalms, the manuscripts circulate. Marlowe's *Doctor Faustus* and *Edward II*. Daniel's *Delia*.

1593: b. George Herbert; b. Izaak Walton; d. Christopher Marlowe (murdered in tavern brawl). Church attendance required. Henry of Navarre becomes Roman Catholic, saying "Paris is worth a Mass." Plague forces theatres to close. Queen Elizabeth translates Boethius's *De Consolatione Philosophiae*. In 1544 she had put the 13th Psalm into tetrameters and had written a prose version of Marguerite de Navarre's *Le Miroir de L'Ame Pecheresse (The Mirror of the Sinful Soul)*. The Countess of Pembroke publishes her brother Philip's *Arcadia*, the most popular work of fiction for more than a century. Hooker's *Laws of Ecclesiastical Polity* (I–IV). Marlowe's *Massacre at Paris*. Shakespeare's *Richard III* and *Taming of the Shrew*.

1594: b. Henry (James's son); d. Thomas Kyd; d. William Painter. Henry of Navarre crowned King Henry IV of France. Dr. Roderigo Lopez is falsely accused by the Earl of Essex of attempting to murder Elizabeth and is executed on June 7. Lopez dies as a pawn between the secret services of the queen and Essex. Nashe's *Unfortunate Traveller*. Daniel begins *Civil Wars Between the Two Houses of Lancaster and York*. Shakespeare's *King John* and *Two Gentlemen of Verona*.

1595: b. Elizabeth Avery (religious polemicist); b. Thomas Carew; d. Torquato Tasso. Robert Southwell (a Jesuit) executed. Shakespeare's *Richard II* and *Romeo and Juliet*. Sidney's *Defence of Poesy* published. Spenser's *Amoretti, Colin Clout's Come Home Again*, and *Epithalamion*. Mary Sidney's *Dolefull Lay of Clorinda* appears in Spenser's *Colin Clout's Come Home Again*.

1596: b. Elizabeth (daughter of James I; eventually Queen of Bohemia; poet and letter writer); b. Elizabeth Jocelin (advice book writer); b. Rene Descartes; b. James Shirley; d. George Peele; d. Sir Francis Drake. Essex destroys Spanish fleet. Sir John Davies's *Orchestra*. Shakespeare's *Midsummer Night's Dream*. Spenser's *Faerie Queene* (IV–VI), *Prothalamion*, and *Fowre Hymns*.

1597: b. Rachel Speght (polemicist, pamphleteer). New Poor Law. Aemilia Lanyer encounters Simon Forman, the astrologer who writes about his viewing of several of Shakespeare's plays. Lanyer visits Forman to learn whether her husband's voyage will be profitable. Lanyer, according to A.L. Rowse, is Shakespeare's Dark Lady from the *Sonnets*; Rowse's evidence, however, is circumstantial and has often been questioned. Elizabeth Vernon, Countess of Southampton, starts at about this time to write letters about her relationship with the Earl of Southampton, Shakespeare's patron. Vernon's letters appear in Violet Wilson's *Society Women of Shakespeare's Time*. Bacon's *Essays*. Shakespeare's *1 Henry IV* and *Merchant of Venice*.

1598: b. Lady Eleanor Douglas (pamphleteer and mystic); d. William Cecil. Bodleian Library endowed. Religious wars in France end. Queen Elizabeth translates Horace's *Ars Poetica*. The Countess of Pembroke publishes Philip Sidney's *Astrophil and Stella*. She is the most significant female literary figure of her generation in England—mainly because of her editing and publishing of Philip Sidney's works, as well as for her own writing and her patronage of Edmund Spenser, Abraham Fraunce, and Samuel Daniel. She influences Spenser to write *The Ruine of Time* and *Astrophel*. She influences Thomas Moffet's *Nobilis* (on Sir Philip Sidney's life and death). Pembroke writes two poems commemorating the death of her brother: "The Dolefull Lay of Clorinda," which appears with other elegies for Sidney in Spenser's *Colin Clouts Come Home Again* (1595) and "To the Angell Spirit of the Most Excellent Sir Philip Sidney." Jonson's *Every Man in His Humour*.

1599: b. Oliver Cromwell; d. Edmund Spenser. Essex fails in Irish military campaign, returns, enters Elizabeth's bedchamber without permission, and is arrested. Satires and erotic poems censored in England. Ecclesiastical order that all polemical works by Thomas Nashe and Gabriel Harvey be confiscated and no more printed. Burbage takes apart The Theatre because of lease problems and rebuilds it nearby, renaming it The Globe. Lady Falkland translates *Le Miroir de Monde (The Mirror of the World)*. She later translates the works of Cardinal Du Perron and the writings of Blosius, a Flemish Benedictine monk. The Countess of Pembroke writes a poem in praise of Queen Elizabeth: "A Dialogue between two shepheardes … in praise of Astraea"; she had previously written another poem praising the Queen, "Even Now That Care." Esther (Hester?) Kello's *Ecclesiastes*, which includes her self-portrait. Dekker's *Shoemaker's Holiday*. Jonson's *Every Man out of His Humour*. Shakespeare's *As You Like It, Henry V*, and *Julius Caesar*.

1600: b. Lady Brilliana Harley (writer of approximately 200 letters covering the years 1625–1643); b. William Prynne (Puritan pamphleteer and MARTHA MOULSWORTH'S GODSON); b. Charles I; d. Thomas Deloney; d. Richard Hooker. Essex convicted of disobeying the Queen's orders by returning to England without permission. Shakespeare's *Twelfth Night*.

1601: b. Lady Elizabeth Brooke; d. Essex; d. Thomas Nashe. Essex rebellion fails; he is executed. Southampton convicted but not imprisoned. Donne imprisoned for secret marriage to Ann More. Shakespeare's *Hamlet* and *Twelfth Night*. Margaret Clifford, Countess of Cumberland's epitaph for Richard Candish, engraved upon his tomb.

1602: Jesuits ordered out of England. Bodleian Library opens. Elizabeth Cary (Lady Falkland) marries Henry Cary (member of Privy Council, Lord Chief Deputy of Ireland). She begins writing after her mother-in-law seizes all her books because she reads too much. She writes a verse history of Tamburlaine and a tragedy (neither one is extant). The Countess of Pembroke's "Dialogve between two Shepheardes ... in praise of Astraea" appears in *A Poetical Rhapsody*, ed. Francis Davison. Elizabeth Weston's *Poema ... Studio Ac Opera*.

1603: d. Queen Elizabeth; d. Elizabeth Grymeston; d. Elizabeth Caldwell. James I ascends the throne of England upon Elizabeth's death. End of Tudor dynasty and beginning of Stuart governance. The Watson and the Cobham Plots attempt to overthrow James. Ralegh imprisoned in Tower for treason, possibly on false charges. Millenary Petition (Puritan attempt to modify Anglican Church). Mountjoy subdues Ireland. Plague in London. Lady Falkland writes *Mariam, the Fair Queen of Jewry*. Elizabeth Melville Colville, a Scottish poet, publishes *Ane Godlie Dreame, Compylit in Scottish Meter be M.M. Gentlewoman in Culros, at the requeist of her freindes*. This is the Scottish version; she publishes the English version in 1606. Elizabeth Caldwell publishes a letter in *A True Discourse of the Practises of Elizabeth Caldwell (and Others) on the Person of Ma. T. Caldwell in the County of Chester, to Have Murdered and Poysoned Him, with Divers Others. Together with Her Maner of Godly Life during Her Imprisonment, Her Arrainement and Execution, with Isabell Hall Widdow. Lastly a Most Excellent Exhortatorie Letter, Written by Her Owne Selfe Out of Prison to her Husband, to Cause Him to Fall into Consideration of his Sinnes, etc. Serving Likewise for the Use of Every Good Christian. Being Executed the 18 of June 1603*. Lady Katherine Paston begins *The Correspondence of Lady Katherine Paston 1603-1627*. Florio's translation of Montaigne's *Essays*. Heywood's *Woman Killed with Kindness*. Jonson's *Sejanus*.

1604: d. John Whitgift. Hampton Court Conference. Law banishes Jesuits. Elizabeth Grymeston's advice book *Miscelanea, Meditations, Memoratives*. Marston's *Malcontent*. Shakespeare's *Measure for Measure* and *Othello*.

1605: b. Isabella Twysden (diarist); b. Anne Smyth (writer of petition to the House of Commons); b. Sir Thomas Browne; d. John Stow. Gunpowder Plot (Catholic plan to blow up the king and Parliament) fails. James passes laws restricting Catholics and Puritans. Elizabeth Cooke Hoby Russell, Anne Bacon's sister, publishes her translation from French, *A Way of Reconciliation of a good and learned man, touching the Trueth, Nature, and Substance of the Body and blood of Christ in the Sacrament*. In her dedication to her daughter, Anne Herbert, Russell includes all the conventions expected of female writers in the Renaissance, as Elaine Beilin points out: "she is pious in her concern for the true religion; she is obedient in having her translation approved by the original author; she is essentially private, because the work was not intended for publication, and only the respect for the dead compelled her to change its course; and she is a devoted mother, eager to contribute to the spiritual well-being of her child with her 'last Legacie, this Booke. A most precious Jewell to the comfort of your Soule ....'" Bacon's *Advancement of Learning*. Shakespeare's *King Lear*.

1606: b. Gertrude (Grace) More (Catholic spiritual writer); b. William Davenant; b. Edmund Waller; d. John Lyly. Oath of Allegiance. Act against recusancy. James tries unsuccessfully to unite England and Scotland. Elizabeth Melville Colville publishes *A Godlie Dreame, Compyled by Elizabeth Melvill, Ladie Culros yonger at the request of a friend*. This is the English version (Scottish version 1603). Elizabeth Weston's *Parthenicon E.J.W., Virginis Nobilissimae*. Jonson's *Volpone*. Cyril Tourneur's *Revenger's Tragedy* (sometimes attributed to Thomas Middleton). Shakespeare's *Macbeth*.

1607: English settlement in Jamestown, Virginia. Beaumont and Fletcher's *Knight of the Burning Pestle*. Shakespeare's *Antony and Cleopatra*.

1608: b. John Milton; d. Thomas Sackville. Parliament rejects another bid by James to unite England and Scotland.

1609: b. Barbara Blaugdone (Quaker writer who in 1691 published her *Account of the Travels, Sufferings and Persecutions of Barbara Blaugdone. Given Forth as a Testimony to the Lords Power, and for the Encouragement of Friends*); b. Rebecca Travers (Quaker who preached, wrote polemical tracts, and organized women's meetings); b. Henrietta Maria (letter writer; eventual wife of Charles I); b. Sir John Suckling; d. Cecelea Bulstrode, (author of *Newes of My Morning Worke*, which appears in the ninth edition of *The Conceited News of Thomas Overbury*. Ben Jonson and John Donne wrote compassionate poems about her upon her death, even though she and Jonson had quarreled). Spain exiles the Moors. Jonson's *Epicoene, or the Silent Woman*. Catholic translation of Old Testament in English at Douai. New Testament translated in 1582. Shakespeare's *Sonnets* published by Thomas Thorpe without Shakespeare's authorization. Lady Anne Clifford marries Richard Sackville, Earl of Dorset. By denying her contact with her children, he forces her to cease the lawsuit she initiated in 1605 (her father had willed his estate to his brother rather than his wife and children, which was contrary to law). Esther Kello's *Octonaries upon the Vanitie and Inconstancie of the World*. Thirty-five of Kello's manuscripts are extant.

1610: b. Ursula Quarles (poet); d. Lady Anne Bacon (translator and letter writer). Henry of Navarre assassinated. Beaumont and Fletcher's *Maid's Tragedy*. Jonson's *Alchemist*. Shakespeare's *Winter's Tale*.

1611: b. Giles Fletcher (the elder); d. Maria Thynne. King James Bible published. Arminian Baptists publish their first Confession. Donne's *First Anniversary*. Lanyer's *Salve Deus Rex Judaeorum*, one of first volumes of poems in English by a woman. The book contains poetic addresses to several noblewomen, including the Countess of Pembroke. The book includes "The Description of Cooke-ham" and "Eve's Apologie In Defence of Women." Lanyer's book, which may have been written for a largely female audience, presents a feminist perspective and is designed to combat misogyny. For instance, in "Eve's Apologie," Lanyer blames men, not women, for The Fall and attacks current gender double standards. Middleton's *Chaste Maid of Cheapside*. Shakespeare's *Tempest*. Elizabeth Shirley's *Life of Mother Clement*.

1612: b. Anne Bradstreet (poet); b. Bathsua Makin (polemical writer); b. Rosamond Saltonstall (letter writer); b. Samuel Butler; d. Joan Thynne; d. Robert Cecil; d. Sir John Harington; d. Henry (King James's oldest son); d. Elizabeth Weston. Trial of Lancashire Witches. Donne's *Second Anniversary*. Heywood's *Apology for Actors*. Webster's *White Devil*.

1613: b. John Cleveland; b. Richard Crashaw; b. Jeremy Taylor. James approves divorce of the Countess of Essex so that she may marry the king's favorite, the Earl of Somerset. When Thomas Overbury opposes the new marriage, the Countess has him poisoned in the Tower. Francis Bacon becomes Attorney General. Elizabeth Cary, Lady Falkland publishes *The Tragedie of Mariam, the Faire Queene of Jewry*, the first full-length original play ever published by an Englishwoman. Lady Jane Cornwallis begins her correspondence, *The Private Correspondence of Lady Jane Cornwallis; 1613–1644*. Shakespeare writes his last play (*The Two Noble Kinsmen*) with John Fletcher. Globe Theatre burns down after the cannon is set off during a production of Shakespeare's *Henry VIII*.

1614: b. Margaret Fell (Quaker pamphleteer). Second Globe Theatre opens. Jonson's *Bartholomew Fair*. Ralegh's *History of the World*. Webster's *Duchess of Malfi*.

1615: d. Robert Armin. Donne becomes Anglican clergyman. Publication of Jane Grey's *Life, Death and Actions of the Most Chast, Learned, and Religious Lady, the Lady Jane Grey, Daughter to the Duke of Suffolke*. Anne Turner's *Mistris Turners Farewell to All Women*.

1616: d. Margaret Clifford, Countess of Cumberland; d. Francis Beaumont; d. Cervantes; d. Richard Hakluyt; d. Philip Henslowe; d. William Shakespeare; d. Arabella Stuart. Shakespeare dies. William Harvey formulates theory on the circulation of blood. Somerset and wife convicted of murder. *The Works of Benjamin Jonson* published in folio. Dorothy Leigh publishes her advice on motherhood, *The Mothers Blessing: Or, The godly Counsaile of a Gentlewoman*. Leigh's book undergoes fifteen editions from 1616 to 1630. Elizabeth Arnold translates Thomas Tuke's *Treatise Against Painting*. Joseph Swetnam's *Arraignment of Lewd, Idle, Forward and Unconstant Women* first published. The book, a nasty and vicious anti-feminist work, enjoys enormous popularity and by 1634 has undergone ten editions. See 1617 for Rachel Speght's reply.

1617: b. Mary Simpson (Presbyterian spiritual writer). Ralegh travels to Guiana in search of gold but returns unsuccessful. Rachel Speght responds to Swetman's attack on women (see the listing under 1616) by writing *A Mouzell for Melastomus*. "Melastomus" means "slanderer, black-mouth." Speght is the first Englishwoman in her generation, while employing her own name, to reply to the popular and financially successful literary attacks on women. She employs the Bible to advocate the importance of women in society and to demand rights for married women; Speght writes, "For man was created of the dust of the earth ... but woman was made of a part of man after that he was a living soul. Yet was she not produced from Adam's foot, to be his too low inferior; nor from his head to be his superior; but from his side, near his heart, to be his equal: that where he is lord, she may be lady." Two other published responses to Swetnam's misogynistic attacks claim female authorship: Esther Sowernam's *Ester hath hang'd Haman* and Constantia Munda's *The Worming of a mad Dogge*. The pseudonym "Esther" signifies Sowernam's desire to redeem her people (instead of the Jews, she wishes to save women; the Persian Haman represents misogynists such as Joseph Swetman who write anti-female tracts. The surname Sowernam is the antithesis of Swetnam). Sowernam criticizes Rachel Speght for publishing an ineffective rebuttal and feels compelled to compose her own. Sowernam claims, "I doe in the first part of it plainely and resolutely deliver the worthinesse and worth of women, both in respect of their Creation, as in the worke of Redemption." Constantia Munda praises Speght for responding to Swetnam and discusses the issue of whether females possess the right to defend themselves publicly: she decides that "though feminine modesty hath confin'd our rarest and ripest wits to silence, wee acknowledge it our greatest ornament, but when necessity compels us, tis as great a fault and folly" to refrain from responding. The fact that Munda and Sowernam employ pseudonyms indicates a reluctance to acknowledge themselves publicly for fear of their reputations. In fact, some scholars have suspected that the authors may have been men interested in fanning the flames of controversy.

1618: b. Grace Barwick (Quaker and spiritual writer); b. Thomasina Pendarves (Baptist letter writer); b. Richard Lovelace. Ralegh executed for treason. Francis Bacon named Lord High Chancellor.

1619: b. Winefrid Thimelby; d. Samuel Daniel; d. Anne of Denmark. Aemilia Lanyer operates a school.

1620: b. Lucy Hutchinson (biographer, autobiographer); b.? Elizabeth Calvert (publishes radical, sectarian literature in the 1640s and 1650s, is arrested several times, writes letters, dies in 1675); d. Grace Mildmay (diarist). Puritans (Pilgrims) aboard *The Mayflower* arrive at Plymouth Rock in Massachusetts. The Court of Chancery starts to enforce marriage contracts, eventually allowing women to have a separate estate; widows and heiresses thus acquire some financial protection from covetous husbands and are not as much dependent financially on their spouses. Bacon's *Novum Organum*.

1621: b. Mary Cary; b. Lady Jane Cavendish (author of account books and letters); b. Anne King (poet and sister of poet Henry King; she writes poems such as *Under Mr. Hales Picture*); b. Andrew Marvell; b. Henry Vaughan; d. Margaret Clifford, Countess of Cumberland (b. 1560; author of poetic epitaph); d. Thomas Hariot; d. Mary Sidney (Countess of Pembroke). Bacon dismissed for accepting bribes. Donne becomes Dean of St. Paul's cathedral. Burton's *Anatomy of Melancholy*. Massinger's *A New Way to Pay Old Debts*. Middleton's *Women Beware Women*. Lady Mary Wroth publishes and then immediately withdraws *The Countess of Montgomeries URANIA*. The work is the first sustained work of prose fiction by an Englishwoman. The novel, modeled after *The Countess of Pembroke's Arcadia*, possesses a female protagonist and satirizes events at court (the reason why it is withdrawn and not republished in her lifetime). Lord Denny castigates her, declaring that women should not devise tales but may translate. Wroth never publishes again. Ironically, her aunt, Mary Sidney (Countess of Pembroke), had encouraged her to write. *The Countess of Montgomeries URANIA* contains an appendix, *Pamphilia to Amphilanthus*, a collection of one hundred poems and sonnets by Wroth. Her letters to Dudley Carleton in 1619 indicate that she circulates her works in manuscript. Wroth also had written *Loues Victorie*, a pastoral romance and had performed in masques, such as Jonson's *Masque of Blacknesse*. Contemporaries such as George Chapman, Joshua Sylvester, and Ben Jonson praise Wroth's poetry. Jonson dedicates *The Alchemist* to her and praises her in *Epigrams 103* and *105*. He lauds her husband in "To Sir Robert Wroth" and her parents in "To Penshurst." Rachel Speght publishes *Mortality's Memorandum*, an allegorical dream in which she asserts her right to be a female writer and attacks critics who believe that her father must have written her *Mouzell for Melastomus* in 1616. *Mortality's Memorandum* is autobiographical. Lady Amie/Anne Blount, fearful that William Holt (a man who owes her money and has lost to her in court but has delayed payment by appealing) will not pay her what the court orders him to pay, writes *To the Honorable Assembly of the Commons House. The Humble Complaint of the Ladie Amie Blount Daughter of George Late Earl of Castle-Haven*.

1622: b. Lady Anne Halkett (devotional writer, autobiographer); b. Martha Simmonds (Quaker polemicist who contested male Quaker governance); b. Anna Trapnel (Baptist spiritual writer); d. Elizabeth Jocelin (nine days after the birth of her daughter). Puritan moral theologian William Gouge writes *Of Domesticall Duties*, in which he demands that wives call their spouses "husband" and refrain from calling their husbands by their first names (which would symbolize an equality of status) and from using terms of endearment such as "sweetheart" and "love." Gouge also says that "though an husband in regard of equal qualities may carry the image of the devil, yet in regard to his place and office, he beareth the image of God .... We cannot but think that the woman was made before the Fall that the man might rule over her." *Countess of Lincolnes Nurserie* published. The Countess, mother of eighteen children, provides advice about the nursing of children. Two of her eighteen children later sail with Anne Bradstreet and John Winthrop to New England. Middleton's *Changeling*. Peacham's *Compleat Gentleman*.

1623: b. Margaret Cavendish (Duchess of Newcastle, poet, playwright, biographer); b.? Anna Cromwell (poet); b. Jane Lead (mystical writer); b. Elizabeth Walker (autobiographer); d. Countess of Lincoln. Shakespeare's *First Folio* published. M.R.'s *The Mothers Counsell, or, Live within Compasse,* an advice book for mothers.

1624: b. Mary Rich (1625?), Countess of Warwick (diarist, autobiographer); b. Anne Whitehead (Quaker polemicist and one of the first female preachers); d. Richard Sackville. Elizabeth Jocelin's *Mothers Legacie, To her vnborn Childe* is published posthumously. Jocelin writes the advice book for the benefit of the unborn child she carries because she fears that she will not survive its birth. She dies nine days after giving birth to her daughter in 1622. The book, first published in 1624, is printed seven times by 1635. Elizabeth Dale's *Petition to Parliament.* Lady Grace Darcie's *To the honourable assembly of the Commons house in Parliament.* Middleton's *Game at Chess,* despite its popularity, is banned because of its anti-Spanish propaganda.

1625: b. Lady Ann Fanshawe (biographer); d. Bessie Clarkson (co-author of religious treatise in dialogue form). Accession of Charles I following James's death. Charles marries Henrietta Maria of France. England wars with Spain.

1626: b. Lady Elizabeth Brackley (stepdaughter of Margaret Cavendish); b. Anne Venn (Presbyterian spiritual writer); d. Francis Bacon; d. Sir John Davies; beginning of recorded activities by Katherine Chidley, radical Protestant author of Civil War pamphlets. Bacon dies of pneumonia, perhaps while using snow to conduct experiments on refrigeration. Davies dies after his wife, Lady Eleanor Douglas, predicts his death. The prophetess predicts correctly when he will die after he burns her manuscripts. See entry for 1644. Elizabeth Cary (Lady Falkland) converts to Roman Catholicism without her husband's permission, ruining his political career. He leaves her, takes their eleven children with him, and removes everything from the house. Katherine Chidley, the first woman to defend religious independence in print, along with other females at St. Chad's parish in Shrewsbury in the refusal to be churched after giving birth.

1627: b. Dorothy Osborne (letter writer); b. Anne Audland; d. Helen (Eleanor?) Livingston, Countess of Linlithgow; d. Thomas Middleton. Privy Council orders Lord Falkland to support his wife, but he fails to comply. She kidnaps two of the children. John Marston and Michael Drayton dedicate works to her, and John Davies writes a poem in her honor. Lady Falkland's *History of Edward II.*

1628: b. Elizabeth Andrews (owner of draper shop who lost her goods for opening her shop on Christmas Day and refused to pay "Sunday shillings" [tithes], precipitating the document *An Account of the Birth, Education and Sufferings for the Truth's Sake of that Faithful Friend Elizabeth Andrews;* b. Patience Ashfield, Quaker and second wife of important Army officer Colonel Ashfield; in 1686 she signed the general testimony for Anne Whitehead in *Piety Promoted*; b. John Bunyan; d. Lady Katherine Paston. Murders of Buckingham and Greville. Petition of Right. Translation by Francis (Catherine) Greenway, Catholic nun, of *A short relation of the life, virtues, and miracles of S. Elizabeth*, by F. Palaudanus. William Prynne's (MARTHA MOULSWORTH'S GODSON'S) *Unlovelinesse of Love-lockes ... prooving the wearing and nourishing of a locke or love-locke, to be altogether unseemely and unlawfull unto Christians....*

1629: b. Hester Biddle. Charles I dismisses Parliament and begins eleven years of personal rule. John Eliot jailed. Ford's *Broken Heart*. Helen Livingston's, Countess of Linlithgow's, *Confession and Conversion of My Lady of L[inlithgow]*, published posthumously. She previously writes a letter using the name Eleanor Hay) to King James (published by D. Laing).

1630: d. Anne, Countess of Arundel (author of commemorative poem). War with Spain ends. Lady Anne Clifford remarries. Her new husband, Philip Herbert, Earl of Pembroke, also stops her from continuing her lawsuit. Clifford's lawsuit, in which she demands the estate her father has left to his brother, spans from 1605–1643. After Herbert's death in 1650, Clifford begins writing again (*Diary of Lady Anne Clifford* and *Clifford Letters of the Sixteenth Century*). She also later founds an almshouse for homeless women and a school and becomes the "Sherriffwich" in Westmorland. She dies in 1676. Lady Falkland translates and publishes *The Reply of the Cardinall of Perron, to the Answeare of the Most Excellent King of Great Britaine*, which is then ordered to be burned publicly. Anne Bradstreet sails from England to Massachusetts on the *Arbella*; her father becomes governor. Bradstreet is the first great American poet. Despite performing household chores and raising eight children, she finds time to write poetry—even though many Puritans do not approve of women writing poetry. Bradstreet writes, "I am obnoxious to each carping tongue / Who says my hand a needle better fits." A poem by Dorothy Berry appears in Diana Primrose's *Chain of Pearl, Or a Memoriall of the Peerless Graces, and Heroick Vertues of Quene Elizabeth of glorious Memory. Composed by the Noble Lady Diana Primrose*. This collection includes ten poems by Primrose that laud the virtues of the late queen. Beginning of recorded activities by Constance Fowler (letter writer). Anne Prowse's translation *Of the Marks of the Children of God, and of Their Comforts in Afflictions*.

1631: b. Mary Boreman (Quaker writer); b. John Dryden; d. John Donne; d. Michael Drayton. Lady Elizabeth Brooke writes *Observations, Rules for Practice*. Anne Phoenix's *The Saints Legacie* is published without her consent.

1632: b. Viscountess Elizabeth Mordaunt (who convinced Oliver Cromwell to save her husband's life and who authored *The Private Diary of Elizabeth, Viscountess Mordaunt*, edited by the Earl of Roden); b. Katherine Philips (poet); b. Mary (Martha) Beale (writer and artist whose psalms appear in Samuel Woodforde's *Paraphrase of the Psalms* and who writes *Discourse on*

Friendship; b. Elizabeth Camfield (writes *Many are the Testimonies* in Anne Whitehead's *Piety* [1686]); b. Sarah Wight (religious writer and visionary); b. John Locke; d. Elizabeth Compton (letter writer). MARTHA MOULSWORTH, at the age of fifty-five, writes "The Memorandum of Martha Moulsworth / Widow," one of the earliest extant autobiographical poems by an Englishwoman. Bessie Clarkson's *Conflict in Conscience of a Deare Christian Named Bessie Clarkson in the Parish of Lanark, which She Lay under Three Year and an Half. With the Conference that Past Between Her Pastor and Her at Diverse Times....* Agnes More translates *Delicious Entertainment of the Soule: Written by the Holy and Most Reverend Lord Francis de Sales, Bishop and Prince of Geneva. Translated by a Dame of Our Ladies of Comfort of the Order of St Bennet in Cambray.* Another translation of More's (but not from the same year) is *The Ruin of Proper Love and the Building of Divine Love*, by Dame Jeanne of Cambrai. Translation by Alexia Gray, Catholic nun (1606–40) of *The rule of ... Saint Benedict.* Ford's *'Tis Pity She's a Whore.*

1633: b. Samuel Pepys; d. Gertrude More; d. George Herbert. William Prynne (MARTHA MOULSWORTH'S GODSON) publishes his *Histrio-Mastix: the Players Scourge, or Actors Tragoedie .... Wherein it is largely evidenced ... by the authorities of ... 55 Synodes and councels, of 71 fathers and Christian writers ... of 40 heathen philosophers ... that popular stage playes ... are sinfull, heathenish, lewde, ungodly spectacles.* Donne's *Poems* published. Herbert's *Temple* published. Alice Sutcliffe's *Meditations of Man's Mortalitie. Or, a Way to True Blessedness*, which contains dedications in verse from Ben Jonson, Thomas May, and George Wither.

1634: b. Grace Bathurst (spiritual writer; contributed to her stepdaughter Elizabeth Bathurst's *Truth's Vindication* [see entry for 1655]). William Prynne (MARTHA MOULSWORTH'S GODSON) is imprisoned for his attacks on the episcopacy; his ears are cropped. Milton's *Comus.* Jane Owen's *Antidote Against Purgatory.*

1635: b. Mary Rowlandson (writer of captivity narrative, 1676); b. Mary Anderdon (a Quaker who wrote of her imprisonment: *A Word to the World. From the Spirit of Truth as a Tender Visitation of My Father's Love etc. From Exon. Gaol, the 23rd of the 9th month, 1662, where I am a Prisoner for Truth's Sake ....* Magdalene Augustine [Catherine] Bentley translates Luke Wadding's *History of the Angellicall Virgin Glorious S. Clare.*

1636: b. Margaret Baxter (diarist); d. Lady Anne Southwell. Sarah Burton arrested for presenting her husband's sermons to lords in Parliament.

1637: b. Thomas Traherne; d. Ben Jonson; d. John Webster? Mary Fage's *Fames roule* (anagrams, acrostics on names of British nobility). Milton's *Lycidas.* Elizabeth Middleton's poem *The Death and Passion of Our Lord Jesus Christ, as it Was Acted by the Bloody Jews, and Registred by the Blessed Evangelists.*

1638: Lucy Hutchinson marries Colonel Hutchinson; the wedding had previously been postponed because she contracted smallpox on her original wedding day. Hutchinson later translates Lucretius and writes her memoirs and those of her husband. Mary Rich temporarily loses her financial allowances after she angers her father by refusing to marry the man he selects for her. Her father attempts to marry her off for political and financial gain. Ann Brockman writes a medical book. Lady Elizabeth Lindsey's letter to her father. *The confession of ... Lady Bridget Egerton, 1638* (published 1871).

1639: d. Elizabeth Cary (Lady Falkland). Lady Falkland dies and is buried in chapel of Queen Henrietta Maria. Bridget Paget's *To the Most Illustrious & Most Excellent Lady, Elizabeth, Queene of Bohemia, Countesse Palatine of the Rhine, &c*, which appears in John Paget's (her husband's) *Meditations of Death.*

1640: b. Aphra Behn (playwright, poet, novelist, and government spy; her works include *Oroonoko, The Rover, Abdelazar, The Feign'd Curtizans*, and *The Widow Ranter*); d. Robert Burton; d. Thomas Carew. Judith Man's translation of John Barclay's *Epitome of the History of Faire Argenis and Polyarchus.* Lady Elizabeth Lindsey writes letter in which she refuses to watch a court masque for Twelfth Night.

1641: Mary Rich marries the Earl of Warwick. After her son and daughter die during infancy, she practices birth control but feels guilty about it later. In 1666, she begins her spiritual diary, which she continues until her death in 1678. She writes spiritual meditations (she is a Puritan), despite her husband's disapproval of her religious devotion. She attributes the causes of the Great Fire and the plague to Divine Providence. In 1672, she writes her autobiography, perhaps inspired by that of the Duchess of Newcastle. Jane Lead has her first mystical vision. She later writes about the female aspects of God and claims that God possesses male and female attributes. She also writes that prior to The Fall, Adam had been androgynous. She anticipates The Third Coming, ending the gender split (into male and female) that occurred during The Fall. Bathsua Makin, considered the most learned Englishwoman of her generation, tutors Charles I's daughter, Elizabeth. Makin also is a scholar and school mistress who strives diligently for females to be allowed a quality education. In 1641 she begins her correspondence with the Dutch scholar Anna Maria Van Schurman, the author of *De Ingenii Muliebris.* Van Schurman's work inspires Makin's *Essay to Revive the Antient Education of Gentlewomen.* Katherine Chidley's *Justification of the Independent Churches of Christ ... Being an Answer to Mr Edwards His Book*, later known as *Reasons Against Independent Government of Particular Congregations.* The following petition is from 1641: *A True Copy of the Petition of the Gentlewomen, and Tradesmens-wives, in and about the City of London.*

1642: d. Sir Isaac Newton; d. Sir John Suckling. Civil War starts. Closing of theatres in England. Margaret Cavendish's house is looted by supporters of the Commonwealth. She goes to work for Queen Henrietta Maria. 400 women petition the Houses of Lords and Commons for an alteration in economic policy. When the Duke of Richmond mocks them, they assault him. Browne's *Religio Medici* published. The following petition is from 1642: *The Humble Petition of Many Hundreds of Distressed Women*.

1643: from 1643–80, recorded activities by Mary Carey, author of unpublished autobiographical meditation and poetry.

1644: b. Elizabeth Bury (proficient in medicine, philology, heraldry, French, and Hebrew; she later writes a Puritan diary from 1693–1720). Second Globe theatre torn down. Milton's *Areopagitica*. Lady Eleanor Douglas's *From the Lady Eleanor, Her Blessing to her Beloved Daughter*. Lady Eleanor Douglas's second husband, Sir Archibald Douglas, dies after she predicts his death upon his burning of her manuscripts. See related entry for 1626. Lady Eleanor accurately predicts the death of both her husbands and the birth and gender of King Charles I's son Henry. She believes that the spirit of Daniel possesses her, and Queen Henrietta Maria consults her for predictions. Douglas is imprisoned and fined for illegally prophesying and, while in prison, is allowed no paper, writing implements, books, or Bible. Katherine Chidley's *New Yeares Gift, or a Brief Exhortation to Mr Thomas Edwards* and *Good Counsell, to the Petitioners for Presbyterian Government*. Chidley preaches at William Greenhill's Independent church. Anna Hume's translation of Petrarch's *The Triumphs of Love, Chastity, and Death*. Rosamond Saltonstall writes letter about spiritual beauty to her brother.

1645: d. Aemilia Lanyer; d. Mary Ward; d. Ursula Quarles. Mary Cary's *Glorious Excellencie of the Spirit*. Elizabeth Warren's *The Old and Good Way Vindicated: In a Treatise Wherein Divers Errours (both in Judgment and Practice, Incident to these Declining Times) Are Unmasked, for the Caution of Humble Christians*. Isabella Twysden's *Diary of Isabella, Wife of Sir Roger Twysden ... 1645–1651*, edited by F.W. Bennitt. Elizabeth Warren's *Ladies Legacie to Her Daughters. In Three Books*. Ursula Quarles's *Short Relation of the Life and Death of Mr Francis Quarles*.

1646: D. MARTHA MOULSWORTH. Bathsua Makin's concern for unmarried women and her desire for their monetary independence prompt her to pen *The Malady and Remedy of Vexations and Unjust Arrest and Actions*. Colonel Hutchinson, husband of Lucy Hutchinson, serves in Long Parliament that judges Charles I. Lady Eleanor Douglas's *Day of Judgements Modell*. Crashaw's *Steps to the Temple*. Herrick publishes *Hesperides* and *Noble Numbers*. Lady Elizabeth Brackley's play *The Concealed Fansyes*. She also wrote a poem and meditations on pregnancy, childbed, and other topics that appear in *Loose Papers Left by Y. Right Hobl. Elizabeth Countess of Bridgwater*. Dorothy Burch writes *A Catechism of Several Heads of the Christian Religion, Gathered Together in Question and Answer, it Being Intended Onely for Private Use, but now Published for the Good and Benefit of Others; by the Importunitie of Some Friends*. Elizabeth Warren's *Spiritual Thrift. Or, Meditations wherein Humble Christians (as in a Mirrour) May View the Verity of their Saving Graces, and May See How to Make a Spirituall Improvement of all*

Opportunities and Advantages of a Pious Proficiencie (or a Holy Growth) in Grace and Goodnesse. And wherein Is Layd Open Many Errours Incident to these Declining Times. Posthumous publication of Ursula Quarles's *Judgment and Mercy.* Elizabeth Lilburne's *To the Chosen and Betrusted Knights, Citizens and Burgesses, Assembled in the High and Supreme Court of Parliament. The Humble Petition of Elizabeth Lilburne, Wife to the Lieut. Coll. John Lilburne, who Hath Been for Above Eleven Weeks by Past, Most Unjustly Divorced from Him, by the House of Lords, and Their Tyrannical Officers, Against the Law of God and (as She Conceives) the Law of the Land.*

1647: b. Ursula Cartwright (author of *The Case of Ursula Cartwright, Widow, and of Thomas and Roda Cartwright the Children of William Cartwright Esq; Deceas'd, by the Said Ursula His Second Wife, Defendants, to the Appeal of Fulk Grosvenor Esq; and Mary His Wife, and Dorothy Cartwright, Against a Decree and Dismission and Several Orders Made in the Court of Chancery* in 1680); b. John Wilmot, Earl of Rochester; d. Mary Simpson. Elizabeth Avery publishes Scripture-prophecies Opened, Which Are to Be Accomplished in these Last Times, Which do Attend the Second Coming of Christ; In Several Letters Written to Christian Friends. Her brother, Thomas Parker, publishes a letter in response (see the reference to Parker in 1648). Mary Cary's *Word in Season to the Kingdom of England.* Elizabeth Whitehead writes letter to Thomas Alcock, later published in *Aspinwall Notarial Records from 1644 to 1651,* in which she seeks information regarding her sons. Hannah Allen and Henry Overton publish *The Exceeding Riches of Grace Advanced by the Spirit of Grace,* which relates the words of Sarah Wight, a Baptist woman undergoing a religious reverie as she fasts. Mary Pope's *Treatise of Magistracy, Shewing the Magistrate Hath Been, and for ever Is To Be the Cheife Officer in the Church.* Mary Overton's *To the Right Honourable, the Knights, Citizens, and Burgesses, the Parliament of England, Assembled at Westminster, the Humble Appeale and Petition of Mary Overton, Prisoner in Bridewell,* which relates her arrest for stitching copies of *Regall Tyrannie Discovered.* Overton and her six-month old baby were mercilessly stoned, and the baby died. The tract is probably by her although it is possible that her husband wrote down her words.

1648: WILLIAM PRYNNE (MARTHA MOULSWORTH'S GODSON) elected to Parliament. Katherine Philips, 16, poet, marries James Philips, 64. Lady Anne Halkett helps Colonel Joseph Bampfield and other royalists to rescue the Duke of York (later James II) from his imprisonment by dressing the prince in girl's clothing. Halkett in 1677–1678 writes her *Memoirs* and pens over twenty manuscript volumes. Lady Eleanor Douglas's *Lady Eleanor: Her Remonstrance to Great Britain.* While Dorothy Osborne stays with her brother at an inn on the Isle of Wight, he writes inflammatory remarks about the government on a window pane. Both, along with William Temple (who also stays there), are arrested. Although her brother is guilty, she confesses and convinces the officers that it is merely a woman's folly. Temple is impressed with her gumption, and they begin a correspondence. Thomas Parker publishes a letter to his sister in which he declares that his sister claims to be "above Ordinances, above the Word and Sacraments, ye above the Blood of Christ himself, living as a glorified Saint, and taught immediately by the Spirit"; "your printing of a Book, beyond the custom of your Sex, doth rankly smell." Mary Cary's *Resurrection of the Witnesses; and England's Fall from (the Mystical Babylon) Rome*. Alice Rolph's *To the Chosen and Betrusted Knights, Citizens, and Burgesses Assembled in Parliament at Westminster. The Humble Petition of Alice Rolph, Wife to Major Edmond Rolph, Close Prisoner at the gate-house Westminster, etc.* Mary Pope's *Behold, Here Is a Word or, an Answer to the Late Remonstrance of the Army. And likewise, an Answer to a Book, Cal'd the Foundation of the Peoples Freedomes, Presented to the Generall Counsell of Officers. With a Message to All Covenant-breakers, whom God Hates*, which her son wrote down for her. Mary Pope's *Heare, Heare, Heare, Heare, A Word or Message from Heaven, to All Covenant Breakers (whom God Hates) with All that Hath Committed that Great Sinne, that Is, as the Sinne of Witchcraft*.

1649: d. Richard Crashaw. Charles I beheaded. Interregnum begins. Women petition Parliament about poor economic conditions and demand that Levellers be freed from prison. Parliament declares that it has already provided responses to the petitioners' husbands, who legally are their only constituents (husbands govern wives as members of Parliament represent the husbands), and advises the women that they should "go home and look after your own business and meddle with your housewifery." The women respond that "we are no whit satisfied with the answer you gave unto our husbands." Lady Eleanor Douglas's *New Jerusalem at Hand*. Johanna Cartwright's *The Petition of the Jewes for the Repealing of the Act of Parliament for Their Banishment out of England*. Katherine Chidley collaborates on a women's petition. Elizabeth Warren's *A Warning-Peece from Heaven, Against the Sins of the Times, Inciting Us to Fly from the Vengeance to Come. Or, Mournful Meditations of Revealed Wrath, Appearing in the Progresse of Our Sins and Sorrows*. Mary Simpson's *Faith and Experience: Or, a Short Narration of the Holy Life and Death of Mary Simpson, Late of Gregories Parish in the City of Norwich; Who Dyed Anno 1647. In or about the Thirtieth Year of Her Age, After Three Years Sicknesse and Upwards. Containing a Confession of Her Faith, and Relation of Her Experience, taken from Her Owne Mouth*. Mary Pocock's *Mystery of the Deity in the Humanity*, which supports John Pordage, a curate. Thomasina Pendarves's letter of support for Elizabeth Poole, which appears in Poole's *Vision: An Alarum of War, Given to the Army, and to Their High Court of Justice (so Called), Revealed in a Vision*.... Elizabeth Poole's prophecy appears in *The Manner of the Depositions of Charles Stewart ... Also the Words of a Woman, who Pretends to Have Seen a Vision, to the Generall Councell of the Army*; Poole's writes her account of the event, *A Vision: The Summe of what Was Delivered to the Generall Councel of the Army, December 29 1648*. The following three petitions are from 1649: *Mercurius Philo-monarchicus*, regarding the widows of soldiers; *A Modest*

Narrative of Intelligence, concerning widows who lost their husbands while in government service; and *To the Supreme Authority of England the Commons ... the Humble Petition of Divers Well-Affected Women.*

1650: Anne Bradstreet's collection of poems, *The Tenth Muse Lately Sprung Up in America,* is published in England and becomes a financial success. The poems, published without her knowledge, are provided to a publisher by her brother-in-law, John Woodbridge. The collection is the first book of poems published by a settler in America. Her revised and new poems are published posthumously in 1678. Frances Cook's *Mrs. Cook's Meditations. Being a Humble Thanksgiving to Her Heavenly Father, for Granting Her a New Life, Having Concluded Her Selfe Dead, and Her Grave Made in the Bottome of the Sea, in the Great Storme Jan 5 1649 Composed by Her Selfe at Her Unexpected Safe Arrivall at Corcke.* Cook's husband prosecuted Charles I. Mary Walker's *Case of Mrs. M.W., the Wife of Clement Walker Esq.,* an appeal to the House of Commons. Anne Smyth's *Case of Anne Smyth, the Wife of Daniell Smyth, One of the Daughters of Sir John Danvers of Culworth in the County of Northampton Kt., Deceased, Truly Stated.* Mary Moore's *Wonderfull News from the North. Or, a True Relation of the Sad and Grievous Torments, Inflicted upon the Bodies of Three Children of Mr George Muschamp. Late of the County of Northumberland, by Witchcraft: and how Miraculously it Pleased God to Strengthen Them, and to Deliver Them: as also the Prosecution of the Sayd Witches, as by Oaths, and Their Own Confessions Will Appear, and by the Indictment Found by the Jury Against One of Them, at the Sesions of the Peace Held at Alnwick, the 24 Day of April, 1650.* Vaughan's *Silex Scintillans.* The following petition is from 1650: *To the Supreme Authority of this Commonwealth, the Parliament of England. The Humble Petition of Severall Wives and Children of such Delinquents, whose Estates Are Propounded to Be Sold, as the Petitioners Are Informed.*

1651: d. Lady Mary Wroth. Milton goes blind. Lady Eleanor Douglas's *Dragons Blasphemous Charge Against Her.* Lady Ann Fanshawe's husband, Richard, is captured after the Battle of Worcester; she works diligently for his release. They flee England and are taken prisoner in Ireland. She is almost made a slave to Turks but escapes by wearing men's clothes. Katherine Philips's first published poem appears in a book written by William Cartwright. Hobbes publishes *Leviathan.* Elizabeth Alkin, polemical journalist known as "Parliament Joan," writes (c. 1651–1654) for payment for spying and nursing. Alkin also publishes two government newspapers and the royalist *Mercurius Scotius.* Mary Cary's *Little Horns Doom and Downfall; or, a Scripture Prophesie of King James, and King Charles, and of the Present Parliament, Unfolded,* with *A New and More Exact Mappe or, Description of New Ierusalems Glory.* Katherine Chidley provides government troops in Ireland with 5,000 pair of stockings. Publication of *To the Parliament of the Common-wealth of England, the humble petition of Elizabeth dutchesse (dowager) of Hamilton and her four orphan children.* Anna Weamys's *Continuation of Sir Philip Sidney's Arcadia, Written by a Young Gentlewoman,*

Mrs. A.W. Catherine Thimelby's *To Her Husband on New-Years-Day, 1651.* Thimelby's letters, along with those by Winefrid Thimelby (author of *Meditation on the Principal Obligations of a Christian* and whose letters are from 1650–1690), appear in *The Tixall Letters; Or the Correspondence of the Aston Family and Their Friends During the Seventeenth Century,* edited by A. Clifford. The following petition is from 1651: *The Womens Petition, to the Right Honourable, His Excellency, the Most Noble and Victorious Lord General Cromwell.* Publication of Lucy Knatchbull's autobiography. Mary Love's four petitions on behalf of her husband, *Love's Letters, His and Hers.*

1652: b. Jane Barker (poet and novelist); b. Agnes Beaumont (writes *The Narrative of the Persecution of Agnes Beaumont in 1674* regarding her conflict with her father as she struggles to obey her religious convictions). Lady Anne Clifford's *Great Books of the Records of Skipton Castle* (a history of the Clifford family from King John's reign to the present). Margaret Fell becomes a Quaker after meeting George Fox. Dorothy Osborne begins writing letters to William Temple that will later be published in 1836 and 1888. Elizabeth Hooton (c. 1600–1671/2) published in *False prophets and false teachers described;* author of other religious tracts.

1653: John Bunyan's spiritual conversion. Margaret Fell begins writing letters to England's rulers, asking for religious toleration. Margaret Cavendish publishes her first book, *Poems and Fancies* (writings about animals and fairies). Cavendish also publishes *Philosophical Fancies* (collection of poetry). Elizabeth Avery, Mary Barker, Anne Bishop, Sarah Barnwell, Mary Burrill, Elizabeth Chambers, Frances Curtis, Tabitha Kelsall, Elizabeth Marrow, Ann Megson, Rebecca Rich and Mary Turrant publish their "experiences" in John Rogers's *Ohel or Beth-Shemesh,* in association with the Baptist church. Mary Cary's *[Twelve Humble] Proposals to the Supreme Governours of the Three Nations Now Assembled at Westminster.* Katherine Chidley presents petition with 6,000 names to the Commons to release from prison John Lilburne. Frances Clark's and Elizabeth Worsopp's *A Brief Reply to the Narration of Don Pantaleon Sa,* in which she petitions that the murderer of her brother be punished. An Collins's *Divine Songs and Meditations Composed by An Collins.* Prudence Harding's, John Moon's, Elizabeth Newton's, Martha Platt's, Hannah Reckless's, John Reckless's, William Smith's, and Sarah Watstone's *Real Demonstration of the True Order in the Spirit of God, and of the Ground of All Formality and Idolatry,* which appears in William Smith's *Works.* Jane Turner's *Choice Experiences of the Kind Dealings of God Before, In and After Conversion; Laid Down in Six General Heads. Together with some Brief Observations upon the Same. Whereunto Is Added a Description of the Experience.* Hester Shaw's *Mrs Shaw's Innocency Restor'd, and Mr Clendon's Calumny Retorted, Notwithstanding His Late Triumph; By Sundry Depositions, Making out more than ever She By Discourse or Writing Did Positively Charge upon Him (in Respect of the Unjust Detention of Certain Sums of Money) etc.* and *A Plain Relation of My Sufferings by that Miserable Combustion, which Happened in Tower-Street through the Unhappy*

Firing of a Great Quantity of Gunpowder there the 4. of January 1649. An explosion destroyed her house, killing her three grandchildren and her son-in-law; money found at the property was sent to her preacher, Mr. Clendon, for safekeeping, but Shaw insisted that he only returned some of it to her and kept the rest for himself. The following petition is from 1653: *To the Parliament of the Commonwealth of England: The Humble Petition of Divers Afflicted Women, in Behalf of M. John Lilburn Prisoner in Newgate.*

1654: b. Elizabeth, Duchess of Albemarle, author of *The Case of Elizabeth Dutchess of Albemarle, and Christopher Monke Esquire, Appellants* (1688), which concerns the inheritance of the previous Duke of Albemarle; d. Lady Elizabeth Lindsey; d. Anne Venn. Mary Pocock defends curate John Pordage before the reading Assizes. Susanna Bastwick authors her ninth petition to release her husband from prison: *To the High Court of Parliament of the Commonwealth of England, Scotland, and Ireland. The Remonstrance and Humble Petition of Susanna Bastwick (the Distressed Widow of John Bastwick, Doctor of Physick) and Her Children.* Mary Blaithwaite publishes *The Complaint of Mary Blaithwaite Widdow; Setting Forth Her Sad Condition, Occasioned by the Late Dissolution of the Parliament, and Neglect of Justice ever Since,* which reports of the physical and emotional abuse she and her husband suffer by the hands of Royalists when they are caught distributing pamphlets supporting Parliament; the abuse leads to her husband's early death. Anna Trapnel's *Cry of a Stone or a Relation of Something Spoken in Whitehall by Anna Trapnel,* which is her prophecy in verse. The same year Trapnel writes *A Legacy for Saints: Being Several Experiences of the Dealings of God with Anna Trapnel; Anna Trapnel's Report and Plea. Or a Narrative of Her Journey from London into Cornwall;* and *Strange and Wonderful Newes from Whitehall: Or, the Mighty Vision Proceeding from Mistris A. Trapnel ... Concerning the Government of the Commonwealth... and Her Revelations Touching... the Lord Protector, and the Army.* Margaret, Countess of Somerset, writes *To the Parliament of the Commonwealth of England, Scotland, and Ireland. The Humble Petition of ....* Mary Stirling's *To the Supream Authority of the Nation the Parliament ... the Humble Petition of Mary Countess of Stirling* and *An Answer to a Printed Paper; Entituled, Some Considerations.* Katherine Stone's *To the High Court of Parliament, of the Commonwealth of England, Scotland, and Ireland. The Humble Petition of Katherine Stone, Widdow and Henry Stone, Her Son.* Katherine Pettus's *Katherine Pettus Plaintiffe, Margaret Bancroft Defendent in Chancery.*

1655: b. Elizabeth Bathurst (later wrote *Truth's Vindication, or, a Gentle Stroke to Wipe Off the Foul Aspersions, False Accusation and Misrepresentations Cast upon the People of God, Called, Quakers* [1679]; wrote *An Expostulatory Appeal to the Professors of Christianity Joyned in Community with Samuel Annesley* [1679] in which she defends the right of women to preach: "Yea, though we have not all the Gift of Prophecying [vocally] bestowed on us, yet by our upright Carriage, we shall every one become Preachers of Righteousness amongst our Neighbours, whereby we shall reach to the

Witness, they hath slain in the Consciences, and shall cause it to arise and stand upon its Feet, and Prophesie in their Streets"; and wrote and compiled *The Sayings of Women, Which Were Spoken upon Sundry Occasions, in Several Places of the Scriptures, etc.* [1683]); d. Agnes More. Margaret Fell's *False Prophets, Anticrists [sic], Deceivers*. Elizabeth Cowart and Margaret Newby share with the reader the pain they suffer while in the stocks in Evesham that year; Cowart dies and Newby dies two years later from injuries suffered during the experience. Margaret Cavendish publishes *The World's Olio*—essays, including one denying the charge of plagiarism. She also publishes *The Philosophical and Physical Opinem*. The work expresses a feminist perspective; Cavendish writes, for example, that "by an Opinion, which I hope is but an Erroneous one in Men, we are Shut out of all Power and Authority, by reason we are never Imployed either in Civil or Martial Affairs ...." Dorothy Osborne marries William Temple. Both sets of parents had disapproved of the marriage, and the Osbornes had tried to marry Dorothy to Henry Cromwell, the Protector's son. Osborne helps Temple in his diplomatic career and travels with him. Charles II commends her for her courage when she, along with Temple, are on a ship attacked by the Dutch navy. She is praised by Jonathan Swift (her husband's secretary) in his "Ode Occasioned by Sir William Temple's Late Illness and Recovery" (1693): Swift calls her "Mild Dorothea, peaceful, wise and great." Thomas Macaulay praises William Temple's diplomatic correspondence, *Memoirs of the Life, Works and Correspondence of Sir William Temple* (first published 1836), but Osborne is actually the author. In 1888, the book is republished with a new title, *Letters from Dorothy Osborne to Sir William Temple*. Virginia Woolf says of Osborne, "Had she been born in 1827, Dorothy Osborne would have written novels; had she been born in 1527 she would never have written at all. But she was born in 1627, and, at that date, though writing books was ridiculous for a woman, there was nothing unseemly in writing a letter." The following two statements by Osborne regarding Margaret Cavendish's numerous publications offer insight into Osborne's views on publications by women: there are "many soberer People [than Cavendish] in Bedlam." Osborne also remarks, "Sure the poor woman [Cavendish] is a little distracted, she could never be so ridiculous else as to venture writing books .... [I]f I could not sleep this fortnight I should not come to that." Two of Katherine Philips's poems appear in Henry Lawes's *Second Book of Ayres*. Philips's literary circle included Charles II's Master of Ceremonies, theologian Jeremy Taylor, Abraham Cowley, and Henry Vaughan. Philips's literary works consist of 120 original poems, five poems translated from French, and translations of two of Corneille's dramas (*Pompey* and *Horace*). *Pompey* is published twice in 1663 after its successful run in Dublin. *Horace* appeared at court and in the theatre in 1669. 74 of her poems are published without her consent in 1664. Philips's collected works are published posthumously in 1667. Four of her letters are published in 1697. Anne Audland is acquitted by a jury of blasphemy charges but suffers imprisonment for eight months anyway. Audland contributes to *The Saints Testimony Finishing Through Suffering*—a work concerning the debate about female speakers. She, along with Jane Waugh, writes *A True Declaration*. She later pens *Anne Camm, Her Testimony Concerning John Audland* (1681), which appears in *The Memory of the Righteous Revived* (1689), *The Admirable and Glorious Appearance of the Eternal God* (1684) with Thomas Camm. Audland also writes a testimony in 1687 and *The Life and Death of Robert Widders* in 1688. Mary Cole's and Priscilla Cotton's *To the Priests and People of England, We Discharge Our Consciences, and Give Them Warning*, a work that deals with the debate about whether women should have the right to speak out about religion. Cole and Cotton, both Quakers, write their treatise in Exeter gaol, where they are sent after priests assail them for their religious beliefs. Margaret Beck pens *The Reward of Oppression, Tyranny and Injustice, Committed by the Late Kings and Queens of England, and Others; By the Unlawful Entry, and Unlawful Deteiner of the Dutchie Lands of Lancaster. Declared in the Case of Samuel Beck, an Infant ... Margaret Beck ... Mother and Guardian to the Infant.* The manuscript concerns Beck's desire to attain the duchy for her son, who she believes is the rightful heir. Margaret Braidley's *Written from the Spirit of the Living God, Margaret Braidley, One, whom the World Calls a Quaker*—bound with Christopher Taylor's *Certain Papers which Is the Word of the Lord*. Martha Simmonds's *When the Lord Jesus Came to Jerusalem* and *Lamentation for the Lost Sheep of the House of Israel*. Damaris Strong's *Having Seen a Paper Printed*, which demands a woman's right to own the right to publish her deceased husband's (especially a clergyman's) works. Margaret Killam's (Killin's?) *Warning from the Lord to the Teachers and People of Plymouth. With a Few Queries to the Parish Teachers of This Nation, That Have Great Sums of Money for Teaching the People.* During this year, people in Plymouth who disapproved of Killam's Quaker beliefs tied her feet under the belly of a horse and her hands behind her back. Mary Knight's lyric "To the Most Honoured" appears, set to music by Henry Lawes, in his *Second Book of Ayres and Dialogues*.

1656: b. Lady Mary Chudleigh (poet, essayist); b. Anne Bathurst (Quaker, writer of memoir and spiritual diary in 1679). Margaret Fell's *For Manasseth-Ben-Israel*; *A Loving Salutation*; *A Testimonie of the Touch-Stone*. Margaret Cavendish's *Natures Pictures Drawn by Fancies Pencil to the Life* (tales of heroines). Cavendish publishes *Playes* (consisting of fourteen dramas) in 1662. She is the most frequently published female writer in England in her time. Susanna Bateman, a Quaker, writes an untitled work that attacks religious backsliders. Priscilla Cotton's *As I Was in the Prison-House*. Anne Culpepper's *To the Reader* in Nicholas Culpepper's (her husband's) *Treatise of Aurum Potabile* show her anger toward a publisher who has written two epistles and attributed one to her and one to her husband. Dorothy Waugh's *Lamb's Defence Against Lies*. Sarah Wight's *Wonderful Pleasant and Profitable Letter Written by Mrs. Sarah Wight*. Martha Simmonds's *O England, Thy Time is Come*, which contains Hannah Stranger's Quaker treatise *Consider I Beseech You How Clearly the Scripture is Fulfilled in Our Days*.

Margaret Killam's (Killin's?) and Barbara Patison's *Warning from the Lord*. A poem by Mary Oxlie, in which she lauds William Drummond, is published in his *Works*. Elizabeth Major's *Honey on the Rod; or a Comfortable Contemplation for One in Affliction; With Sundry Poems on Several Subjects*. Publication of two works by Anne Gargill: *A brief discovery of that which is called the popish religion* .... and *A warning to all the world*.

1657: d. Margaret Newby; d. Isabella Twysden; d. Richard Lovelace. Marvell appointed as Milton's secretary by the Commonwealth. Browne's *Hydriotaphia, Urn-Burial*. Jone/Jane Bettris writes *A Lamentation for the Deceived People of the World. But in Particular to Them of Aylesbury* and *A Short Discovery of His Highness, the Lord Protectors Intentions Touching the Anabaptists in the Army, and all such as Are Against His Reforming Things in the Church*. Elizabeth Moore's *M^ris. Moores Evidences for Heaven, Composed and Collected by Her in the Time of Her Health, for Her Comfort in the Time of Sickness*, which appears in Edmund Calamy's *Godly Mans Ark*. Gertrude (Grace) More's *Holy Practises of a Divine Lover, or the Sainctly Ideots Devotions*. Margaret Killam's *Short Account of the Barbarous Sufferings*. Lady Elizabeth Lowther's letters regarding her eldest son, Thomas. *A remarkable letter of Mary Howgill to Oliver Cromwell*.

1658: b. Susannah Blandford (Quaker writer); d. Beatrice Digby (letter writer); d. Catherine Thimelby (poet); d. Oliver Cromwell. Oliver Cromwell's death leaves the Protectorate without an effective political leader. Richard Cromwell succeeds his father as leader of the Protectorate. Sarah Blackberry/Blackborow publishes *A Visit to the Spirit in Prison*. Publication of Anne Venn's *Wise Virgins Lamp Burning; or Gods Sweet Incomes of Love to a Gracious Soul Waiting for Him. Being the Experiences of Mrs. Anne Venn (Daughter to Col. John Venn, & Member of the Church of Christ at Fulham:) Written by Her Own Hand, and Found in Her Closet after Her Death*. Anna Trapnel's *Voice for the King of Saints* and a book of poems. Lady Eliza Southcote writes letter to her uncle, Herbert Aston, after the demise of his wife. Winifred Newman's *Fruits of Unrighteousness and Injustice Brought Forth by ... the Rulers in Hampshire, Against the Innocent People of God, Called Quakers* ... Gertrude More's *Spiritual Exercises of the Most Vertuous and Religious Dame Gertrude More, of the Holy Order of St. Bennet, and English Congregation of Our Ladie of Comfort in Cambray*. Anna Kemp's pastoral, *A Contemplation of Bassets Down-hill by the Most Sacred Adorer of the Muses Mrs A.K.* Barbara Lamb's letter to Richard Baxter regarding her husband's spiritual problems.

1659: b. Anne Wharton (poet, translator, dramatist); d. Lady Jane Cornwallis; d. Alice Osborne. Richard Cromwell abdicates. Margaret Fuller's *A Paper Concerning Such as Are Made Ministers; To the General Councel, and Officers of the Army*. Anne Wharton, one of the most publicly honored female poets of the Restoration, is born. Edmund Waller and Aphra Behn write poems honoring her and correspond with her. She is the niece of the Earl of Rochester, and at fourteen she marries Thomas Wharton, who later becomes a Whig leader. Behn, Dryden, and Tate publish her works in books they publish after her death. Wharton writes a blank-verse tragedy that is never published. She also writes *Love's Martyr, or Witt above Crowns*— semi-autobiographical poems to Behn and Wolseley that manifest the problems that women encounter when their reputations do not measure up to societal expectations. Margaret Abbott writes *A Testimony Against the False Teachers of this Generation by One who Is Come from under them, unto the True Teacher and Shepherd of the Soul.* Theodosia Alleine forced against her desires to marry. Alleine in 1671 publishes her story of the persecution she and her second husband suffered under the Act of Uniformity and the Five Mile Act and how she nursed him in prison: *A Full Narrative of His Life (from His Silencing to His Death)*, which appeared in *The Life and Death of the Excellent Minister of Christ Mr. Joseph Alleine.* Mary Westwood publishes Grace Barwick's message from God, *To All Present Rulers, Whether Parliament, or Whom-soever of England.* Hester Biddle begins writing (1659–1662) her eight broadsides and pamphlets (e.g., *Wo to Thee City of Oxford, Thy Wickedness Surmounteth the Wickedness of Sodome* and *Oh! wo, wo, from the Lord*). Arrested for preaching in the street, Biddle told the judge, "Phoebe was a Prophetess, and Phillip had four Daughters that had prophesied, and Paul wrote to his Brethen that they should take care of the women that were fellow labourers with him in the Gospel." Katharine Bull, Mary Stout (who uses the name Sanderson), Rebecca Travers, Rebecca Ward, and Mary Westwood sign the tithing petition. Priscilla Cotton's *Briefe Description by Way of Supposition.* Anna Gold's (Gould's?) *Epistle to All Christian Magistrates and Powers in the Whole Christendom, and Professors and Teachers, and Christians that Witness the End of the Law ....*, which Humphrey Bache, Daniel Baker, George Fox, Robert Hasle, and Mary Webb sign. Rebecca Travers's *This Is for Any of that Generation that Are Looking for the Kingdom of God.* Ann Sherwood, a Quaker, writes letter to Quaker leaders. Mary Smith's *Here Is Another Warning which was Given forth some Years Before, to the Majestrates and Ministers (so Called) of the City of York, Written from Ouse-bridge the 9 Day of the 7 Moneth 1659.* Susanna Parr's *Susannas Apologie Against the Elders. Or, a Vindication of Susanna Parr; One of those Two Women Lately Excommunicated by Mr Lewis Stucley, and His Church in Exeter. Composed and Published by Her Selfe, for the Clearing of Her Own Innocency, and the Satisfaction of All Others.* The following petition is from 1659: *These Several Papers Was Sent to the Parliament 1659 ... Being above Seven Thousand Names of the Hand-maids and Daughters of the Lord.* Margaret Lynam's *For the Parliament Sitting at Westminster.*

1660: b. Anne Killigrew (poet, painter); b. Jane Barker (poet and novelist); b. Daniel Defoe; d. Ann Brockman; d. Frances Cook. Restoration of monarchy and the accession of Charles II, who had lived in exile in France and brought back with him the influence of French theatre. Charles II provides William Davenant and Thomas Killigrew with a monopoly on theatrical productions in London as the theatres re-open. The Act of Indemnity and Oblivion creates the land settlement and establishes the rights of private property owners. Samuel Pepys begins his diary. Margaret Fuller's *The Citie of London Reprov'd. A Declaration and Information from Us; An Evident Demonstration to God's Elect; This Is to the Clergy; This Was Given to Major Generall Harrison; A True Testimony from the People of God.* Fuller is imprisoned from 1664 to 1668 for complaining too vigorously about the need for government to stop persecuting The Friends (Quakers). Sarah Blackberry/Blackborow publishes *The Just and Equal Balance Discovered: With a True Measure Whereby the Inhabitants of Sion Doth Fathom and Compasse All False Worships and Their Ground ...* (1660), which contains her statement that "Christ was one in the Male and in the Female; and as he arises in both." She later publishes *The Oppressed Prisoners Complaint of Their Great Oppression* (1662). Anne Clayton's *Letter to the King,* which welcomes the return of Charles II to England. Clayton, a Quaker, was imprisoned and whipped several times for preaching in the streets. Dorothy White's *Visitation of Heavenly Love unto the Seed of Jacob ....* The following petition is from 1660: *The Royal Virgine: Or, the Declaration of Several Maydens in and about the Once Honourable City of London.*

This chronology would not have been possible without help from the following sources:

Abrams, M.H., et al. *The Norton Anthology of English Literature.* 6th ed. 2 vols. New York: Norton, 1993. Vol. 1.

Beilin, Elaine V. *Redeeming Eve: Women Writers of the English Renaissance.* Princeton: Princeton University Press, 1987.

Bell, Maureen, George Parfitt, and Simon Shepherd, eds. *A Biographical Dictionary of English Women Writers 1580–1720.* Boston: G.K. Hall, 1990.

Evans, Blakemore. *The Riverside Shakespeare.* Boston: Houghton Mifflin, 1973.

Stone, Laurence. *The Family, Sex and Marriage in England 1500–1800.* Abr. ed. New York: Harper and Row, 1979.

Todd, Janet. *British Women Writers: A Critical Reference Guide.* New York: Continuum, 1989.

Index of Women Mentioned
in the "Chronology of Texts and Contexts"

Index